The Politics
and Development
of the Federal
Income Tax

The Politics and Development of the Federal

Income Tax

John F. Witte

The University of Wisconsin Press

Published 1985

The University of Wisconsin Press
114 North Murray Street
Madison, Wisconsin 53715

The University of Wisconsin Press, Ltd.
1 Gower Street
London WC1E 6HA, England

First printing

Printed in the United States of America

For LC CIP information see the colophon

ISBN 0-299-10020-9

For

John M. Witte
(1918–1961)

Edwin E. Witte
(1887–1960)

The only tragedy of my life
is not having had the
opportunity to talk
with these men as an adult.

Contents

Figures

Tables

Preface

When I began this project many years ago, I set out to accomplish three things. First, I wanted to test, analyze, and evaluate the incremental policy-making model for a specific policy field over a long period of time. Second, I wanted to create new facts that might be useful to scholars and practitioners in the important field of taxation. Third, I wanted to promote a method for studying public policy that integrates political theory, political practice, and policy analysis. And, of course, I wanted all of this to be definitive for tax policy, but I also wanted the reader to realize the implicit lessons for public policy in general.

Having completed final revisions, I am pleased with the product, but my expectations, in one sense, have declined. I believe that this broad method of viewing public policy and the "facts" on tax policy may prove useful to those studying and making policy decisions. However, I have also come to understand how complex evaluating public policy can be. I have become particularly aware of the difficulty of analyzing the normative criteria on which policy evaluation ultimately rests. I have presented strong conclusions, but they turn on somewhat narrow normative threads. And I can understand how others, utilizing the same facts that I present, might arrive at different conclusions. That is not a comfortable admission, but it is honest, and points to the critical importance of analyzing values in public policy. That means a concentrated effort to merge political philosophy with the analysis of public policy and political behavior.

Over the years, several organizations and many people have aided and supported this project. The research was supported by a National Science Foundation grant (No. DAR 8011902). The Russell Sage Foundation provided an accommodating year to write in an intellectually stimulating environment. The Wisconsin State Historical Society offered a place to work, a magnificent collection, and patient experts in government documents. Comments and intellectual and moral support were provided by Clara Penniman, Charles Anderson, Dennis Dresang, Leon Epstein, Leon Lindberg, Malcolm Feeley, Ira Sharkansky, Robert Lampman, Jack Knott, Aaron Wildavsky, Charles Lindblom,

David Mayhew, and Daniel Throop Smith. The research and production efforts were aided by Janet Stevens, Dona Fischer, Bob Kaestner, Lloyd Velicer, John Peterson, Debi Hegerfeld, Chris Willard, Mark Rom, and Ann Grady. The University of Wisconsin Press has been magnificent and patient. Among others, I thank Gordon Lester-Massman, Jane Barry, and Jack Kirshbaum. Finally, I thank my wife, Mary, who has put up with the long hours, the travel and the pressure of getting it done on time.

John Witte
Madison, Wisconsin
September 19, 1984

Introduction

          This book is about the politics of the United States federal income tax. It is a study of the development, changes, and long-term consequences of income tax policy and politics from the inception of the tax through 1982. However, the book is also about political theory and, in particular, the incremental theory of policy making. It is this aspect of tax policy that stimulated the study in the first place. I was concerned that although the incremental model corresponded to my personal experience in observing and studying specific, short-term political decisions, the types of problems that might emerge in a policy area over a long period of time and the range of interests that ultimately benefit had not been adequately studied.

    This combination of tax policy and political theory has, as a colleague put it, the look of "red wine with fish." The word "taxes" conjures up images of practical-minded accountants, lawyers, and experts in public finance, all totally immersed in real-world policy analysis. "Political theory" suggests a college professor thumbing tattered volumes of Plato and Aristotle and, at best, barely tolerating the encroachment of the real world on the universe of ideas. Images aside, the style and content of scholarly work in these two fields are certainly very different. Most writing on taxes takes the form of relatively standard policy analysis in which emphasis is placed on concrete and very specific policy options, either analyzing or speculating on the consequences of a particular provision or method of taxation. These consequences are then judged against a string of values, such as horizontal and vertical equity, market distortion, and administrative efficiency. The method has been very successful, and the field, broadly labeled public finance, has had vast direct impact on actions at all levels of government in the United States.[1]

    Whereas discussions of taxes concentrate on real or anticipated consequences of policy actions, the puzzles for political theorists are the problems of how decisions are or should be made; how governments should be organized; the analysis of values; and the creation, rather than the application, of general principles. Although there are those who would argue that political theory long ago ran its course and that

there is little left to discover or propose, twentieth-century political theory, with its new emphasis on decision making and the empirical analysis of political systems, has made substantial and important contributions to an ancient subject.

Thus, while I have little quarrel with the methods or accomplishments of either policy analysis or political theory, there is a point at which each needs the other. Policy analysis without consideration of process or behavior, often results in hypothetical policy proposals that may be innovative, but that also may be of little use in the real world. Similarly, policy analysis undertaken without consideration of political constraints or policy history, may be based on and perpetuate important myths and assumptions in a policy field. For example, I will argue in later chapters that the progressive rate structure of the federal income tax is not necessarily evidence of a deep commitment to progressivity or income redistribution as many tax analysts assume. Rather, it is a historical accident characteristic only of periods of war and financial crisis.

Conversely, the ultimate tests of political theories are, in a sense, the outcomes that result from recommended political structures. There is the strong temptation for political theorists to concentrate exclusively on the structure, balance, and uses of power in theoretical or empirical terms and to fail to anticipate the concrete policy outcomes of the political process. Thus, in case studies of decision making the researcher often considers only who has what degree of influence and how that influence is used. In his community power studies, for example, Robert Dahl focused on the question of who has influence at what point in the policy process.[2] As Theodore Lowi later pointed out, even if the policy process has laudable characteristics, the ultimate results might prove undesirable on a number of other grounds.[3] Although Lowi pushed this point to an extreme and argued that the characteristics of a policy field actually determine the nature of the political process, a critical result for political theory is the weaker observation that various formulations of political power and different rights and access to a system may have specific effects on the types and limits of policy outcomes that develop. James Q. Wilson raised the same general issue when he argued that we have to know not only who governs, but what difference it makes.[4] Thus, the political theorist may learn a great deal by paying close attention to the analysis of outcomes, which is the stock in trade of the policy analyst.

If studying political processes in conjunction with policy outcomes is of general importance, why select taxation as a policy field to investigate? The reasons are: (1) there is a long policy history that can be

analyzed; (2) policy changes and the distribution of benefits can be more precisely estimated in this field than in many others; (3) taxation involves the interesting question of economic equality; and (4) taxation is a crucial and perpetual public policy field that grows in importance as government expands.

The historical aspect is important in understanding the development of a policy field. The analysis of a single policy decision or a small set of decisions may either give a false impression because of the unique nature of the selected case or may misrepresent the long-term character of policy outcomes because of the narrowness of the focus. The historical analysis that follows, first in a narrative and then in a more rigorous, quantitative form, is based on the assumption that although individual policy decisions should be documented in their own context, longer-term patterns and the evolution of a policy field will become evident only when one considers a large set of such decisions.

Because of the quantitative nature of taxes and the statistics available, it is easier to understand who is helped or harmed by a specific provision than is true of many other policy fields (e.g., housing, education, job programs). For the same reason, the cumulative impact of tax policy can be described, understood, and judged relative to some appropriate practical and normative standards. This does not mean that all potentially relevant outcomes can be precisely estimated even with the wealth of quantitative data available. For example, while some estimation of distributional effects can be made and the clarity and complexity of the tax code can be assessed as it evolves, it may be much more difficult to specify exact effects of tax provisions on economic behavior or market allocations.

The issue of taxation is important in a theoretical sense because of its direct bearing on the problem of economic equality. The conflict between economic equality and the type of liberty that some would argue is the cornerstone of liberal democracy is a lasting intellectual problem. The use of the tax system either to further redistribute income or to provide an ameliorative alternative to the direct government support system created during the 1960s and 1970s is supported by numerous commentators on both ends of the political spectrum.[5] Additionally, as will be discussed in detail in chapter 1, the problem of equality of outcomes looms as perhaps the major question within the incremental/pluralist model of American democracy.

Finally, as has been the case for over a decade prior to publication of this book, tax policy remains in the center stage of American domestic policy. In addition to the continuing concern over income distribution, in recent years tax policy has increasingly been viewed as a vehicle for

government induced incentives in other policy areas. However, the central factors ensuring that tax policy will remain a crucial domestic issue are the disparate impulses toward government growth on the one hand, and continuing resistance to tax increases on the other. The most conservative administration in fifty years has been unable to limit expansion of the government budget. It has, however, perpetuated the historical bias toward tax reduction. The persistence of these trends, and the budget deficits that result, ensure that tax policy will remain an important issue in the years ahead. That these diverse tendencies are inherent in our political process is a central argument of this book.

These reasons tilt toward the political theory side of the policy analysis–political theory dichotomy. The basic issues that will be discussed in detail below are issues that originate in political theory, not in the literature on taxation. Unlike a number of excellent studies already published, this study does not include detailed explanations of, or arguments for or against, specific income tax provisions. There is also no effort to present either grand or modest designs for reforms of income taxes, although in later chapters I will discuss the implications of the politics of taxation for such questions as the capacity and limits of the income tax for raising revenue, its potential for redistributing income, and the unlikely prospects for "reform."

This does not mean that the book is devoid of information that may be of use and interest to more practically inclined policy analysts (or their teachers). There has been a conscientious effort, stimulated by the slight but terrible possibility that someday, someone may inquire into the collective utility of social theory, to return to an older model of scholarly research in which information that may be of use to a wider audience is conveyed in return for the luxury of theoretical excursions. In this case, that information centers on the historical development of the federal income tax and a detailed analysis of the size, growth, and distribution of the large number of tax reduction provisions that serve to "erode" a hypothetical tax base. In addition, chapter 16 contains an analysis of thirty years of public opinion about various aspects of the income tax.

The book is organized in five sections. The first outlines incremental theory as practiced in a pluralist political setting. An effort is made to describe the "standard" critiques of that theory and to suggest additional and contradictory claims that will guide the basic argument of the book. The second section presents a history and analysis of normative theories of taxation. Chapter 2 reviews the major prescriptive theories that have been developed in an effort to come to grips with the problem

of a just method of taxation and an appropriate rate structure. The third chapter focuses on what has been the primary concern of income tax theorists since World War II: the debate over what is known as a comprehensive, or broad-based, income tax. The purpose of these chapters is to give the reader an appreciation of the normative complexity of tax policy, as well as to argue that a simple, broad-based income tax is a reasonable standard against which the development of the income tax can be judged.

The third section of the book is a chronological history of the development of the income tax. This section, which began as a historical overview grew to seven chapters, with an additional chapter summarizing strong historical patterns. These chapters trace the income tax from the Civil War through 1981, with emphasis on modern developments that are not covered by previous tax histories. Although the presentation shares with earlier histories a chronological format and a detailed description of political events, it differs in its theoretical emphasis and in its continuing focus on results over a long historical period. Each major revenue bill from 1894 on is analyzed point by point (with some limitations on corporate tax changes), mapping the political history of changes in over one hundred tax provisions. (The lists of tables and figures will give the reader an idea of the types and scope of historical data used in the presentation.)

The fourth section of the book is a more systematic analysis of the major tax provisions as they have developed over time. These tax reduction or "tax expenditure" provisions, which consist of income exclusions, deductions, credits, and other devices that serve to reduce taxes, are analyzed in terms of their growth in numbers and revenue loss, their distribution, and their legislative histories. The provisions have been classified by size, policy rationale, and income-group effects to aid in the interpretation of what is otherwise an unmanageable set of data. A taxonomy based on the primary policy rationale for each provision is presented in chapter 13, which also analyzes the growth of tax expenditures. Chapter 14 considers the distributional effects of the tax reduction provisions for which data are available. Chapter 15 focuses on the legislative process through which tax expenditures are created and modified. The intent of the chapter, which analyzes what types of changes are made and how often, the institutional origins of change, and the adequacy of deliberation, is to assess the procedural legitimacy of tax politics.

The final section evaluates tax politics relative to three standards: (1) responsiveness to public demands; (2) the effectiveness of the process in terms of the incremental/pluralist model; and (3) the effectiveness of

income tax policy as it has developed over seventy years. Chapter 16 summarizes what is known of public opinion on the income tax and considers how well the political parties ensure responsiveness. Chapter 17 returns to the issues of chapter 1. The overriding issue is the long-term consequences of incremental politics. The unconventional argument is made that the democratic impulse to represent broad and diverse sets of interests, which is facilitated by an incremental/pluralist process, in the long run jeopardizes the basic purpose and legitimacy of tax policy.

Section I.
Theoretical
Issues

Chapter 1.
Incremental
Theory and
Income Tax
Policy

The Incremental Model

The intellectual roots of incre-
mental theory are less obvious than the modern origin and meaning of
the term. The roots are imbedded in American pragmatic philosophy,
which arose as a rebellion against utilitarianism and other philosophical
efforts to construct formal moral systems and rules. For pragmatists,
value determination is meaningless apart from actions and applications.
There is an emphasis on problem solving, learning, and experimenta-
tion rather than on achieving predetermined ends. Knowledge is acquired in a continuous process as individuals interact with and adapt to
their environment. In the process of doing, of making and implement-
ing policy, values are clarified and priorities established through democratic agreement.[1] This approach to knowledge and value underlies the
incremental theory of decision making.

The history of the term "incrementalism" provides a useful framework for explaining the model's basic approach and assumptions. It was
first used in 1953 in a book by Charles Lindblom and Robert Dahl. The
book, *Politics, Economics, and Welfare*, was an elaborate exposition of
the interplay of values, control structures, decision-making techniques,
and strategies in public policy making.[2] It is best known as the first
formal presentation of the theory of polyarchy, which Dahl later expanded and elaborated.[3] However, the book also contained a critique of
the feasibility of long-range, comprehensive planning, which had become an important theoretical issue beginning in the 1930s with the
creation of welfare economics and the conception of a general welfare
function. The issue was politically relevant in the cold war era because

3

of the Soviet experiments with economic planning before and after the war and because of the support for comprehensive planning in the West generated by successful wartime planning. The book also utilized emerging behavioral theories of control and organizational decision making, including those of Chester Barnard and Herbert Simon.[4] In contrast to the assumption of calculated, perfectly informed rationality that typified both classical economics and rational planning models, those studies had emphasized psychological factors in decision making and the practical limitations that faced actual decision makers. Thus, the foundations for incremental theory were laid in this early book, and the argument was made for short-term, politically derived solutions to problems. The term "incrementalism" was used only in a general sense, however, and the theory was never fully developed.

In a seminal article published in 1959, Lindblom presented the incremental, or "branch," approach as an alternative to the "root" approach.[5] In later works, the "root alternative" is aligned with a formal and comprehensive welfare function, and the label is changed to the "synoptic ideal." The synoptic ideal as a contrast to incrementalism is repeated in one form or another in all subsequent presentations of the theory. In *A Strategy of Decision*, written with David Braybrooke, Lindblom's description of this ideal is based on the work of a Dutch economist, Jan Tinbergen, although the description is accomplished by picking unconnected sentences from one of Tinbergen's books. The description of the synoptic ideal reads as follows (the original page references are given in brackets):

> In his *Economic Policy: Principles And Design*, he [Tinbergen] prescribes the following procedures for an ideal analytical process: (1) The policy maker should pursue an agreed-upon set of values [pp. 11 ff.]; (2) the aims of policy should be clearly formulated in advance of choosing among alternative policies [p. 6]; (3) the policy maker should attempt a comprehensive overview of policy problems and of alternative policies [p. 8]; (4) co-ordination of policy should be made the explicit function of the policy maker [p. 220]; and (5) economists as policy analysts should be comprehensive in considering economic variables and values [p. 8]. . . . Such a conception of ideal policy analysis is not unusual; its prescriptions are so "obvious" as to be the first things that come to anyone's mind.[6]

These are obvious perhaps, but other examples Braybrooke and Lindblom offer are hardly straightforward. For example, they quote a

hypothetical model from James March and Herbert Simon, which these authors had also set up as a counter-ideal:

1. When we first encounter him in the decision-making situation, he [the decision maker] already has laid out before him the whole set of alternatives from which he will choose his action. . . .

2. To each alternative is attached a set of consequences. . . .

3. At the outset, the decision maker has a "utility function" or a "preference-ordering" that ranks all sets of consequences from the most preferred to the least preferred. . . .

4. The decision maker selects the alternative leading to the preferred set of consequences.[7]

Having stated this theory, Braybrooke and Lindblom proceed to destroy the synoptic ideal quickly and efficiently, concentrating on its requirements for comprehensiveness in consideration of alternatives and consequences and on the need for lengthy, precise, and a priori preference orderings. They find several faults with the synoptic ideal:

1. The synoptic ideal is not adapted to man's limited problem-solving capacities.

2. The synoptic ideal is not adapted to inadequacy of information.

3. The synoptic ideal is not adapted to the costliness of analysis.

4. The synoptic ideal is not adapted to failures in constructing a satisfactory evaluative method (whether a rational deductive system, a welfare function, or some other one).

5. The synoptic ideal is not adapted to the closeness of observed relationships between fact and value in policy making.

6. The synoptic ideal is not adapted to the openness of the systems of variables with which it contends.

7. The synoptic ideal is not adapted to the analyst's need for strategic sequences of analytical moves.

8. The synoptic ideal is not adapted to the diverse forms in which policy problems arise.[8]

In contrast, and in response to the problems encountered in attempting synoptic decision making, they prescribed the following conditions as the incremental alternative:

1. MARGINAL AND DEPENDENT CHOICE—Rather than making a comprehensive analysis of policy issues, decision makers concentrate on marginal changes from the status quo.

2. CONSIDERATION OF A RESTRICTED NUMBER OF POLICY CHOICES.

3. CONSIDERATION OF A RESTRICTED NUMBER OF CONSEQUENCES.

4. ADJUSTMENT OF OBJECTIVES TO POLICIES (Reconstructive analysis)—In many cases it is impossible to state and concentrate analysis on a specific policy problem, working directly toward a solution. Rather ends are often adjusted to means and defined and altered as a policy develops.

5. SERIAL ANALYSIS AND EVALUATION—Policies are best conceived as a series of attacks on problems.

6. REMEDIAL ANALYSIS—The incremental method encourages analysts to identify situations or ills from which to move away rather than goals toward which to move.

7. ANALYSIS SHOULD BE DONE AT MULTIPLE POINTS AND LEVELS.[9]

It was also emphasized that policy knowledge was cumulative and that as policies were developed at multiple locations, ideas and information could be exchanged and borrowed.

The model was presented as an empirical description of how the vast majority of real world decisions are made, particularly in government, and it was justified normatively as the most rational, if still imperfect, method of reaching decisions. Its advantages were inherent in the logic of its conditions. The incremental approach offered simplifying mechanisms so that complex problems could be solved. By approaching value judgments not as a priori considerations, but as elements to be considered and defined in the decision-making process itself, the sticky problems of defining and achieving consensus on comprehensive preference orderings were circumvented. And, finally, by conceiving of decision making as an ongoing process occurring at multiple points in the system, error correction and the wisdom of balanced views were built into the process.

When first introduced in 1959, Lindblom's theory said little about the characteristics of decision makers, the methods by which conflicts were resolved and policy choices coordinated, or the political system in which the decision strategy was to be imbedded. Theoretically, the incremental strategy need not apply solely to public or even collective decisions. Many individual decisions (e.g., selecting a breakfast cereal) are likely to be highly incremental. Similarly, governments and organizations that are not thought to be democratic in any sense may still often proceed in an incremental fashion. However, from the first incrementalism was linked primarily with public decisions and a specific political model.

Lindblom discussed the nature of decision makers and coordinating strategy in policy making in works published in 1961 and 1965. The central concept in these formulations was *partisan mutual adjustment*, which Lindblom defined most concisely in *The Intelligence of Democracy*.

> In a group of decision makers, a decision maker is partisan with respect to others if (a) he does not assume that there exists some knowable criterion acceptable to him and all the other decision makers that is sufficient, if applied, to govern adjustments among them; and (b) he therefore does not move toward coordination by a cooperative and deliberate search for and/or application of such criteria or by an appeal for adjudication to those who do so search and apply.[10]

He later added a critical dimension to this definition: "A partisan decision maker is therefore one who makes decisions to *serve his own goals*, not goals presumably shared by all other decision makers with whom he is interdependent."[11]

A long, detailed, and somewhat cumbersome list of methods for achieving coordination between decision makers was then outlined, expanding and elaborating the discussions of control mechanisms and bargaining techniques that had appeared a decade earlier in *Politics, Economics, and Welfare*. More relevant for this study are three major types of partisan mutual adjustment that Lindblom proposed in a paper discussing decision making on taxes and spending:

> *Atomistic.* Each decision-making group simply ignores the repercussions of its decision on other groups in deciding upon its own policies.
>
> *Deferential.* Each decision maker avoids any policy that would constrain or adversely affect another group.

Strategic. Decision makers manipulate each other in a variety of ways, including reasoned verbal appeals, exchanges of threats or promises, or actions beyond the policy making arena.[12]

It is the last of these types of partisan mutual adjustment that Lindblom greatly elaborated in the 1965 book. He emphasized that while these methods are analytically distinct, in practice they may well occur simultaneously. The distinction is important because the third strategy is most likely to lead to countervailing influence and hence restraints on the demands of specific groups. If deferential adjustment is the dominant force, such restraint will be lacking; demands should be more easily filled and benefits more difficult to remove once conferred.

The final element of the political model, the structure of influence in which decisions are reached, was less clearly defined, although as far back as 1953 Lindblom had aligned himself with what I will risk labeling the "pluralist" tradition. The term "pluralism" has generated so much controversy and confusion that Robert Dahl, whose work is also often associated with the concept, at one time advocated purging it from the political science vocabulary.[13] However, such terms are not easily forgotten. One of the problems is that the term is generic, describing cultural, social, and economic characteristics as well as political ones, although it is most often used in the context of political systems. In this book it refers to a political system characterized by: (1) numerous, diverse, and autonomous interests; (2) multiple individual and institutional actors and decision points; (3) competition between elites over questions of public policy and access to public office, and (4) widespread opportunity to participate, either directly or through intermediary groups, in elections of officials and (to a lesser extent) policy debates. Lindblom links incremental theory to pluralism in *The Intelligence of Democracy*, in which he argues for a system with autonomous political parties, interest groups, and executive agencies operating at multiple levels and with periodic elections serving as the key mechanism of accountability. He admits that his proposed system is very similar to the American political system. It also reflects the description of polyarchy that he and Dahl had worked out a number of years before.

Dahl and Lindblom's early work, while emphasizing the imperfect nature of democracy in practice, still paints an optimistic portrait of the results of the marriage of incrementalism and pluralism. Lindblom specifically hypothesized the following outcomes:

1. "Any value held to be important by any group of people can be made influential on policy making."

2. "A satisfactory weighting of conflicting values or interests" is achieved.

3. "The weighting of interest in mutual adjustments meets the requirements of consent."

4. "Citizens' perception of their own preferences and leadership's knowledge of citizen's preferences" are clarified.

5. "Conflict stemming from narrow or hastily considered views of group interests by group members" is often dissipated.

6. "Whether mutual adjustment is or is not more coercive than centrally achieved coordination depends upon the rules of the game by which the mutually adjusted groups play."[14]

The major critiques of the incremental/pluralist model, to which Dahl and Lindblom have themselves contributed in recent years, stem in part from challenges to these hypotheses.

Standard Critiques of the Model

Critiques of the incremental model and the assumptions of a pluralist framework are numerous, and I cannot hope to cover all of the subtle arguments that have been launched in response to these theories. However, several types of critical arguments seem to persist over time, even though the political unit in question may shift (e.g. from an urban to a national setting). These "standard" critiques, which overlap to some extent, involve: (1) the question of change; (2) bias in favor of the wealthy; (3) misrepresentation; and (4) inadequate decision-making procedures.

The Question of Change. Research and writing since the initial formulation of incremental theory have unfortunately tended to focus predominantly on changes in outcomes as the primary test of incrementalism. Although there are crucial questions concerning the extent of change, two types of literature miss the critical points. The first of these has to do with the definition of an "increment." The basic argument seems to be that the precise measure of an increment is a matter of speculation, and thus the theory is indeterminant: that is, it is impossible to tell an incremental decision from some other type of decision. This argument, in fixating on the label, simply misses the whole point of incremental theory.[15] Incrementalism is a method or strategy for solving problems. It rests on a series of conditions or criteria for decision making rather than simply the pattern of change that results from a decision. The only one

of these criteria that directly involves change is the principle that alternatives depend on existing policy and are marginal adjustments of it. Even this criterion does not necessarily involve the *amount* of change produced. For example, changes were made in tax law to meet the revenue demands of World War II. One of the major changes was a lowering of the personal exemption in a series of steps. This change was accomplished by changing one number in a tax code thousands of pages long. However, this one change had an enormous impact on revenue, on the number of people subject to taxes, and consequently on the nature of tax politics from that time forward. The series of changes was marginal, dependent on existing policy, remedial, serial, and limited—in other words, incremental. However, the result was a radical change in policy.

As an example of the problem of fixating on changes in outcomes rather than how decisions are reached, the literature on budget policy and politics has been devoted almost exclusively to analysis and statistical modeling of changes in budget totals. As a consequence "incrementalism" has been sorely reduced in meaning. Following Aaron Wildavsky's groundbreaking study, *The Politics of the Budgetary Process*, which concentrated on decision-making strategies and tactics, a series of quantitative models of changes in budgets over time were created.[16] These models have been useful in their own right, both in advancing the art of mathematical modeling and in understanding and hence predicting changes in the budget. However, they have little to do with the theory of incrementalism, at least as originally outlined by Lindblom and applied by Wildavsky. Again, by concentrating solely on changes, even in a case where the results tend to demonstrate a regular and steady pattern, we learn little about the decision process or the problem-solving strategies employed by political decision makers.

There is, however, an important critique of the incremental method that involves the notion of change. It is the claim that the method is basically conservative in the sense that both the direction and the amount of change possible over time are constrained by an incremental process. This is not, as are the above arguments, a challenge to the clarity or reality of the incremental method, but rather a challenge to the limits of the method: specifically, a charge that the method works slowly and produces a few substantial changes over a long period. Braybrooke and Lindblom acknowledged this critique, but denied it:

> It is possible to have a quite different impression of the strategy—indeed, the reverse impression. Is not the strategy prepared for a world for which John Dewey said education must

be designed, thereby scandalizing conservative people? Once launched with the strategy on a course of changing policy, where is the stopping-place? Is there any limit to the changes to which it might lend itself? The very word "incrementalism" may awaken the same sort of fears that call forth declamations against "creeping socialism." Surely (from this point of view) it cannot be regarded as a coincidence that the New Deal should be fertile in examples of the strategies being applied.[17]

Despite this rejoinder, the claims persisted. Years later Lindblom, writing with Dahl, admitted that the problem was real:

Granted that the sequences of incremental change proceed too slowly, we believe that the pace can, by appropriate reform, be speeded—for example, by removal of many of the veto powers widely distributed in the American system. How further to raise the frequency of incremental change is an appropriate major target for research and thoughtful discussion.[18]

Lindblom, in a reappraisal and response to critics on the twentieth anniversary of his 1959 article, reiterated his initial faith in progress under an incremental system:

Moreover, incrementalism in politics is not, in principle, slow-moving. It is not necessarily, therefore, a tactic of conservatism. A fast-moving sequence of small changes can more speedily accomplish a drastic alteration of the "status quo" than can an only infrequent major policy change.[19]

However, he also suggested that a curious problem might develop because of the range of changes that are possible:

Incremental changes add up; often more happens than meets the eye. If, on the one hand, this is an objection to incremental politics, this feature of it also suggests that a skilled reformer may learn paths of indirection and surprise, thus reaching objectives that would be successfully resisted were his program more fully revealed. This possibility of course raises important issues in political morality.[20]

He also argued that because of the prevalance of veto mechanisms in the political system and the privileged position of business, in-

crementalism is poorly adapted to solving larger problems of society, such as energy shortages, employment, and inflation. Moreover, he felt that the national agenda was set in such a way as to preclude consideration of such central issues as alternatives to the current distribution of income, reorganization of the distribution of political power, or change in the basis of corporate ownership, prerogative and control.[21] Thus, the problem of change has become a serious question even for those scholars inextricably linked to the concept of incrementalism.

The question of change is important enough that we need to be very clear and precise about what the issues are. The objections to incrementalism stated above come from a liberal tradition, which Lindblom, Braybrooke, and Dahl share and which seems to be based on the premise that government inaction or failure to produce certain types of outcomes is inherently bad. However, it is not clear in any a priori sense that inaction is a failure according to other norms and ideologies. Granting that over time incrementalism does not produce significant results in specific policy areas (for example, ending discrimination, reducing vulnerability to Soviet attack, or redistributing income), an evaluation of this "failure" still depends on other factors: one's appraisal of the desirability of the ends and the costs of reaching them; one's conception of government's role in society; and the disposition of the populace toward the change. Thus, even if incrementalism does not lead to change it could still be working extremely well in a situation where the more ambitious reforms are merely expressions of the personal goals of a critical minority. Evaluation of progress toward many liberal policy goals of the last twenty or even fifty years depends on this question. Has school busing failed because incrementalism failed, or because it succeeded?

Judging the limits of incremental change is not as simple as some would have it, and many judgments seem to be based on premises that may not be uniformly shared. However, there are two possible standards on which broad agreement is possible. The first is the capacity for change, or maintaining the capability in a policy field for effecting change if the need and will arise. To establish this as a standard, one need only imagine that at some point in the future change will be demanded by a political majority. Note, however, that the change required may be retraction as well as expansion of government action. Thus, the failure of incrementalism may not be its inability to produce solutions to problems through government action, but rather its inability to resist government involvement and demands for government benefits from sets of minority interests.

The second standard is more difficult to state precisely and straddles

the issue of economic bias to be discussed below. The direction of policy change should be neither consistently biased in favor of a single powerful minority, particularly when the outcomes of that policy also affect wider segments of the population, nor biased against an affected minority by consistently ignoring its claims. The former possibility could arise either because a specific group has direct control over decision makers or because it controls social or economic institutions or beliefs that have an indirect effect on decision makers. In either case change could be directed through the organization of the agenda or through the management of conflicts that arise as decisions are reached. As the passages quoted above indicate, this concern for change is shared by Lindblom, who views corporate power as the major culprit. The latter problem, bias against an affected minority, can arise because the minority is powerless as the result of a lack of organization or political or economic resources or because those representing the majority consciously disregard its claims. Thus, incremental change is bracketed by these two potential hazards, both as old as the notion of representative government itself.

Bias in Favor of Economic Power. Among the most persistent critiques of American democracy in general and the incremental/pluralist model in particular is that the system is biased in favor of those who control economic resources. Although theories about the exact mechanisms and strategies promoting such a bias have varied, the argument itself has not changed appreciably since the Progressive Era. At times it centers on the role of wealthy families or a broader "power elite," but more often it turns to the power of corporate officials, power derived naturally from their crucial roles in production, investment, and employment. The more sophisticated versions of the argument propose subtle forms of influence. Rather than using coercive power, economic elites exercise power by controlling values and limiting the scope of alternatives considered in political decisions (i.e., by limiting the definition of what is politically possible). This control of the "agenda," which serves to limit the bounds of government action, is not seriously opposed because of mass inculcation of capitalist values.[22]

The incremental model is a theoretical sitting duck for such charges. It admits a dependence on the status quo; a primary condition is a limited horizon in terms of both alternatives and analysis; and the emphasis on multiple actors and fragmented decision making affords bountiful opportunity for economic elites to block threatening actions. However, actual tests of such propositions give more equivocal results. More than twenty years ago Robert Dahl responded to a new wave of

power elite theories by posing a rigorous test of decision bias that required that for a suitable sample of decisions it be shown: (1) that an identifiable power elite existed; (2) that its position was at odds with the will of the majority; and (3) that its alternatives were successful in a significant proportion of cases.[23] Although logically precise and correct, the task posed by Dahl is enormous for even a single decision, let alone the adequate sample he specifies. Although the problem is somewhat easier when the focus is narrowly on corporate power, sorting out preferences, locating majorities, measuring influence, and determining successful outcomes is often difficult. In practice the intellectual debate goes on interminably, with one's stance usually determined by individual values and perceptions rather than by reference to a specific body of evidence.

The approach in this study is less rigorous than that implied by Dahl, but it does make an effort to analyze who benefits from a historical series of decisions. It also attempts—less successfully, I fear—to determine whether those outcomes match the preferences of a minority, sets of minorities, or an aggregated majority. Although economic bias may produce a mismatch between preferences and policy outcomes, it is not the only source of distortion.

Misrepresentation. In idealized notions of democracy, public policy mirrors the policy preferences of the majority of citizens. However, many modern democratic theorists have been uneasy about this idealized formulation. Although electoral competition, party differences, and interest groups may be conceived of as political institutions that translate population preferences into policy choices, pluralist theory does not necessarily require an exact fit between preferences and policies. What is important in these theories is open political competition either in elections or between interest groups. This competition serves to check excess power and moderate extreme outcomes.[24] Indeed, several theorists are openly dubious of the impact of mass preferences on policy decisions. For example, Joseph Schumpeter, in a famous passage, totally rejected this idealized notion:

> Thus (in the classical doctrine) the selection of representatives is made secondary to the primary purpose of the democratic arrangement, which is to vest the power of deciding political issues in the electorate. Suppose we reverse the roles of these two elements and make the deciding of issues by the electorate secondary to the election of the men who are to do the deciding. To put it differently, we now take the view that the role of

the people is to produce a government, or else an intermediate body which in turn will produce a government, or else an intermediate body which will produce a national executive or government. And we define: the democratic method is that institutional arrangement for arriving at political decisions in which individuals acquire the power to decide by means of a competitive struggle for the people's vote.[25]

Robert Dahl, in *A Preface to Democratic Theory*, while supporting Schumpeter's general position, objects to his trivializing of the role of elections in determining policy outcomes, stating that elections are "crucial processes for insuring that political leaders will be somewhat responsive to the preferences of some ordinary citizens."[26] However, earlier in the same work, he claims "that in no large nation state can elections tell us much about the preferences of majorities and minorities, beyond that bare fact that among those who went to the polls a majority, plurality, or minority indicated their first choices for some particular candidate or group of candidates."[27] The best explanation for this apparent contradiction is that individual candidates will be responsive to what they perceive as the needs and preferences of voters in their geographic districts, but that elections as a whole convey little because these needs, which may not be explicit in the first place, are summed across a series of individual elections. Dahl stresses that final policy outcomes are likely to be moderate because of the incremental bargaining and compromise that characterize the system.

Since these early statements, survey research results have been more encouraging, at least as regards the importance of policy issues in the voter's choices between candidates. For example, V. O. Key's last book makes an eloquent and convincing argument to the effect that elections actually have a greater connection to policy issues than studies of elections up to 1963 have shown. His basic argument, which he calls "perverse and unorthodox," is that there is evidence, based on analysis of those who switch parties and those who stand pat between elections, that issue congruence between candidates and voters is an important factor in electoral choice. Key's point is that voters are not fools (or perhaps that many are not fools) and that the electorate is "moved by concern about central and relevant questions of public policy, of governmental performance, and of executive personality."[28] Since Key's death, the importance of issues as determinants of election outcomes has been the subject of a large amount of contested and very technical research. However, there is general agreement that issues played a significant role in the presidential elections of 1964, 1972, and 1980.[29]

We are only beginning to look at the relationship between congressional elections and issue positions, a focus that one could argue is more important in many policy areas.[30]

Even with Key's analysis and the later mixed evidence on the importance of issues in electoral outcomes, there is little to suggest that elections provide anything more than the most general exchange of policy information between candidates and voters. Theoretically, however, interest groups may make up for some of the shortcomings of electoral competition in translating preferences into policies. According to theories that generally applaud the role of interest groups, such groups serve as a valuable link between decision makers and the mass population (or at least subgroups in the population).[31] These groups establish communication on specific issues, providing information, initiating action, and protecting member interests. Although there are questions about the type, quality, and range of information provided, this link has several theoretical advantages. First, it offers solace to those who are cautious about conferring too much power on leaders, elected or otherwise. Interest groups serve as permanent watchdogs and are thus a constraining influence in what may be a very complex legislative process easily co-opted by legislative specialists.

Second, it offers an outlet for expressing intense preferences on the few issues that might be of interest to any single faction in society. From the Croatian Society, interested in Yugoslav political prisoners, to the American Petroleum Institute, lobbying for decontrol of oil, an avenue is opened that is not available through electoral mechanisms alone. Thus, interest groups at least indirectly serve to increase the range and frequency of interaction between the population and their leaders; provide specific and ongoing information in the policy process; and allow individuals a mechanism for registering preferences on certain issues. Combined with the electoral theory, these models provide a theoretical answer to the problems of adequate representation of diverse interests and a reasonable degree of political equality in the actual decision-making process. Or do they? There are some relevant counterarguments.

Two important problems with the hypothesized links between policy decisions and citizen preferences involve the structure of preferences themselves and the adequacy of the translation actually provided by elections and interest groups. Three basic issues are involved in the question of citizen preferences. The first, which has bred a great mass of social science research, is whether citizens have adequate knowledge and information and opinions that readily translate into policy choices.

Although a review of the literature is beyond the scope of this chapter, the trend is from early pessimism to a more optimistic view of the abilities and knowledge of the mass public.[32] Unfortunately, much of the research is limited by the types of policy questions provided in national surveys. These surveys tend to ask relatively general questions on a number of issues, and thus it is difficult to explore attitudes on any single issue in depth. This study concentrates on a single issue, and will review the attitude information that is available. However, because of the way questions are phrased and, more importantly, because of the complexity of the opinions on taxes, the results are subject to differing interpretations.

This latter point—the complexity of issues and thus the demand for complex preferences—poses a second problem in translating citizen preferences into policy outcomes. Policy choices usually involve a series of questions rather than a single question, and reasonable answers to each individual question may be inconsistent. Often there may be general agreement on a broad goal for a policy, but fierce disagreement when it is necessary to trade off goals or to agree whether a goal is worth a specific price. In the case of taxes, for example, the issues include the preferred form of taxation, the appropriate level of taxes, the distribution of burdens, and the exact structure of a tax code. Reasonable opinions on each of these questions may logically conflict and may also fluctuate considerably when other implications are introduced. For example, to no one's surprise, most people feel that taxes should be lower, but when this desire is matched against a loss of services or a budget deficit, the attitudes shift considerably. Thus, even the best-informed and concerned citizen faces, with considerable uncertainty, the same kind of difficult trade-off choices that face decision makers. Preference complexity aggravates other difficulties in translating mass attitudes into policy choices.

A third difficulty is the problem of preference aggregation. The problem goes beyond the simple notion of trying to "sum" complex preferences and determine a majority opinion, although this is no trivial undertaking in its own right. Several theorists have argued that for important policies that lack an underlying distribution of moderate and unimodal opinion, pluralist solutions will be difficult. The contrasting example is usually an extreme bimodal split in opinion, particularly when cleavages on sets of issues reinforce each other, thus separating the population into relatively permanent opposing and hostile camps.[33] Such a distribution makes compromise, bargaining, and marginal change unlikely. On a potentially redistributive policy such as taxation,

such differences in opinion are likely. Indeed, as will be shown in chapter 16, there is evidence to indicate that such distributions characterize important attitudes toward taxation.

Another preference structure that can cause difficulty is one in which attitudes are widely dispersed, both in preferences and intensities. Specifically, the case may arise where groups have very narrow but intense concerns on a particular policy and little interest in other, perhaps related, issues. Pluralist democratic theory poses this as the problem of the tyranny of the majority, in which the demands or interests of the narrow minority may be permanently overridden by majority rule. However, the argument presented in this study will be the opposite one: that decision makers cannot resist such narrow interests, with a devastating cumulative effect on policy.

A final potential problem in the representation of policy preferences in an incremental/pluralist system is that electoral competition and interest group representation may be inadequate or badly distorted. A rigorous theory of electoral translation of policy preferences requires that voters have specific policy preferences and that party and candidate choices exist that mirror those preferences. If parties and candidates fail to articulate distinct policy choices, the link dissolves. A weaker theory might assume that party labels convey sets of values and support for particular groups that will give voters some assurances that future policy choices will be in their interests.[34] However, even this weaker version, which seems more credible for a more complex policy such as the income tax, requires some differentiation of parties. For example, if one party consistently favors tax reforms that reduce the burden on lower income groups, without knowing details a low income voter can reasonably select a candidate based on party. If historically such differentiation does not exist, any linkage is doubtful. In the chapters ahead, partisan differences on tax decisions will be an important issue.

The problem of interest group distortion is usually phrased in terms of economic bias, which was discussed above. Thus, the proposition that the economically well-off, particularly business groups, have undue access and influence through their lobbying efforts is the leading issue in analyzing this aspect of tax politics. However, I would also note that another problem may be that certain groups purport to express "citizen interests" while in reality representing what an elite has interpreted as citizen preferences. Because of the complexity of preferences on tax questions, this is an especially relevant distinction.

Inadequate Procedures. Procedural critiques of incrementalism can be easily misconstrued. A common argument is with the method itself—that is, that the range of opinion and alternatives is very limited, and

thus the decision process is too restrictive. Of course it is restrictive—that is the point and a principal argument in favor of the incremental method. The relevant questions involve the openness of the process, the care taken in analyzing alternatives, the number and influence of decision makers, and the registering of formal and public choices.

Questions can be raised, and often are in the case of tax politics, with each of these conditions. Rather than open and public debate, it is argued that crucial decisions are made in committees, often in closed executive sessions. Careful analysis and debating of proposals may precede some policy changes, but others are passed quietly as part of lengthy policy packages with only perfunctory examination. In contrast to the broad and fragmented decision process assumed by incremental theory, actual policy making may be dominated by a handful of executive branch experts, powerful congressional leaders, and influential committee members. Finally, rather than formal, open voting procedures, which signify agreement and provide some potential for accountability, many decisions escape voting at all, while others end in ambiguous votes on large policy packages. In fact, for most tax legislation, specific procedures are adopted to ensure that tax provisions are not the subject of floor amendments and separate votes. Thus, there is a conscious effort to constrain democratic procedures and limit the scope of debate.

These procedural critiques reached a peak in the early 1970s and culminated in significant changes in Democratic Party procedures in Congress.[35] The tax committees, then headed by Rep. Wilbur Mills (D-Ark.) and Sen. Russell Long (D-La.), were the most frequently cited examples of procedural aberrations and were particular targets of "reform." The effects of these on tax policy will be outlined and evaluated in subsequent chapters.

The Arguments of this Study

Relinquishing the potential for dramatic suspense, I will state briefly the major arguments of this book, most of which run counter to the critiques outlined above. With one important exception, which will be discussed last, the arguments follow the issues described in the last section.

The Question of Change. Contrary to the standard critique, which centered on the conservative bias of incremental decision making, as Braybrooke and Lindblom anticipated, in the area of taxation a highly incremental process has produced radical policy changes over time.

Indeed, the problem with the incremental approach is that the process allows *too much* change—that over time political resistance to a broad range of demands wears thin and eventually disappears. Among the results of this persistent hyperresponsiveness are the ever-increasing number of tax reduction devices and the unbelievable complexity of the tax system. Ironically, these trends have created a situation in which the future capacity for change in the income tax has been eroded. Because of the scope of tax reduction provisions and the complexity of the code, it is doubtful: (1) that the income tax can meet potential revenue demands in the future; (2) that it could be used to redistribute income, even if the political will to do so existed; and (3) that it can be "reformed" to expand the tax base and/or simplify the system. Thus, the radical nature of change over time and the inability of the system to resist change create a policy morass that is perpetuated by its own structure.

Bias in Favor of Economic Power. Determining the extent of bias favorable to the economically powerful is difficult in any policy area, even one like the income tax where the benefits of policy changes can be reasonably apportioned. Direct influence is impossible to measure and probably varies significantly according to economic circumstances and political regimes. However, by estimating historical change in aggregate tax burdens, and by analyzing detailed policy changes that affect different income and economic groups, some inferences concerning the patterns of bias can be made.

The results of these analyses suggest conclusions somewhat more complex than the one-dimensional critique described in the previous section. There is no question that in normal times, which generally means peacetime, corporations and those in higher-income groups benefit considerably from incremental changes in tax legislation. However, the effects of wars and crisis periods cannot be overlooked because of the extreme increases in rate progressivity that they introduce, increases consistently eroded in subsequent periods of peace. This pattern also challenges the commonly stated assumption that the income tax represents a historical commitment to income redistribution. Whether the lack of such a commitment is a result of indoctrination or "false consciousness" is impossible to determine, although relevant public attitudes are analyzed in chapter 16. What does seem apparent is that legislated tax reduction and reduced progressivity are the historical norm, breaking down only in periods of crisis.

The apparent fragility of our political commitment to a progressive tax system does not necessarily mean that the rich control the tax system.

Indeed, many conservatives bemoan the steeply progressive rates, which they judge to be unfair and detrimental to economic growth. Although these claims usually misrepresent the actual effective rates paid and the normal historical trend toward lower nominal rates, one point that they stress is correct: the well-off pay most of the income taxes in the United States. Additionally, detailed analysis of changes in tax policy clearly establishes that, by any of a number of indicators, policy changes benefiting the rich are usually hard fought politically— much more so than changes in those provisions that benefit lower-income groups (and there are a number of such provisions). In the broadest historical terms, this produces a tax system that essentially exempts the poor, taxes the broad middle class at a very stable rate, and taxes the rich at varying rates depending on political and ideological shifts. Thus, rather than arguing that the rich control tax politics, the conclusion of this study is that the principal problem is that *no one* controls tax policy and that the tendency is for politicians to confer as many benefits on as many groups as is politically feasible.

Misrepresentation. My arguments related to the problem of representing mass preferences in policy choices are closer to the standard critiques than those on the issues of change and bias. I have concluded, however, that it is very difficult, either theoretically or empirically, to state precisely the relationships between preferences, party positions, and outcomes in an area as complex as tax policy. From one perspective it will be shown that there is an uncanny match between aggregate preferences and both the actual burden of taxes and the structural features of the tax code. However, if one focuses on different survey questions, this image changes dramatically. There is also evidence of bipolarity on the issue of progressivity, at least among those expressing an opinion. Thus, I argue that preferences on income tax issues are nebulous and that there is, and probably should be, great latitude for politicians to define preferences as they see fit.

My second argument is more troublesome and very much in line with the position that party differences are mostly symbolic. It will be shown that the public perceives and expects sharp differences between candidates and parties on tax issues. However, although at times there is evidence of real partisan conflict, more often the differences are rhetorically exaggerated exercises in symbolic distancing. Although "critical votes" sometimes produce partisan splits, these are misleading in terms of the amount of underlying consensus on most sections of tax bills that run to hundreds of pages. Whatever partisan differences exist are outweighed by the common incentives that operate in tax politics. And

these bipartisan incentives generate constant pressures for change and bias the system in favor of conferring specific tax benefits at the expense of general revenues.

Inadequate Procedures. My argument relating to procedures is again perverse in relation not only to the standard critiques, but also to what I believe is the prevailing attitude among contemporary democratic theorists, who advocate increased openness and participation. In general I argue that the image of tax politics as closed, careless, and narrowly dominated by powerful elites has been overdrawn, particularly in recent years. As is demonstrated in section II and chapter 15, major tax policies are seldom enacted carelessly, quietly, or in haste. In addition, the closed-committee system, with limited floor voting, which often prevailed in the first sixty years of income tax politics, has not prevailed in the last ten.

The important issues are what the results of these procedures have been and how this "democratic" trend should be evaluated. I will argue that the results have been disastrous and the inverse of what congressional reformers had in mind. Further, I will argue that these results are not idiosyncratic but were readily predictable, and that opening up the system and making it more responsive to political demands is moving in the wrong direction. Indeed, what should be considered is an attempt to stabilize the tax system by insulating it from politics.

The Long-Term Consequences of Incremental Policy Making. With rare exceptions, neither critics nor advocates of the incremental/pluralist model have had much concern for the long-term consequences of policy decisions.[36] The reason goes back to the division between policy analysis and political theory with which this book began. Theorists are mostly interested in either the nuances of specific decisions or the institutions and behaviors that structure the decision process. Empirical research derived from theoretical issues conforms to this emphasis. Research takes the form of decision case studies, the study of institutions and procedures, or the detailed observation of political actors. All of this is commendable and useful, and it greatly increases our knowledge of politics. However, these studies are rarely concerned with outcomes, and those that are are confined to a very narrow time frame. On the other hand, those concentrating on outcomes (e.g., in the budget field) have been primarily concerned with statistical modeling of the process and less concerned with substantive effects, especially of a cumulative nature. What is missing, unfortunately, is enormously important be-

cause of the simple fact that incremental decision making, by design and intent, is long term and cumulative.

This cumulative aspect of incrementalism is theoretically one of its greatest assets, but may also prove its greatest liability. For tax politics it is the latter. It is an asset to the extent that mistakes can be corrected, identifiable problems can be continuously patched, and radical changes can result. The detrimental aspects of cumulative change, which may be peculiar to tax policy but seem more pervasive, are that policies can be predicted to expand in scope, cost, and structure. The results of this expansion are likely to be increasing complexity, limited options, and an unintentional but unavoidable undermining of the original and primary purpose of the policy. For tax policy this means the development of a tax system of enormous complexity, which may have reached the limits of legitimacy, the capacity to meet revenue demands, and the capability of reform. Although there are benefits in the policy structure that has developed, a very strong case can be made that the disadvantages far outweigh the advantages. The first task is to consider this case in the context of more general normative theories of the income tax.

Section II.
Theories of
Income Taxation

The two chapters that make up this section provide both a summary and a critical evaluation of selected theories of income taxation. The discussion is not meant to be comprehensive; rather, it concentrates on the tax philosophies that are the most important historically or that seem to have the greatest impact on actual policy debates. The presentation is slanted toward the normative issues in incremental theory, and particularly the intrinsic difficulties in applying a priori value orderings to public policy decisions.

This slant leads to the chapter division into "prescriptive" and "pragmatic" approaches to income tax theory. By "prescriptive" I mean the quest for general principles that provide definitive rules for the structure and form of taxation. The theories covered range from the somewhat dated efforts of utilitarian theorists to deduce principles of tax progressivity to the more elaborate recent efforts by "optimal tax" theorists to integrate concern for equity with concern for economic efficiency. Incremental theory rests on the presumption that such prescriptions will not be persuasive—a presumption supported by my arguments in chapter 2. The "pragmatic" approach begins with an analysis of Henry Simons' theory of a comprehensive tax base, which concentrates on defining an income base against which various tax levies can be assessed. Although there is an element of pragmatism in this approach in that it allows significant leeway for political decision making, I argue that Simons' position ultimately rests on an unclear set of value premises. Chapter 3 ends with a defense of a comprehensive or broad-based income tax, but one that rests on a more instrumental set of values than that employed by Simons.

Chapter 2.
Prescriptive
Theories of
Taxation

The goal of this chapter and the next is to provide the reader with a sense of the normative problems that envelop tax issues. Since theories of taxation date back to the Roman empire, any review of tax philosophy must be selective and somewhat superficial. Fortunately, other excellent summaries exist for those who wish to delve further into the problem.[1] The theories reviewed here concentrate on the income tax and are limited to three traditions in that theoretical literature. The oldest, utilitarian theories, and the newest, optimal tax theory, are the specific subjects of this chapter; the one most often referred to in political debates, the comprehensive tax base approach, is the subject of the next. However, before describing and evaluating these traditions, it is instructive to review the scope of questions and alternatives that would be involved in a truly comprehensive analysis of tax policy. In other words, just briefly I want to treat seriously the notion of a "synoptic ideal" for taxation. Although Lindblom equated synoptic decision making with the grandiose goals of a social welfare function (see chapter 1), even the much more restricted normative assignment of designing a comprehensive tax system from scratch provides an appreciation of the incremental method.

A Synoptic Analysis of Taxation

Imagine having the power to design a complete tax system for a modern industrial society. What would a comprehensive, synoptic evaluation entail? At a minimum, the design would have to include consideration and analysis of: (1) the type or object of taxes; (2) the unit to be taxed; (3) the distribution of the tax burden; and (4) the exact structure and administrative apparatus appropriate for each type of tax. For each of these issues a set of diverse values or criteria would need to be consid-

ered. A brief description of these design features and some of the
normative criteria by which alternatives might be evaluated verifies the
scope and complexity of the task. It is instructive to note that for each
issue most of the options mentioned are not imaginary. Rather, the
examples are drawn from actual taxes that have developed over time or
from proposals that have received political consideration.

The Object of Taxation. What can be taxed by government is finite,
but just barely. And, further, within each category of objects, there are
often numerous subcategories that could and perhaps should be treated
separately. For example, taxes on property are very old. At one time it
was common in the United States to tax not only private residences,
land, and structures, but also personal property such as automobiles,
furniture, jewelry, and other possessions. Numerous categories and
subcategories of commercial property and equipment can also be taxed.

Taxes can also be levied on various forms and types of consumption.
A consumption tax can be based on a flow of income, much like an
income tax. This type of tax, currently being discussed as an "expenditure tax," depends on the theoretical separation of income into consumption and savings. An expenditure tax subtracts (in any of several
complex ways) the latter from income and taxes the remainder. However, consumption taxes need not be based on income flows, and
historically have not been in this country. Usually they take the more
common form of sales and excise taxes and customs duties. Another
consumption tax, common in Europe and recently proposed in Congress, is the value-added tax, which levies taxes on successive stages of
the production process rather than taxing final sales or personal expenditures.

In addition to property and consumption, taxes can also be levied on
inheritances, on income flows (in accordance with any of a number of
definitions of income), or on particular actions or services. Action taxes
often take the form of license fees (to get married, drive a car, transfer
stocks, etc.). However, we also tax such deviant behaviors as gambling,
smoking, drinking, and driving at excessive speeds, and we have proposals pending for taxing pollution and the purchase of gas-guzzling
automobiles. In other words, the scope of things that can be taxed is as
varied as the economic and behavioral patterns of modern society.

The Taxable Unit. For most types of taxes, the taxable unit is also a
controversial issue. Common income tax examples distinguish between individuals, families, and corporations. However, the tax code
further splits these categories into a bewildering array of family types

and legal entities that distinguish various categories of profit and non-profit organizations, including numerous types of partnerships, holding companies, foundations, and so on. Consumption and action taxes also vary, depending on the unit. Excise taxes on tires differ from automobiles, trucks, and motorcycles; so do the tolls they pay. In many countries taxes on products vary considerably depending on how much of the product was produced within the country, thus distinguishing foreign from nonforeign units. Personal property and sales taxes often distinguish between "luxuries" and necessities. Inheritance taxes are replete with exceptional conditions for different types of property and different forms of transfer. Farms are treated differently from residential property or tangible assets; property left to children or to charity can be considered differently from that left to a spouse.

Tax Burden. Tax systems must identify not only the object and unit of taxation, but also relative rates to be paid. The most common distinction is between levels of income or wealth: should income or inheritance taxes be progressive, proportional, or regressive? However, rate structures and thus tax burdens can involve much more than this one-dimensional reference. For example, the history of excise and customs taxation is a history of political struggle over burdens to be borne by various products and regions. One variant of a consumption tax briefly proposed in the midst of World War II would have taxed consumption progressively. European value-added taxes often apply varying rates to different types of products, usually based on their necessity. The theory of effluent charges is also based on increasing burdens for types and levels of pollution. One might also theoretically propose that the taxes on liquor or cigarettes increase as consumption rises. Even with the income tax, the question of burden goes well beyond the specification of simple rates to the consideration of endless special pleadings. For example, should excessive medical and casualty losses be deductible? Should retirement, public assistance, and unemployment benefits be taxed? Should the number of children matter? Should small businesses pay different rates from large corporations, regardless of the income flow in a given period? Abstracting the problem of tax burdens from these related questions, as is done in the tax theories that follow, greatly simplifies the problems that must be resolved in practice.

Administration. Policy formulation all too often neglects policy administration; in taxation it cannot. A tax that cannot be collected, or one that is very inefficient, is of little use. The design of a tax system must take into account a number of administrative issues. For example, withhold-

ing and filing features distinguish major types of income tax and expenditure tax schemes.[2] Similarly, the ultimate distinction between sales taxes and value-added taxes is the manner of collection, with a critical argument centering on the invisibility of the latter. Administrative capabilities and costs affect not only decisions to initiate new taxes (a value-added tax has been successfully resisted in the United States in part because of such costs), but also subsequent development. For example, as a tax code becomes more complex and tax avoidance more feasible amd more tempting, information sources, auditing functions, and data-processing capabilities loom as critical factors.

Normative Criteria. This complicated set of factors suggests a bewildering array of potential tax systems. In a synoptic analysis, each possibility would be evaluated against a set of agreed-on criteria. The list of criteria most often used is also extensive, often unclear, and in part logically inconsistent. The list always begins with equity, which is traditionally subdivided into vertical and horizontal equity. The former refers to the distribution of tax burdens between various income classes, the most common assumption being that the burden should increase as income increases. The latter refers to the principle that similar cases should be equally taxed. The difficulties of clearly specifying and convincingly arguing for either of these criteria will be discussed in detail in this and the following chapter. However, other criteria are also very important in tax analysis.

The effect of taxes on economic efficiency usually follows equity as a primary value and concern. By this some mean the distorting effect of taxes on market allocation of production factors. Taxes raise the prices of labor, capital, land, and equipment, and thus the natural market or equilibrium mix of components is disturbed. Other tax theorists and decision makers are more concerned with the specific problem of changed incentives. High income taxes might reduce incentives to work; ironically, negative income taxes might have the same effect. Similarly, a refrain heard often in recent years is that taxes on capital retard the incentive to invest, particularly in new, high-risk ventures. Judging by the actions of states and municipalities in the last decade, a major concern at those levels is the effect of property, use, and corporate taxes on company incentives to locate or retain facilities in particular areas.

Criteria other than equity and efficiency may be less prominent but are nevertheless important in tax debates. One major theorist, Richard Musgrave, has resurrected in modern form the old principle that taxes should be levied in relation to the benefits received from public goods.

This benefit theory is usually associated in practice with fees for services or specific forms of excise taxes (such as hunting licenses or taxes on tires and airline tickets). However, the basic proposition also plays a prominent role in property tax debates (often pitting those with school-bound children against those without) and even in analyses of income taxes where the issue is who benefits from broad government programs.[3]

Other values considered include administrative efficiency, which can be conceived of (if not always measured) as the administrative cost per dollar of revenue collected, and the simplicity of the tax system. Although the two are often related, there is a justification for distinguishing them as separate criteria. Administrative efficiency is important on a simple cost-benefit basis but also because of its effects on the accuracy, impartiality, and integrity of the tax system. Simplicity is related to some of these effects, but many other factors (information sources, audit capability, data-processing capacity, etc.) also affect administrative efficiency in these areas. Similarly, a complex tax system has costs associated with it apart from the administrative ones. Complicated systems require tax experts to compute and plan strategies for individuals and organizations, thus reducing taxpayer understanding and diverting resources to activities some consider unproductive. More important, complexity, and the public's perception of that complexity, may affect the legitimacy of the tax system. These consequences may extend to general attitudes toward the rule of law and government actions and institutions. Although they may be difficult to measure accurately, they are an important normative consideration nonetheless.

A final point, which I will not belabor, is that the various criteria often conflict. The trade-off between vertical equity and economic efficiency is the most prominent example; however, there are others.[4] It will be argued in the following chapter that the pursuits of horizontal and vertical equity are often inconsistent in both theory and practice. Moreover, benefit principles may conflict with both equity and efficiency. For example, public education probably disproportionately aids the poor, but taxing them would run counter to the idea of vertical equity.[5] Also, while proponents of benefit theories argue that they are less distorting of market transactions than other types of taxes, relying solely on users' fees would certainly have delayed—or prevented—the construction of the interstate highway system, airports, and other collective public works that undoubtedly aid economic growth. Other examples of conflict abound. A simple tax system makes little provision for distinctions commonly accepted on equity grounds (such as deducting the cost of doing business or consideration of different taxing units).

It would also fail to distinguish between types of income and activities (such as savings or capital gains) that on efficiency grounds would be treated differently.[6] In all of these examples, and numerous others, the various values must be weighed against each other—a very difficult task if one adheres to a comprehensive ideal.

Given these complicated sets of potential alternatives and the range and inconsistency of values, it will come as little surprise that in practice policy makers proceed in a highly incremental manner. Rather than building or reforming tax systems from the ground up, they begin with what they have, concentrate on a few alternative modifications, try to reach agreement on the options (perhaps stressing different values), and hope that disastrous choices can be corrected and unfulfilled goals resurrected later. The historical section that follows describes this process in considerable detail for the income tax. However, other types of taxes at different levels of government have also developed incrementally, and the result has been an unbelievable maze of varying tax structures.

Theoretical analysis of tax issues is also usually nonsynoptic, although a minority of theorists portray their solutions and conclusions as if they resulted from a synoptic analysis. This reduction in theoretical scope is accomplished either by concentrating debate on a specific form of taxation (as in a symposium on the value-added tax) or by trying to generalize arguments related to one or perhaps several of the value criteria. Examples of the latter include efforts to develop or argue for tax systems relating taxes paid to benefits from government action, efforts to develop theoretical prescriptions or principles specifying appropriate tax burdens, and the hypothetical trade-off between equity and efficiency. The discussion to follow is restricted to narrow arguments over value criteria applied to the income tax. Even with that reduced focus, the severe problem of prescribing principles to decide value issues will become clear.

Classical Utilitarian Theories

As issues of equality exploded in the industrialized world of the nineteenth century, there was a parallel expansion in theories of income taxation.[7] Although some of these theories, particularly the earlier ones, proposed equal or proportional taxation, there was an acute awareness of the impending prospect of progressive, and hence redistributive, tax rates. It is safe to say that none of these theories have sustained the test of time and policy development. But their failure is

more than a matter of historical interest; it is relevant to current debates over taxation and income redistribution and what we might expect from them.

Utilitarian tax theories are based on the notion that happiness or well-being is the fundamental value to be considered in policy choices. Utility as a general concept has since been challenged as vague, unmeasurable, and not comparable from one individual to another.[8] Utilitarian tax theories are somewhat immune to this critique, however, in that, unlike more global theories of felicity, they relied on income as the standard of utility. Still, as we shall see shortly, the exact relationship between income and utility remains a critical question.

Assuming some positive relationship between aggregate income and aggregate happiness, taxes, considered apart from benefits, reduce happiness and thus induce sacrifice. Around this notion were developed the theories of equal, proportional, and minimal sacrifice. *Equal sacrifice* was defined as an equal or constant loss of utility for each taxpayer. *Proportional sacrifice* meant a loss of utility that ensured that the ratio of after-tax utility between taxpayers was equivalent to the before-tax ratio. Finally, the *minimal sacrifice* theory proposed a tax structure that minimized the aggregate utility loss when totaled for all taxpayers.[9]

A series of classic studies in tax theory demonstrated the sensitivity of these theories to the exact functional relationship between utility and income. The first important contribution was made by a Dutch mathematician, Arnold Jacob Cohen-Stuart. Writing in the late nineteenth century, when the most widely accepted general notion was that taxes should reflect a "leave them as you found them" ideal, he argued in favor of a progressive rate structure. He demonstrated that if it is assumed that the utility curve follows a "rectangular" or logarithmic form (known at the time as the Bernoulli curve), then equal sacrifice would imply a constant percentage rate, but proportional sacrifice would require progressive rates. The assumption that $U_i = \log(Z_i)$, where U_i is the utility at income Z_i, implied that utility was the inverse of income ($1/Z$). This was not only simple, but also consistent with the widely held assumption that marginal utility decreased as income rose.[10] Because proportional sacrifice was more consistent with the ideal of neutrality, Cohen-Stuart argued, tax rates should be progressive. Since income taxes were then under consideration in both the United States and Europe, his contribution received wide attention, at least among academic tax experts.

However, British economist F. Y. Edgeworth quickly destroyed Cohen-Stuart's formulation by demonstrating that other utility functions, which also assumed decreasing marginal utility for income,

would yield inconsistent tax rates for the principles of equal and proportional sacrifice alike. For example, if it is assumed that utility was equivalent to the square root of income, it turns out that equal sacrifice requires a regressive rate structure and proportional sacrifice a constant percentage rate.[11] For more complex but still marginal decreasing utility functions, it was further shown that equal sacrifice could lead to progressive rates; for others, proportional sacrifice implied regressive rates. Thus, depending on the exact functional relationship assumed, equal and proportional sacrifice might mean regressive, constant, or progressive rates.

Edgeworth further argued that, assuming marginal decreasing utility, the only principle that avoids this inconsistency is minimal sacrifice: because each increment to income has less utility than that preceding it, taxing the highest incomes will produce the least amount of utility loss, regardless of the exact functional relationship between utility and income. He also argued that minimal sacrifice was normatively justified in that it maximized after-tax utility or happiness.

Although Edgeworth's formulation was ingenious and widely cited in support of progressive tax movements, it was not without significant flaws. Unfortunately, several prominent and general critiques of sacrifice principles confuse the issues when they are applied to Edgeworth's theory. One such critique focuses on the charge that utility cannot be calculated or quantified and thus all utility principles are necessarily vague. For example, Walter Blum and Harry Kalven concede that the idea of declining marginal utility makes intuitive sense and would be accepted by most people, but declare that: "The error lies in trying to translate money, which can be measured in definite units, into corresponding units of satisfaction or well-being. In the end, satisfaction in the sense of happiness defies quantification."[12] Other prominent theorists, such as Henry Simons and Harold Groves, also denounce utility theories on similar grounds.[13]

However, although the problem of quantifying and measuring utility creates havoc for most theories of welfare economics, it does not affect the clarity of the minimal sacrifice theory. All that is required is some form of continuous declining marginal utility of income. If this is accepted, whether we know the exact shape of that curve or not, a specific prescription for a progressive tax system is forthcoming, and that fact makes minimal sacrifice a dominant theory relative to equal or proportional sacrifice. Indeed, it is precisely because we cannot measure utility exactly that minimal sacrifice is dominant. The prescription that follows from a rigorous application of minimal sacrifice is that required taxes should be extracted exclusively from the individuals in

society with the highest incomes, that group continuously expanding as the top incomes become equal. Given any continuous function that fulfills the requirement of decreasing marginal utility, the income thus extracted will represent a minimal loss of utility. Whether utility is quantifiable in practice or not, the prescription is exact.

Another variant of the argument against minimal sacrifice is that the vagueness of the utility concept and the lack of specification for utility functions leads to such a broad array of possible alternatives that the theory is useless. This challenge is an appropriate critique of equal and proportional sacrifice theories, as has been shown, but not of minimal sacrifice. In fact, the opposite is true: it is because the minimal sacrifice theory is so devastatingly exact and robust that it is open to criticism.

There are two fundamental weaknesses in the minimal sacrifice theory. The first is the radical prescription that it offers. Taxes would be borne only by the wealthiest members of society, the tax system continuously bringing them down to a level equal with at least some of their fellows. The extreme nature of this outcome led even the most dedicated proponents of minimal sacrifice to suggest that the rates be modified. Cohen-Stuart, who after Edgeworth's critique supported minimal sacrifice, argued for a subsistence exemption with progressive rates that decline to proportionality at higher incomes. He couched his argument in an elaborate explanation that for the very rich, who have satisfied all personal wants, the utility of income ceases to decline marginally, suddenly and mysteriously providing constant utility (presumably at a minimal level).[14] Edgeworth was not at all persuaded by this argument, as he coyly commented: "The mathematical reader who is not convinced by Mr. Cohen-Stuart on this point will hardly defer to others."[15] However, he then stated: "Practical reasons, not deductions from any form of the first principle, would thus lead to a 'digressive progression' culminating in a simply proportionate tax of the higher incomes, such as in fact seems to be coming into vogue."[16] The practical reasons he discussed are the consideration for "other disutilities," such as disincentives to work, produce, or invest.

Unfortunately, once such an admission is allowed and the prescription is violated, the general principle becomes vague and ambiguous. Although Edgeworth went on to create "formulae" for aiding policy makers in setting tax rates (formulae they did not particularly welcome),[17] he provided no convincing analysis to support either the break points or the steepness of the progressive rates. Once the anchor of minimal sacrifice is raised, the ship quickly founders. Thus, the radical result of minimal sacrifice theory destroyed its practicality. The underlying reason is that the concept of utility could not be stretched far

enough to encompass all relevant values. Exclusive taxation of the rich, at probably close to confiscatory rates, violated even minimal considerations of fairness based on merit or just dessert.[18] Moreover, as Edgeworth understood, the analysis supporting minimal sacrifice also disregarded the effects of taxation on economic efficiency and investment.

The importance of including the economic effects of taxation in a utilitarian calculus was fully understood by theorists of that day. T. N. Carver, a contemporary of Edgeworth and a fellow utilitarian, made this explicit: "The evils of taxation are of two kinds: (1) the sacrifice to the one who pays the taxes; (2) the repressive effect which a tax may have on industry and enterprise. Therefore in accordance with the principle of utility, the burdens of taxation should be so distributed that the sum of these two forms of evil—should be as small as possible."[19] Carver went on to describe the dilemma that emerged because the minimal sacrifice theory minimized the first evil, while equal sacrifice minimized the second.

Once it is assumed that sacrifice and economic effects must be folded into one calculus, the problem of accurately estimating each variable on some common dimension becomes an issue. It is at this point that the attacks on utility as nonempirical, nonquantifiable, and inherently vague are appropriate. Without some measure of the trade off between the evils Carver describes, utility theories provide absolutely no guide to an appropriate tax rate: regressive, constant, or progressive rates with endless combinations and kinks are all reasonably possible. It is this problem that is being directly addressed for the first time by contemporary optimal tax theorists.

Optimal Tax Theory

Optimal tax theory begins where classical tax theory left off. That the research that falls under this rubric begins almost a century after Carver's declaration is indicative of how little the issues have changed and perhaps how intractable are the problems to be resolved. The general thrust of this utilitarian revival is to expand the notion of utility derived from income by including in the calculation of utility such values as leisure, educational investment, and capital investment. The models and the specific variables included are also specified in such a way that some empirical estimation of labor and capital supply and similar factors can be made. Finally, in a fascinating innovation that makes allowance for political value differences, models have been created that permit various solutions to be formulated based on the weight a society wishes to place on the value of income equality.

As in classical theories, optimal tax theory assumes a general welfare function that includes both income and tax functions. One way to conceive of total welfare in the sense used by classical utilitarians is to begin by dividing society into levels and types of ability. For each class of person so defined, utility can be simply conceived of as earnings minus taxes paid, or $U_n = Z(n) - T(n)$, for ability type n with income Z and taxes T. If this utility is then multiplied by the frequency of type n ability in society, or $f(n)$, we have total utility for that class. If we repeat this for all groups in society and sum the results, we get total utility, or total welfare, W. This can be expressed mathematically as

$$W \sum_{n=1}^{N} [Z(n) - T(n)] f(n)$$

for N levels of ability in society.[20]

The object of the Edgeworth minimum sacrifice theory was, given a total tax to be raised, to choose a function $T(n)$ to maximize W. Assuming declining marginal utility, the answer was that the wealthiest in society alone would bear the tax burden. The ultimate result as taxes increased was that incomes would be equalized. As argued above, the two major criticisms of this theory were the drastic nature of the solution and the problem of calculating overall utility, including the possible disincentives of taxation. Optimal tax theories try to correct each of these problems.

The first effort was by J. A. Mirrlees, who balanced one disincentive, the fact that taxation can produce the choice of leisure over work, by asserting that leisure also has a utility value.[21] The general utility function is

$$W = \sum_{n=1}^{N} U_n [x(n), y(n)] f(n)$$

where $y(n)$ is the proportion of each day spent at work for an individual of type n, and where $x(n)$ is after-tax income, or

$$x(n) = z(n) - T[z(n)].$$

Before-tax income, $z(n)$, is a function of both the hours worked and the wage rate for different ability levels. Thus, if the ability level, n, is thought of as a wage rate for a unit of time,

$$z(n) = n y(n).$$

The problem is to specify a tax rate for different ability (or wage) levels, $T(n)$, which maximizes total welfare, W. Such a calculation requires

specification of: (1) the distribution of abilities in society, $f(n)$; (2) the utility function, $U(n)$, which varies with after-tax incomes at different ability levels; and (3) the trade off or replacement rate for income and leisure as tax rates change.

Because of the complexities involved, Mirrlees found it impossible to arrive at any clear definition of the general properties of $T(n)$. He concluded: "The optimum tax schedule depends upon the distribution of skill within the population . . . in such a complicated way that it is not possible to say in general whether marginal tax rates should be higher for high-income, low-income, or intermediate-income groups."[22] He was able to come to definite conclusions only by making a number of simplifying assumptions about the forms of $U(n)$ and $f(n)$. The utility function he explored in detail was the classical log function to include both income and leisure, the importance of each to be weighted through the use of a parameter. Using this special case, represented as $U = \log_e[x^a(1 - y)]$, and assuming a lognormal function for $f(n)$, he was able to work through several numerical examples, calculating $T[z(n)]$ to maximize total utility W for several values of a.[23]

Mirrlees admitted that the results were very sensitive to these assumptions and used the term "heroic" to describe the assumed rate at which leisure replaced work as tax rates were changed. While this was certainly so, he accomplished two things that eluded classical theorists: he specifically introduced the disincentive to work as a variable in his model, and he expressed utility in terms of variables that might be actually measured (i.e., wage levels and hours worked). In addition, the inclusion of a parameter for the trade off between work and leisure allowed calculations based on varying assumptions concerning the rate of exchange at different income levels. Although the ultimate shape of the individual utility curve remained a question, future empirical research conceived in these terms could help clarify the appropriate functional form. In the meantime, simulations could be generated by varying the assumed work-leisure relationship and the value for a.

Further theoretical works quickly followed Mirrlees' initial contribution. In each case a new dimension was added to the original model. Both R. C. Fair and A. B. Atkinson incorporated the notion that earnings were a function of both ability and education. Both models were very specialized. Fair concentrated on trying to calculate a tax rate that would optimize income distribution; thus, he included a guaranteed minimum income in the form of a negative income tax.[24] Atkinson limited his analysis to a flat rate that would maximize lifetime income.[25] Both were interested in how tax rates would affect and be affected by investment in education ("human capital"). As in Mirrlees' study, they

theoretically assumptioned functional relationships between income, education, and utility.[26] Additional contributions by Martin Feldstein added varying wage rates that depended on the tax rate; a lump sum government subsidy that became part of the utility function (the previous assumption had been that the revenue constraint should be zero); and, most importantly, the assumption that tax rates would affect capital accumulation. Like Mirrlees, Fair, and Atkinson, he assumed very simple theoretical labor and capital supply models.[27]

The substantive findings of all these studies were never a serious issue, as each author carefully cautioned readers that the results were extremely sensitive to theoretical assumptions, which they admitted were extreme simplifications. The intent of each was to push optimal tax theory closer to reality by expanding the models to include variables that affected utility and in turn were affected by varying tax rates. These efforts demonstrated both how far it was necessary to go in order to create a theory that embodied the relevant factors, and how quickly, once this was done, the models became complex and the range of assumptions increased. All of these models were theoretical to the extent that functional relationships were assumed and no real data were directly used. Before we turn to more recent empirical research, which concentrates on restricted parts of these puzzles, one more interesting theoretical idea must be discussed.

In an early paper on equality, Atkinson stated that the social welfare function might be generalized as follows:

$$W = (\Sigma U_i p)\frac{1}{p}$$

where W is social welfare and p is a parameter that represents the egalitarian preference of society. This is a transformation of the original utilitarian calculation, in that for $p < 1$, higher weights are given to the increments of those with less utility. The classical utilitarian model is achieved when $p = 1$. As p approaches zero, utility differences between ability levels or classes become nonexistent, and thus little gain in utility is derived from inequality.[28]

Atkinson revived this idea in reviewing the work of Mirrlees to demonstrate that Mirrlees' results were very sensitive not only to the work-leisure trade off, but also to his selection of the classical utility model, or the equivalent of $p = 1$. He concluded that as p decreased, "the marginal utility of income diminished more rapidly and the 'cost' of inequality (in terms of the loss of aggregate utility) increased."[29] Atkinson also took the next step and reformulated an earlier proposal of Musgrave's that this calculation could be done simply by using after-tax income

rather than utility, thus placing a *social* value on different incomes dependent "on the degree of aversion to inequality in society."[30]

These ideas represent something new and something old. By weighting individuals differently as long as the "true" underlying utility function is unknown, Atkinson really is merely varying the utility function in a different, more complex way. In this sense, the statement quoted above is not at all new but merely a restatement of what Cohen-Stuart and Edgeworth had discovered seventy years earlier. In other words, Atkinson reestablished that tax rates are very sensitive to assumptions concerning utility functions. And to the extent that the utility function is indeterminant, optimal tax theory is subject to the same kinds of criticism as classical utilitarian theories.

However, several interesting possibilities are introduced with Atkinson's formulation. In the first place, by precisely specifying a parameter representing equality, various ranges of solutions can be generated and models can be compared for roughly equivalent notions of intended equality. This type of exercise, used in articles by Atkinson, Feldstein, and Rosen, could ultimately prove useful as a policy-making tool.[31] If credible models could be developed, decision makers could select the value of equality desired, and the models would then crank out the appropriate tax rates. By allowing for a weighting parameter, p, the welfare function is transformed from a mere counting operation, wherein each individual's utility is counted equally, to a political or social calculus for arriving at p.

These simple examples of optimal tax theory demonstrate if nothing else the revived interest in utilitarian-based tax theory. Classical models have been updated to include additional variables and the idea that parametric representation of critical trade-offs allows precise simulations of optimal tax rates under differing assumptions. However, there are major difficulties both with purely theoretical work that has been done and with the prospect of moving from the theoretical world of assumed functional relationships to the real world of actual effects and influences.

In purely theoretical terms, several prominent tax experts, including Feldstein and Musgrave, who are sympathetic to the cause, have noted the complete disregard for considerations of horizontal equity, or a like tax for equal incomes. Using different approaches, they have demonstrated that in certain not unlikely circumstances, optimal tax solutions directly violate reasonable definitions of this not always clear concept.[32] Other problems, ironically, are that the models being developed are on the one hand overwhelmingly complex, but are on the other hand too restrictive in terms of the assumptions being made to be used as a practical guide for policy makers.

The mathematical models employed require numerous assumptions and produce complicated arrays of conditional alternatives. At the simplest level this makes it difficult even to understand when different prescriptions should apply. If one wishes to go further and judge the validity of the various conclusions, substantial knowledge of mathematics, economics, and statistics is required. There is not yet in optimal tax theory the relatively simple translation into logical principles that classical theories and the comprehensive tax-base approach (see chapter 3) offer those unschooled in these advanced arts, politicians being not the least important in this category. Furthermore, if the brief history to date is any indication , theories will become more, not less, complex as additions and adjustments to the models are produced.

From Theory to Empirical Research

There is no question that optimal tax models to date are too specialized and simple to provide estimates that could be used for policy recommendations.[33] At this stage of research, however, this may not be critical, because more general models might not yield results specific enough to guide further research.[34] If there is one conclusion that has emerged so far, it is that the tax rates derived are extremely sensitive to assumptions concerning the elasticity of substitution of labor for leisure, capital accumulation, and other factors. If these models are ever to have a practical use, empirical knowledge of these relationships must improve considerably. But the difficulty of this task can be understood by reviewing the scope of the problem for both labor and investment incentives based on recent empirical research into the economic effects of taxation.

Labor Incentives. The relevant labor supply question is what effect different tax structures have on the amount and intensity of work. Pure theory is of limited help. Workers confronted with a tax on earnings that lowers the net wage may choose to work less (or, put another way, to substitute leisure for work) because their after-tax wages have declined, *or* they may choose to work more to make up for the decline in total income. The first of these actions is called a substitution effect, and the latter an income effect. Although labor studies to date have dealt only with hours of work, presumably the same dilemma applies to intensity of effort. A critical problem in labor-supply studies is separating out these two factors.

This is far from the only problem, however, because the behavioral context of decisions on how much or how hard members of a family

work is very complex. The potential factors that affect labor effort are numerous, and understanding the effects of each factor is by itself a major research problem. A noncomprehensive list of variables affecting labor choices would include the following:

1. *Income other than wage income.* It is not only the amount that may have an effect but also the type of income. For example, tax-free transfer payments, particularly when income-tested, create special situations.

2. *Type of job.* Some jobs allow for flexibility in schedule; some do not. Part-time wage earners can be expected to react differently from full-time workers.

3. *Taste for leisure versus work.* Attitudes toward work and the use to which leisure may be put—e.g., education or training—are important.

4. *Career position and age.* Taxes may have a different effect depending on the position of individuals on their career paths, paths that themselves will be varying and complex.

5. *Education or skill level.* This is particularly relevant for spousal work but may affect the primary earner's choices as well.

6. *Health*

7. *Current level of work effort.* There is a limit on hours and effort. How close one is to that limit affects possible changes in work effort.

8. *Family circumstances*:

   a. *Family size*

   b. *Financial responsibilities/debt.* This factor becomes increasingly important as housing costs consume greater proportions of disposable income.

   c. *Fixed costs associated with a working spouse.* Child care and transportation costs, for example, may be an initial barrier to a spouse's employment, particularly in a low-paying part-time job.

9. *Inflation and future expectations.* Decisions concerning work effort, education, and training are conditioned not only

on current income, marginal net wages, and other circumstances, but also on future expectations of income, income security, and living standard goals.

Not only is this system of variables complex; it is also susceptible to considerable change over time. Job structures, family sizes, tastes for leisure, willingness to invest in education, and future expectations for inflation and economic prosperity had undoubtedly changed enormously in the last several decades, and we can anticipate increasing changes in the future. This means that models based on outdated information or behavioral assumptions will produce distorted results.

An additional problem is that tax effects on work effort vary significantly across the population, whereas optimal tax models usually employ single population estimates based on measures of central tendency. This problem is the basis of a serious criticism of one of the most advanced labor supply estimation models, constructed by Jerry Hausman. Hausman included in his model a wide range of control variables (including many on the list above) in an effort to predict varying hours of work in a national sample. Contradicting previous findings, he found a significant aggregate responsiveness to progressive tax rates that reduced work effort.[35] However, Gary Burtless, commenting on the Hausman paper, demonstrated that the result was primarily due to a small minority of husbands who were very responsive to tax rates and argued that in fact "most individuals are not very responsive to taxation and suffer very modest reductions in well-being as a consequence of the progressive nature of the tax schedule."[36] Thus, an aggregate result masks important differences within the population. If these differences were neglected in policy formulation, the result could be reduced equity for many in exchange for increased work effort for a few. Although this may be an appropriate outcome, these detailed effects are nonetheless relevant political facts that can be easily overlooked in emphasizing the aggregate result.

Until very recently, this complex set of factors and problems seemed to eliminate any hope of providing accurate measures of labor loss due to taxation. Early studies were limited to very weak tests relying on surveys of specialized populations in which respondents were asked about changes in work effort following tax increases. The often-cited conclusions were that higher rates and progressivity have little if any impact on work effort, even at the higher levels of income on which these studies focused.[37] Until the early 1970s the impact of taxes was never considered in empirical labor supply studies dealing with a larger population. Even in a major volume on the highly publicized negative

income tax experiments, labor-supply effects were calculated using market wages rather than after-tax wages.[38] However, since the first attempts to introduce taxes as a factor in choices concerning working hours, there has been considerable progress. A number of technical problems in model specification and estimation procedures have been overcome, and the number of variables included in models has expanded.

The road to practical application, however, is long and winding. The difficulties extend beyond the problems of changing factors and values and the task of coping with varying distributions of responses. At the very core is the issue of "taste" for work versus leisure. In response to the Hausman research described above, Michael Boskin demonstrated that the conclusions were extremely sensitive to the assumed distribution of tastes built into the model.[39] An additional complication is that labor incentives affect not only hours of work, but also work intensity. This adds a dimension even more difficult to analyze, and one that may well work in opposite and offsetting directions to hours worked (as anyone who has observed tired overtime workers can testify). Finally, labor supply is strongly affected by macroeconomic conditions, and macroeconomic conditions in turn are affected by tax levels and the distribution of the tax burden. Without incorporating macroeconomic effects into the models (which implies time series data), major questions remain. Thus, both theoretically and empirically, predicting the effects of tax rates and the general level of taxes on labor supply variables is a task of enormous proportions.

Investment Incentives. It is difficult to draw generalizations from the empirical research on the effects of taxes on investment because the amount of research is so massive. I will be content merely to outline the range of subjects and issues involved and mention what appear to be the general conclusions of relatively recent studies. The major thrust of past research has been aimed at the effects of taxes on various types of savings or on corporate investment decisions. As Boskin has pointed out, however, consideration of tax effects on investment in human capital must also be included.[40] The issue here is the time frame involved. Labor supply studies invariably consider short-term effects on income, ignoring both future expectations and future increases in income due to education and training. Although estimates of human capital have been made, they are relatively crude, and one would suspect that the incorporation of a single parameter applied across the population masks a great deal of variation between occupations.[41] Further, I leave it to the reader to imagine how convincing evidence

might be marshalled on the distribution of future values of education in a society that seems poised on a number of technological thresholds. Econometric estimates based on either current cross-sectional data or past time series seem hardly adequate.

Determining the effects of taxes on savings and corporate investment shares some of these same problems, although in general measurement is less of a problem than specifying appropriate models. Academic debate on the effects of taxes on savings appears recently to have entered a new round. For several decades few challenged Edward Denison's "law" that private savings (the sum of personal and corporate savings) are a constant percentage of national income during periods of full employment. This is explained by the fact that personal and corporate savings are inversely related; thus, as corporate saving declines, individual saving increases.[42] Paul David and John Scadding extended Denison's original work (from 1929 back to 1898) and showed further that tax-financed government consumption (in terms of transfer payments, etc.) is considered by taxpayers as a substitute for personal consumption, and hence their net savings rate is unaffected by it—thus the conclusion that taxes have no effect on personal savings.[43]

The rationale behind what has been labeled "ultrarational" behavior is that the link between taxes and transfers is so regular and predictable, given the business cycle, that individuals and corporations can anticipate fluctuations, and hence substitutions become automatic. In a recent paper in the Brookings collection on taxes and economic behavior, George von Furstenberg challenges this latter assumption by concluding that unanticipated increases in both government spending and taxes (balanced budget expenditures) may indeed have a negative effect on personal savings because they stimulate consumption. He arrives at this conclusion by including the interaction effects of the three saving sectors in his econometric models. This entails the use of three sets of very complicated models, all of which were criticized as inadequate by those commenting on the paper. Von Furstenberg himself begins a summary of his conclusions with the comment: "Empirical analysis of aggregate U.S. time series has not, and in my opinion cannot, provide conclusive evidence regarding the effect of saving incentives on the personal saving rate. The reason is that the relevant explanatory variable, the expected after-tax real rate of return on household net worth, cannot be measured precisely."[44] A final difficulty with his paper, and with the general modeling problem, is that, as with labor supply, most believe that expectations play a large role in determining outcomes, but expectations are extremely difficult to measure and are dependent on a large number of exogenous factors. Thus, while von

Furstenberg's study parallels Hausman's in that it questions the long-standing conclusion that taxes have negligible effects on efficiency, there is reason to suspect his results and, by his own plea, not to take them too seriously.

The final link in the optimal tax theory chain is between taxes and corporate investment. Again the literature that brings this issue to the concrete level of policy effects is relatively new. The first important series of papers was published by the Brookings Institution in 1971. The literature is too broad to review here because it has been aimed at a number of different measures of investment using a wide range of econometric models. Some concentrate on capital stock, and some on changes in investment in either machinery or land; some include effects on total output and prices, while others do not. In addition, as I have observed in other areas, the number of factors that can enter a model is staggering. Some of the factors affecting corporate investment decisions at the firm level are: (1) expected future sales; (2) initial capital costs, to be decomposed into interest costs and taxes; (3) capacity utilization; (4) technology and the ease of substituting capital for labor; (5) plant and equipment replacement costs; (6) the ratio of replacement costs to equity plus assets; and (7) expectations concerning both future capital costs and technological developments. Not surprisingly, the results of these studies have varied widely. Lester Thurow, in an effort to come up with an estimate of the effects of corporate tax reduction on corporate investment, reviewed seven studies that attempted in the mid-1960s to estimate the increased investment that would result from a 1 percent reduction in corporate taxes. The estimates ranged from zero to $0.8 billion. (Thurow simply takes $0.4 billion as a useful number, continues with his macro estimates of total efficiency losses due to taxes, and fails to comment on this striking spread.)[45] Arnold Harberger, after commenting on the progress achieved by using theoretical economics for policy purposes, summarized the 1967 Brookings studies by saying: "I cannot help reflecting on the disparity of the results emerging from four treatments of the relation of tax incentives to investment behavior." He then elaborates on this point, describing how slight differences in models, different data bases, and different statistical techniques led to very different conclusions.[46] In 1981 Emil Sunley, commenting on another paper that attempted to measure tax effects on investment, quoted Harberger's earlier statement as still appropriate.[47]

From the point of view of optimal tax theory, there is an added difficulty in estimating efficiency losses in terms of savings and investment. To be useful in an optimal tax formula, investment and savings

effects, even if they can be estimated using econometric techniques, must be translated into personal income. This requires a macro model, and there is significant difference of opinion on how the various components fit together to predict changes in real income. For example, in a period of low-capacity utilization, will investment in new or replacement equipment enhance economic growth and hence the growth of personal income? Similarly, great hope is placed on investment in new technologies, and there is no doubt that the income of some will be considerably increased by such investment. However, as is becoming painfully clear, others, particularly those in unionized industrial jobs, will suffer substantial wage reduction. There is significant disagreement on the aggregate effects on personal income in both of these cases, and many other examples could be cited.[48]

The controversy between supply-side and demand-side economists over the role of savings is of the same order. According to Keynes's analysis of the depression, excess savings do not necessarily lead to growth; rather, they stifle consumption, which is the engine that stimulates economic activity. The policy argument that follows from this analysis is that one should reduce taxes, but reduce them for the poor and the middle class, who consume the most. Supply-side theorists stress the need for investment and an increase in savings to fuel corporate expansion. The corresponding policy recommendation is again to cut taxes, but in this case the taxes of upper-income groups that have a higher propensity to save and greater capital to invest. Both schools are concerned about inflation, but there is no consensus on which strategy is more harmful in this regard, or what the effects on real income will be once monetary policy, government spending, productivity, and other factors are taken into account. As will be shown in the historical chapters that follow, the politics of taxation is critically affected by shifting concerns about deficits and shifting theories about how dangerous or beneficial they are. Economists currently seem to be little better off than politicians in their ability to agree on such effects. Thus, the success of optimal tax theory is very much tied to the success of macroeconomic modeling. From the perspective of a respectful outsider, there appears to be an enormous and very complex research agenda ahead.

The difficulties faced in empirically estimating efficiency losses should not lead to an underestimation of either the current use of these studies or their future potential. The former I view with alarm, and the latter with hope. This research is producing specific numbers for readily understandable dependent variables such as labor and capital supplies. And numbers tend to drive out non-numbers in the policy-making

process. What is alarming is that the uncertainty of the estimates and the qualifications that are a part of scholarly discourse may be lost as unqualified users zero in on simple aggregate conclusions to build and support political arguments. The other danger of this research is that the emphasis in the empirical studies is on efficiency losses, and the equity side of the equation can be easily lost.[49] This is bound to weight the outcome in favor of less progressivity and lower taxes. What is almost certain to happen is that these studies will be used not in any general reform effort but rather in isolated considerations of specialized provisions such as depreciation and exclusion of savings. The hope is that the research will continue to progress as rapidly as it has in the last few years. This will, at the very least, generate a plurality of research conclusions and at the same time advance the more ambitious promises of optimal tax theory.

Conclusion

There is little in the preceding pages that can be used to argue convincingly for any general principle of or prescription for taxation. In this sense, probably to the surprise of very few, the assumptions of incremental theory are correct. Even very limited efforts at the prescription of appropriate tax rates or levels founder. Although at some point in the future optimal tax theorists may change this, the grand scope of their enterprise and the ultimate need for empirical evidence in addition to theory indicate that such an outcome is not likely in the near future. What is more likely is that information from studies of various pieces of the optimal tax puzzle will be used in an incremental fashion as arguments for or against specific proposals that apply to investment, savings, or labor supply. With this prospect, we move to another level and a very different type of tax theory—the argument over the appropriate income tax base.

Chapter 3.
The Uneasy
Case for a
Comprehensive
Income Tax
Base

With the exception of optimal tax theory, in which there has been some recent interest, the types of prescriptive theories discussed in the preceding chapter had run their course by the 1930s. Utilitarianism came into disrepute with the rise of pragmatic philosophy and the increasing importance of empirical research. In 1938 Henry Simons, a professor of economics at the University of Chicago, published a short book called *Personal Income Taxation: The Definition of Income as a Problem of Fiscal Policy*, which epitomized this transition.[1] The theory presented in this book, which had an immediate impact on the field of public finance, continues to have enormous influence on current discussions of income tax theory. The broad-based definition of income as the basis of income taxation that he presented has inspired tax reform proposals at regular intervals since World War II, the last appearing in 1977 under the title *Blueprints for Basic Tax Reform*.[2] Those who have subscribed at least in part to his basic formulation include liberal tax reformers of the 1960s, such as Stanley Surrey, Assistant Secretary of the Treasury for Taxation from 1960 to 1968; conservatives, such as William Simon, Treasury Secretary under Nixon and the moving force behind the 1977 tax reform proposal; and Norman Ture, an Undersecretary for Taxation for the Reagan administration.[3]

The influence of Simons on the actual course of tax policy is another matter. Of the detailed reforms he proposed in 1938, few have been put into practice, and many of the provisions that he felt needed to be reformed have by his standards actually been made worse. Further, the basic idea he promoted of a very broad-based measure for income with

few exclusions, deductions, exemptions, or credits for tax purposes has moved farther and farther from reality, to the point that it is now little more than a mythical goal. Explaining what led to this result is an important function of this book. This chapter is devoted to explaining Simons' theory, analyzing its logical weaknesses, and offering a different form of defense for a broad or comprehensive base for the income tax.

Henry Simons' Theory of the Income Tax

For Henry Simons the task of the tax philosopher was not to create a deductive principle of taxation that would lead to prescriptive formulas like those proposed by utilitarian theorists, but rather to determine the appropriate basis for taxation in more general and pragmatic terms. Indeed, Simons began his book by briefly and ruthlessly dismissing utilitarian theories. His attack dealt with a number of points, but the fatal flaw as he saw it was the confused notion of hedonism or pleasure seeking, a central concept in utilitarianism. In a delightful parody that drew a derogatory parallel between utilitarian theory and studies of criminality based on dimensions of the head (the "cephalic index"), which had become an intellectual joke of the time, Simons wrote:

> Let us imagine a world where people, while substantially equal in other respects, display enormously different efficiencies as pleasure machines. Let us imagine also that these efficiencies vary inversely as the cube of the cephalic index. In such a world the criterion of least sacrifice would require that taxation leave the longheads with very large incomes; and a consistent policy would require that all impecunious longheads be generously subsidized. Now to support such a scheme, one finds an appropriate theology not only convenient but utterly indispensable. The criterion implies that the primary objective of policy on earth should be that of generating *through* the human population the maximum output of pleasure for the contemplation of some external Spectator; and the appropriate supporting religion would assert that this Spectator dispensed blessings and punishments to humanity according to the adequacy of the pleasure output.[4]

Having dispatched utilitarian theories, Simons turned to what were known originally as "faculty theories," which had been translated into

vague proclamations that taxes should be related to "ability to pay."[5] He summarized this class of theories in the following brusque passage:

> Whereas the question is as to how taxes should be allocated with respect to income, consumption, or net worth, the answer is that they should be proportional to ability or faculty, which cannot be conceived quantitatively or defined in terms of any procedure of measurement. Such an answer indicates that the writer prefers the kind of taxation which he prefers; that he is unwilling to reveal his tastes or examine them critically; and that he finds useful in his profession a basic "principle" from which, as from a conjurer's hat, anything may be drawn at will.[6]

While Simons repudiated these earlier attempts to establish a principle of progressive taxation, he did not ignore the problem himself. Indeed, as is sometimes forgotten by commentators who misperceive Simons' theory as "neutral" relative to the ultimate tax burden, he offers an unflinching argument for progressivity in the tax system. However, his argument is based on a completely different and much simpler notion than those that preceded it. Following the work of a German theorist, Adolph Wagner, he simply assumes that the prevailing inequality of income and wealth was unjustified in terms of merit and thus inappropriate, and that the tax system was the most convenient vehicle for altering that situation. Why was it "inappropriate"? Simons' famous answer was: "The case for drastic progression in taxation must be rested on the case against inequality—on the ethical or aesthetic judgment that the prevailing distribution of wealth and income reveals a degree (and/or kind) of inequality which is distinctly unlovely."[7] And essentially that was it. In the pages that follow, he admits that progressivity could have negative effects on work and investment, but argues that these should simply be considered costs of alleviating inequality and that, if necessary, lost productive power could be made up by direct government production. In the tradition of pragmatic philosophy that Simons' work reflects, statements of value take this form. The discussion of vertical equity in taxation could go no further than this simple expression of faith and belief. He turns rather to the task of defining the appropriate base for taxation and to analysis of a number of specific tax provisions.

Following the earlier work of German economist George Schanz, which had been translated into English and elaborated by Robert Haig in 1921, Simons elects to use market power or market rights as the basic

standard for defining personal income and, hence, the appropriate base for the income tax. According to Simons, this standard allows for the relative measurement during a specific period of economic activity—activity directed toward the exercise of control over society's scarce resources. To be accurate in this relative sense, all sources of increasing market power had to be included in the tabulation of income. Thus, he adopts what is now known as the Haig-Simons or accretion definition of personal income, which he stated "as the algebraic sum of (1) the market value of rights exercised in consumption and (2) the change in the value of the store of property rights between the beginning and end of the period in question."[8] Personal income is thus a combination of consumption and accumulation of wealth over a given period. This definition includes direct income from all sources, including savings and investments, realized capital gains, earnings on tax-exempt bonds, earnings on life insurance, and so on. It also includes income-in-kind, such as the imputed rental value of a house[9] and unrealized increases to wealth accruing during the period, which would include undistributed corporate profits or unrealized capital gains.[10] By measuring gains from all these sources in terms of market value, an objective metric of relative comparisons between taxpayers would be established.

In the remaining sections of the book, Simons first defends his definition against others and then goes through detailed arguments for the inclusion of specific items in the income tax base. Throughout the book Simons avoids the phrase "ability to pay," which he so scornfully rejects in the passage cited above. Rather, he repeatedly makes his case on grounds of horizontal equity, by which he means "fairness between and among persons of similar economic circumstances."[11] Only in the last chapter does he briefly return to the other standard for judging taxation, which is the effect on the degree of economic inequality in society. The difference between this standard and the "ability to pay standard" is important, and the merging of the two terms by many of Simons' subsequent disciples has created more confusion over the theory than Simons' extremely careful presentation deserves.[12]

Dubious Arguments for the Comprehensive Tax Base

Just as classical utilitarian tax theories remain relevant because they provide a bridge to contemporary optimal tax theory, Simons' comprehensive tax base notion remains important because it continues to fuel current, more practical debates over the proper structure for the income

tax. In the transition from Simons' primarily academic treatise to the quasi-official reports, conferences, and symposia of today, some of the supporting arguments have been changed, and most are less rigorous and more moderate than the unflinching propositions promulgated by Simons himself. He reasoned that tax systems should be judged solely on two criteria: "(a) their effects upon the degree of economic inequality, and (b) their fairness between and among persons of similar circumstances."[13] The system he proposed was an income tax based on inclusion and equal weighting of all forms of income and additions to accumulated wealth, which would then be taxed at progressive rates. In the process of advocating what are currently, and perhaps less precisely, termed vertical equity and horizontal equity, Simons brushed aside considerations of economic efficiency by straightforwardly admitting that efficiency losses might result from equally including investment income in the tax base and using the tax system to redistribute income.[14] He was simply willing to accept these consequences as necessary costs.

In the following pages I will argue that his arguments related to vertical and horizontal equity and economic efficiency are dubious or merely statements of preference. The arguments below involve more than simply a critique of Simons' book, although as the most sophisticated argument to date for a broad-based income tax, it is an appropriate focal point for a critique. The intent is to demonstrate in more general terms that equity and efficiency, however defined, are problematic standards for judging tax policy. Before discussing each of these criteria individually, it is useful to analyze in more detail the concept of market power, which formed the central theoretical core of Simons' philosophy.

The Concept of Market Power. In contemporary accounts of Simons' famous definition of income, the importance of the concept of market power is often overlooked. However, whether Simons' personal income formulation is an adequate index of market power and whether market power is the appropriate normative basis for the income tax are absolutely essential issues for the integrity of the theory. His formulation of market power differed from that of E.R.A. Seligman, writing forty years earlier. Seligman was also concerned with market power in the form of "productive capacity." However, his basic idea, flippantly ignored by Simons, was that productive capacity increased at a greater rate than income.[15] Although Simons' concept of market power is broader than Seligman's concept of productive capacity in that market power applies to both consumption and production, the Seligman notion was anath-

ema to the dollar-for-dollar accounting that Simons felt was the critical ingredient in creating an index to measure relative economic gain in a given period. For Simons each dollar of personal income contributed equally to one's market power; for Seligman, higher levels of personal income were weighted more.

Both of these propositions seem arbitrary and depend on clouded concepts of market power. Simons never precisely defined his notion of market power, although he did use it synonymously with the term "rights." One reasonable interpretation, which is consistent with both modern conceptions of "power"[16] and Simons' continuous references to choices, is to define market power in terms of the ability to exercise economic preferences. Within this context, Simons' devotion to equal weighting of income and his refusal to make allowances for different circumstances surrounding types of income or consumption needs imply that each increment to income produces a similar increase in one's ability to exercise market choices. And he is absolutely adamant that different consumption patterns or the choice to delay consumption (i.e., to save) are matters of personal taste. In his words: "The market asserts that property rights are just property rights, whether they permit one's eating eggs or clipping coupons. . . . Why he may have bought claims to future goods, services, or funds, rather than that which he might eat or drink at the moment, the market does not inquire."[17]

The proposition that all income adds equally to the exercise of market choices seems wholly untenable. The ability to exercise preferences varies dramatically for different income levels. Choices available to the poor are simply much more constrained than those available to the rich. Not only do the poor not have the same options when it comes to the choice between savings and consumption, but their choice of consumption items is also limited. Further, any such disparity in one time period is likely to be exaggerated in subsequent periods. Distortion in the metric Simons proposes is also affected by other circumstances. Family size, medical problems, debts, and whether one is employed (and able to expand income) or retired or unable to work—all these place constraints on available choices and limit one's market power.

Contemporary supporters of a general comprehensive tax base approach, faced with a tax system that makes numerous allowances for varying economic circumstances, are more lenient in the exceptions they allow. Not only are they willing to allow exceptions related to the problems outlined above, but they also admit that other uses of the tax system and other values must be considered. For example, Richard Musgrave defends the deductions that allow for disaster expenses, such as casualty losses and medical expenses:

The purpose is not to exclude specific income sources but to allow for situations where taxpayers with equal incomes and family size have strikingly different needs. . . . By allowing for disaster situations, the equity goal, far from being offended, can be achieved more fully.[18]

Similarly, in an exchange with Boris Bittker, who attacked Simons' definition of income as too comprehensive, Joseph Pechman chides Bittker for misinterpreting what proponents of Simons had been saying:

But he [Bittker] fails to mention that departures from comprehensiveness are permitted by the proponents, and that they have stipulated the conditions under which departures would be tolerated. These conditions are, first, that the departure must promote a major national objective and that the tax mechanism is the most efficient method of achieving it; second, that it is impractical to tax the particular item.[19]

Finally, Richard Goode returns to the notion of ability to pay, emphasizing the idea of hardship.

An equitable tax system must take proper account of ability to pay. This may be defined as "the capacity for paying without undue hardship on the part of the person paying or an unacceptable degree of interference with objectives that are considered socially important by other members of the community."[20]

Although each of these statements seems reasonable, once exceptions are allowed, as Simons well understood, the theory rapidly dissolves because there are no logical limits to what constitutes acceptable special pleadings. What Musgrave considers a "disaster" others may not. What possible limit can be built into Pechman's notion of "a major national objective"? And, once defined, how could we know whether the tax system is the most efficient method of pursuing the goal? The same vagueness applies to Goode's terms "undue hardship" and "socially important" objectives.

This theoretical unraveling has left modern proponents of a comprehensive tax base approach in the awkward position of seemingly supporting exceptions based on arbitrary or personal values. Thus, liberals may be supportive of need-based exceptions, while conservatives are more interested in special treatment for savings and investment income. The essential problems are the uncertainty of the metric that

transforms income into market power and the question whether market power alone should be the basis for structuring an income tax. Both of these problems have a direct bearing on the common references to vertical and horizontal equity and economic efficiency.

Vertical Equity. The problems of judging tax systems in terms of vertical equity were discussed in the last chapter. The difficulty of specifying a relationship between income and utility was emphasized, both in the narrow individual sense and across populations. It is more typical of modern tax experts (optimal tax theorists excepted) to support a progressive broad-based income tax by reference to a vague notion of ability to pay, much as is done by Richard Goode in the passage quoted above. This is a major departure from Simons, who carefully distinguished his criterion of "economic inequality" from any notion of ability to pay. His notion of inequality applied to relative income between broad classes in society and not to individual cases. He understood that a tax system based on a comprehensive definition of income would necessarily conflict with ability to pay if the focus was on individuals and their differing circumstances. The simple reason is that once individual cases are considered, ability to pay implies not only market power, but also circumstances of need. Needs do not fall neatly in line relative to a measure of personal income but rather come in discrete packages and in an impossible assortment of combinations. The wealthy widow facing immense medical deductions; the high-income family whose uninsured house burns to the ground; the disabled veteran; the farmer whose income shifts from abundance to naught depending on the weather; or the family without children versus the one with four or five—these combinations cannot be ranked in any linear fashion relative to underlying income; in fact they cannot be ranked in any intelligible or predictable fashion at all.

Simons' vision, vaguely but inconsistently supported by broad-based income tax reformers, was of a simple, all-inclusive tax base devoid of exceptions that would appropriately redistribute income through a progressive rate structure. However, he understood that once ability to pay became a criterion, the base would erode, and erode without logical limits. This is precisely why he opted for economic equality as the goal, rationalizing his position by simply stating his preference. It was a deviously clever argument and avoided the pitfalls awaiting sacrifice, faculty, or ability-to-pay theories.

Unfortunately, as a rationale for a comprehensive tax base it is weak in two important senses. First, what aesthetically pleases Simons may not please other people, who might reasonably place greater value on

"just" market rewards, labor or capital incentives, or simply the pleasure or interest to be derived from an unequal but heterogeneous
society. One does not have to be an insensitive, anticommunal egotist to
have a different preference on this critical matter. Second, the arguments for special treatment in certain cases are very powerful and
certainly politically magnetic. While the notion of ability to pay is
inconsistent, vague, and impossible to cast as a concise prescription, it
has a commonsense logic that may supersede the academic urge to
discover general principles. However, that conclusion also is a matter of
preference and speculation. In other words, there is no principle or
specific criterion of vertical equity apart from an expression of preferences. Simons' preferences just happen to be somewhat more neatly
packaged than those based on the complexities of ability to pay.

Horizontal Equity. As mentioned previously, Simons was clever
enough to concentrate his argument on the more universally accepted
notion that equal income should be equally taxed. The horizontal equity
criterion remains a common standard for judging tax policy as well as
policies in other areas. However, the complicated determinations that
must be made to identify like economic cases has a devastating impact
on horizontal equity, much as they do on any consistent notion of
vertical equity. Simons' position rested on the assumption that a broad-
based definition of income is an adequate metric of market power,
which is the sole standard of relative equality. Those with equal income
have equal market power, and in fairness they should be taxed equally.
However, as I argued above, if the link between income and market
power is dubious, the standard crumbles into complicated comparisons
between families of different sizes, different economic circumstances,
and different types of income.

To employ any sort of standard of horizontal equity, one must fore-
sake the notion of prescription and fall back on a case-by-case analysis.
As the circle of relevant differences is enlarged, decisions will rest on
bargaining and negotiation rather than the application of a strict rule
such as the one provided by the comprehensive tax base. Simons
directly addressed this distinction when he wrote:

> Thus one faces the choice between following a rule in spite of
> its occasionally unfortunate consequences and, on the other
> hand, admitting a mass of caustic distinctions and exceptions.
> Stressing the view that the levy must be fair among persons,
> one inclines toward the latter choice. This view can never be
> ignored; and it usually guides one well through particular

issues. But it must never be trusted implicitly or permitted the status of a court of last resort. Otherwise, one removes the whole inquiry to a world of dialectic populated only by doctrines of ability, faculty, sacrifice, maximum social advantage, and their kind; and from this realm there is no bridge back to a real world of tax legislation and administration.[21]

It is unclear precisely who is in the real world and who is not. Nonetheless, Simons chose to stick with the rule, however limited its utility. One can hardly blame others for disregarding it and responding rather to the diversity of circumstances among "equals."

Economic Efficiency. The relationship between the comprehensive tax base and economic efficiency is theoretically unclear and again seems to rest on a preference that is not without a competitive counterpoint. The theoretical difficulty is that the term "efficiency" is used in two ways that can be merged in economic theory but may lead in different policy directions. The most consistent use treats efficiency as a measure of distortion in factor inputs in the economy. An "efficient" tax system in this sense would minimize changes in pretax ratios between labor and capital, labor and leisure, or consumption and savings. It is often suggested, with few counterarguments, that the comprehensive tax base will be more efficient in this sense than taxes that selectively affect components of the economy.[22] When wages, gains from capital, and interest on savings are included on an equal footing, relative prices will be unaffected and thus factor ratios should be stable. Although there may be different effects for various patterns of rates, as discussed in relation to optimal tax theory above, this is another matter, unconnected to the specification of the base.

In theory, "efficient markets" also lead to maximum economic growth. Since the Depression, however, economic growth and output have not been left, in theory or in practice, to the workings of the "efficient" market. The government has assumed clear responsibility for maintaining adequate growth, appropriate levels of employment, and, more recently, tolerable levels of inflation. The term "economic efficiency" is therefore also used (sometimes loosely) to refer to economic growth, however achieved. Economic management to promote sustained growth can be done through macroeconomic policy that is concerned primarily with the level of taxation relative to spending and not with specific components that contribute to sectoral growth or to the alleviation of particular economic problems. As a macroeconomic tool,

the comprehensive tax base also has merit because the broad base allows for fluctuations in revenue with minimal changes in marginal rates.

However, at least in recent years, there is rarely a consensus among economists about the appropriate macroeconomic strategy. This division, plus the natural political tendency to disaggregate problems, stimulates policy proposals of a more targeted nature. To the extent that policy makers desire to focus their concerns on specific aspects of the economy (such as employment, savings, or productivity) or specific sectors, the comprehensive tax base tends to tie their hands. If the problem is seen as one of shortage of investment, special tax provisions to encourage savings and investment are a possible method for achieving that result; if agricultural production is lagging, tax benefits targeted for that sector can be designed; and if unemployment among a certain category of workers is an identifiable problem, a tax credit is a natural and convenient option for policy makers.

Simons was aware of the negative consequences that his theory would have on economic efficiency, and he discussed them not in terms of market distortion or general economic performance, but in terms of jobs, savings rates, and work incentives. In keeping with the toughness of his position, he was willing to accept losses in those areas as unfortunate consequences of greater equality. He justified his position, however, by suggesting that they could be corrected with positive government intervention through public employment, direct subsidy of production, or actual government ownership.[23] What was never directly discussed was why, if those were legitimate problems to be addressed by government, the tax system should not be used to address them.

An Alternative Defense

If the preceding analysis is correct, it is difficult to evaluate tax systems in terms of their effects on equity or economic efficiency. That conclusion is also consistent with the previous analysis of utilitarian and optimal tax theories. The underlying problem is that, because these terms have multiple meanings and because they are applied to complex situations, it is virtually impossible to utilize them as general norms that can be operationalized when policy choices need to be made. Further, even if they could be precisely defined, they would still conflict, and Simons' definition does not accommodate the inevitable political trade offs that must be made. To Simons' credit, he seems to have understood

these problems better than many of his later followers and was willing simply to place his preferred values above others and accept the costs implied by his choices.

Thus, equity and efficiency seem to be inappropriate defenses of an income tax based on a comprehensive definition of income. On the other hand, the alternative, which one can expect to be a complicated tangle of exceptional provisions, is equally unpleasant. Another approach is to assume that the comprehensive tax base is an imperfect and indeterminant norm in terms of equity and efficiency, but that it promotes other, more rudimentary and instrumental objectives or consequences. A list of such goals would include the capacity to raise revenue, administrative efficiency, certainty, simplicity, and legitimacy. Although perhaps less dramatic than equity and efficiency, these pragmatic goals are easily understood, internally consistent, and widely accepted, and the advantages of a comprehensive tax base for each value are relatively straightforward.

Revenue capacity is not necessarily equivalent to high taxes but rather implies the ability to raise taxes to meet desired levels of revenue. A broad-based tax system can raise taxes more easily and quickly than a system based on a narrow population that is replete with income exclusions and reduction devices. Convincing evidence of this fact is provided in chapter 6, which depicts the transition of the income tax from an elite to a mass tax during World War II. This was accomplished primarily by lowering the personal exemption to broaden the base. The result was an expansion in revenue that was beyond imagination prior to the war. One of the basic arguments in the upcoming chapters will be that as the complexity of the income tax increases and tax reduction provisions expand, it will become increasingly difficult to raise necessary taxes through the income tax system.

The question of the *administrative efficiency* of a comprehensive tax base is not as simple. There is no doubt that a system rigidly following Simons' definition would contain some provisions that would be virtually impossible to administer. For example, inclusion in yearly income of unrealized appreciation of assets would be not only difficult, but also costly, to administer. Procedures for valuation would need to be established requiring complicated rules and probably negotiated settlements. Inclusion of the imputed rental value of housing would pose similar problems: home values would have to be established, and certain expenses of home ownership not incurred by renters (interest payments, maintenance, etc.) would have to be deducted as expenses. Other provisions might impose similar difficulties on administrators. Joseph Pechman has argued that there is no reason why these items

cannot simply be excluded from the base on the grounds that they are infeasible to administer.[24] A problem would arise if there were large numbers of provisions that fit this category, since allowing many exceptions based on administrative infeasibility or cost would lead to the same types of uncertainty and special treatment that emerge from considerations of equity and efficiency. I simply do not think that this is the case, however, and as we begin to explore the history, size, and distribution of the tax reduction system as it presently exists, I invite the reader to consider the administrative difficulties that would accompany the elimination of each provision and ask whether the code would be generally easier or harder to administer in its absence. Although the administrative costs of an ideal tax system would be difficult, if not impossible, to estimate, and as it turns out even comparing administrative costs of different existing taxes is questionable,[25] to argue that the current income tax is less costly to administer than one with a comprehensive tax base seems totally unrealistic. The more appropriate issue is the degree of savings involved in the shift.

Certainty in taxation obviously involves political and economic factors other than the form of the tax system and the definition of the base. What a comprehensive tax base would do, however, is narrow the range of uncertainty because the number of parameters that could be manipulated would be greatly reduced. The individual contemplating selling a capital asset would not have to estimate the possibility of the exclusion level's being lowered or the holding period's being altered; the businessman considering investment in new equipment would not have to worry about extension or change of investment credits, or asset depreciation, or the longevity of the new tax credit/leasing provisions.[26] In these and literally hundreds of other examples that could be drawn, tax rates and exemption levels would still be potentially variable. However, so much more of the tax code would be set that the relative certainty of an income tax built on a comprehensive tax base cannot be denied.

The *simplicity and legitimacy* of a broad-based income tax, which treats each dollar of income on an equal basis and disallows complicated deductions and exclusions, would undoubtedly be greater. Although, as Boris Bittker, a leading tax lawyer and scholar, has pointed out, a comprehensive tax base would not eliminate all complexities,[27] it is difficult to argue that it would not be a significant improvement overall. Currently, large fortunes are made by legal and accounting specialists who concentrate on small sections of the tax code. Efforts to simplify the rules and tax forms are ongoing but losing propositions. We do not know the exact consequences of large numbers of people not understanding the taxes they pay or the effects of uneven knowledge that

rewards some at the expense of others. It is clear in theory, however, that deviating from the comprehensive tax base impairs the legitimacy of the income tax and hence compliance with its provisions. For some writers, such as Charles Galvin, the flaws of the prevailing structure are obvious and dramatic: "Of one thing I am certain. The monstrous complexity of the present system in this country and the inequities wrought on upper and lower income groups alike will bring the whole structure crashing down around us unless we think seriously of innovative and far-reaching changes."[28]

Although the crash has yet to occur—in fact, a long-term erosion is more likely—the point is well taken. Even with modern data-processing methods and vastly improved information sources and cross-checking capabilities, there is overwhelming consensus among tax experts that voluntary compliance is absolutely essential in collecting income tax revenues. Voluntary compliance depends both on the capacity of taxpayers to understand the tax code, and on their willingness to comply. The complexity of an income tax system loaded down with the sort of tax-reducing and tax-delaying devices that characterize the U.S. system affects compliance and legitimacy in several ways. As emphasized above, it is difficult for many people to understand the intricacies of the tax system that is extracting their money. The system also gives an impression of special privilege—of "loopholes" that exist primarily for the wealthy, who can afford high-priced tax lawyers who manipulate the tax code by creating dubious methods of sheltering income. Books like *The Great Treasury Raid* and *The Rape of the Taxpayer* play on, and enlarge this image.[29] Although the truth is that it is not only the wealthy who benefit from the tangle of tax-reduction devices, some of the unfavorable images of the tax code, which will be described in chapter 16, certainly result from deviations from the Simons model.

Additionally, while we know little about the psychology of tax avoidance, it is reasonable to assume that the easier it is to go undetected, or the easier it is to escape punishment once caught, the greater the temptation. Complexity allows both in that it makes the task of enforcement significantly more difficult, and it makes it easier to plead ignorance or error when the intent was truly fraud. This does not mean that complexity alone stimulates tax avoidance efforts. Certainly the tax rates, general economic conditions, and the perceived legitimacy of government expenditures also play important roles. However, the complexity of the code provides a convenient vehicle and a rationale: as others are believed to be gaining illicit benefits, it becomes easier for each taxpayer to decide to do the same. The ultimate fear of administrators is that tax avoidance is not a linear progression. Perhaps once it

reaches a certain point, it increases in a curvilinear pattern. It is certainly worth considering where on that curve we now rest.

Conclusion

Simons' comprehensive tax base approach still provides a reasonable and pragmatic ideal to guide tax legislation. It is reasonable not because it is necessarily fairer than other systems (although it might be), or because it enhances economic efficiency, but rather because in comparison with the alternative, it is more likely to preserve the revenue-raising capability of the income tax, improve administrative efficiency, enhance the certainty and comprehensibility of the tax code, and maintain the legitimacy necessary for voluntary compliance. It is pragmatic in the sense that it defines the structure or form of the income tax but allows, within that framework, for political judgments concerning the level and incidence of taxes. Unfortunately, Simons' theory, while continuously referenced in calls for tax reform, has not guided historical events. He ended his 1938 book with ten specific recommendations, which paraphrase as follows:[30]

1. All exclusions from income, notably interest on government obligations, should be eliminated.

2. Income in kind, specifically imputed rent, should be included as taxable income.

3. All gifts, inheritances, and bequests should be included as current income.

4. A supplementary tax on recipients of gifts should be enacted to eliminate the possibility of gradually dispersing property to heirs.

5. Gains on assets that have appreciated in the owner's possession (i.e., unrealized capital gains) should be fully included.

6. Full realization of capital gains at death should be made.[31]

7. A rebate system should be devised to create a form of income averaging to alleviate the problem of lumping gains.

8. Tax rates in the lower brackets should be sharply increased, with an initial rate of about 20 percent after exemptions.

9. Federal revenues from the states should be shared with the states on the basis of state collections.

10. Excepting gasoline taxes and several others, eliminate all tariffs, duties, excises, license fees, and so on.

Of this list, numbers 2, 3, 4, and 10 have not been acted on in any significant way since 1938. With exceptions for the war years, policy has moved in the *opposite* direction from Simons' recommendations 1, 5, and 8. Number 6 was enacted in 1976, delayed in 1977, and repealed without being implemented in 1980. Number 9, revenue sharing, was enacted with a different formula and as a minor transfer, not a replacement for other state taxes, as Simons envisioned it. And number 7 was enacted in the form of income averaging in 1939. Notice that the only recommendations that were acted on in any form were those that conferred benefits, while those that threatened more taxes (without contigent action on the rate structure) were either ignored or reversed. Thus, policy makers, although continually reminded of his theory in reform proposals, have ignored it in practice. It would appear that tax policy has much more to do with politics than with theory.

Section III.
The Historical
Development of
the Income Tax

The practice of systematically recording and analyzing legislative history in various policy fields has become rare in the last several decades. Through the 1950s social science journals regularly published annual updates written by leading scholars in major policy and institutional fields. With better information sources (such as the *Congressional Quarterly*) and more sophisticated techniques that promised a science of politics and public policy, these efforts were abandoned. The following chapters are an attempt to resurrect that lost art and to construct and update a legislative history for the income tax. It differs from past efforts in that the history is guided and pointed specifically toward the theoretical issues previously discussed and is thus, hopefully, more an analytical than a merely chronological narrative. In alliance with the past, however, it is also my purpose to suggest that much, and perhaps even most, of what happens in the real policy-making world is complex, often inconsistent, and rarely subject (without great loss of information and understanding) to the rigors of mathematical models.

The chapters that follow become progressively more detailed as they move through the post–World War II period. This is because published legislative histories end just after World War II and because the war marks the beginning of the income tax as a mass tax. Since tax issues have become increasingly important in the last decade, there is even more emphasis on these later years, with an entire chapter devoted to the 1981 Economic Recovery and Tax Act. For the convenience of the reader not enamored with the minutiae of legislative conflict, summaries are provided at the end of most chapters. Chapter 12 is a summary and elaboration of the stronger historical patterns that characterize the politics of taxation.

Chapter 4.
The Income Tax Through World War I

The Civil War Experience

It is consistent with subsequent history that the first income taxes in the United States began with a crisis in revenue.[1] The first proposal for a national income tax was made during the War of 1812, which by 1814 had produced an unheard-of national debt of $100 million. At the onset of the war, most taxes were raised through customs duties on foreign goods, which had been doubled in 1812 but actually produced less revenue because of the decline in trade. Internal revenues consisting of excise taxes on goods and commodities and taxes on houses, slaves, and land were instituted, and income and inheritance taxes were proposed by the time the war ended in 1815. Following the war, all the new taxes were dropped, and the debt was eventually retired as a result of a high protective tariff passed in 1816.

The first federal income tax was enacted during the Civil War, and again the stimulus was a dire need for revenue.[2] Lincoln's administration began in bad financial condition, with a debt of almost $75 million in March of 1861. The first efforts to raise revenue by Lincoln's Secretary of the Treasury, Salmon Chase, a former senator from Ohio, were along traditional lines. Federal bonds and notes were issued, the tariff was doubled, sales of public lands were increased, excise taxes were raised and new excises passed, and license fees were instituted. These taxes were all classified as direct taxes and therefore fulfilled the constitutional requirement of being "direct and uniform." The taxation of income was not so considered.

The political push for the income tax began when the powerful chairman of the Ways and Means Committee, Thaddeus Stevens (R-Pa.), proposed an additional direct tax on land in each state, with each state's share to be apportioned by population. This tax, combined with

the earlier tariffs on basic commodities (tea, coffee, and sugar), generated a congressional rebellion, led by states in the South and West. This geographical division, which established a basic political alignment on tax issues that would not be broken until the late 1930s, pitted the wealthy industrial North and Northeast against the poorer agricultural regions in the rest of the country. The regional positions were a simple response to different economic circumstances: the Northeast favored first tariffs (which protected their industrial goods from competition), and excise, license, and land taxes if needed; the South and West resisted all these taxes, whose impact fell disproportionately on them, and favored taxes on income and wealth, of which they had little.

Faced with deteriorating financial conditions and the resistance of the agricultural states (led on the House floor by Schuler Colfax, R-Ind.), Stevens was forced to relent after the bills he proposed were recommitted twice with instructions to reduce the direct tax on land and add taxes on income and wealth. On July 29, 1861, a bill was reported that contained a tax of 3 percent on all incomes over $600 a year. On the same day the Senate adopted an amendment to the tariff bill calling for an income tax of 5 percent on all incomes over $1,000. The compromise offered by the Conference Committee was a 3 percent tax on incomes over $800. It was specified that net rather than gross income was to be taxed, but the specification of appropriate deductions was left up to the Secretary of the Treasury. The bill also contained the first "loophole," a special 1.5 percent rate on interest on government securities to encourage the purchase of bonds, which were the major means of financing of the war effort.

At the time of its passage, the income tax occupied much less congressional time and attention than the tariff changes and direct land tax. This may have been one reason why, by the spring of 1862, no income tax revenue had been raised and no real effort was under way to implement the law. The financial requirements of the war had increased by early 1862, and Chase had resorted to massive sales of bonds to cover finances. In this atmosphere, when a new revenue bill was prepared in the House in the spring of 1862, little attention was paid to the inclusion of another income tax provision similar to that passed in 1862 but with an exemption of $600. The same provision was initially included in the Senate bill. However, after direct taxes on land were defeated on a floor vote, it was later altered to include a progressive rate structure. To make up the revenue lost by defeat of the land tax, progressive rates were set at 3 percent on incomes between $600 and $10,000; 5 percent between $10,000 and $50,000; and 7.5 percent over $50,000. The rate for bond interest was 1.5 percent, and deductions

were allowed for all other taxes paid. The conference committee later eliminated the 7.5 percent rate. Also included in the act was the first inheritance tax, although the rates were very modest. In contrast to the first act, the income tax provisions were quite specific (with less left up to the Treasury), and there was no doubt that it was to be implemented.

Two things should be noted about the relatively quiet birth of the income tax. First, it was passed under conditions of economic emergency: the national debt had risen to $505 million. Second, progressivity was introduced not out of concern for equity, but rather to increase revenues. Sidney Ratner summarized these events as follows: "The principle of progressivity was not adopted for its own sake but as a by-product of the increase in rates. Since a tax of 7.5 per cent on all income above $600 would have been regarded as an excessive and unjust burden on the small incomes, the Senate was forced to apply higher rates to higher income."[3] With some slight exceptions, these two conditions continued to be essential elements in the development of the income tax through the Korean War.

A second Civil War income tax was passed in 1864, and this time with a great deal more interest and debate. By that time the national debt totaled $1.8 billion, with a deficit of over $600 million in 1864 alone. The debate over the income tax provisions was bitter. Rates were altered by a floor amendment to increase the graduation of the tax to a maximum of 10 percent. This led to an unsuccessful protest by Justin Morrill of Vermont, the founder of the Republican Party and the head of the tax subcommittee of Ways and Means:

> The very theory of our institutions is entire equality; that we make no distinction between the rich and the poor man. The man of modest means is just as good as the man with more means, but our theory of government does not admit that he is better, and I regard it as an evidence of the spirit of agrarianism to present a law here which shall make such distinction. It is seizing the property of men for the crime of having too much.[4]

In addition to raising the progressivity of the income tax, more complex exceptions and special provisions were also added. Rent was made a deductible expense; gains from real estate were taxable only if the property was both purchased and sold in the tax year; and a series of complex and beneficial provisions for farm income were included. As the stakes increased, and as legislators and lobbyists came to understand the income tax, complications and exceptions for special circumstances quickly followed.

Agitation for repeal of the war taxes began almost immediately after the war ended. The income tax was a main target of congressmen from the Northeast, particularly from New York—and for good reason. By the time the tax was finally terminated in 1872, New York had paid approximately one-third of the tax collected. The final votes for repeal in the House reflected this regional and economic split. Seven New England states plus California, which had collectively paid 70 percent of income tax revenues, voted 61 for repeal, 14 against; the fourteen southern and western states plus New Hampshire, which, combined, paid only 11 percent of the tax, voted 5 for and 61 against.[5] The early politics of the income tax was hardly based on altruism or a sweeping movement for equality.

The Enactment and Repeal of the Income Tax of 1894

Following repeal of the Civil War taxes, the tariff and excise taxes again carried almost the entire burden of government revenue. Some agitation for an income tax began in the 1870s and continued through the 1880s both outside and within Congress. Several proposals were introduced but were easily derailed by the Republican leadership in the House. The 1880s was a period of considerable prosperity, and government revenues soared, creating annual surpluses of over $100 million. At the same time, however, great fortunes were being created, and those fortunes and some of the darker aspects of unrestrained capitalism were well publicized. In the West and the South, the Populist movement began. In 1892 the Republican reign ended with the election of Grover Cleveland as president and the shift to Democratic control of both the House and the Senate. However, party was not to play as important a role in the battle over the income tax as region and economic conditions.

The prosperity of the eighties ended swiftly and completely with the panic and depression of 1893, a depression that would continue (with a slight recovery in 1895) through the end of 1897. The panic of 1893 was caused by a run on gold and fears in the eastern financial community that the nation would go off the gold standard for the dollar. Agitation to repeal the gold standard came from the poor and debtor states of the West and the South. It was firmly resisted by the wealthy Northeast, which was afraid that without the gold standard the dollar would inflate and debts would be paid off in cheap money. In the previous twenty years, the reverse had been true in that the dollar had nearly doubled in value, much to the chagrin of debtors. The run on gold demonstrated

the financial weakness of the government, and the panic was averted only when a consortium of eastern banks purchased gold to replenish extremely low government reserves.

The financial situation, combined with the Democratic Party's fear of losing ground to the Populists in the West and South, created a precarious tax position that led to the introduction of the income tax.[6] At the same time that there was a need for increased revenue, there was also pressure to lower the extremely high rates of the McKinley tariff (1890), particularly on necessities. It was this combination of forces plus the decisive actions of a few men in the House and the Senate that led to the passage of an income tax as an amendment to the tariff bill of 1894. Although Cleveland was opposed to an income tax on individuals (supporting a modest tax on returns on corporate investment), he could not veto the bill because of the favorable tariff provisions; rather, he left it unsigned.

The political maneuvering that led to the final adoption of an income tax makes an interesting story, but one that has been reported several times before and need not concern us here.[7] Those instrumental in the passage of the tax were mostly from the Middle West and South. The Chairman of Ways and Means, Benton McMillin (D-Tenn.), William Jennings Bryan (D-Neb.), and Uriel S. Hall (D-Mo.) led the fight in the House. Two Populists, William V. Allen (Neb.) and James H. Kyle (S.D.), led the floor debate in the Senate. The opposition came almost exclusively from the East, with two key Democratic orators from New York, David Hill in the Senate and Bourke Cochran in the House, leading the floor attacks for the opponents. The debate that surrounded passage was magnificent, and although the geoeconomic factors were raised, the issue was also posed as one of rich versus poor and the rights of property versus the specter of socialism.

David Hill began the debate in the Senate in the spring of 1894 by cataloging the evils of the income tax with meticulous order and clarity. It would cause economic ruin in that incentive would be dampened and wages lowered; it was unnecessary to raise the revenue needed; it was class legislation because the exemption of $4,000 would place the entire burden on a very small number; it would be inquisitorial and generate fraud and corruption; it would be unequally borne by the states (and would particularly oppress his home state of New York); and, most importantly, it represented an ill-advised attempt to follow Europe down the path to socialism.[8] The most stringent reply to Hill came in late June from William Allen, who defended not only the income tax but also the Populist program in general. He struck repeatedly on the theme that income and wealth were extremely skewed and that taxes should reflect

this distribution. He then linked this distribution to the charge of sectionalism: "Mr. President, it is said that an income tax is unjust and sectional. It is sectional because the people of a certain section of this country have the greatest number of incomes which are taxable."[9] This was followed by a reading into the record of a list of 119 New York millionaires, with John D. Rockefeller, several Astors, and three Vanderbilts leading the list. Next to their incomes was printed the 2 percent tax they would have to pay. The exchanges with Mr. Hill that followed were increasingly caustic and personal, ending with Allen stating that Hill had purchased his Senate seat and Hill accusing Allen of lying and—what was worse—being a former Republican.[10]

In the House one of the classic congressional debates of all times was waged between Bourke Cochran and William Jennings Bryan. Cochran began his arguments with an appeal to what we call in the 1980s "supply-side economics." He argued that the estimates of revenue by the Treasury were low, because the government failed to consider that tariff reduction would in fact increase revenues by increasing trade activity. He quickly moved on to his major point: that by levying a tax on only 85,000 people out of 65 million, the government deprived the vast majority of the patriotic right and privilege of supporting it and so removed the "moral ground for insisting that the control be equal." Not only was the income tax an opening wedge of socialism that taxed only those "who had made the best use of the benefits common to all," but it endangered the Republic itself.[11]

Bryan replied to this argument with a flourish:

> Why, sir, the gentleman from New York [Mr. Cochran] said that the poor are opposed to this because they do not want to be deprived of participation in it, and that taxation instead of being a sign of servitude is a badge of freedom. If taxation is a badge of freedom, let me assure my friend that the poor people of this country are covered all over with the insignia of freedom. . . . The gentleman says he opposed the tax in the interest of the poor! Oh, sirs, is it not enough to betray the cause of the poor— must it be done with a kiss? (Applause) Would it not be fairer for the gentleman to fling his burnished lance full in the face of the toiler, and not plead for the great fortunes of this country under the cover of a poor man's name? (Applause)[12]

It was fair that the main burden of the income tax fell on the very wealthy, since the tariff, twenty times greater, fell disproportionately on the working man, Bryan said. He ended his speech with a reply to Ward

McAllister, who had recently published a letter in the *New York World* arguing that if the income tax was passed, many of the wealthy might take up residence abroad.

> If some of our best people prefer to leave the country rather than pay a tax of 2 per cent, God pity the worst. (Laughter)
>
> If we have people who value free government so little that they prefer to live under monarchial institutions, even without an income tax, rather than live under the stars and stripes and pay a 2 per cent tax, we can better afford to lose them and their fortunes than risk the contaminating influence of their presence. (Applause)
>
> I will not attempt to characterize such persons. If Mr. McAllister is a true prophet, if we are to lose some of our best people by the imposition of an income tax, let them depart, and as they leave without regret the land of their birth, let them go with the poet's curse ringing in their ears.[13]

Mr. Bryan then recited "My Native Land" and received a standing ovation, which was followed by a vote for final passage.

The votes on the internal revenue provision of the tariff bill reflected regional lines, although in the House most Republicans abstained. The Democrats split geographically almost exactly along the North/Northeast versus South and Middle West lines. In the Senate, in the critical vote for repeal that was defeated 40 to 24, not a single northeastern senator supported the income tax. The bill as finally passed was trivial in scope and simple in structure. It levied a flat 2 percent tax on income from all sources, including dividends, interest, rents, sales of real estate and property, and gifts, as well as wages and salaries. It exempted only interest on federal bonds that were issued with a prior exemption from taxes and the salaries of state and local officials, federal judges, and the president. Its structure was the epitome of what was later to be called the comprehensive tax base model and was undoubtedly the closest the United States was ever to come to that ideal. However, it affected very few people because of the high exemption of $4,000. It was in the beginning, as its opponents had so bitterly claimed, truly a class tax.

The tax was not destined to last long. In 1895, after two separate hearings, the Supreme Court overturned the income tax as unconstitutional.[14] The critical issue was whether the taxes on various sources of income were to be considered "direct" taxes. If they were, the Constitution specified that they had to be assessed uniformly, which meant in proportion to state population, a condition that the income tax

obviously would not meet. The ruling in both cases was that the taxes on income from rents and personal property were direct taxes and hence invalid. The tax on municipal bond interest was also ruled invalid because it infringed on state and local taxing powers. On the other hand, taxes on wages, professions, and trades were not considered direct taxes, and the tax on those sources of income would have been valid had not the entire tax amendment been ruled illegal in the second hearing because of the other unconstitutional provisions. The ruling was front page news throughout the country, and analysis of the opinions continued in the popular press and academia for over a decade, ceasing only in 1913 with the passage of the permanent income tax.

In the years between 1895 and 1909, interest in the income tax waned considerably. The Populists, led by Bryan, took up other causes, although they briefly tried to resurrect the income tax as a means of financing the Spanish-American War. However, firm Republican control of Congress and the difficulty of writing legislation within the confines of the court ruling defeated the effort. In 1908 the issue became credible again when Teddy Roosevelt made a radical proposal for both an inheritance tax and an income tax. In Congress, it came to life in 1909.

Although there was sympathy in the House, where Cordell Hull (D-Tenn.), beginning an illustrious political career, had become a supporter of and expert on the income tax, efforts were thwarted by the iron parliamentary rule of Speaker Cannon. In the Senate, Republican leadership under the control of Nelson Aldrich (R-N.Y.) had consistently resisted the income tax in favor of very high tariffs. In the spring of 1909, however, a new group of liberal Republicans who became known as the Insurgents joined earlier Progressives like Robert La Follette, who had been elected in 1906. This group of eight to ten senators, mostly from the Middle West, defied Aldrich's campaign to drum them out of the Republican Party and fought diligently but unsuccessfully against extension of the high tariff rates. During the proceedings they also introduced two income tax proposals that directly challenged the 1895 Supreme Court ruling. The first, by Bailey of Texas, was an exact copy of the 1895 statute except that it excluded interest from state and local bond issues as taxable income. The second, introduced by Albert Cummins, the former radical governor of Iowa, was more extreme, with an exemption of $5,000 and progressive rates ranging from 2 to 6 percent. A compromise was reached, and a group of nineteen Republicans and all the Democrats in the Senate agreed to the proposed amendment to the tariff bill. Anticipating defeat on the issue, Aldrich managed to delay a vote on the amendment for two months, during

which time he and several other key Republicans appealed to President Taft for intervention. The administration's suggested compromise was offered ostensibly to defuse a potential constitutional crisis between Congress and the Supreme Court. It proposed (1) a constitutional amendment that would specifically allow an income tax without equal apportionment among the states, and (2) immediate passage of an "excise" tax of 4 percent on corporate profits.

The intense debates that followed in both houses of Congress featured the unlikely combination of conservative Republicans reluctantly supporting the corporate income tax and radical Republicans and Democrats opposing it as an unjust tax and a treacherous substitute for the personal income tax. Hull described this strange turn of events as follows:

> During the past few weeks the unexpected spectacle of certain so-called "old-line conservative" Republican leaders in Congress suddenly reversing their attitude of a lifetime and seemingly espousing, though with ill-concealed reluctance, the proposed income tax amendment to the Constitution has been the occasion of universal surprise and wonder.[15]

Both branches of Congress accepted the proposals by almost unanimous votes. A very modest but permanent corporate income tax was born, and the path to the individual income tax was set.[16]

The Individual Income Tax of 1913

Ratification of the Sixteenth Amendment was slow. Only Alabama ratified it in 1909, but Georgia, Illinois, Kentucky, Maryland, Mississippi, Oklahoma, and Texas soon followed. The regional pattern is consistent with the geographical support for the income tax from the very beginning. However, although the eastern states were slower in acting, and there was somewhat greater opposition, many eventually ratified the amendment: even New York did so on its second try. In most states there was little opposition, and the votes in favor of ratification were lopsided. The last states to ratify were Vermont, New Hampshire, and Massachusetts, with the thirty-sixth state voting on February 3, 1913.[17] The timing was appropriate, for a major political transformation had taken shape since 1909, culminating in the sweeping Democratic victories of 1912.

From about 1906 onward, the Progressive movement had been grow-

ing nationally, leading to the election of the Insurgent Republicans so instrumental in the passage of the 1909 income tax provisions and a growing number of radical Democrats under the leadership of William Jennings Bryan. The movement encompassed a range of issues including government reform, direct democracy, and women's suffrage, but it hit hardest at the practices and power of big business and the resulting accumulation and distribution of wealth and income. Studies of the power of monopolies and trusts began in earnest. Several of these studies, such as Ida Tarbell's exposé of Standard Oil and the report of the Pujo Committee (which studied the banking system and proclaimed the existence of a "money trust"), received a great deal of publicity. Studies showing that the income distribution had significantly worsened since 1890 and tracts on rural and urban poverty were also widely circulated.[18]

The radical trend affected the political balance at the national level. The most important effect was the split in the Republican Party in 1912. The Progressives and Insurgents, following the new-found radicalism of Theodore Roosevelt, attempted unsuccessfully to wrest the Republican presidential nomination from Taft and the conservative Republicans. Their failure led to the creation of the Bull Moose Party, with Roosevelt as its presidential candidate. The Democrats capitalized on this split. Woodrow Wilson, aiming his campaign at small businessmen, farmers, and laborers, promised reforms of big business, lowered tariffs, and an income tax. He was elected by a plurality of 6.3 million votes to Roosevelt's 4.1 million and Taft's 3.4 million. Democrats outnumbered Republicans by 291 to 128 in the House (with 15 Progressives and an Independent), and 51 to 44 in the Senate (with 1 Progressive).

This realignment led to immediate action on revenue legislation. In his inaugural address, given in March 1913, Wilson called for tariff reform and reduction with an income tax to make up the lost revenues. He asked for and got an emergency session of Congress to enact such legislation.[19] The Ways and Means Committee, under the leadership of Oscar Underwood (D-Ala.) and with a Democratic majority of 14 to 7, reported a bill by April 7. The second part of that bill was an income tax provision that had been drafted by a subcommittee headed by Cordell Hull. Reflecting Hull's moderation and the conservatism of the majority of the Democrats in the House, the provisions were modest. Hull originally wanted a flat rate but yielded to the arguments of John Nance Garner (D-Tex., and later Franklin Roosevelt's vice president) on graduation of the rates. An exemption of $4,000 was granted, with rates of 1 percent as a "normal tax" on incomes up to $20,000 and "surcharges" of 1 percent on income between $20,000 and $50,000, 2 percent on

income between $50,000 and $100,000, and 3 percent on higher incomes.

Hull explained the provisions and responded to questions and the debate on the floor. He forcefully defended the tax as based not on consumption, as the tariff and excise taxes were, but on ability to pay. There was no opposition voiced to passage of the income tax, although unsuccessful efforts were made to raise or lower the exemption. With the exemption at that level, very few people would pay anything, a fact that contributed greatly to the political popularity of the tax. Several amendments were offered to increase the rates, the most drastic of which was Representative Copley's proposal to set a top rate of 68 percent. When defeated by a wide margin, Copley responded that "within twenty years, the country would see such a law."[20] It did not take that long.

There was also confusion over the meaning of several provisions, including the one dealing with the sale of property. Hull asserted that only profits on goods bought and sold in the tax year would be taxed. This initial confusion began the protracted legislative history of the complex provisions governing capital gains. Insurance was another problem, particularly the status of dividends on mutual insurance policies, which the industry claimed were really rebates on premiums. In many of these confusing areas it was felt that the broad powers given to the commissioner of Internal Revenue would allow later administrative clarification. The debate lasted two days, and no separate vote was taken on the income tax provisions. At the time the tax was accepted as a natural and inevitable culmination of the constitutional amendment. It was not deemed as important as the tariff bill itself. The income tax section occupied only 8 pages of an 814-page report.

The debate in the Senate was much different and ironically led to a more radical bill, even though the Democratic majority was smaller. The Finance Committee bill made a precedent-setting adjustment in exemptions, allowing everyone a deduction of $3,000 with an additional $1,000 if married and $500 for each dependent. Thus, in consideration of ability to pay, family size was introduced for the first time as a factor in the income tax. After a struggle, the Democratic caucus limited dependent exemptions to two children. The major fight, however, came over the degree of progression in the rates. The western radicals, led by La Follette of Wisconsin, Borah of Idaho, Bristow of Kansas, and Poindexter of Washington, all proposed various increases in rates. These proposals were greeted by hostile remarks, typified by Henry Cabot Lodge's characterization of the proposals as "confiscation of property under the guise of taxation" and "the pillage of a class."[21] Although the amend-

ments offered were all defeated on floor votes, a large enough coalition was formed by the radicals to force a compromise in the Democratic caucus that added three brackets, with a top surcharge of 6 percent on incomes over $500,000. This was accepted by the Senate as a whole and eventually survived the Conference Committee to become law. As in the House, no separate floor vote was taken on the income tax section. The full bill was passed by an almost straight-line party vote of 44 to 37 with only two defections on each side.

The final income tax provisions that emerged from conference and became law on October 3, 1913, were a blend of compromises and adjustments to accomodate legal precedents, political divisions, and the demands of several interest groups. The exemption for dependent children was dropped, but the marriage differential remained, as did the graduated rate structure that the radicals forced through the Senate. Thus, the top rate became 7 percent, including both a normal tax and a surtax. A number of sources of income were excluded: interest on state and local bonds, salaries of all state and local employees, and the income of the president and federal judges were excluded out of deference to previous court rulings; gifts and inheritances were excluded because a separate inheritance tax was planned; and proceeds of life insurance policies were excluded to appease the life insurance lobby. A series of deductions were also allowed as "expenses" of doing business: direct business expenses (but not personal living expenses); interest paid on indebtedness; all taxes; uncompensated casualty losses due to fire, storm, or shipwreck; uncollectible bad debts; a depreciation allowance for wear on property; and dividends paid on stock (for computation of normal taxes only). That all of these deductions are still part of the income tax laws is testimony to the importance of policy precedents and the staying power of tax reduction provisions.

Thus, fifty-two years after the first income tax was passed during the crisis of the Civil War, the individual income tax became a permanent statutory reality. It began as a modest amendment to a high tariff bill, designed to fill a small revenue gap between excise taxes and the tariff and affecting only a small percentage of the working population (less than 2 percent of the labor force filed returns in the years 1913–1915). It was created in the best tradition of incremental politics. The process was torturously slow, including four major political tests involving all branches of the federal government, states, and localities. The final legislation was borrowed from past experience and the experience of states and other countries, and it was carefully adapted to the political and constitutional restraints that had developed over time.[22] Through its varied provisions the law acknowledged particular circumstances of

ability to pay as well as conditions and expenses affecting the creation of income. The final rates were a very modest expression of the Progressive ethic that had captured at least part of the nation. The movement toward equality was slow and easy, with a tax that had no effect on 98 percent of the population. The importance of the tax was to be dramatically enhanced by World War I, but its "elite" impact would not be permanently altered until the Second World War.

World War I — Discovering the Income Tax

Those who model policy changes, particularly in terms of budget expenditures, often use time series data that either begin after World War II or exclude war periods as deviant events or external shocks.[23] To do either with the income tax, or the study of taxes in general, is to ignore the single most important influence on the formation and structure of the tax code. In analyzing the impact of wars on public finance, one has to stretch the meaning of the term "marginal change" to accurately describe the shifts that were rapidly introduced in the revenue structure and tax burden during the war years. Figure 4.1, which displays the percentage breakdown of federal revenue by source from 1880 to 1980, vividly portrays the effects of wars on federal taxes. Prior to World War I, over 90 percent of federal revenues came from either excise taxes or customs. Between 1913 and 1915, the income tax had almost no influence on tax collections, partly because the initial estimates of revenue to be raised were woefully optimistic. By 1916, however, individual and corporate income taxes accounted for 16 percent of revenues, which expanded to an average of 58.6 percent for the years 1917–1920. As figure 4.1 indicates, the war virtually ended the importance of the tariff as a source of revenue and greatly diminished the role of excise taxes, although they would again become significant for a brief period during the Depression.

Almost immediately after the passage of the 1913 tariff bill, revenue needs due to the war in Europe increased. The initial pressure on revenues came from short-term declines in custom duties following the outbreak of the war in Europe. The revenue bill of 1914 made no changes in the income tax and primarily raised excise taxes, using legislation adopted during the Spanish-American War as a guide. A boom in the economy that began in late 1914 made it unnecessary to pass further revenue bills until 1916 when a serious effort to build up the armed forces began. Political debate over the Emergency Revenue Act of 1916, finally passed in September after almost a year of discus-

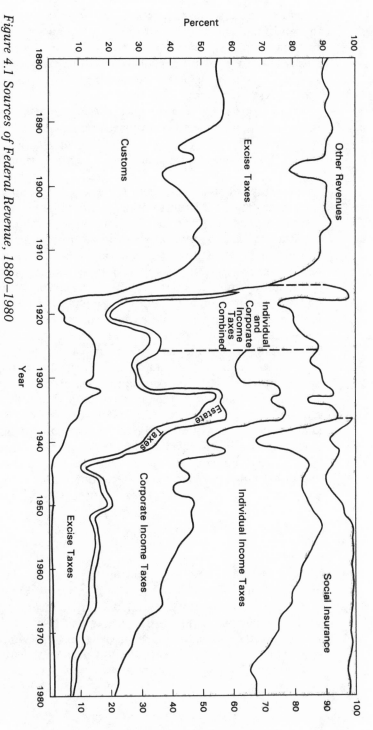

Figure 4.1 Sources of Federal Revenue, 1880–1980

Sources: Bureau of the Census, *Historical Statistics of the United States: Colonial Times to the Present*, series Y352–57, Y358–73, Y343–51 (Washington, D.C.: Government Printing Office, 1976); *U.S. Statistical Abstract, 1980* (Washington, D.C.: Government Printing Office, 1980), p. 260, table 434.

Note: Only combined corporate and individual income tax totals are reported for 1918 to 1924. All corporate income taxes include excess profits taxes. From 1880 to 1936 statistics are based on the administrative budget. From 1940 on, cash receipts were used. For 1937–1939 Social Security receipts were added to the administrative budget totals.

sion, revolved around three controversial provisions: increases in the income tax; imposition of a tax on the production of munitions; and initiation of the first federal inheritance tax.

The debates on the internal revenue measures were along familiar lines. The House Ways and Means report, written under the tutelage of Hull and Claude Kitchin (D-N.C.), chairman of the committee, stressed that revenue should be collected from "the incomes and inheritances of those deriving the most benefit from the government."[24] A reply came from Nicholas Longworth (R-Ohio, and Theodore Roosevelt's son-in-law), who criticized the proposed rate increases of the income tax without a lower exemption as pure class legislation. He recommended lowering the exemption to $1,000, but was defeated on a floor vote by the Democratic majority.[25] The debate was similar on the inheritance tax, which the Democrats had set at a graduated rate of 1 to 5 percent but with a $50,000 exemption, which again excluded the vast majority of the population. A munitions tax of 12.5 percent, modeled after similar taxes in Denmark, Sweden, Canada, Great Britain, Germany, and France, was placed on producers of armaments making a net profit over 10 percent of their invested capital. Since defense of war profiteering was difficult for anyone, few Republicans objected to this tax in either the House or the Senate.

Action in the Senate was more lively, primarily as a result of the efforts of the Progressives, who were intent on publicizing the income tax returns of very wealthy individuals. The outcome, as in 1913, was to push the bill to a more radical level. While neither the House nor the Senate bill lowered the exemption or the rate at which the surcharge became effective, as Wilson and some Republicans and moderate Democrats requested, both increased income tax surcharge rates. In the House, the normal tax was increased from 1 to 2 percent, and the top surcharge rate to 10 percent. The Senate pushed the top rate to 13 percent, and its option won in the conference committee. Several other important changes were made, expanding the taxation of stock dividends and allowing a depletion calculation for oil, but the crucial result was the discovery of how easily and quickly large sums of revenue could be raised through the income taxes.

Although ideology, geography, and partisanship all played an important role in the legislative process in 1916, a budget deficit of $177 million between 1915 and 1916 was the basic moving force. Secretary of the Treasury McAdoo and President Wilson were determined from the beginning to pay for as much of the defense expenses as possible, and this feeling was shared by both congressional parties.[26] That taxes were to be raised significantly was never in question. As changes in tax

provisions were considered, the revenue effects were a continuous element of the debate. This does not mean that the debate neglected the issue of progressivity or that the bill had no influence on the distribution of tax burdens. However, those choices were forced on the political system by the dictates of war, and there is little evidence of an independent interest in redistributing income through the tax system.

What began in 1916 was carried to remarkable extremes in 1917, primarily by simple but dramatic extensions of the new taxing devices that had been created in the previous four years. In December 1916, following Wilson's defeat of Charles Evans Hughes in the presidential election, Secretary of the Treasury McAdoo announced that without further revenue measures there would be a deficit of $185 million by June 30, 1918. His estimate was to be low by many billions of dollars, but his message was enough to spur Congress, under the quavering leadership of Claude Kitchin, to consider expansion of the newly enacted war munitions and inheritance taxes. The most significant change was the adaptation of the war munitions tax, which as passed in 1916 applied only to corporations directly producing arms, to an "excess profits" tax that applied to all corporations and partnerships (therefore including lawyers, doctors, financial firms, etc.). Such a tax had already been passed in fifteen other countries. Whereas the 1916 munitions tax was a flat 12.5 percent on net profits for armaments producers, the excess profits tax applied to profits "over a reasonable return on invested capital." The reasonable rate of return was set at 8 percent, as was the tax rate on profits over that amount. This was in addition to the existing munitions tax and the corporate income tax, which at that time was 2 percent. The Ways and Means Committee also proposed increasing by 50 percent the inheritance rates, which had become law less than six months earlier. The 1917 rates were graduated from 1.5 to 15.0 percent.

The political opposition to these changes was heightened by a report, played up in the press, that Kitchin, who was from North Carolina, had declared in the Democratic caucus: "You can tell your people that practically all of this will go north of the Mason and Dixon line. The preparedness agitation has its hotbed in such cities as New York."[27] While the report of this comment led to indignant cries from northern newspapers and congressmen, the bill in the House was debated for only a single day, and most of that debate was a discussion whether the government should pay for preparedness through the tariff or income taxes. Although Representative Fordney (R-Mich.) objected vehemently to the excess profits tax and all of his Republican colleagues ended up voting against the bill, the Democrats, with their slim major-

ity, held fast in an extremely partisan vote.[28] The day after passage of the House bill, the Germans pressed forward their policy of submarine warfare against shipping that aided their opponents. With U.S. entry into the war apparently close at hand, the Senate rushed to approve the House bill, forestalled only by a brief filibuster by Senator La Follette who favored much steeper income and inheritance taxes rather than an excess profits tax that he felt would be impossible to administer. As in the House, both the vote to recommit the bill to the Senate Finance Committee and the vote on final passage were nearly straight-line party votes.[29] The bill was signed by the president, but before it could go into effect it was made obsolete by U.S. entrance into the war on April 5, 1917.

In the wake of the overwhelming congressional vote to declare war, a bipartisan atmosphere and a willingness to go along with administration revenue requests prevailed in Congress. Up to this point detailed income tax legislation had, for the most part, been left up to Congress, with most of the power delegated to the revenue committees. In early April, however, Secretary McAdoo came before Congress with specific estimates of revenue needs and a detailed set of requests for raising the revenue. His initial cost estimates, to be revised upward several times during the year, were $3.5 billion for the U.S. war effort and $3.0 billion in loans to the allies. He proposed that 50 percent of this sum be raised through taxes and the rest through bonds and borrowing. The major income tax proposals, which were to account for a little less than half the increases in revenue were: (1) a surcharge of 50 percent on all taxes retroactive to 1916; (2) an increase in surtax rates up to a maximum of 40 percent; (3) a reduction for the first time of the exemptions of $3,000 for single and $4,000 for joint returns (they were cut in half); and (4) an increase in the excess profits tax.

The general approach of financing the war through heavy taxation was supported by most of the academic community, which sent a letter to Congress outlining the advantages of this course.[30] Curiously, the question of equity or justice was addressed only in terms of the inappropriateness of laying the burden of war debts on returning servicemen and succeeding generations. Although the proposed changes in the income tax would clearly increase progressivity, changes were not accompanied by calls for income redistribution. The need for revenue ruled the discussion.[31]

The political history of the 1917 War Revenue Act is complicated, and the details have been adequately reported elsewhere.[32] Although final passage in both the House and the Senate was by overwhelming bipartisan majorities, the exact form and degree of the increases was worked

out over six months of struggle and compromise. Kitchin and a small group in the House tried to radically increase individual and corporate rates without lowering the exemption, but the Ways and Means Committee rejected that approach as Longworth and others argued that it would impose the tax burden on only one-half of one percent of the population. Moderates claimed that only by lowering the exemption could the needed amount of revenue be raised. In the Senate the excitement was generated as always by the radicals led by La Follette, and again the most extreme amendments for steeply increased taxes on the wealthy, offered by the group that included La Follette, Borah, and Hiram Johnson (R-Cal.), were defeated. However, their efforts did succeed in pushing the Senate bill in a more radical direction. La Follette's personal efforts on the floor were hurt by charges that he was an enemy of democracy because of his antiwar stance and vote against the declaration of war in April.

The result was a revenue bill that overwhelmed any previous financial action by the government in terms of both the amount of revenue eventually collected and the distribution of the tax burden. It also marked the shift of the finances of the United States from a base of customs and excises to one of income taxes. The final bill was long and complicated. Major changes were as follows:

1. *Income taxes.* Exemptions were lowered to $1,000 for single persons and $2,000 for married couples. A normal tax of 2 percent was set on all income above that level with an additional 2 percent on income over $3,000 ($4,000 for married couples) and surtaxes that reached a maximum of 50 percent on incomes over $1 million.

2. *Corporation taxes.* The normal tax on corporations was increased from 2 to 4 percent after exemptions of $3,000 for corporations and $6,000 for partnerships. A graduated tax on excess profits was created. The tax was levied on profits greater than 7-9 percent return on investment for a base period from 1911 to 1913. Rates began at 8 percent and ended at 60 percent on profits above 32 percent of the base period earnings. Excess profits derived from personal or professional services were limited to 8 percent above a $3,000 exemption ($6,000 for a married couple).

3. *Other taxes.* Numerous excise taxes were increased, with liquor and tobacco producing the most revenue. Postal rates were increased by 50 percent. Inheritance taxes were in-

creased in a range from 0.5 percent for estates above a $50,000 exemption to 10 percent on estates over $10 million. (These increases were actually lower than those approved in the March bill.)

These internal revenue measures produced an increase in revenue from $0.8 billion in 1917 to $3.7 billion in 1918. Of this increase, 87 percent was contributed by the income and profits taxes.[33] The profits tax proved to be even more fruitful than anticipated because of a very successful business year, particularly for those producing armaments and exporting goods abroad. In the spring of 1918, the administration began asking for additional revenue measures, although this time there was some reluctance in Congress to believe that expenditures could not be controlled so that current rates would be sufficient. At Wilson's urging, following specific proposals by McAdoo, the House produced a bill that increased normal rates to 5 percent on incomes below $4,000 and 12 percent on those above. Surtaxes were increased to a maximum of 65 percent. A number of complicated changes were also made in the excess profits tax, which had drawn a large amount of hostile testimony in House hearings and was the central focus of the debate on the House floor. Following the pattern set by the 1917 act, the bill was passed on September 22 by a unanimous vote. The Senate, however, did not finish drafting its changes to the War Revenue Act of 1918 before the elections and the Armistice on November 11, 1918.

With the end of the war, a second drafting was done based on new recommendations by Secretary McAdoo. La Follette again fueled the debate in the Senate with an entire substitute package that proposed even more extreme rates on profits and on the wealthy, with surtaxes for individuals reaching a maximum of 78 percent for a total rate of 90 percent. He was soundly defeated by a vote of 55 to 6, and in February 1919 the Senate passed the 1918 Revenue Act (as its name remained) by a voice vote. The final bill contained increases in the individual income tax as passed in the House bill, but with automatic reductions in the normal rate to take effect in 1919 and 1920. The bill created a maximum rate of 77 percent, including normal taxes and surcharges. The excess profits tax was altered in several ways, but the most important was the addition of a war profits tax that was based on changes in profit (rather than return on capital) from the prewar period. While short-lived, lasting only for the 1918 tax year, the provision fulfilled the administration's desire to limit profiteering on the war effort. The regular excess profits tax was also slightly increased, but automatic reductions were built in for 1919 and beyond. Rate changes in the bill were

less dramatic than those in 1917, but because normal taxes were raised, affecting large numbers of taxpayers, the bill's yield was considerably higher than that of the 1917 acts. Because of these rates and a steep upturn in personal income in 1920, the income and profits tax combined accounted for $2.8, $2.6, and $4.0 billion in 1918, 1919, and 1920.[34]

World War I was a turning point in the history of public finance in the United States. It marked the end of the tariff and excise as the dominant sources of revenue. The revenue-generating capacity of income taxes and the ease with which they could be expanded were undeniable. Consumption taxes fostered long, fragmented political struggles between specific groups of producers and consumers. This made it difficult to raise large amounts of revenue quickly. In contrast, the income tax had the appearance of universal applicability, and at that time few special interest ties had been formed to restrain its effects. The tax's appeal was enhanced by its progressivity—the first real progressivity in American tax history. For the years 1917 to 1919, although less than 1 percent of the returns reported income over $20,000, that group paid an average of 70 percent of the income taxes.[35]

During the war years the cries of "ability to pay" and "war profiteering" drowned out pleas for defense against "class legislation." In effect the income taxes were class legislation—a fact explaining some of their appeal. For 1920, the year in which the most returns were filed, there were only 5.5 million taxable returns for a population of 106 million and a labor force estimated at 41.7 million (see figure 6.2). By the end of 1920, however, the election had produced a sweeping reversal of the Democratic majorities that had existed since 1912, and the political mood in the country had changed dramatically. Reflecting that change in its call for a return to normalcy, the new Republican administration placed the dismantling of the war taxes high on its agenda. And dismantle they did for almost twelve years, until another series of crises reversed the trend once again.

Summary

The creation of the income tax followed a distinctly incremental path. It was originally instituted as a reaction to revenue needs created by the Civil War. It was later reborn at least in part as a response to the dire financial condition of the government during the panic and depression of 1893. By the time the income tax was permanently enacted, it had been thoroughly reviewed by all branches of the federal government

and approved by three-quarters of the states as a constitutional amendment. The idea and the structure of the permanent income tax were borrowed from other countries and based on previous federal taxes and state income taxes. The Civil War tax, the 1894 act, and the tax of 1913 all began modestly, accounting for very little revenue relative to other sources, affecting very few people, and imposing very low rates.

The stimulus for the income tax in 1894 and 1913 was a combination of revenue demands, Progressive ideology, and geoeconomic divisions that pitted the industrialized North and Northeast against the rest of the nation. The rural South, Middle West, and Far West, having less income than the Northeast, bore a disproportionate burden of consumption taxes (tariffs and excise taxes). These states, in which the Populist and Progressive movements were centered, led the campaign for the income tax. Enactment of the permanent income tax in 1913 coincided with a shift toward Democratic control of the White House and Congress. However, the die had been cast for the income tax with the proposal of a constitutional amendment in 1909. The 1913 bill was to some degree anticlimactic.

World War I was a shock to government finances that dramatically and permanently affected the internal revenue system in the United States. What began as a modest income tax with a very large exemption, a maximum tax rate of 7 percent, and a negligible share of revenue expanded in four years to a tax accounting for close to 60 percent of all revenue and having a maximum rate of 77 percent. The flexible revenue capacity of income taxes was proven during the war, and although the next decade would be devoted to slowly undoing the war tax system, the income tax would never again be a minor source of revenue.

Throughout these early years, evidence that the income tax was ever intended to redistribute income or that it was a symbol of a commitment to greater income equality is at best mixed. There can be no question of this commitment on the part of some of those who were instrumental in the passage of the tax in driving up war rates. But there is also evidence that most of the time these radical "Bryan Democrats," Progressives, and Insurgent Republicans were in a minority. Rather, revenue needs and regional divisions served to shift the consensus at critical moments. The initial commitment to equality was modest, and real progressivity came only with the winds of war.

Chapter 5.
The Interwar
Years

The 1920s—A Partial Return to Tax "Normalcy"

In the 1920s there was a gradual but persistent trend toward lower and less progressive income taxation. This trend had, by the end of the decade, reduced maximum income tax rates from a wartime high of 77 percent to 24 percent.[1] There was a clear consensus in 1920 that taxes should be cut and that surtax rates were too high. Wilson himself questioned the high rates in his last message to Congress: "The Congress might well consider whether the higher rates of income and profits taxes can in peace times be effectively productive of revenue and whether they may not, on the contrary, be destructive of business activity and productive of waste and inefficiency." This was a rhetorical restatement of Secretary of the Treasury Carter Glass's post-war declaration: "The upmost brackets of the surtax have already passed the point of productivity." Wilson's last Secretary of the Treasury, David Houston, raised the same objection in a different way: "It seems idle to speculate in the abstract as to whether or not a progressive income tax schedule rising to rates in excess of 70 percent is justifiable. We are confronted with a condition, not a theory. The fact is that such rates cannot be successfully collected."[2] He then went on to describe how the income of the wealthy was being shifted to the purchase of tax-exempt state and local bonds.

In keeping with the rise in business influence following the Republican sweep of 1920, President Harding appointed a Pittsburgh industrialist, Andrew Mellon, as Secretary of the Treasury. Although he was at first viewed in Washington as an outsider, a businessman who knew nothing about government finance, he was destined to become one of the most powerful men in Washington and probably the most influential Secretary of the Treasury in modern times. As he approached the later years of his twelve-year reign over Treasury, the standing joke was that three presidents had served under Andrew Mellon. Because of his

influence and also because of the parallels being drawn in the 1980s with this historical period—an examination of his philosophy, which he dutifully recorded in a 1924 book entitled *Taxes: The People's Business*, is a worthwhile venture.

Mellon's lasting legacy was his ability and desire to cut taxes. Partly in concert with Wilson, Glass, and Houston (as he pointed out), he based his arguments for lower taxes and lower surtax rates on the grounds that: (1) high surtaxes led to evasion through either trickery or investment in government bonds (which he felt was a poor use of capital); (2) high rates actually led to lower tax collections; and (3) a high level of taxation sapped initiative and work effort. His most celebrated passage expresses the last idea:

> Any man of energy and initiative in this country can get what he wants out of life. But when initiative is crippled by legislation or by a tax system which denies him the right to receive a reasonable share of his earnings, then he will no longer exert himself and the country will be deprived of the energy on which its continued greatness depends.[3]

A less well known argument but one of more current relevance is Mellon's supply-side theory of revenue accumulation:

> It seems difficult for some to understand that high rates of taxation do not necessarily mean large revenue to the government, and that more revenue may often be obtained by lower rates. There was an old saying that a railroad freight rate should be "what the traffic will bear"; that is, the highest rate at which the largest quantity of freight would move. The same rule applies to all private business. If a price is fixed too high, sales drop off and with them profits; if a price is fixed low, sales may increase, but profits decline.[4]

Mixed in with these standard and at that time widely held, conservative positions were other beliefs that were less conventional and some that were actually quite liberal. For example, although he and nearly everyone else favored repealing the war excess profits tax, he was also committed to the idea that corporations should pay a healthy share of the income tax, and he proposed that corporate rates should be raised as excess profits taxes were eliminated. As with most of his initiatives, this one was successful, and unlike individual rates, corporate rates remained high throughout his tenure. He also was adamantly opposed to

tax-exempt securities and began a campaign for repeal of the exclusion that has been taken up unsuccessfully by almost every administration since that time. But what perhaps separates him the farthest from the Republican philosophy of the 1980s was his belief that "earned" and "unearned" income should be distinguished and the former taxed at lower rates. In a very sympathetic passage revealing the advantages of wealth (which he enjoyed), Mellon makes as compelling a plea as any before or since for designing taxes to discriminate between different sources of income and different conditions of need:

> The fairness of taxing more lightly incomes from wages, salaries or from investments is beyond question. In the first case, the income is uncertain and limited in duration; sickness or death destroys it and old age diminishes it; in the other, the source of income continues; the income may be disposed of during a man's life and it descends to his heirs.
>
> Surely we can afford to make a distinction between the people whose only capital is their mental and physical energy and the people whose income is derived from investments. Such a distinction would mean much to millions of American workers and would be an added inspiration to the man who must provide a competence during his few productive years to care for himself and his family when his earnings capacity is at an end.[5]

The Revenue Acts of 1921 and 1924. The tax proposals Mellon put forward in 1921 and 1924 were consistent with these philosophical positions. In 1921 he argued for repeal of the excess profits tax, which was a foregone conclusion for all but the most radical congressmen. However, he also proposed that repeal be compensated for by either a modified corporate profits tax or a flat corporate income tax without any exemption. His other major proposal was to reduce the surtax rates so the minimums were 40 percent in 1921 and 33 percent thereafter. The House in 1921 voted for even more extreme cuts in personal income taxes, lowering the rates so that the highest marginal rate was 32 percent. In the Senate, however, where 33 of the 60 Republican members came from states west of or bordering the Mississippi, the top rate was moved back to 50 percent and that rate prevailed in the Conference Committee. The critical issue in 1921 was a proposal by Senator Smoot (R-Utah) to replace the lost revenue from the excess profits tax with a national sales tax. After an extended debate, which split along regional and party lines, the Democrats and progressive Republicans narrowly defeated his amendment by one vote.

As finally passed, the bill repealed the excess profits tax while increasing the normal corporate tax from 10.0 percent to 12.5 percent. The final surtax rates were lowered to the Senate level of 50 percent, but the normal rate was unchanged. Of the other provisions, by far the most important was one initiating a special maximum rate of 12.5 percent for capital gains held more than two years. The Senate Finance Committee proposed a different method of taxing capital gains, by excluding 60 percent of the gains and taxing the remainder at normal rates, but the Conference Committee adopted the House option. In later years these methods were to be combined.

Reaction to the bill was mixed, but very few were totally satisfied. As Roy and Gladys Blakey wrote: "The disappointment over the new law was almost universal; it seemed to please no one."[6] A good deal of the disappointment came from tax experts who had hoped for grand revision and simplification, but instead got more special provisions and complexity. T. S. Adams, a Yale economist and the leading tax expert of his time, led the movement for simplification and in a letter to the Ways and Means Committee adequately expressed the general frustration at the failure to accomplish that goal.

> They [the practical and experienced Congressmen] propose "to narrow some of these holes at this session of Congress and close some more of them in the future." I do not sneer at this position. It is one that an honest and intelligent man could conceivably take. But it overlooks and forgets one crucial fact. It assumes that, four or five years from now, when we get around to the task of patching up holes in the income tax, we shall have the kind of income tax that can be patched up. *The probability is strong that in four or five years the income tax will, as a matter of practical politics, be past patching.* [Italics in the original.][7]

At this early point in income tax history, the course of the 1921 bill was thought to be an aberration of the political process. Cordell Hull explained it as follows:

> It was most unfortunate that the attempted revision legislation of 1921 degenerated measurably into a wrangle between champions of large income taxpayers and those of smaller taxpayers, each striving to see which could unload the largest amount of taxes first. The legislative situation thus became so

confused and demoralized that but scant opportunity for consideration of comprehensive, scientific tax revision was afforded.[8]

That "scientific revision" was, of course, never to come, but neither was the immediate disaster feared by Adams and others.

The 1924 legislation lowered taxes incrementally, but with several interesting twists introduced by Mellon. Because of the excellent fiscal conditions—there were surpluses totaling $2.3 billion from 1920 to 1923—Mellon proposed further tax cuts, notably a reduction in the normal tax from 6 to 3 percent and a lowering of surtax rates to a maximum of 25 percent. However, he also proposed a tax credit of 25 percent for earned income,[9] and action against abuses of capital gains and interest deductibility regulations that allowed taxpayers to claim losses in excess of their income from these sources. As with the 1921 bill, Congress wanted and got more cuts than Mellon wanted to allow and in the process opened up several new reduction provisions that would prove very costly in the years ahead.

The parties struggled to outbid each other in terms of tax reductions. The Ways and Means Committee, headed by William Green, a moderate Republican from Iowa, began the bidding by proposing an immediate 25 percent tax reduction on all 1924 taxes and by defining all income below $5,000 as "earned" and thus eligible for the permanent 25 percent credit proposed by Mellon. This proposal was challenged on the House floor by a substitute package offered by John Garner that would have meant a much larger loss in revenue but a more progressive tax cut. He proposed a lower and graduated normal tax, increased exemptions, and tax surcharge reductions that reached a higher peak of 44 percent but began at $10,000 rather than $6,000. Since the Republicans were split and Garner's bill offered greater overall benefits, it was passed on a floor vote of 221 to 196. A compromise substitute for Garner's bill, introduced by Nicholas Longworth after lengthy negotiations with the radical factions, was ultimately accepted, but it was closer to the Garner plan than to the original Ways and Means bill.[10]

The Senate Finance Committee, in contrast to its previous habit, came out with a bill more conservative than the House's and closely adhering to Secretary Mellon's original proposals. On the floor, however, the Democrats were able to increase the surtaxes to a maximum of 40 percent by calling an unexpected vote when a number of Republicans were not present. The Republicans were unable to overturn this measure on a later vote. These rates survived conference and were the effective surtaxes until 1926. Another startling amendment that was passed with considerably less than a full Senate present was the one

offered by Senator Jones (D-N.Mex.) to tax corporations at a graduated rate depending on the percentage of their profits that they distributed to shareholders in terms of cash dividends. He had offered this before, but it was never accepted. On this occasion, although accepted on the Senate floor by a vote of 43 to 21, it was dropped in conference. It would be revived under Franklin Roosevelt as a principal component of his attack on corporate wealth in 1935.

The final provisions of the 1924 act further reduced normal rates and surcharges from their World War I peak and added an additional reduction for "earned" income. The act made two important changes in capital gains taxation, which had already become an important and controversial issue. On the one hand, it restricted the benefits accruing to capital gains by following Mellon's suggestion that losses be limited to 12 percent of the total capital gains. On the other hand, as a result of a Ways and Means proposal accepted on the floor, capital assets no longer had to be property used for profit or investment to qualify for the special rate. This provision was instituted specifically so that the sale of residences would be treated as capital gains. Other provisions opposed by the administration raised the estate tax (at the instigation of the Democrats and progressive Republicans) and then added a gift tax to prevent evasion of the estate tax.[11] The bill also created a Board of Tax Appeals to hear tax complaints. The latter was to grow into a special tax court that to this day handles the great bulk of legal claims arising from the tax system. The estate and gift taxes became the critical issues in the revenue bill of 1926.

1926—Unconstrained Tax Reduction. The 1926 Revenue Act was a direct response to the elections of 1924, which gave the Republicans control of the White House and solid majorities of both houses of Congress. The election also marked the end of the Progressive and Insurgent challenge to the Republican Party, even though La Follette's bid for the presidency had received 4.8 million votes (14 percent of the total). Coolidge received a plurality of 2.5 million votes over the combined totals of La Follette and the Democratic challenger, John W. Davis. The Republicans ended up with a 60-seat majority in the House and a 17-seat advantage in the Senate. In the House they were so strong that the radical Republicans were not invited to the party caucus and hence were not given seats on the important committees, including Ways and Means. The party had campaigned on a platform of support for business and further tax reductions. Thus, most of the administration-sponsored provisions of the tax bill that began to wind its way through Congress in early 1925 were accepted as a *fait accompli*. The

opposition was posturing more than anything else—awaiting a better day rather than seriously expecting to change most of the proposals. It was successful in combating only one major provision.

Consistent with the slogan that "big business was in the saddle" following the 1924 elections, Mellon's proposals reflected the antagonism of business interests and numerous "tax clubs" toward the estate and gift taxes and high surtax rates. Mellon proposed abolishing the gift tax immediately and the estate tax over several years and lowering the surtax from 40 to 20 percent. The only proposal affecting lower-income groups was one to make the normal tax rates 5 percent (rather than the current graduation of 2, 4, and 6 percent), which would have harmed those with taxable incomes under $8,000. His other major proposal, to drop excise taxes on automobiles, entertainment, admissions, and jewelry, was of course viewed favorably by affected industries and high-income consumers. Mellon got most of what he wanted, but, as with most major non–war tax legislation, he got additional provisions as well.

The mood of Congress favored cutting taxes, and cutting them even further than Mellon proposed. Adding to the political dynamics was the federal surplus which had existed since 1920 and had almost reached the billion-dollar level for 1924. However, the Mellon program appeared to be a little too one-sided even for this conservative Congress. Following the lead of Representative Green, the moderate chairman of Ways and Means, the House reacted to the Mellon program by sweetening the pot for the lower-income taxpayers. This was done by lowering all the normal rates, increasing the exemption levels $500 for single people and $1,000 for heads of households, and increasing the upper limit for what was considered "earned" income from $10,000 to $20,000. It was estimated at the time that the exemption increases alone would eliminate one-third of the 7.3 million taxpayers who filed returns in 1924.[12] The only important direct challenge to the Mellon proposals was in the area of the estate tax, which the Democrats managed to save by agreeing to a 50 percent reduction in rates and, more important, an increase in the credit allowed for payment of state inheritance taxes from the current 25 to 80 percent.[13] Although the Senate voted for total repeal, the House provision was upheld in Conference.

The Senate did very little with the bill beyond altering depletion provisions for mineral resources. The current method, evaluating the worth of the property at the time of discovery, had proven an administrative nightmare; the new provision simply required the calculation of a depletion allowance based on gross income from the property.[14] This provision was in the final bill (set at 27.5 percent for oil and gas), and

although it was to remain essentially unchanged for almost fifty years, it was under constant attack for most of those years and came to epitomize the tax "loophole." In both houses, votes to maintain higher surtaxes for more stringent estate tax provisions were rejected by large margins. Votes on final passage in each case were close to unanimity, with most Democrats joining the tax reduction effort.

Winding Down. Another tax act was passed in 1928, and a joint resolution was enacted at Mellon's request in 1929. The former act had little effect on the individual income tax, its primary provision being a cut in the corporate tax from 13.5 to 12.0 percent. Mellon and Coolidge had initially asked for cuts in individual taxes and full repeal of the estate tax, basing their request primarily on the continuing surpluses between 1924 and 1927. Congress was more cautious, however, and insisted instead on retiring more of the war debt. The 1929 resolution, in response to Mellon's request and with little discussion, lowered normal tax rates and dropped the corporate tax a further percentage point, but it limited these decreases to one year.

In retrospect, Mellon's rationalization for this temporary reduction was ironic: "The surplus of the fiscal year ended June 30 last and the current year's probable surplus was and will be due to a very large extent to the unusual increase in taxable incomes reported by individuals, although corporations enjoyed a very prosperous year in 1928, and all reports indicate that their 1929 income will exceed that of 1928."[15] Contrary to that prediction, the rapid decline in business activity in late 1929 and 1930 turned the Treasury surplus around so that by the first quarter of 1931 there was a projected *deficit* of $750 million. The reality of the depression swept the nation. The recommendation of nearly all the experts was to raise taxes to cover the deficit. Although Hoover resisted at first, by the middle of 1931 the deficit for the year was clear, and an overwhelming consensus had formed that taxes had to be raised. It was an ironic ending to Mellon's tenure at Treasury that one of his last actions was to propose undoing much of what he had accomplished in the previous decade.

The 1920s marked the first transition period in the history of the income tax. The Armistice ended the period of extraordinary demands on revenue and ushered in a period of prosperity. The political transition that occurred simultaneously provided ideological support for tax reduction, but some degree of tax cutting would have resulted even if the Democrats had remained in power. Although parallels are often drawn between the 1920s and the 1980s, in several respects the reductions were very different from those in recent years. The highest proportion of

wartime tax increases fell on corporations and thus their repeal was a direct incentive for corporate investment. The relatively modest reductions being discussed in the 1980s are not parallel to the stimulus afforded by the return to peace in 1918. (The magnitude of the shifts is portrayed in the next chapter in figure 6.1.) In addition, the reduction process was conservatively paced over eight years, and a watchful eye was kept on the budget balance the whole time. Although Andrew Mellon expressed a belief in the rudiments of supply-side theory, he was too cautious to act on faith.

Income Taxes During the Depression

Early Revenue Bills. In broad terms, the direction and form of tax policy is determined by a combination of revenue demands and ideology, with the former generally dominating the latter. If ever there was evidence for this predominance, it was the Revenue Act of 1932. After eleven straight years with a budget surplus, during which time almost $9 billion of public debt had been retired, there was a deficit of $461 million in 1931, and the financial situation was deteriorating so rapidly that the Treasury was predicting a $2 billion deficit for 1932. (It was actually $2.7 billion.) The administration planned its revenue and expenditure policies in the summer and fall of 1931 as it awaited the return of Congress in December. One of the first projects of the congressional session was taxation, and Andrew Mellon, in his last appearance before Congress, presented the administration's proposals with the aid of Ogden Mills, who would replace him as secretary in February. In essence, the proposals were a retreat to the tax law of 1924, eliminating the major tax reductions that had been granted in 1926 and 1928. They lowered exemptions and increased normal taxes and surtaxes to the 1924 levels. They also proposed raising the estate tax that the administration had in earlier years tried so desperately to eliminate. Finally, excise taxes were to be placed on numerous items and postal rates increased. In the annual Report of the Treasurer, Mellon explained the need for these proposals as follows: "The country knows the burdens to be expected under such a law [the Revenue Act of 1924]. It paid taxes under that law and . . . found that these taxes did not constitute an unbearable burden nor prevent prosperity. . . . We are convinced that in the long run lower rates are more productive than higher ones. But these are not normal times."[16]

The consensus in Congress was similar to that in the administration. There was no question that taxes were to be raised, and raised dramati-

cally; the questions were how, and who should bear the brunt of the increase? The Treasury proposals spread the burden, with the rich paying through higher surtaxes and estate taxes and the poor through the increased exemptions, normal rates, and sales taxes. The Ways and Means Committee, applauding this effort in a nonpartisan atmosphere, approved these proposals with only slight modifications. However, it added an increase in the taxation of corporate dividends and a 1.5 percent increase in the corporate tax rate and, against the Treasury Department's wishes, reduced the benefit of the earned-income provision by making it a deduction rather than a 25 percent tax credit.[17] The most controversial change was the imposition of what amounted to a national sales tax but was called by the committee a "manufacturer's excise tax." The administration opposed the tax, as did liberals, who had long objected to sales taxes because of their undue burden on lower-income groups.

The mood and partisan makeup in the House had changed. The Republican majorities of the previous decade were gone: there were now 220 Democrats and 214 Republicans. As with the revenue legislation of the war years, progressive Republicans and Democrats, often reflecting the geographical cleavages of earlier years, changed the committee bill in a more radical direction. The key battle was over the sales tax, which was finally rejected by a vote of 223 to 153 in which only 40 Democrats joined the chairman of Ways and Means. In voting for the tax,[18] Representative Ramseyer (D-Iowa) proposed, as he had in past Congresses, higher estate tax rates. This time he won. The changes would have been more radical had it not been for a dramatic appeal by John Garner (by then Speaker of the House) for a compromise during a period of extreme crisis. He got it, and the bickering that had been going on for weeks was quickly halted as the bill was approved on April 1, 1932, by a vote of 327 to 64.[19]

The Senate, despite a one-vote Republican majority, pushed for even more extreme measures. In the Finance Committee, a progressive Republican named James Couzens (R-Mich.) proposed returning to the wartime surtax rates of the 1918 revenue bill, with a maximum of 65 percent. Although this proposal was defeated, a compromise settled on the rates applicable in 1922, with a maximum surtax of 55 percent. In addition, corporate rates were increased to 14 percent, the earned income credit was dropped altogether, and many items that had been put on an excise list in the House were dropped. All these changes were accepted by the Conference Committee with some adjustment of the sales tax list.

Thus, the last piece of tax legislation in which the Republican Party

would have significant influence over the next fourteen years called for a major increase in taxes and allocated tax burdens in a much more progressive fashion than had the laws developed over the previous decade. As with the extreme rates of World War I, progressivity was reluctantly increased at a point of financial crisis.

Given the solid victory of Franklin Roosevelt and the large Democratic majorities in both houses in 1932, one might have expected more radical progressivity. Such changes were to come, but until World War II they came very slowly and cautiously, and in fact the Roosevelt administration initially adopted a conservative stance on tax issues. Several early pieces of New Deal legislation had tax implications. The Agricultural Adjustment Act, for example, included taxes on food processing, and, more important, the National Industrial Recovery Act levied a 5 percent tax on dividends and revived the wartime excess profits tax at a modest level. However, the next major revenue act, in 1934, was enacted with minimal administration involvement, and that involvement was decidedly conservative in tone and substance.

The Revenue Act of 1934 was primarily a technical and administrative bill that arose out of a congressionally mandated study of tax evasion carried out by a subcommittee of Ways and Means. The subcommittee reported in December 1933 and made a series of recommendations to which the Treasury Department, headed by Henry Morgenthau, responded. The responses, discussed before the committee by Roswell Magill, provided an intriguing glimpse of the new administration's ambivalence on tax policy. The subcommittee's major recommendations were unanimously devoted to tightening special provisions, thus creating increased revenues, or increasing the progressivity of the code, or both. Of the nine major proposals addressed in their report, the Treasury Department objected to five, all of which were clearly liberal proposals. These were:

1. reduction of depreciation and depletion allowances by 25 percent;

2. elimination of the right of corporations to consolidate returns with their subsidiaries;

3. elimination of special beneficial provisions governing corporate reorganizations;

4. prevention of the deduction of partnership losses from personal income taxes;

5. taxing the undistributed profits of personal holding com-

panies that were being established to allow accumulation of earnings as a means of avoiding individual surtax rates.

Although the administration's arguments for opposing these reforms varied, the most frequent was that tightening taxes in these areas would restrict economic recovery. Treasury opposition was effective on the first four proposals, which were either dropped from the final Ways and Means bill or severely restricted.[20] The committee bill, which passed the House unamended, did make several important changes. Its major provisions:

1. altered the normal tax and surtax rates in a slightly more progressive manner (raising the maximum to 59 percent, but lowering the normal tax to a flat 4 percent so that the combined top rate remained 63 percent);

2. changed the method of taxing capital gains from a reduced rate of 12.5 percent to a method allowing exclusion of a portion of the gains, depending on how long the asset was held;

3. restored the earned income credit that had been eliminated in the 1932 act (but at 10 percent rather than the previous 25 percent);

4. imposed, against administration wishes, a 35 percent tax on undistributed profits of personal holding companies.

When Senate hearings began in March 1934, for the first time in the history of income tax legislation, no witness for the administration appeared. The Senate, following the lead of a rejuvenated group of radicals,[21] agreed to more extreme provisions increasing income and estate tax rates, eliminating consolidated corporate returns (which had been dropped by the House), and improving public access to tax return information. Most of these provisions were dropped in Conference, but the bill still made numerous important changes in the mass of complex provisions that had developed in the twenty-year history of the income tax. In later years such an act would be labeled a "tax reform" bill: one meant to tighten up provisions that had come to be abused rather than to make major structural changes in the code. That Congress felt such a measure was necessary is evidence that income taxation had at this early stage become an extremely complex business, susceptible to legal maneuvering by which some taxpayers, usually the wealthy, substantially reduced what others felt was their just or statutory tax obligation.

This fact was not lost on the new administration, which would soon launch its own attack on tax "loopholes." At this point, however, the administration was hesitant and decidedly conservative; indeed, its actions were much more restrained than the last efforts of the Hoover administration, which had so dramatically restructured the code in 1932.

Roosevelt's Attack on Wealth. The Roosevelt conversion came in 1935. The reason for it is not clear. In his annual message to Congress in January, the president stated that no new taxes would be needed in that year. On June 19, however, in a surprise tax message to Congress, that shocked both Congress and the business community, Roosevelt attacked the revenue system as having "done little to prevent an unjust concentration of wealth and economic power." John Morton Blum paraphrases the critical passage of Roosevelt's speech:

> "Wealth in the modern world," Roosevelt said, "resulted from a combination of individual efforts. In spite of the great importance in our national life of the . . . ingenuity of unusual individuals, the people in the mass have inevitably helped to make large fortunes possible. The transmission of these fortunes from generation to generation," he argued, "was not consistent with American ideals. Accumulation of wealth, moreover, perpetrated great and undesirable concentration of control in a relatively few individuals over the employment and welfare of many, many others."[22]

When the Senate clerk finished reading the speech only Huey Long of Louisiana, the organizer of a movement to share the wealth, responded: "Mr. President, before the President's message is referred to the Committee on Finance, I wish to make one comment. I just wish to say 'Amen!'"[23]

The president's specific proposals, which led to what came to be known in the press as the "Wealth Tax of 1935," were: (1) an inheritance tax to go along with the existing estate tax, the proceeds of which would go toward retirement of the national debt; (2) a graduated corporation tax; (3) a tax on intercorporate dividends (which were being used to avoid corporate taxes); and (4) an increase in surtaxes, but only for incomes over $1 million. Although the Progressives and radicals in Congress embraced these proposals, there was also some suspicion that the intent was more to display concern about disparities in wealth than actually to redistribute it. Senator Borah, who supported the proposals,

nevertheless claimed that as measures to redistribute the wealth they were "fakes." Long sent a pointed letter asking Roosevelt to spell out his intentions and specify what limits to wealth he believed were appropriate, what the minimum family income should be, and so on. No reply was made public, and following Roosevelt's dramatic speech the administration again became hesitant. Morgenthau was noncommittal in hearings before both tax committees. His diaries contain the following dialogue between himself and Roosevelt in the midst of congressional debate on the bill:

> "Mr. President," Morgenthau asked, "just strictly between the two of us, do you or do you not want your Inheritance Tax program passed at this session?"
>
> "Strictly between the two of us," Roosevelt said, "I do not know, I am on an hourly basis and the situation changes almost momentarily."[24]

In spite of Roosevelt's hesitancy, however, the Ways and Means Committee, anxious to adjourn and under the leadership of a devotee of the administration, Representative Doughton (D-N.C.), reported out a bill that substantially fulfilled the president's requests. The overwhelming Democratic majority in the House, plus the heat of an unairconditioned summer, made for swift passage on the floor without substantive revisions. This encouraged Roosevelt, and while Morgenthau made a very noncommittal appearance before the Senate Finance Committee, his aides began to press more strongly for the president's proposals, particularly the restoration of a graduated corporation tax, which was the one area on which the House bill had been weak.[25] Although the Senate, which had a 44-seat Democratic majority, was eager to comply with the "soak the rich" aspects of the bill, Finance was not ready to accept a totally new tax on such short notice. Thus, rather than support an inheritance tax, on a vote of 10 to 8 it opted for increased estate taxes. The committee did, however, slightly widen the graduation in the corporation tax. As in the House, floor debate was short, and no important amendments survived conference. The key issue in the Conference Committee was the inheritance tax provision, on which the House relented. The final bill was satisfactory to the administration in that it incorporated a graduated corporation tax (from 12.5 to 15.0 percent); it taxed intercorporate dividends; it increased the estate and gift tax rates considerably; and it increased the surtax rates on incomes above $50,000, with a top rate now to be 75 percent for incomes over $500,000. Although this change affected very few taxpayers, the sym-

bolic effect was lost neither on Roosevelt supporters nor on conservatives. The latter feared what might come next.

As 1936 began, Roosevelt had no next plan and no intention of proposing that taxes be raised in an election year. Thus, no tax increase was suggested in his State of the Union speech. However, revenue needs again dictated action. The Supreme Court had overruled the Agricultural Adjustment Act and thus the $500,000 in taxes it raised annually. More important, Congress had passed, over Roosevelt's veto, payment of cash bonuses for veterans of World War I. These bonuses, with accrued interest, amounted to a government obligation of $2 billion. The question facing the administration was how to raise the revenue, and its answer was bold. It revived the notion of taxing undistributed corporate profits, although it would do so indirectly by graduating corporate taxes according to the percentage of profits distributed to shareholders. This new tax was to replace all existing corporate taxes and be set at a level high enough to yield an amount equal to what would be collected if all profits were paid out as dividends and thus taxed as personal income. The administration argued that this would prevent corporations from accumulating profits as a way of avoiding high personal surtax rates. It also felt that forcing such a pay-out would have a great stimulative effect, creating needed demand in the economy. It was, of course, a way to raise revenue in an election year without increasing the taxes of the vast majority, a point that the administration did not stress but that the Republicans bitterly understood.

This proposal involved a radical change in the tax structure, and it was introduced quickly, with Treasury statisticians working around the clock to meet demands for estimates of the effects of different plans. As in 1935, the administration got most of what it wanted in the House, although this time Doughton was not at all happy with the proposed tax. The House bill created a graduated corporate tax ranging from 1.0 to 29.5 percent, depending on the percentage of net income distributed to shareholders. It repealed existing corporate taxes and excess profits taxes. Given the overwhelming Democratic control and the power of committees, the House as a whole accepted the bill with little debate. As Randolph Paul, then a Treasury official, was later to write: "Three quarters of the members were absent . . . and it is doubtful whether more than a handful of those who remained on the floor understood the complicated 236 page measure."[26] It was passed in a highly partisan vote of 267 to 93.[27]

The House Bill was passed on April 29, less than two months after Roosevelt addressed Congress. The reaction in the Senate was much different. Opposition had been mobilized in the business community.

Charging that the proposal was moving the nation toward "Tugwellian socialism," opponents challenged the numbers generated by the Treasury and calculated the negative impact of the law on specific companies. The charge was made that the tax would stifle corporate investment and place large, already well-capitalized companies like American Telephone & Telegraph at a competitive advantage. While Roosevelt insisted on some form of taxation of undistributed profits, Morgenthau began to get jittery over the radical nature of the change. He wrote: "I have come to the decision, that I cannot take the risk of giving up something that I have in hand, namely: $1,320,000,000 in revenue, for a possibility of getting roughly $1,700,000,000. It seems to me there are too many dangers surrounding the possibilities."[28]

Senator Harrison (D-Miss.) was unable to hold the Finance Committee to the proposal; its bill included only a mild graduation based on undistributed profits and did not eliminate the other corporate taxes. The committee maintained that position in Conference, and the deadlock was broken only when Roosevelt and Morgenthau accepted an undistributed profits tax as an addition to the existing structure. The final law added a graduated surtax (from 7 to 27 percent) on the corporate rate, which was set at a flat 13.75 percent. However, the bill also raised the tax on intercorporate dividends to 15 percent and made dividend income fully taxable at normal rates. The excess profits tax was reduced somewhat. All in all, the bill added significantly to corporate income taxes. Although Roosevelt was able to use the tax issue to his advantage against Alf Landon's attacks in the 1936 campaign, the undistributed profits tax that Morgenthau later wrote was a "sort of revolution . . . a cornerstone for a new America" was to have a very brief life.[29]

A combination of factors—Roosevelt's desire to prevent wealthy individuals and corporations from abusing the tax laws, changing economic conditions and revenue needs, and a switch in Congress toward a more conservative and anti-Roosevelt philosophy—pushed tax legislation in diverse directions in the late thirties. Revenue legislation was passed every year from 1934 through 1945, with two bills each in 1939 and 1940. The 1937 act was stimulated by the administration, again after it had begun the year by announcing no new tax legislation. Insider accounts indicate that several incidents, including reports that wealthy individuals were sheltering money in foreign holding companies and that private yachts were being incorporated to escape taxation, angered Roosevelt and led to a stepped-up attack on those whom he had termed "economic royalists" in his 1936 nomination acceptance speech.[30] The attack was made specific in a proposal to Congress in June 1937 listing

nine tax "loopholes" that the administration wanted tightened or elim- inated. The proposal included a number of detailed suggestions for provisions governing personal, domestic, and foreign holding com- panies and the incorporation of yachts and estates and a series of regulations relating to family trusts, pension plans, and family part- nerships, which at the time were attractive and legal devices for wealthy individuals to avoid high surtaxes and estate taxes.

Congress immediately appointed a special Joint Committee on Tax Evasion and Avoidance. Within a week its hearings were producing case histories of abuses and outlining the devices used by sixty-seven very wealthy families to avoid taxes. The hearings generated a great deal of publicity and stimulated the quick passage of a bill to tighten many of the provisions of concern to the administration. The major provisions of the bill, which was not debated at any length and passed both houses without roll call votes, were adjustments to the special provisions governing personal holding companies that had been autho- rized in 1934 against Treasury advice.

The holding company provisions are an excellent illustration of the cat and mouse nature of incremental policy adjustment in taxation. The 1934 law was a reaction to the invention of personal holding companies, which avoided high individual surtaxes by incorporating professional, family, and other sources of personal income. It forced tax attorneys to develop new legal maneuvers to keep corporations outside its definition of a "personal holding company." The 1937 law responded to these maneuvers by broadening the definition and other rules governing the personal holding companies. The changes enacted were unimportant in terms of either revenue and distribution of tax burdens, and certainly they did not put an end to the cat and mouse game. In fact, this piece of tax legislation marked the beginning of what is now a tangle of tax provisions that few people other than specialized tax attorneys can comprehend. Nevertheless, the symbolic effect of the blitz to close "loopholes" was not unimportant, and such campaigns were to recur at regular intervals, at times sparking significant legislation. This one may have evoked a different sort of reaction, for in 1938 Congress turned against the administration and, in the face of a serious economic down- turn, reduced many of the taxes that the administration had previously enacted.

Congress Attacks Roosevelt. A major recession began in the fall of 1937, and administration programs and policies came under attack from many quarters. The business community was the most vocal on tax policy. Like the excess profits tax in the years immediately following

World War I, the undistributed profits tax was the particular target of business lobbying in 1937. The declining economy and growing congressional ambivalence about Roosevelt fueled the debate in Congress. Business interests and some noted economists argued that the heavy tax burden had contributed significantly to the economic downturn.

The initial agenda of the Revenue Act of 1938 was based on a report of a subcommittee of Ways and Means appointed by Chairman Doughton in August 1937 just after passage of the 1937 act. The subcommittee's report contained sixty-three proposals, most of which affected corporations but many of which affected individuals as well. The major and most controversial proposals were (1) maintenance of the undistributed profits concept, but with greatly reduced rates and total exemption for businesses with net incomes under $25,000; (2) further refinement of the regulations governing personal holding companies, this time posing a special tax on "closely held" corporations that, unlike personal holding companies, were stock companies, but companies with ten shareholders or fewer; and (3) changes in the method of taxing capital gains, generally lowering rates and encouraging longer-term holding of assets.

Although lengthy hearings were held on these proposals, they did little to dissuade the full Ways and Means Committee, which reported a bill very close to the recommendations of the subcommittee. Understanding that the mood of Congress favored reduced tax burdens for high-income groups and businesses, the committee had put together a compromise package that had the approval of the administration: a weakened undistributed profits tax, but not full repeal; lower corporate taxes for small businesses but stricter regulation of personal holding companies; and a distinction between long- and short-term capital gains, lowering rates on the former and raising them on the latter. The conservative reaction in Congress was sharp, however, and the bill unraveled in several important areas during passage. The House removed the provisions defining and taxing closely held corporations. The Senate Finance Committee eliminated the undistributed profits tax altogether, going back to a flat corporate rate of 18 percent. It also removed the distinction between short- and long-term capital gains and went back to a flat tax of 15 percent, which reduced the total tax on capital gains considerably relative to the House bill.

Action on the Senate floor was fast-paced. Roy and Gladys Blakey describe the scene: "As the clerk speedily read the bill for amendments, the chairman punctuated his steady flow of words with the formula, 'Without objection amendment agreed to,' spoken as though it were one long word. At the end of twenty minutes Vice President Garner turned

the gavel over to Minton with the remark that they had already passed 224 pages of the measure."[31] Objections were offered by Majority Leader Barkley (D-Ky.), and Senator La Follette proposed amendments restricting capital gains reductions and reinstating the undistributed profits tax (which he had been instrumental in enacting two years earlier), but they were easily defeated. Very minor, although more easily understood, issues occupied more floor time. The bill was passed without major amendment by voice vote with no audible "nays" on April 9, 1938.[32]

The Conference Committee bill was a compromise as usual. The undistributed profits tax was retained but reduced in scope and limited to one year. Originally, it provided for a surcharge ranging up to an additional 27 percent of net income depending on the percentage of corporate profit paid out. The 1938 act reduced this to 2.5 percent. The regulations governing closely held corporations were never considered. The capital gains provision, which was the only major change affecting individual income taxes, was a complex compromise that distinguished three classes of gains by the length of time the asset was held. It applied different inclusion percentages and rates to each class, and treated losses differently for each. The compromise, which resolved the differences in the two bills by adding together features from both, created a complex set of provisions. The result was not illogical. There was a consensus that the existing taxes were too severe and caused assets to be held for too long, creating a major obstacle to permanent economic recovery. The effort to produce changes sufficiently fine-tuned to meet these problems, yet satisfactory to the various actors involved, resulted in a set of provisions much more complex than those of the previous law.

The final pieces of tax legislation before World War II were relatively minor. The first was the Public Salary Act of 1939, which repealed the exclusion from the income tax (dating from 1913) of the salaries of state and local government employees and federal judges. The bill was initiated by the administration after several Supreme Court cases upheld both the right of states to tax federal employees and the federal government's right to tax state and local employees. Roosevelt also asked that tax-exempt securities be banned on the basis of a much less clear court case, but Congress refused, as it had in nearly every session since the Wilson administration. Constitutional uncertainties aside, the issue for Congress was (and remains today) the cost of financing state and local government. Congress feared political opposition from the states more than it feared the Court. The bill, without mention of tax-exempt securities, passed through Congress with little opposition.

Its chief importance lies in the fact that it gives a rare example of the removal of a specific tax reduction benefit. The income exemption for state and local government salaries was removed easily because once the constitutional question was settled, there was no real basis for the special treatment.

Like the Revenue Act of 1938, the Revenue Act of 1939, the final legislation before the war, was passed against Roosevelt's wishes. The critical issue in the bill was the final repeal of the undistributed profits tax, which the adminstration fought for months to retain in some form. When it became clear that Congress was not about to retain the tax, the president relented, bargaining instead for provisions that controlled the amount of capital accumulation within corporations. The undistributed profits tax was replaced by a flat 18 percent corporate tax on net income with lower, graduated rates for small companies. The bill also lowered capital gains for corporations by allowing greater flexibility in accounting for losses. Arguments pressed by a persistent business lobby stressed again that corporate taxes were retarding economic expansion. Congress, led by an emerging coalition of Southern Democrats and Republicans, was then a willing partner to the business demands, although the climate was to change drastically in the months ahead. The only measure to have any real effect on personal income taxes was a provision to allow individuals to average income over a five-year period. As noted in chapter 3, this was the only one of Henry Simons' widely circulated recommendations that was enacted in his lifetime. Ironically, some of his strongest arguments were in support of the taxation of undistributed profits, which was eliminated in the bill. There was little discussion of the bill in either house (less than four hours), and it was passed by an almost unanimous vote in the House and a unanimous voice vote in the Senate.

In the area of taxation, Roosevelt's reversals were as marked as his success. He began with a very conservative position and a willingness to leave revenue questions in the hands of Congress. As his ideology shifted, the administration's activism in tax matters increased. Although he achieved some notable successes in raising taxes on corporations, increasing estate taxes, tightening some of the more glaring "loopholes," and sensitizing the nation to the tax avoidance issue, the most important structural changes he proposed—a federal inheritance tax and the undistributed profits tax—never became a permanent part of the tax code. Indeed, the changes that had the most effect on revenue in the thirties were those enacted by the Hoover administration in 1932 and the large increases in excise taxes that were mostly passed on congressional initiative. The latter changes accounted for an increase in

the share of federal revenue from excise taxes (see figure 4.1). The 1932 act accounted for most of the progressive shift in effective income tax rates that occurred during the period (to be described in detail in chapter 12). Nevertheless, Roosevelt was to oversee the most important transition in the history of the income tax, although it was not to be as much his doing as that of the Third Reich.

Summary and Conclusions

Income tax legislation in the interwar years set the pattern for most future tax legislation. First, the policy-making process during these years was highly incremental. Rate and general tax decreases in the twenties were enacted in small stages, as were the increases of the thirties; existing policy provisions were the basis for the changes, and the major innovations that were proposed either were not enacted or were short-lived; many adjustments were reactions to difficulties caused by previously enacted provisions, such as those governing personal holding companies and capital gains; and, finally, the process was a continuous exercise in negotiation and compromise between Congress and the administration, between the various factions in Congress, and between the two houses.

Second, one result of incrementalism was increasing complexity. Corporate income taxation was split into numerous branches depending on the nature, size, and type of business. Whole bodies of law were developed to deal with partnerships or domestic, foreign, or personal holding companies. A permanent trend toward special provisions benefiting small businesses as opposed to large ones appeared. And certain industrial groups, such as mineral and life insurance companies, benefited from a series of special tax provisions. For individuals, distinctions built into the law concerned family size, how one earned one's income, where one earned one's income (foreign income was treated differently from domestic), and the year-to-year pace at which income was acquired. Further, if one was lucky enough to have income from the sale of property or from stock dividends, a whole different set of rules applied. For each of these cases, behind each of these distinctions, there is some measure of logic. Rationales were not fabricated, and they did not emerge through covert use of power—indeed, most were approved by overwhelming consensus. They emerged as the natural outcome of an incremental process.

Third, the interwar years offer little evidence for a commitment to progressivity in the tax system. There were, to be sure, consistent advocates of progressivity who at times won the day; however, the basic

trend following World War I was toward lower taxes and lessened progressivity. In the twenties, maximum rates for individuals were dropped from a wartime high of 77 to 24 percent, and corporate taxes were slashed by almost three-fourths. Although that trend was reversed in the early thirties by the same administration, the basic impetus was not equality, but rather a desperate need for revenue. Roosevelt's efforts to increase the burden on corporations and the owners of capital and to tax the passage of wealth between generations were not very successful, in part because of his own initial hesitancy, and in part because of later opposition from his own party in Congress.

Finally, basic patterns emerged in the politics of taxation in the first three decades of the income tax. The most obvious pattern is that tax agendas are greatly influenced by revenue demands, whether wartime needs or the need to balance the budget. This tends to generate a broad consensus on the direction of tax increases or decreases, although not on the structural formula by which it should be accomplished. Another pattern suggests that political parties do make some difference in tax policy. The crude evidence is that with the return of Republicans to power in 1920, there was a significant downward trend in taxes and progressivity; once the Democrats regained control of Congress, a shift occurred in the opposite direction; and over the years, as Democratic majorities increased, that trend became more extreme. However, several anomalies indicate that the relationship between party and tax policy is not that simple. The Democrats were pointing toward the same policy as the Republicans in 1920; the Hoover Treasury recommended the bulk of the tax reforms in 1932; Roosevelt's initial stance was strikingly conservative; and by the late thirties, Democrats were voting with Republicans against Roosevelt's efforts to defend the progressive tax policies that had developed.

The influence of various institutional actors also seems to vary considerably. The executive branch initially had a limited role in tax policy. Even during World War I, the administration focused its requests on the level of revenue to be raised rather than the method by which it should be raised. Andrew Mellon changed that when his office became the prime mover behind revenue legislation in the 1920s. The Roosevelt years began and ended with Congress taking the initiative, but the administration was again the major actor in the important tax bills of 1935 and 1936. Even in these years, however, Congress was rarely acquiescent. The details of revenue bills were worked out in the tax committees, and administration proposals were often either dropped or modified. Congressional dominance would return as a defining characteristic of postwar tax politics.

Chapter 6.
The War Years
From an Elite
to a Mass Tax

The First World War had an important impact on the income tax, rapidly transforming it from a highly contested but insignificant source of revenue into a major tax. Rate and provision adjustments made over several years turned what was almost a proportional tax into one with a highly progressive nominal rate structure. Although these rates were reduced in the twenties and only slightly increased in the thirties, they rose quickly in response to the outbreak of war in Europe. There was to be a major difference, however. Although the top rates during World War I rose to almost confiscatory levels, the tax never reached the vast majority of citizens. That situation changed with the much larger revenue needs of World War II, and, most important, the mass wartime income tax remained after the end of the Korean War.

Another important facet of World War I taxation was the tremendous increase in revenue resulting from relatively minor changes in tax laws. It was demonstrated in World War I that the income tax could be rapidly expanded by augmenting the corporate tax with an excess profits tax and by adjusting rates and exemptions for the personal income tax. The same approach was taken in World War II. Although numerous additional forms of revenue were proposed, including national sales taxes, spending taxes, and other forms of capital taxes, none were enacted. The revenue system continued to rest on gift and estate taxes, excises, and corporate and personal income taxes. As shown in figure 4.1, however, the burden once again shifted toward the income taxes in 1941. The only major innovation of the war period was the enactment of withholding at the source—deducting individual income taxes from wages and salaries. This had both an immediate and a lasting impact on the individual income tax. Other changes essentially involving simple modifications of critical tax parameters were made in a series of revenue acts beginning in 1940.

Taxes for Rearmament

In World War I most of the increase in revenue came from increases in the corporate income tax, mostly in the form of an excess profits tax. That option was the first to be considered in the Second World War as well. A proposal for an excess profits tax was made in the terrifying spring of 1940, when the German armies swept across Europe. In May, a month before the fall of France, the president reacted to the crisis by asking Congress for $1.2 billion for defense. Congress acted rapidly, with Ways and Means reporting a bill in two weeks. The bill was quickly passed in the House, where it had been brought to the floor under a Rules Committee ban on substantive floor amendments. This "gag," or "closed rule," was to remain a feature of revenue bills in the House through 1975. A Republican minority could do little in the six hours allotted for debate other than attack past Democratic spending and deficits, which they did with vehemence but no effect. The final vote was 396 to 6: some Republicans were reluctant to support the bill but unwilling to risk the appearance of obstruction in a time of crisis.[1]

In order to speed passage of the bill, in accordance with a preagreement between Chairman of Ways and Means Doughton (D-N.C.) and Senate Finance Chairman Harrison (D-Miss.), the House bill did not contain an excess profits tax; rather, it raised the corporate tax a modest 1 percent. This became the issue in the Senate, and Progressive Senators La Follette (R-Wis.) and Norris (R-Neb.) proposed and won a floor amendment enacting an excess profits tax. It was eliminated in conference but immediately became an issue again when the second revenue bill of 1940 was proposed.

By the time the first bill became law on June 25, 1940, Italy had joined the Axis, France had fallen, and the long summer assault on Britain had begun. Whereas the first tax bill of 1940 primarily affected individuals, adding a 10 percent surcharge on incomes between $6,000 and $100,000 and lowering exemptions (from $2,500 to $2,000 for married couples and from $2,000 to $800 for single people), the second bill was directed at corporations. The centerpiece was a very complex excess profits tax combined with special accelerated amortization rates for investments in defense-related facilities. Impetus for the excess profits tax came from Roosevelt, who endorsed the concept and in a May press conference had vowed that "not a single war millionaire would be permitted as a result of the war disaster."[2] Senate floor action on the first bill confirmed that a majority would support this tax, which had proved highly successful in meeting revenue needs in the First World War.

The issue from the beginning was the base upon which the tax would rest. How were "excess" profits to be defined? One method, favored by the Treasury, was to base calculations on rates of return on invested capital. Under this method, "excess" could be defined either relative to returns on capital in a base period or simply as profits in excess of an arbitrary profit-to-investment ratio. The other method would base the tax on actual earnings before the war (the years 1936–1939 were the base period used in all calculations). The former method was favored by economists because they felt that it measured true excess; the latter was favored by congressional politicians because it was easier to understand and related to direct changes in profits. The differential impact of these methods was important. For example, companies with little profits in the base period could be taxed very heavily if the earnings method was adopted, while more profitable companies, which included armaments companies selling to Europe in the 1930s, would not be taxed as much. On the other hand, a return-on-investment approach favored large, heavily capitalized corporations. The final resolution, typical of many compromises in tax legislation, was simply to accept both methods, allowing corporations to choose which one to use. In the Senate La Follette strenuously objected, favoring only the capital approach, but his amendment was defeated by a vote of 41 to 20.[3] Although the final bill was graduated up to 50 percent of excess profits as Roosevelt had requested, Treasury was unhappy with the outcome.[4] It was anticipated that further changes would be required very soon.

There were two tax bills in 1941. The first was a minor bill that essentially corrected errors and made necessary adjustments in the excess profits tax that had been hastily inacted in late 1940. The second bill, which called for a major tax increase, followed a resolute announcement by the administration that revenue demands could be expected to grow at a rapid pace in the coming months. Roosevelt signed the Lend Lease Act to support Britain in March, and when Secretary of the Treasury Morgenthau went before the Ways and Means Committee in May, a budget deficit of $14 billion was projected. Morgenthau stated that the administration's goal was to pay for two-thirds of the war expenditures with taxes and the rest with borrowing.[5] This firm stand was greeted with enthusiasm by conservatives and hailed by most of the newspapers in the country.[6] This support soon vanished as the amount of taxes needed and the method of extracting them began to be understood.

The administration proposed to increase all major sources of taxes. Excess profits were to be raised, and the option of basing the tax on changes in earnings relative to profits in the base period was to be

eliminated. In addition, the regular corporate tax, excise taxes and the surtaxes on individuals were to be increased, while the exemption applicable to the surcharge was to be reduced. The Ways and Means Committee acted quickly and generally favorably on these proposals. The exception was that they kept the option in the excess profits tax and actually voted several new escape provisions. A 10 percent increase in all the excess profits brackets was granted, so that the top rate was now 60 percent. The House debate mostly concerned a very controversial provision, removed on a floor vote, that would have required husbands and wives to file joint returns. Indignant congressmen and newspaper editorialists had a field day defending the dignity of marriage, which was being threatened by a regulation making it more profitable to stay single or get divorced. Although the issue may seem trivial in relation to the other aspects of the bill, it foreshadowed problems over the differential treatment of family units that remain important today.[7]

By the time Senate hearings were in progress in August, two important developments had occurred. First, the war was going badly, and the fall of Britain was widely predicted; second, the war economy had produced sustained prosperity for the first time in more than a dozen years, but with prosperity came inflation. By July there had been five straight months of significant price increases. These two factors led the administration to request that the Senate add to the bill a lower exemption. One argument in favor of the lowered exemption was that all should contribute to the war effort, but it was the need to increase revenue and reduce purchasing power that dictated the outcome. The Finance Committee accepted this proposal, dropping the exemption for joint returns to $1,500 and that for single returns to $750. The effect was to add 5 million people to those required to file a tax return—an increase of 30 percent. The average American worker was beginning to feel the income tax, and married couples were proportionately harder hit.[8] The committee also adjusted and increased the surtax structure and combined gift and estate taxes. Although it considered sales and purchase taxes and withholding personal income taxes at the source, a majority did not support any of these dramatic changes.

When the bill reached the Senate floor, conservatives, led by Senator Vandenberg (R-Mich.) directed a perfunctory attack against past Democratic spending but generally supported the lower exemption as a means to raise additional revenue and control inflation. The most vehement attack came from the left in the ever-present form of Robert La Follette, Jr., who proclaimed the bill "inadequate," "inequitable," and "indefensible." He leveled his most severe criticism at the change in the exemption and the failure to correct the "loopholes" in the excess profits

tax. To address the latter issue he resurrected a 1917 proposal of his father's to base excess profits solely on invested capital. It lost by a vote of 47 to 19. His effort to eliminate the lower exemption, which cost the poor proportionately more than the wealthy, also failed by a vote of 43 to 23.[9] Final passage of the bill was by an overwhelming vote of 67 to 5, with La Follette as one of the five.[10] The bill was expected to raise $3.5 billion in additional revenue and pay for 60 percent of war expenditures. It was by far the largest revenue bill in history, but it would soon be easily surpassed.

Taxes for War

By 1942 both the need for revenue and the problem of inflation were much more extreme. Following Pearl Harbor the war situation abruptly changed as all theoretical opposition to arms increases immediately evaporated. In Roosevelt's January 6 State of the Union message, he called for massive increases in armaments, listing one by one the number of planes, tanks, and other weapons that were going to be built in 1942 and 1943. The vast majority of the public was supportive, the allies were jubilant, the Nazis called the proposals a bluff, and Congress, which would have the ultimate responsibility for raising the revenue needed, was stunned. With U.S. entry into the war, production of military goods took precedence in all sectors of the economy, and the effect on prices of consumer goods was immediate and dramatic. During 1940 and to some extent 1941, the expansion in production had filled plants and facilities long idle. By 1942, however, production was approaching full utilization, which meant a squeeze on output. The balance between arms and consumer goods shifted toward the military side, thus producing further consumer shortages. At the same time, America was once again back to work, or in the military, and family incomes were growing steadily, which further fueled demand. The combination of war and inflation pointed in one direction—increased taxes. The question was, which taxes, in what form, and who should bear the burden? The answer would turn out to be that only existing types of taxes would be used; that the basic forms of these taxes would change little; and that the burden would be borne by all. Although the system would become highly progressive, lower- and middle-income groups would bear much more than in the past.

For the most part these outcomes were not those proposed by the administration. The formal Treasury proposals, put before the Ways and Means Committee in March 1942, included increases in Social

Security and income taxes. Social Security withholding was to be increased $1 billion to control inflation. Morgenthau argued that the increases would be used after the war to extend benefits and create a social welfare system with broad coverage of health and unemployment insurance. Taxes were to be raised a total of $7.6 billion by increasing individual rates in a steeply progressive manner. While personal exemptions were to remain the same, at Roosevelt's insistence, marginal tax rates were to be raised to 100 percent for anyone with current after-tax income of over $25,000. For most brackets the recommended changes were approximatley proportional, thus preserving the progressivity built into the 1941 bill.

There was also an emphasis in the proposed bill on "tax reform" or closing "loopholes." The recommendations included elimination of the exclusion of interest on state and local bonds, mineral depletion allowances, special provisions for capital gains, and, once again, the option of filing separate returns for married couples. At the suggestion of Randolph Paul, the leading tax expert in Treasury, however, several new "relief" provisions (as opposed to "loopholes") were suggested. These included deductions for some medical expenses, a tax credit for parents of children between the ages of eighteen and twenty-one attending school, and special credits for child care and household help costs for working women. These provisions were rationalized as necessary relief for the lower- and middle-income groups that began paying income taxes for the first time in 1942. Finally, the administration recommended increases in the basic corporate rate and the excess profits tax, as well as changes in the treatment of income from life insurance companies and partnerships that also meant higher taxes. Increases were also proposed in estate taxes and excise taxes on tobacco, alcohol, gasoline, and certain entertainment events.[11]

The administration argued against imposing a national sales tax, although some in the administration favored the idea.[12] Instead, at Roosevelt's personal request, it was suggested that Congress consider a scheme that had been imposed in Canada and Great Britain in which part of the income tax increase would be set aside in a special fund to be rebated to taxpayers after the war, thus temporarily removing money from the economy in order to control inflation.

The reaction to this program was universally hostile. Randolph Paul, who was responsible for many of its provisions, described the response:

Most of the Secretary's recommendations other than the relief provisions aroused bitter opposition in many quarters. . . . The common denominator of protest was that the Treasury's recom-

mendations did not dip deeply and widely enough into the
lower income brackets; the *New York Herald Tribune* typically
complained that the fundamental weakness of the Treasury
plan was its failure to reach more than half the nation's
income.[13]

Congress quickly remedied that. Chairman Doughton of Ways and
Means had told administration officials early on that eliminating mineral depletion and tax-exempt securities and other loophole-closing
provisions could not pass his committee, or the House, and thus they
were scrapped. Although an amendment dropping tax-exempt status
for state and local bonds was passed on the floor of the Senate, the
House prevailed in Conference after a warning by New York's Representative La Guardia that such a change would jeopardize already
shaky state and local finances. Equally unpopular was Roosevelt's
proclamation that "to win the war, no American citizen ought to have a
new income, after he has paid his taxes, of more than $25,000 a year."[14]
This was labeled by some a "CIO proposal." More than one commenta-
tor argued that it was political demagoguery and not intended to be
enacted. It was quickly dropped as Ways and Means began to write its
own bill.

Following public testimony by approximatley 350 witnesses (nearly
all complaining about one or another proposed change), a bill was
reported that addressed the issue of broadening the base and dipping
deeper into the incomes of lower-income groups. First it lowered the
exemption, inducing a reluctant administration to endorse the change.
Then it increased the normal tax from 4 to 6 percent and more than
doubled the lowest surtax backet rates from 6 to 13 percent. The top
marginal rate was raised only from 77 to 82 percent. Following Treasury
officials' testimony on abuse of the 1941 excess profits provisions, the
committee was disposed to be somewhat harder on corporations. It
raised the total normal and surtax rates from 31 to 45 percent and the
top excess profits rates from 60 to 90 percent. Excise taxes were
increased to a higher rate than the administration had requested.
Proposals for new types of taxes, including several variants of sales
taxes, and Roosevelt's request for a refundable income tax fund were
rejected. Incrementalism served better than innovation when the
stakes were high and the need to raise revenue and control inflation was
immediate. The bill was reported under a closed rule allowing only
committee amendments, two of which favorably supported the committee recommendations to raise corporate taxes to the levels specified.

After three days of debate laden with calls for sacrifice in the face of war, the bill was passed 395 to 2.

Several interesting events took place in the Senate. The first was total rejection of an administration plan to use the income tax to tax spending as well as income. The spending, or consumption tax proposal began when the House opposed the administration's request to raise Social Security taxes and passed a freeze instead. In rebuttal, Paul and others in Treasury concocted a plan in which income going to consumption would be taxed by an additional levy. As in current proposals for an "expenditure" tax, the base for the tax would have been calculated by subtracting from income all savings, life insurance premiums, pension payments, and debts paid during the year. After allowing other deductions for equity reasons (taxes paid, dependent exclusions, rent, etc.), what remained was to be taxed in a graduated manner. Progressivity was defended on the assumptions that higher spending did greater harm to the war effort (by promoting inflation) and that higher expenditures represented unnecessary purchases of luxuries. This alternative to a sales tax was summarily dismissed after one session. It was reported that not a single legislator was for it. The *Washington Post* dubbed it: "Morgenthau's morning glory. It opened Tuesday morning and closed before noon."[15] This was not the year for major innovations in the tax system.

Of more importance for the final outcome of the bill was the Senate's conservative stance on corporate increases. It added numerous exceptions to lower the effective rates of the excess profits tax and lowered the regular corporate rate from the 45 percent passed by the House to 40 percent. In addition, further broadening the base and reducing the progressivity of the individual income tax, Senator Walter George (D-Ga.), Chairman of the Finance Committee, gained approval of a flat 5 percent "Victory Tax" to be collected from anyone with a gross income over $624, regardless of whether he or she paid any other income taxes. In partial accordance with the original administration suggestion, part of this amount was to be rebated following the war. All of these changes further shifted the burden of taxes to the lower- and middle-income classes. The bill passed the Senate after only five days of debate by a vote of 77 to 0.

In its final form the Revenue Act of 1942 had an enormous effect on the tax structure of the United States. It broadened the base by over 100 percent, with the number of taxpayers expected to increase from 13 million to 28 million for regular taxes and to 50 million if the Victory Tax was included. However, it also cut deeply into those it reached. Surtax

rates had reached 82 percent for a total marginal rate of 93 percent, including normal and Victory taxes. At the lower end, the exemption dropped to $1,200 for couples and $600 for single taxpayers, and the first-bracket rates more than doubled. In 1941 those in the first bracket, which began at a higher income, paid 10 percent. Under the new law they would pay 24 percent, with a 1.25 percent rebate after the war. Corporations did not escape, although some in the administration and elsewhere thought that they came out relatively well given the profits being made in many industries because of war manufacturing and the general economic recovery. The corporate and excess profits rates were raised, and numerous complicated provisions were added to correct deficiencies, alleviate differences in the effects of the tax on one or another industry, and prevent the abuses and special privileges that had developed. The complexity of the total bill was overwhelming. As Paul notes:

> The act devoted 42 pages to clarification and definition of ex-
> isting provisions to enable more equitable enforcement. Out of
> its 173 provisions, 104 were corrective. In pages, this was
> nearly 78% of the act, 162 pages out of 208. . . . The rate struc-
> ture had reached the point where loopholes resulted in drastic
> loss of revenue, and where inequities and discrepancies
> threatened to be not only troublesome, but even disastrous to
> taxpayers.[16]

The decision was made by members of the administration to accept the bill even though it fell short of their revenue requests, ignored many of their specific recommendations, and was in some respects inconsistent with the ability-to-pay philosophy that they proclaimed. Congress considered little in the way of tax reform unless one counts the passage of several relief provisions affecting lower- and middle-income taxpayers. There was also little in the way of tax innovation despite a wide range of proposals from Congress, the Treasury, and the White House itself. Only a very weak form of Roosevelt's plan to refund taxes after the war was incorporated as part of the Victory Tax.

Even without new taxes, however, the bill was large, technical, and complicated. At the cabinet meeting in which it was decided to accept the bill, Roosevelt was both amused and bemused: "He said, 'The bill might as well have been written in a foreign language.' He did not understand it and did not think the Treasury understood it. . . . He was told to sign it that day in order to save some $60 million revenue, so that

he was forced to sign it without reading it. He made quite a joke of the whole thing."[17]

Though 1942 was not a satisfying year for the Roosevelt administration on tax policy, compared with 1943 it would be viewed as a stunning success. The first order of business in 1943 was to create a means by which the taxes passed in the previous two years could be collected. This meant withholding at the source of income. In both 1941 and 1942, the administration, anticipating collection problems with so many new taxpayers, had recommended the introduction of withholding in 1943. Randolph Paul succinctly summarized the situation: "The existing income tax payment system was poorly adapted to the budgets and flow of income of 44 million taxpayers. The lag in payments had become a serious problem with the war expansion of the income tax, the backbone of the Federal system."[18]

The problem of collections was aggravated by high inflation, and thus the need to remove some of the rapidly increasing purchasing power from the hands of the American public, and also by the persistence of one Beardsley Ruml, treasurer of R. H. Macy and Company and chairman of the Federal Reserve Bank of New York. In 1942 Ruml had advanced a plan to solve the problem of back payments by simply forgiving income taxes owed and starting afresh. The administration strongly opposed the plan, and Congress defeated it, although there was broad support for the idea, not only in Congress but also in the press. In 1943 Ruml continued to lobby, citing cases of retired executives and employees content to live on modest pensions but unable to pay their back taxes. A similar case was the soldier drawn from lucrative private employment into noble but low-paying service to his country. Ruml's efforts, supported by a Congress nervous about the astronomical increases in taxes (one congressman claimed that the rate of increase in the previous four years had been 1,500 percent—and no one disputed the figure), were to win the day in an awkward trade for a system of withholding taxes at the source of income.

The year began in confusion as the president's budget message emphasized the need for putting income taxes on a "pay-as-you-go" basis, which the press misinterpreted as a suggestion for tax forgiveness as well as a call for withholding.[19] While Treasury worked to correct this impression, tax collections fell off, and Congress began its deliberation. Behind the leadership of Chairman Doughton, the administration was successful in getting Ways and Means to report a bill specifying withholding without a forgiveness clause. A minority report, however, backed by the Republicans on the committee, proposed tying withhold-

ing to the Ruml plan of forgiving all tax liabilities remaining from 1942. In the complicated floor actions that followed, full 100 percent forgiveness was twice passed, only to be later defeated. Committee bills were twice recommitted until a compromise version that forgave approximately 60 percent of 1942 tax liabilities was finally passed.

The Senate was in no mood to compromise. The Finance Committee rejected the House bill and approved the Ruml plan by votes of 13 to 7. After votes on four other plans, the full Senate adopted the Finance Committee proposal by a vote of 49 to 30 on May 14, 1943.[20] At that point Roosevelt intervened with a letter addressed to conferees denouncing the plan as inequitable in that those with large incomes stood to gain enormous amounts. The final outcome was a compromise presented by Walter George offering 75 percent forgiveness of the lesser of 1942 or 1943 tax liabilities tied to a 20 percent maximum withholding, which was to begin on July 1, 1943. The break came when Chairman Doughton relented in the face of continuous pressure and what he felt were uncertain and confused signals from the administration. The Current Tax Payment Act was a monumental trade off—permanent withholding, which added a necessary but coercive enforcement procedure, in exchange for a one-time forgiveness of past taxes. No loss of cash flow for the year resulted; in fact, the act added $4 billion. However, it was an indication of Congress's nervous reaction to the prevailing rates. The second revenue bill of 1943 provided more direct evidence of that mood.

The underlying forces that drove wartime tax policy, increasing expenditures and inflation, had accelerated even further by the summer of 1943. By June 30 the national debt stood at $136.7 billion, compared with $41.1 billion in 1939. Inflation had risen 25 percent since 1941 and was much higher for many consumer goods. Roosevelt had estimated in his January budget message that $16 billion of purchasing power needed to be removed from the economy to bring inflation reasonably under control. Within the administration the means to that end were hotly contested, and a rift had developed between Morgenthau and Treasury on the one hand and Jimmy Byrnes, head of War Mobilization, and Fred Vinson, director of Economic Stabilization, on the other. Having taken a beating over the Current Tax Payment Act, Treasury wanted to make only general recommendations on revenue needs while again asking for Social Security increases. Byrnes and Vinson, aided by Budget Director Harold Smith, wanted to make explicit recommendations on revenue increases and continued to advocate compulsory savings, as they had in 1942. After a wild and hostile Cabinet meeting in which Roosevelt vehemently reminded those present that "I am the boss," he decided to go ahead with the Treasury plan. The bill that Treasury placed before the Ways and Means Committee on October 4

asked for revenue increases of $10.4 billion, of which $6.5 billion was to come from individuals, 1.1 from corporations, 2.5 from increased excises, and 0.4 from estate and gift taxes.[21]

Randolph Paul, in a considerable understatement, described the reception of this bill in Congress as "cold." Representative Doughton used other words, characterizing the proposal as "an unbearable increased burden" and as "utterly undefensible."[22] Without his help the administration was lost from the beginning. Ways and Means wrote its own bill, completely ignoring Treasury's demands. When it was completed, it was expected to raise only $2 billion in new revenue, mostly from excise taxes. Individual income tax rates and exemptions were not changed. The earned income tax credit that originated in 1924 was dropped, but this revenue gain was offset by a reduction in the Victory Tax. Although the excess profits rate was raised to 95 percent, more exceptions were allowed and the basic profit exemption was raised from $5,000 to $10,000 in response to the demands of small businesses. The Finance Committee later added further insult to Treasury by permanently extending the list of minerals qualifying for depletion allowances by a dozen or so new minerals; defining timber cutting and sales as long-term capital gains; and authorizing special exemptions from excess profits taxes for the natural gas industry. The Senate also added a permanent reduction of 3 percent in the Victory Tax. The bills were passed in both houses with little opposition: by a vote of 200 to 27 in the House in November, and by a voice vote in the Senate in late January 1944. The final bill not only raised less than one-fifth of the amount asked for by the administration, but also repealed a Treasury-backed automatic 1 percent increase in Social Security taxes scheduled for March.

The administration was furious, and the advice of all Roosevelt's key financial aides was to veto the bill. Although at the last minute Morgenthau relented and, fearing an override, urged him to sign, the president vetoed the bill on February 22. It was the first revenue bill to be vetoed in the history of the United States. The language of the veto message was rough, labeling it "not a tax bill but a tax relief bill, providing relief not for the needy, but for the greedy."[23] Congress was outraged. Doughton and George made speeches against the president, and Alben Barkley, Majority Leader for the last seven years, resigned in protest following a dramatic speech on the floor of the Senate. Harold Knutson, ranking Republican and soon to become chairman of the Ways and Means Committee, said: "Congress rejected the president's tax program because it would have wiped out the middle class and jeopardized the solvency of all business."[24] Congress had the votes to override, 299 to 95 in the House and 72 to 14 in the Senate.[25] Roosevelt had suffered a

major defeat, and Congress had demonstrated its resolve to keep taxes that affected the mass of voters as low as possible. That resolve was to be the hallmark of postwar tax history.

The sensitivity of the legislative process to the taxes of the middle class extended to Treasury as well as Congress. Writing in 1944 in what was then an annual review of tax policy in the *American Economic Review*, Edward Allen criticized the initial Treasury proposals with regard to the fight against inflation on exactly these grounds. After noting that those earning between $1,000 and $5,000 received 71 percent of all after-tax income, he wrote:

> The Treasury figures do not make possible a comparison of present and proposed taxes for the $2,000 to $5,000 group, but for the $1,000 to $3,000 group, the proportion of personal taxes to have been paid would have been slightly lower than under existing law and for the $3,000 to $5,000 group only slightly (less than 2%) higher. It follows that *critics were correct in arguing that the Treasury did not have a strong anti-inflation tax program.* That adoption of the Treasury program would have had some anti-inflationary effect cannot be denied, especially when compared with the substitute which was enacted into law early in 1944, over the veto of the President. (Italics in the original.)[26]

The administration's defeat marked the end of major substantive tax legislation until the end of 1945, when its happier task was to prepare for a return to peace by lowering taxes. The issue that consumed Congress's attention in 1944 was simplification of the tax code. Randolph Paul explained the pressing need to simplify income taxes in terms of the rapid expansion that the code had undergone:

> simplicity was imperative if the American tax system was to survive. The necessity of simplifying provisions for the benefit of a large number of taxpayers had intensified in the war years. In 1932 the tax statute had called for slightly less than 2 million taxable returns. By 1943 it called for about 40 million returns. A reasonable number of complications were not fatal to a system which required 2 million returns. To handle complications in more than twenty times that number was a very different matter. While our tax system might safely, though not wisely irritate 2 million citizens, it would run serious risks if it irritated 40 or 50 million.[27]

The act passed that year with little political discussion made a large number of administrative changes, the most important being graduated withholding, calculated using 10 percent of income for deductions; the creation of the standard deduction to eliminate the need for many to itemize deductions; the use of tax tables to determine taxes owed; and a system whereby wage earners could file employer withholding receipts in lieu of filing a tax return. The business community was very supportive of these efforts because its members had been inundated by their employees with requests to aid in calculating and filing returns. These measures would not solve the problem in the long run, however, because the code was to become more, not less, complex.

The final significant event in the war years was a major effort to reduce taxes drastically by repealing the Sixteenth Amendment, which authorized the income tax. Seventeen states passed resolutions to that effect, and only the war seemed to hold back the campaign. Following the passage in 1945 of a minor bill relieving the tax burden on small businesses by raising the exemption on the excess profits tax from $10,000 to $25,000 and major reductions in both individual and corporate taxes later in the year, the pressure to repeal the income tax eased off. However, the depth of opposition—even during a period of national crisis—to high taxes, whether progressive or not, was once again reinforced.

The Magnitude of Change

One indication of the importance of the changes in the income taxes as a result of World War II is the permanent shift in the sources of federal revenue. The changing pattern of revenue was depicted earlier in figure 4.1. As with the First World War, by the end of the war corporate and individual income taxes were carrying approximately three-fourths of the federal tax burden. Prior to the war they accounted for less than 40 percent of federal revenue. After World War I, however, the revenue system partly returned to the prewar pattern, and customs and excise taxes regained their former importance. Following the Second World War, income taxes continued at close to wartime rates. It is only in recent years that Social Security taxes have increased to the point where they rival the income taxes in importance.

Other indicators of the dramatic effect of the war are the size of income tax revenues relative to the Gross National Product and the number of citizens paying taxes. Figure 6.1 portrays income taxes as a percentage of GNP. The increase in World War I, which created such

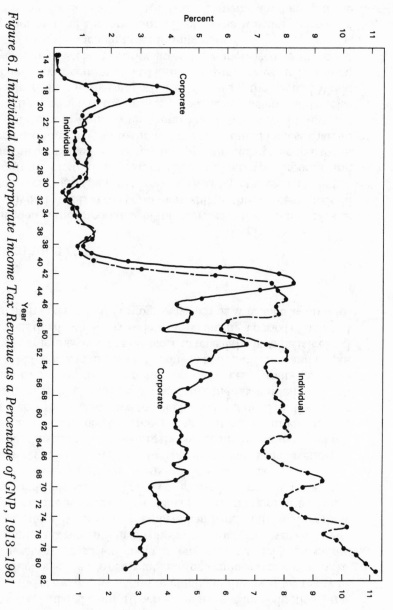

Figure 6.1 Individual and Corporate Income Tax Revenue as a Percentage of GNP, 1913–1981

Sources: Bureau of the Census, *Historical Statistics of the United States: Colonial Times to the Present*, series Y389–90, Y399, Y407; *U.S. Statistical Abstract*, 1980, table 724; *Internal Revenue Service, Statistics of Income* (Washington, D.C.: Government Printing Office, 1970–1981).

Note: Corporate tax totals include excess profits taxes for 1917–1922, 1933–1946, and 1950–1954.

deep controversy at that time, is a "blip" compared with the rise in both corporate and individual taxes in World War II. In the four years from 1939 to 1943, each tax increased from a little over 1 percent of GNP to approximately 8 percent. In contrast to the pattern for World War I, they rose at about the same rate and contributed approximately the same amount to war revenues. The steep drop in corporate taxes after the war was due to the repeal of the excess profits tax, which was reenacted following the start of the Korean War and then permanently repealed. The curious fact is that individual income taxes were not substantially reduced after the Korean War, as they were after the world wars.

The impact of the war on the size of the taxpaying public is indicated in figure 6.2, which portrays the percentage of the total labor force, including the military, filing individual income tax returns and the percentage filing returns that show the payment of some taxes. Because the size of the taxpaying population is greatly influenced by the level of personal exemptions, changes in exemption levels are graphed in figure 6.3. Parallel with the dollar volume of income taxes, the size of the taxpaying public was affected by both wars. Again, however, World War I shows up as a relatively minor distortion, with at most 13 percent of the labor force paying income taxes. Even though exemptions were cut in half during the First World War, income remained low enough that few were affected. Successive legislative changes in the twenties reduced this figure, although never to prewar levels because income expanded substantially during these growth years. Despite the lowered exemption in the 1930s, the rate of filing declined slightly for several years because of poor economic conditions. As recovery set in, the percentages increased slightly in both categories, even though there were no changes in exemption levels. The transition to a mass tax began in 1940 with the U.S. financial commitment to the allies and its own armament efforts. By 1944 the exemption level was reduced to its wartime low of $500 for a married couple and an additional $500 for dependents. As a result, those paying some income taxes increased from 7.1 to 64.1 percent of the population. The consequence was that income tax policies were suddenly transformed from decisions affecting a few to decisions felt by the large mass of citizens.

The war also brought a major shift in the progressivity of the income tax. Although rates began to become more progressive with the Revenue Act of 1932, the war years greatly increased progressivity at all income levels, and particularly at the upper ones, by increasing marginal rates and by lowering and widening brackets. During these years the top marginal rate of 94 percent exceeded the top rates in World War I (77 percent) and the prewar years following Roosevelt's Wealth Tax of 1935 (81 percent). Much more importantly, whereas the earlier rates

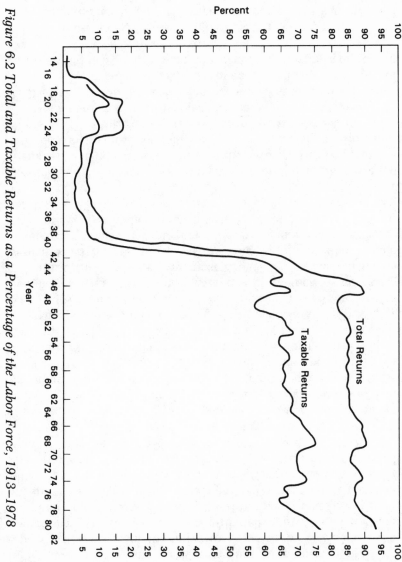

Figure 6.2 Total and Taxable Returns as a Percentage of the Labor Force, 1913–1978

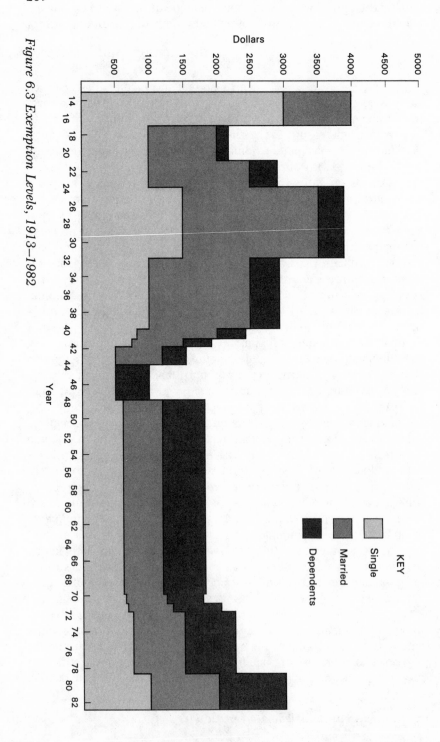

Figure 6.3 Exemption Levels, 1913–1982

applied to income over $1 million and $5 million respectively, from 1942 through 1963 the top-bracket rates applied to income over $200,000 and many times the number of people affected in earlier years. Thus, while earlier progressivity had a mainly symbolic effect, by the end of the war, the rates were real.

Estimating actual effective tax rates is a very complex problem. For a high degree of accuracy, a tax model is required that analyzes actual tax returns augmented by information on excluded sources of income that do not show up on returns.[28] However, rough estimates of the relative progressivity of different tax bills can be obtained by calculating taxes for a family of a given size, either ignoring adjustments and deductions or assuming that they represent a fixed percentage of income. Figure 6.4 is based on the former approach, wherein it is assumed that net income (after adjustments and deductions, but before exemptions) is solely derived from wages and salaries. It thus represents only statutory changes in rates and personal exemptions. This figure, which updates calculations made in 1948 in a seminal article by Richard Musgrave and Tun Thin,[29] provides striking evidence of the effect of World War II tax rates relative to those of other periods. The graph portrays residual after-tax income on a logarithmic scale. The distance between the lines and 45 degrees indicates the amount of taxes paid, and the changes in slopes the progressivity. For both, World War II stands out. Subsequent years show a steady retreat from the wartime high. Since fewer exclusions and deductions were allowed in 1944 than in later years, by ignoring these variables the figure overstates the rates paid in later years; thus, the differences in progressivity are conservative estimates. Further details of historical changes in progressivity are given in chapters 11 and 12, and that evidence is fully consistent with the conclusion apparent from figure 6.4: 1944 and 1945 were the most progressive tax years in U.S. history.

The combination of lower exemptions (and thus greatly increased numbers of taxpayers) and war-induced pressures on progressivity created a situation in which Congress became very sensitive to the effects of taxes on the previously exempted middle class. The congressional rebellion of 1943 was spurred in part by the fear of a backlash by this large voting bloc. That sensitivity would remain a permanent feature of postwar tax politics, serving to stabilize middle-class rates both across income levels and over time.

Summary and Conclusions

Wartime increases in the scope and level of individual and corporate income taxes raised the political stakes in tax policy and permanently

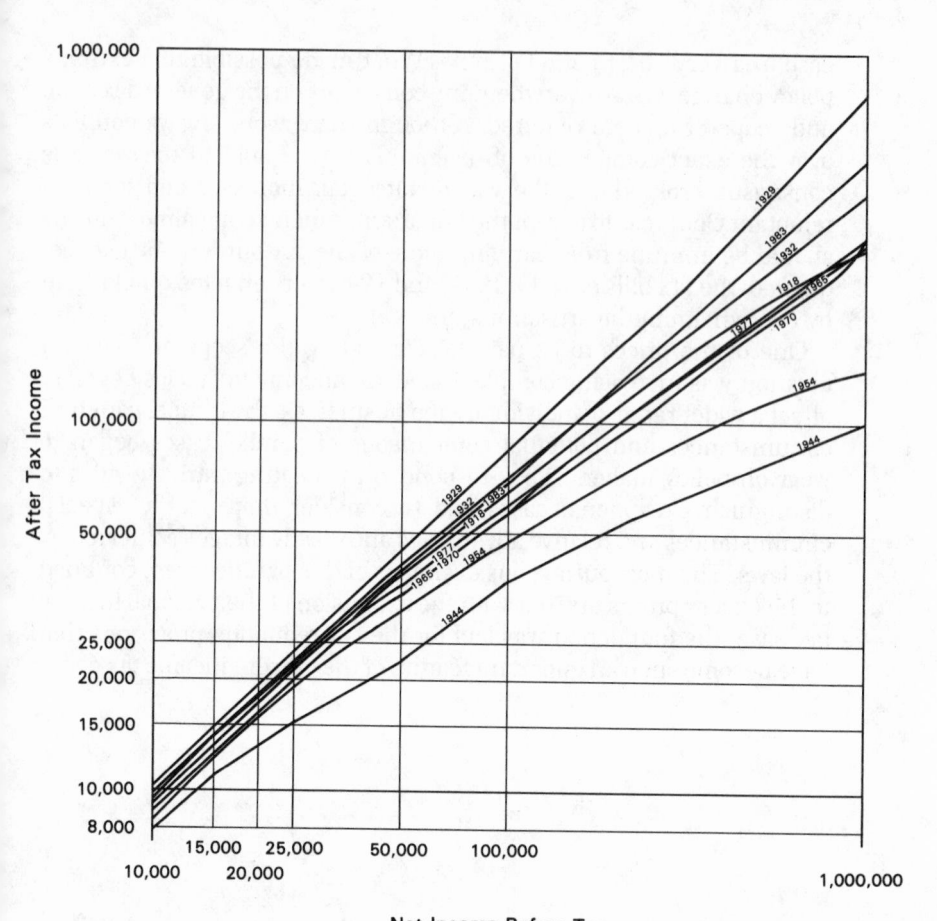

*Figure 6.4 Residual Income Related to Net Income, Selected Years
(Logarithmic scales calculated for a married couple with
two dependents)*

altered the politics of the income tax. Beginning with World War II,
large sums of money and the vast majority of the voting public would be
involved. This conversion was accomplished entirely through a series of
incremental adjustments to existing policies and the adoption of an
excess profits tax similar to that used in the First World War. Never has
there been more convincing evidence for Braybrooke and Lindblom's
contention that incrementalism can lead to massive change—in this

case in a very short period of time. What made possible this extreme policy change was an overwhelming consensus on the general direction and scope of change required. Although there were always conflicts over the exact composition of revenue laws and later in the war this consensus broke down, the war dictated tax increases and forced a reluctant Congress to accept the important principle that almost no one should be immune from carrying some of the tax burden. As a consequence, the tax bills of 1940, 1941, and 1942 were enacted quickly and by overwhelming bipartisan majorities.

One of the prices to be paid for expanding the scope and level of taxation was increasing complexity. As the income tax codes began to affect a wider range of individuals and businesses, the infinite variety of circumstances and potential comparisons of parallel cases began to wear on policy makers. They responded by creating intricate rules to distinguish exceptional cases and to consider more "fairly" special circumstances and relative advantages and disadvantages conferred by the laws. The most outrageous examples of this practice were confined to the excess profits tax, but with the expansion of the personal income tax base, the foundation was laid for the tax reduction provisions that have become such an important feature of the current income tax code.

Chapter 7.
Postwar Tax
Policy

From War to Peace
and Back to War

The first postwar tax legislation passed at the end of 1945 in the euphoria following V-J Day, was foreordained and almost routine. It was enacted in a two-month period with little political oppositon: there was an overwhelming consensus that wartime taxes were to be reduced. The administration proposed to reduce them by $5.65 billion by repealing the excess profits tax, effective January 1, 1946; eliminating the 3 percent normal tax; and cutting back excise taxes to their 1943 levels. Its basic arguments, accepted with little quarrel in Congress, were that these cuts would stimulate investment needed for conversion to a peacetime economy and that they would encourage consumer demand, which was expected to fall.

Congress somewhat altered the form of these reductions, primarily by increasing the reduction for individuals while maintaining most excise taxes at wartime levels. However, the total reduction was very close to the amount requested by the administration, and the bill went through both houses without even token resistance. Passage in the House was almost unanimous, without a vote to recommit, and the Senate passed the bill by voice vote without any divisive floor votes. It appeared as if history was about to repeat itself, with this act as the first of a series of tax reductions similar to those passed in the aftermath of World War I. That was not to be the case, however. First a stubborn president became an obstacle, then another war intervened, and finally a new peacetime role for government began to be acknowledged by both political parties.

Truman's Fight Over Tax Reduction. The years 1946 and 1947 showed all the early signs of another major transition in the history of tax policy. As in 1920 and 1932, the economy was in a period of uncertainty and change. At the beginning of 1945, 22 million people were employed by the government in war production jobs or the armed forces. Unemploy-

ment and recession were predicted by some economists, although others were more optimistic. Inflation was also a potential danger because pent-up demand was expected to swell as soon as wartime controls were removed but before the economy could respond with a transition to consumer goods. Politically the shift away from the New Deal that began in Congress before the war and accelerated in the last two years of the war seemed to have been completed. Republicans won control of both houses with a remarkable swing of 111 seats in the House and 24 seats in the Senate. They held comfortable majorities in each, and the signs were positive for winning the presidency in two years.

The Republicans quickly translated their victory into the tax program that had been a central campaign issue in 1946. As soon as the election results were known, Harold Knutson (R-Minn.), who with the Republican majority became chairman of the Ways and Means Committee, proposed an across-the-board reduction of 20 percent for all incomes below $302,000, and a 10 percent reduction above that figure. He also proposed an additional exemption for those over 65, reflecting the fact that World War II rate increases and lower exemptions required many retired people to pay income taxes for the first time. The rationale for the proposals, which had been a central plank of the Republican campaign, was that they would create incentives, spur production, and force a reduction in government spending. In presenting them, Knutson admitted that a major reason for tax reduction was to "cut off much of the government's income by reducing taxes and compelling the government to retrench, live within its income."[1] Later, on the floor of the House, he pushed the rhetoric a notch higher: the bill, he said,

> puts the ax to punitive taxes designed by alien minds and whizzed through subservient congresses. . . . For years we Republicans have been warning that the short-haired women and long-haired men of alien minds in the administrative branch of government were trying to wreck the American way of life and install a hybrid oligarchy at Washington through confiscatory taxation."[2]

Knutson's changes and proposals met with fierce opposition from some Democrats. A young representative from Tennessee, Albert Gore, who would carry the liberal banner in tax matters for years to come, stated that the proposal came "right out of the Andrew Mellon primer on special privilege."[3] The administration's reaction came in January 1947 when Truman opposed any tax reduction for that year on the grounds

that it would be inflationary and add to deficits; specifically, he opposed the across-the-board reduction because it would distribute relief in an inequitable manner. Senator Taft (R-Ohio) replied abruptly for the Republicans: "The president's real reason for retaining the taxes is obviously to have more money to spend. The best reason to reduce taxes is to reduce our ideas of the number of dollars the government can properly spend in a year, and thereby reduce inflated ideas of the proper scope of bureaucratic authority."[4] It was later shown that of the total reduction proposed by the Republicans, 38.3 percent would go to the 3.5 percent of the taxpayers with net incomes over $5,000.[5] Concern for equity led to a modification of the proposal in Ways and Means that allowed a 30 percent reduction in taxes for those with incomes under $1,000 a year, phasing down to 20 percent at $1,400. The bill was sustained on the floor on a almost perfect party-line vote on recommitting it.[6]

Nine days of hearings followed the expected pattern: business witnesses supported the bill, and trade unions and liberal interest groups opposed it and proposed substitutes based on increased exemptions. The Senate Finance Committee then reported a bill that further compromised the original proposal by lowering the rate reductions in the $79,000–302,000 bracket to 15 percent (rather than 20), leaving a graduated relief schedule from 30.0 to 10.5 percent. In response to concern about inflation and deficits in fiscal 1948, it proposed delaying the bill's effective date from January 1, 1947, to July 1, 1947.

On the floor, the principal challenge came in the form of a substitute offered by Senator Lucas (D-Ill.), minority whip and member of the Finance Committee. His bill would have achieved the reduction by increasing the exemption from $500 to $600, reducing the rates 2 percent in each bracket, and authorizing income splitting for married couples filing joint returns. Together these measures were significantly more progressive than those in the Republican bill. However, the substitute was soundly beaten by a vote of 27 to 58, with 10 Democrats deserting Lucas and only 1 Republican crossing over to vote for his bill. The Republican bill was then passed by a vote of 52 to 34, with 7 Democrats joining Republicans voting in favor of it.[7] Although liberal Democrats objected throughout the Conference Committee meetings and floor debates that the proposed bill was extremely unfair, the Conference bill only slightly altered the House and Senate versions and was easily passed and sent to the president on June 3, 1947.

President Truman, though faced with an election in sixteen months, vetoed the bill not once but, in the end, three times. His veto message in 1947 carried the simple phrase that this was "the wrong kind of tax reduction at the wrong time." His economic arguments centered on

inflation and refuted the theory that economic incentives were needed in view of the extraordinary prosperity that had taken hold of the country since the end of the war. Rather, the task was to control inflation and begin to retire some of the wartime debt. The president also emphasized the inequity of relief under the bill, even in the amended version, which was significantly less regressive than the original Knutson proposal.[8]

Just barely enough congressmen were persuaded to sustain the veto on an override vote in the House. The motion to override failed by two votes, as five Democrats who had supported the orignal bill came to the president's aid. The Republicans, however, immediately proposed a new bill in which the only change was a delay in the tax reductions until January 1, 1948. This bill, which gained the support of several key Democratic members of Ways and Means, easily passed both chambers, only to be vetoed by Truman. This time the House overrode the veto by two votes as two key Democratic representatives, Doughton and Byrd (Va.), managed to carry their state delegations against the president. After fierce lobbying and pressure on swing senators, however, the veto was sustained in the Senate, again by just two votes.[9] Truman and a Democratic minority had forestalled a major tax reduction, but only for a short time.

A new tax bill was one of the first items on the agenda when Congress convened in January 1948. This time the situation was very unfavorable for the administration. Because of the strength of the economy and because taxes were still very close to wartime levels, a government surplus of $6.8 billion had accumulated (the largest ever). Thus, a critical argument for Truman's resistance to tax reduction was lost. The administration proposed, almost halfheartedly, that each taxpayer receive a $40 rebate and that the lost revenue be made up by partial restoration of the excess profits tax. These proposals were embodied in a House bill introduced by Rep. Dingell (D-Mich.), but the bill was ignored and never came to any kind of vote.

Instead, Congress turned to a new bill introduced by Knutson that proved irresistible to nearly everyone. To attract the maximum number of votes, Knutson worked out a compromise that incorporated, as he put it, "the lowest common denominator" of his previous bill and the Lucas Senate floor substitute, which had liberal backing. The bill offered a tax cut for all brackets, but graduated even more liberally than the one in the previous bill. It also increased the exemption from $500 to $600; added an extra exemption not only for the elderly, but also for the blind; and permitted income splitting on joint returns.[10] Thus, a vote against the bill would have meant a vote against lower taxes for everyone, and

particularly for the blind, the aged, and married couples. The cost of the bill was estimated at $6.5 billion, less than the surplus for the past year.

Knutson had done his job well. The compromise, which had the support of Rep. Doughton, the senior minority member on Ways and Means, went before the House under the closed rule, sailed through a recommittal vote, and was passed 297 to 120. The Finance Committee accepted most provisions of the bill, including income splitting, but reduced the percentage reductions, thus lowering the total amount of tax reduction. An effort was made on the Senate floor to reintroduce an excess profits tax, but it was badly beaten by a vote of 58 to 26. The final bill was passed 78 to 11, and the 30 Democrats who supported it fully expected a presidential veto. This time, however, with the support of Ways and Means and Finance leaders of both parties, the veto was overridden. Only one senator (Fulbright, D-Ark.) and three representatives changed their votes to support Truman. For the second time in history, but also the second time in five years, a revenue bill had been passed over a presidential veto.

Senator Millikin (R-Colo.) later explained the bill in bald political terms: "It was deliberately contrived to attract the votes, because we wanted to reduce taxes."[11] A. E. Holmans summarized the process as follows: "What happened was that nearly all Senators were in favor of tax reduction of some sort, and that H.R. 4790 included something of all widely canvassed forms of tax reduction, whereas its predecessor did not."[12] This pattern of constructing approval by broadening benefits was to become common in postwar tax bills. As long as a general consensus exists that taxes should be reduced, coalition building is a process of doling out enough targeted provisions that a majority can find something particularly attractive. Even though there may be disadvantages for some groups in a bill, the complexity of tax legislation allows one to campaign on general tax reduction, highlighting the attractive provisions while ignoring those that are unappealing.

Truman's supporters later argued that he was able to use the tax bill to his advantage in the campaign of 1948, attacking it as "the rich man's tax bill." Although it is not clear how important this issue was in his campaign, his victory and the swing back to Democratic control of both houses forestalled the further tax cuts that would have been attempted if the Republicans had won the presidency and maintained control of Congress as they did in 1920.[13] Indeed, at the beginning of 1949 Truman asked, not for a tax cut, but rather for an increase of some $4 billion to be derived from corporate taxes, estate and gift taxes, and some upward adjustment in personal income tax rates in the middle and upper brackets. The rationale given was the need to balance his

proposed budget increases for cold war defense and for "Fair Deal" programs in housing, public works, health care, and education. Neither side of this program was to be realized in 1949. Congress, although led by Democrats, was much more conservative than the administration and was often controlled by the conservative southern Democratic and Republican coalition that had emerged in 1938 and gave Roosevelt so much trouble in the last years before the war. If there was any consensus in Congress, it was for tax reduction, not tax increases. Moreover, Congress had just gone through a two-year struggle to pass a major tax bill and was not eager to begin again so soon. Furthermore, in 1949 the nation went into the first postwar recession, and by this time enough Keynesian economics had been absorbed that to raise taxes during a recession was to run counter to accepted economic wisdom.[14] Thus, Congress simply stood pat, producing only a minor bill with some technical revisions of the tax code.

The return to something approaching prewar levels that had occurred following every war in U.S. history was stalled after a relatively minor reduction in taxes. A glance back at figure 6.1 confirms that although the 1945 and 1948 acts significantly lowered the revenue derived from both individual and corporate taxes, the reduction left income tax revenues four to six times greater than before the war. This was primarily because normal corporate taxes remained high even after the excess profits tax was repealed and because the personal exemption and individual rates were only slightly modified relative to the changes imposed during the war, even though there were Treasury surpluses in 1948, 1949, and 1950.

Partisanship played a clear role in stalling tax reduction. During the war the executive branch had assumed a more active tax role, and Truman was not averse to high taxes, particularly when relief would disproportionately aid the well-off. The short renaissance of the Republican Party was insufficient to secure the continued downward ratcheting of taxes that had occurred in the twenties. However, factors other than partisanship were also at work. The postwar economic conversion created prosperity so strong that arguments for stimulative tax cuts, which Andrew Mellon had wielded so effectively in the 1920s, were undercut and countered by the Truman administration's emphasis on inflation. Moreover, Keynesian economics justified taxation as a fiscal tool and not just as a price that must be paid for government services. A substantial, progressive income tax served as an automatic stabilizing mechanism, absorbing spending power and thus cooling down the economy and controlling inflation during periods of economic expansion, and stimulating the economy through lower average and marginal

rates in periods of recession. Finally, the basic role of government had changed and with it government spending patterns. The government's responsibility for the economy and the basic well-being of its citizens was established in the Roosevelt years and at least symbolically confirmed in the Full Employment Act of 1946. Regardless of the party in power, this responsibility and the demands it generated would continue to grow. Even if this had not been the case, the outcome of the war, the division of Europe, and the growing fear of the Soviet Union prevented the full demilitarization that had followed previous wars. Although cold war defense spending was controversial at first and military expenditures dropped substantially, with the invasion of South Korea in June 1950 the controversy subsided and the grim task of maintaining high expenditures for defense was widely accepted.

Taxes During the Korean War. The year 1950 was one of the most active and confusing years in the history of American taxation. The year began at a leisurely pace as the administration asked for expenditure increases for domestic programs similar to those outlined but unpassed in 1949. It also asked for a patchwork of revenue changes that would have increased taxes by about $1 billion by raising corporate rates and estate taxes and closing "loopholes" while lowering excise taxes on a range of items. Congress labored over this bill until June, when a Ways and Means bill was approved that, as always, substantially altered Truman's request. It lowered excise taxes more than the president suggested, raised corporate taxes less, and butchered his proposals for closing specific "loopholes." Although it altered provisions regarding life insurance companies and proposed amendments that prevented certain glaring abuses that had developed among tax-exempt organizations,[15] it not only failed to reduce mineral depletion allowances (which was Truman's principal request), but actually increased some depletion deductions and added twenty minerals to the list qualifying for depletion. In addition, against the administration's wishes, the bill lowered the holding period necessary to qualify for long-term capital gains from six months to three, thus increasing the benefit of this provision. As finally passed, the bill had negligible impact on total revenues. This did not matter, however, because it was passed on June 29, two days after the invasion of South Korea, and it was clear that new tax measures would immediately be necessary.

Although the Finance Committee began hearings on the bill on July 5, executive sessions were not held until administration proposals were formally put before the committee by Secretary Snyder in early August. The administration realized that eventually an excess profits tax would

be necessary, but that it would be extremely controversial and would delay the funding that was needed immediately. Snyder therefore requested that Congress postpone consideration of excess profits taxation and instead immediately restore the individual rate structure applicable at the height of World War II, raise normal corporate taxes to 45 percent, and retain all tax-gaining provisions in the current House bill. The Finance Committee, acting quickly in the bipartisan spirit typical of previous early wartime legislation, stuck very closely to the administration's requests. Thus, the increased mineral depletion benefits were dropped (although Truman's proposed reduction was not included), while the provisions tightening up the taxation of life insurance companies and tax-exempt organizations remained. Finance did, however, drop a provision that the House had passed by which dividends would be subject to withholding.

On the Senate floor, operating without the closed rule that had become standard practice in the House, the lengthy debate peaked with the consideration of an excess profits tax proposal offered by Senator O'Mahoney (D-Wy.). Because there was clearly broad support for resurrecting this tax, Senator George, chairman of the Finance Committee, offered a substitute amendment that bound the revenue committees of Congress to report a bill establishing a retroactive excess profits tax at the earliest possible opportunity in the next Congress. George's amendment was accepted on a close vote of 42 to 36, providing an indication of the strength of support for excess profits taxes.[16] Of a score of other amendments offered on the floor, most coming from liberals led by Hubert Humphrey (D-Minn.) and Paul Douglas (D-Ill.), the only substantial amendment accepted was Humphrey's bid to eliminate the House provision lowering the holding period for long-term capital gains to three months. The final bill closely followed the Senate version and raised taxes $4.5 billion. Passage of the legislation took less than forty-five days from the initial administration requests in August.

Action to enact an excess profits tax began immediately after the November elections in a special lame-duck session of Congress. The reasons for haste were the realization that the war would be protracted and the rapid increase in inflation in the months following the outbreak of hostilities. The president sent a message to the Ways and Means Committee on November 14 requesting a tax yielding $4 billion annually. The exact administration proposal offered the next day in testimony by Secretary Snyder closely followed the structure of the excess profits tax formulas of World War II. However, it included liberal modifications (in exempted profits, acceptable rates of returns, and other areas) that reflected the changed economic situation and the relatively small amount of revenue required. The committee bill as

finally approved closely followed administration requests, but the brief partisan clash over the method and speed of enactment was as violent as any in tax history.

Ways and Means, controlled 15 to 10 by Democrats, imposed a strict rule on testimony, limiting comments to fifteen minutes and disallowing discussion of anything other than an excess profits tax. Business witnesses repeatedly made the point that taxation was needed and that corporate taxes should be raised, but that the excess profits tax was unnecessary. Daniel Reed (R-N.Y.), ranking minority member, put before the committee a proposal that had the support of the business community and allowed corporations a choice between increased regular corporate rates of 45 to 55 percent or the excess profits tax as proposed by the administration. This and a number of other amendments were defeated on straight party votes of 15 to 10. Because two Democrats sided with Republicans on several votes related to the percentage of past profits that defined the cutoff for "normal" profits, some slight modifications favorable to business were made. However, the Republicans remained adamant, filed a minority report calling for lower excess profits rates in exchange for increased normal ones, and offered a substitute bill on the floor. The substitute, as part of a recommital motion, was defeated 252 to 145, with only one Democrat (John F. Kennedy from Massachusetts) voting for it and only 10 Republicans voting against. As was standard in war legislation, final passage was close to unanimous at 378 to 20.[17]

Two weeks after passage of the House bill, the Senate passed a final version by a voice vote after only four hours of floor debate in which not a single roll call vote was taken. In that time the Finance Committee had held a week of hearings and a week of closed sessions. The Republicans had given up because of the time constraints of the lame-duck session and the size of the Democratic majority. The Senate had slightly altered some of the major formulas, but its main changes were to add substantially to the list of exempted or specially treated companies. When finally completed, the bill contained complex provisions for fast-growing and depressed industries, for companies with "base period abnormalities" (the profit base was 1946–1949); new corporations; regulated corporations; mining and strategic mineral income; timber, natural gas, shipbuilders, and railroads; and, finally, airlines carrying air mail. It is no wonder that Gordon Keith commented in the *National Tax Journal* some months after passage:

> The Excess Profits Tax Act of 1950 is not a very good law. . . .
> [T]he statute reflects at too many points evidence of the haste
> with which it was drafted, and of the compromises which had

to be made if any bill was to be brought out within the time limits. . . . The question whether the World War II approach to taxation of war profits was the best approach for the present emergency could not even be raised, to say nothing of being given careful consideration.[18]

The incremental practice of borrowing legislation—in this case World War I legislation that had been modeled on European laws—had served its short-term purpose even if the product was complex and imperfect. In signing the bill on January 3, 1951, President Truman lauded Congress for its rapid work and decisive action, while at the same time challenging some of the special provisions and warning that "the task ahead will require more and much heavier taxes."[19] The wartime tax roller coaster had not reached its peak.

As 1951 began, the three basic economic factors that reappear in each war period—expenditures, deficits, and inflation—all seemed to point in the same direction: toward higher taxes. Defense expenditures were projected by Truman to more than double to $41 billion in fiscal 1952, and the subsequent deficit at existing tax rates was estimated at $16.8 billion. Immediately after the outbreak of war in the summer of 1950, there began a run on consumer goods in anticipation of wartime shortages and excise tax increases. The result was an increase of 5 percent in the Consumer Price Index by the end of the year, with much higher levels for some consumer durables. Truman's approach was similar to that of Roosevelt at the beginning of the previous war. The philosophy was to "pay as you go," thus holding down deficits, inflation, and borrowing by raising taxes. In concert with most economists, Truman expressed "the conviction that we must attain a balanced budget to provide a sound financial basis for what may be an extended period of high defense expenditures."[20] Consistent with this maxim, the administration's tax requests in January were for broad increases in all taxes to raise revenues $10 billion. Of this, $4 billion was to be derived from the personal income tax by raising all bracket rates 4 percent, raising capital gains taxes from 25.0 to 37.5 percent, and taxing the interest on state and local bonds. It again proposed reducing the valuation of mineral depletion. Another $3 billion was to be raised by increasing the corporate rate for both large and small corporations (to 33 percent for those with incomes under $25,000 and to 55 percent for those over that level); taxing the profits of cooperatives and savings and loans more fully; and eliminating some of the exclusions in the excess profits tax. The remainder was to come from increased excise taxes (on the usual items, such as liquor, tobacco, gasoline, and consumer du-

rables) and higher gift and estate taxes. The menu was similar to those offered by Roosevelt in 1941, 1942, and 1943.

The legislative process in 1951 was much slower than it had been for the two previous bills, and the administration paid the price for this leisurely deliberation. Over forty days of hearings each were held by the Ways and Means and the Senate Finance committees, and the bill took almost nine months to enact. Over this period there were hundreds of changes and literally dozens of added provisions applying to specific industries and special population and income groups. In the end, except for the basic increases in personal and corporate rates, the final bill bore almost no resemblance to the initial administration proposals. At each stage the amount of the tax increase was reduced. The House bill, passed with almost straight-line party votes for recommittal and passage, would have raised revenues only about $7.2 billion. The Senate bill, in part due to a downwardly revised estimate of expenditures, was projected to raise revenues by only $6.7 billion, or just over half of what Truman had requested.

Debate over the Revenue Act of 1951 was bitter to the very end. Republicans attacked the spending politics of the Truman administration. The senior minority member of Ways and Means, Daniel Reed, representing a conservative upstate New York district, lambasted the act as "a bill to authorize the bureaucrats to turn the taxpayers' pocket inside out." If enacted, he argued, it would fulfill the ambitions of the "hardcore of Socialist planners within the Truman administration."[21] Minority Leader Joseph Martin (R-Mass.) questioned the administration's claim that tax increases were needed to stop inflation: "The Administration's contention that this tax bill is needed to control inflation is economic voodoo talk. No set of controls and no pyramid of taxes ever devised by man will stop inflation in America when the root of the evil is government spending."[22]

Opposition was not restricted to conservatives. A group of liberal senators, led by Humphrey, Douglas, O'Mahoney, and Lehman (D-N.Y.), offered the most persistent and serious opposition that had ever been launched against a Finance Committee revenue bill. The committee had proposed $1.5 billion less in increases than the House bill, and the liberals had estimated that of this reduction, only 8 percent would benefit people with incomes below $5,000.[23] Their arguments attacked not only this general distributive effect, but also the structural changes that permitted those in higher-income groups to legally avoid taxes due. Humphrey singled out income splitting and capital gains provisions as particularly pernicious in this regard. On the latter, he compared the workings of tax lawyers to the attempts of medieval alchemists to

convert lead into gold; the same thing was accomplished in modern times with "an ever-increasing productive program of how to convert earned income into capital gains."[24] Perhaps suprisingly, however, the liberals' most consistent line of argument was fiscal responsibility, echoing Truman's commitment to finance the war without deficits and to use taxes as a major defense against inflation. As in the House, Republicans did not quarrel with the principle but with the administration's spending programs and the ability of this specific set of tax increases to control inflation.

None of these arguments were really new. However, the concern that structural or special tax reduction provisions, were eroding the tax base, often supported by invoking the name of Henry Simons, was more vehement than before and marked a shift in emphasis that would characterize tax reform efforts in the years ahead. As in earlier liberal and Progressive attempts to alter tax legislation on the floor, for all their rhetorical and analytical skill, liberals failed to pass a single important amendment to the bill.

The final bill raised individual income tax liabilities 11 percent for those with incomes under $2,000 and 11.75 percent for those over that level, with a termination date of December 31, 1953. Corporate rates were raised to 30 percent on income under $25,000 and 52 percent on income over that level. These rates would remain for a number of years. The bill was nevertheless highly inadequate from the administration's point of view. Not only were mineral depletion benefits not reduced; they were expanded to cover thirty new mineral groups in classic log-rolling sessions reminiscent of earlier tariff battles. Taxing of cooperatives and savings and loans was partially successful,[25] but withholding of dividends and interest was again dropped in the Senate. Taxing the interest on state and local bonds, proposed regularly since 1917, never appeared in any bill. Estate and gift taxes were not significantly changed, again in keeping with congressional actions since the New Deal. Some excise taxes were raised, but less than one-third of the increases requested by Treasury were granted. And, finally, net changes in capital provisions produced a loss in revenue rather than the increase requested by the administration.

Most important, however, a veritable landslide of special provisions were enacted aiding a wide range of groups. Foreshadowing a pattern that would emerge in all subsequent revenue bills, tax increases in one form were compensated for by conferring tax benefits in another. The following is a partial list of revenue-losing provisions: the profits from the sale of homes were exempted from capital gains taxes, if the proceeds were reinvested in another home; medical expenses for the

elderly were to be deductible up to $2,500; numerous provisions exempting and excluding veterans and GIs from income and estate taxes were passed; mine exploration expenses were given special treatment; the sale of coal resources, unharvested crops, or any livestock was taxed at capital gains instead of regular rates; depletion was extended to everything from "fuller's earth" to clam and oyster shells; income earned abroad was excluded from tax if the citizen had lived abroad seventeen out of the last eighteen months; and, finally, the only unquestionably meritorious provision in the bill excluded income derived from the publishing operations of tax-exempt organizations, such as the one that published the words you read.

This final war revenue bill satisfied no one. The administration objected to the amount of revenue raised and the numerous tax reduction provisions enacted; conservatives objected to the smallness of the cut and the burden imposed on upper incomes and business by the general rate increases; and liberals objected to the special relief provisions afforded to upper-income groups and profit receivers. There was dramatic testimony to this dissatisfaction. Congressional leaders and the administration were shocked when, for the first and only time in the history of the income tax, the House rejected the Conference Committee report. A delighted Republican minority was joined by 65 Democrats, mostly liberals, in defeating the bill 157 to 204. The symbolic nature of the protest became clear when the bill reemerged in several days with only very slight changes. This time the Democrats, at the administration's urging, supported the bill. Truman was far from happy, however, stating on October 20 that he was signing the act only "because we badly need these revenues to help pay for the strong defenses we are building."[26] He criticized the bill as inadequate and unfair, with many unfortunate provisions.

Holmans later summarized this struggle with the comment that: "No evidence was adduced which pointed towards the conclusion that the United States had reached the limit of taxable capacity in any economic sense. The limit to tax increases reached in 1951 was political, not economic."[27] That may well be, but the decision was part of a long-term pattern. In considering the financing of the major wars in this century, Congress began in each case with quick, decisive, and bipartisan action, granting most of what the president requested. As the wars progressed, however, revenue increases became much more controversial, and Congress strongly asserted itself in rewriting administration proposals. The 1951 act did not go as far as that of 1943 because the administration realized that this bill was better than no bill at all or a national sales tax, which had been repeatedly raised as an alternative in

public hearings. What this progression demonstrates is that only in those early months of almost hysterical reaction to crisis can revenues easily be raised in the United States. At all other times, gains will be traded only for losses granted elsewhere in the code, and the trading seems to continue to the point where no one is satisfied but few can afford to see the bill defeated. With several minor exceptions, both the tendency toward revenue reduction and the patchwork quality of the 1951 act have been characteristic of all subsequent income tax legislation.

The Eisenhower Years: The Importance of Inaction

The election of Dwight Eisenhower in 1952 marked another period of political and economic transition, and if one took history as a guide, one would have predicted a series of tax reductions. Unlike the earlier Republican transitions in 1920 and 1946, however, Eisenhower resisted tax reduction just as Truman had. The one major tax bill enacted between 1952 and 1962 consisted of a comprehensive rewriting of the tax code, and there was an automatic reduction in individual taxes and in the excess profits tax, returning to the pre–Korean War rates. Beyond that there was nothing. The tax reduction bills of the twenties were not repeated; exemptions were not increased; and the highly progressive rate structure underlying the tax code remained very close to the World War II peak. Whereas the Second World War established the modern income tax, the inaction of the Eisenhower years sustained it.

The first challenge to the new administration came over the automatic tax reductions that had been built into the Excess Profits Act of 1950 and the Revenue Act of 1951. The challenge came primarily from within Eisenhower's own party. Immediately after the election, Daniel Reed, who had become the new chairman of Ways and Means as a result of the slim majority the Republicans held in the House,[28] introduced legislation to move forward the termination date for the individual income tax increases passed in 1951, from the prescribed date of December 31, 1953, to June 30, 1953. If enacted, the cuts would have coincided with the repeal of the excess profits tax. The administration resisted this effort and proposed rather that the excess profits repeal be moved back to coincide with the December 31 date applicable to individuals. The rationale, put in precise language by Secretary of the Treasury Humphrey, echoed Eisenhower's campaign promise to eliminate deficits as a matter of sound financial planning and as the princi-

pal control on inflation. This was expressed positively as "returning to the people the savings in government expenditure."[29] The immediate argument against Reed's proposal was that the administration must have time to enact its spending reductions before the nation could afford a tax cut. The difficulty was that long-term cuts were never really forthcoming, and after this initial tax reduction, concern for deficits prevented further tax cuts. The Eisenhower position was thus very close to that taken by Truman between 1946 and 1950. As in those years, the size of expenditures, the devotion to balanced budgets, and the fear of inflation proved to be the driving forces behind tax policy.

Reed did not give in easily to the administration's request, and it was only after the administration had his bill bottled up in the Rules Committee that he relented. Extending the repeal date of the excess profits tax required positive legislative action, over which Reed had more control. He refused to bring the administration proposal before the Ways and Means Committee until the Republican leadership, with the consent of the Rules Committee chairman, threatened to bring the bill to the floor without a Ways and Means report—something rarely done with major legislation. The threat worked, and the Ways and Means Committee voted in favor of the administration bill 16 to 9, with 9 Republicans for the bill and 6, including Reed, against. On the floor, liberal and moderate Republicans sided with Democrats to defeat a recommittal motion by 275 to 127. Final passage was 325 to 77. The Senate passed the bill easily, and thus the first tax initiative of the new administration was an effective tax increase. The world had changed a great deal since 1920.

The administration's fiscal stringency persisted in 1954. In Eisenhower's State of the Union and Budget messages, he requested that the war-level excise taxes and the regular corporate income tax, which were due to expire in the coming year, be extended for at least a year and that no further tax reduction provisions be added to the 1954 revenue bill, which was to be presented shortly. The argument was that the $5 billion in reductions resulting from repeal of the excess profits tax, plus the reinstatement of the 1948 individual income tax rates, would put enough strain on the effort to balance the budget.[30] Few agreed with the president's request, but in the end he lost only on the excise taxes. Congress was determined to reduce excise taxes from their war levels, and the consensus this time included Reed, Majority Leader Martin, and the Democratic side of the House. Only a few staunch fiscal conservatives resisted. The administration was finally forced to relent, although it was successful in cutting back on the

reductions as the bill worked its way through Congress. The revenue loss was limited to an estimated $1 billion.

The 1954 Tax Code. The administration was much more successful with passage of the Internal Revenue Code of 1954. Work on this bill, which entirely rewrote the federal income tax code for the first time since its initial passage in 1913, began early in 1953. To review, analyze, and revise the law, it was broken down into fifty major areas, and teams of three to sixteen staff members from Treasury, the Joint Committee on Taxation, the House Office of Legislative Counsel, and the Office of the Chief Counsel of the Internal Revenue Service were assigned to each section. These groups were given the responsibility for proposing technical and policy changes and were in constant contact with executive agencies, outside groups, and the staffs of Ways and Means and Finance. At the same time these committees were meeting, Ways and Means held public hearings on forty specific topics that overlapped the work of the committees. Based on internal committee reports and to a lesser extent, on information gathered during hearings, final decisions on the policy revisions to be included in the formal administration proposals were made by top Treasury Department officials and the long-time staff director of the Joint Committee on Internal Revenue Taxation, Colin Stam. The list of major recommendations comprised twenty-five proposals. Eisenhower underscored the need for major tax revision in his 1954 State of the Union message on January 7 and made specific recommendations in his Budget message later in the month. In the meantime Treasury officials began meeting first with Republican members of Ways and Means and then with the whole committee in executive session.[31]

The result of this careful planning and drawn-out process was that the large majority of the administration's proposals were accepted. One reason for this acceptance was undoubtedly the nature of the recommendations. Although Eisenhower was later to proclaim proudly that: "The new law also closes more than 50 loopholes," the only real source of revenue saving in the bill was the extension of the 52 percent corporate income tax rate. The "price" for this was a slew of revenue-losing provisions that, not unlike those of the 1951 Revenue Act, handed out benefits to a wide range of groups and individuals. Although at that time even crude estimates of the incidence of tax reduction provisions were not available, judging from current knowledge (see chapter 14 below), the benefits were widespread. Of particular importance to taxpayers with moderate incomes were the following: liberalized definitions of exemptions to include unrelated but financially de-

pendent individuals and children over nineteen who are full-time students; increased deductibility of medical expenses; a new tax credit for retirement income; a new deduction for child care expenses; formalization of the existing IRS practice of not including employer contributions to employee health plans as income; exemption of health and accident benefits and sick pay; exclusion of scholarship income; exclusion of combat pay; and the deductibility of interest on installment purchases. For those at the upper levels of the income scale, the amount of income that could be deducted as charitable donations was increased, both a credit and an exclusion for dividend income were created, and certain partnerships were allowed the option of being taxed as corporations.

The wealthy also benefited from a number of provisions aiding businesses, the major ones being significant increases in depreciation allowances, extension of the period in which operating losses can offset profits, and extension of depletion allowances. However, the gains for corporations did not offset the extension of basic corporate rates, at least not in the first year. The tax bill officially sanctioned a number of tax reduction provisions, several of which had been promulgated earlier as IRS rules and all of which were expected to have little initial impact on revenues. Some, however, such as the exclusion of employer contributions to health care plans, now account for enormous loss of revenue. According to estimates by the Joint Committee on Internal Revenue, more revenue reduction went to individuals than corporations, although if the dividend provisions are added to the corporate side, the balance shifts.[32] By any estimation, the bill was carefully balanced so that in some way nearly everyone who paid taxes benefited from it.

Because of the balance and spread of the benefits, almost all of the administration's recommendations were written into the House bill and subsequently enacted with little partisan discussion. Rather, the great debate in 1954 was concentrated on three provisions related to dividends, depreciation allowances, and a Democratic effort to increase tax reduction for the mass of taxpayers either by increasing the exemption level (then at $600) or by providing a flat tax credit to each taxpayer. As usual the bill was brought to the floor of the House under a closed rule that limited debate and disallowed any substantive amendments. The Democrats planned a recommittal vote that stipulated that a new bill should delete the dividend provisions and the new methods of calculating depreciation and include an increased exemption of $700.

The vote was going to be close. Three days before it, therefore, Eisenhower made a broadcast supporting the bill and implied that he would veto any act including an increase in exemptions. To support his

position he brought out an old chestnut reminiscent of Cochran's arguments in 1894 and the wartime rationalizations for lower exemptions:

> When the time comes to cut income taxes still more, let's cut them. But I do not believe that the way to do it is to excuse millions of taxpayers from paying any income tax at all . . . every real American is proud to carry his share of any burden . . . I simply do not believe for one second that anyone privileged to live in this country wants someone else to pay his fair and just share of the cost of his Government.[33]

The vote was almost completely along partisan lines, and the Democrats lost 210 to 204, being able to convince only 8 of the 14 Republicans they needed to support recommittal.

The fight threatened to be even closer in the Senate, where the Republicans had only a single-vote advantage. This led Senator Millikin to suggest a compromise on the floor that reduced the amount of the dividend exclusion and credit and added a proposal for a $20 reduction for each taxpayer and dependent as a strategy to head off Democratic efforts to completely eliminate the dividend provisions and increase exemptions. This strategy, worked out in a Republican caucus, was based on the assumption that the Senate would defeat the $20 reduction but the Republicans could still argue that they had voted for general tax reduction, thus establishing a basis for rejecting an exemption increase. The strategy worked almost perfectly, with votes closely following party lines. The only exception was that, by a surprisingly lopsided vote, the Senate went farther on the dividend provision and completely deleted the dividend credit, rather than reducing it from 10 to 5 percent as Millikin had proposed. It was later restored at 4 percent in the Conference Committee, however—an outcome probably anticipated by the Republicans, since even Millikin supported deletion on the floor vote.[34] Thus, the final bill was very close to the president's request, including a reduced but still substantial break for dividend income, higher rates of depreciation, and the corporate rate extension, but not the increased exemption level sought by the Democrats.

The 1954 revenue bill is typical of postwar tax legislation in several important respects. The bill was long and complicated, and it made alterations in a large number of provisions. However, even though this bill was a major renovation of the entire tax code (the existing code still bears its title), later bills would become even more complex and comprehensive. Although the reasons for this complexity will be reviewed in

more detail later, part of the explanation is certainly the fact that more people in a wider variety of circumstances were now affected by the income tax. Prior to the war there was little need for child care provisions or a retirement credit because most people affected by such rules did not pay any income taxes. Moreover, the stakes of the game had increased for those with higher incomes. When the top marginal rate is 25 percent, whether 20 or 30 percent of adjusted gross income can be deducted as charitable giving does not make that much difference. When the rates are 91 percent, however, it does.

Finally, the U.S. economy had become much more complex by the 1950s, and the rudimentary laws of the early income tax were no longer sufficient. In 1913 there was no social security or unemployment or health insurance, let alone employer contributions to such plans. By 1950 the laws reflected the existence of these programs, and decisions had to be made about how such income, or income-in-kind, should be treated. Similarly, while organizational forms were always complex (perhaps partly in response to the tax laws), they had become much more complicated by midcentury. To match the complexity, the code needed to distinguish between corporations, corporations with income earned abroad, partnerships, holding companies, closely held corporations, and a wide variety of tax-exempt and partially tax-exempt organizations. Complex organizations lead to complex sources and flows of income and costs, which in turn lead to demands for different treatment. Although one interpretation of this situation is that each type of group and organization uses arguments about differential status solely to gain exclusive benefits, another is that such laws are simply based on honest efforts to treat different cases fairly relative to others. Either way, the result is bound to be a long and complex tax code.

Out of the maze of complex changes proposed in the 1954 act, a very restricted set of important issues became the focus of the main political battle. Most of the legislators voting on this bill knew very little about the vast majority of its provisions, and clearly many of these provisions were never mentioned in public debate. Those who subscribe to ideal legislative models of rational deliberation and decision would have been disappointed by the 1954 proceedings. Most decisions were made behind closed doors, initiated by appointed experts unaccountable to voters or legislators. On the other hand, at a different level the parties had an opportunity to express and act on some important differences. How typical this procedure was, and whether such partisan confrontations are pragmatically effective forms of opposition or merely symbolic distancing, will be discussed in subsequent chapters.

Finally, as in 1948 and 1951, the bill added a range of attractive

benefits that appealed to a wide range of individuals and organizations. The bill offered benefits to groups aligned with both political parties and provided individual politicians with a list of provisions that could be used when facing diverse constituencies. In short, there was an acceleration of the tendency that always exists in taxation to generate consensus by giving away the store. In earlier periods the benefits were limited by the range of constituents affected and by the relatively simpler structure of the code. As the number of those affected increased and the code became more complex, the Christmas tree grew.

The Years of Restraint. The 1954 Internal Revenue Code marked the last significant tax legislation for eight years. In 1955 the administration requested that no tax cuts be enacted. Although Eisenhower expressed the hope that such cuts would be possible in the future, all the administration's actions were against any further revenue legislation, with the exception of some minor changes in the treatment of small-business income. In both 1955 and 1957, Democrats made an effort to lower taxes. First there was a belated attempt to extend the debate of 1954 by proposing a flat tax reduction of $20 ($10 for dependents) and repeal of the reduction of the new depreciation rates. The bill narrowly survived in the House on an almost strictly partisan vote in which the whole Virginia delegation, following the advice of Senator Byrd, crossed party lines and voted with the Republicans.[35] However, the votes of four conservative Democrats were enough to defeat the bill in the Senate. The argument of the administration was that the tax reduction would lead to further deficits and set "us right back on the reckless road of inflation."[36] That argument never changed, and to understand its role in maintaining the status quo, it is necessary to understand how expenditures had changed from earlier periods.

Figure 7.1 portrays the shifts in federal expenditures and receipts from the inception of the individual income tax onward. The trend in expenditures helps explain both the longest moratorium on legislation since 1913 and the higher levels of individual and corporate income taxes that this inaction sustained. After World War I, the decline in income tax rates, and thus in the amount of revenue raised, corresponds to a return to expenditure levels varying only slightly from the prewar levels. As outlined in chapter 5, the budget surpluses of that period sustained tax-cutting efforts. The increase in expenditures and growth in deficits of the 1930s are somewhat distorted by presenting expenditures as a percentage of GNP because of the precipitous drop in GNP between 1929 and 1933. However, spending did increase steadily and dramatically in the thirties, more than tripling between 1929 and

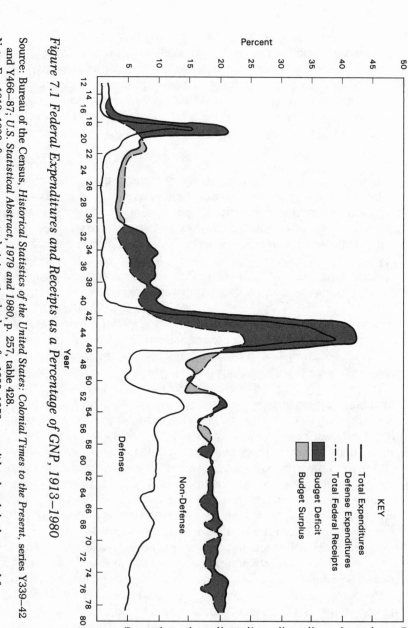

Figure 7.1 Federal Expenditures and Receipts as a Percentage of GNP, 1913–1980

Source: Bureau of the Census, *Historical Statistics of the United States: Colonial Times to the Present*, series Y339–42 and Y466–87; *U.S. Statistical Abstract, 1979 and 1980*, p. 257, table 428.
Note: For 1913–1928, figures represent administrative budgets; for 1929–1953, consolidated cash budgets; and for 1954–1980, unified budgets.

1939. The deficits provided the outgoing Hoover administration and Roosevelt with the motivation for the only legislated peacetime increase in either corporate or individual income taxes prior to 1982. The increases were minor in terms of the revenue generated; most of the growth in federal receipts came from excise tax increases passed against the wishes of the Roosevelt administration.

Massive changes in expenditures and deficits occurred during World War II. Defense needs absorbed most of the increases in both world wars, but even a larger amount in World War II (85.7 percent of the budget in 1945). Yet there was a critical difference in the postwar expenditure patterns. They started similarly, although the time frame for World War II was more extended, with the period from 1919 to 1921 corresponding to the period from 1945 to 1950. In each period there was a sharp decrease in defense spending, followed by a leveling off. In 1922, however, expenditures dropped significantly and a revenue surplus was created, whereas in 1951, with the Korean invasion, expenditures increased sharply. By 1953 defense expenditures had more than doubled from their postwar low, and the budget was again in deficit. With the end of the Korean War, defense expenditures declined, but because of the cold war, the decline did not approach the levels set in 1939 or 1950. Rather, defense consistently absorbed close to 10 percent of GNP between 1955 and 1964.

During the same period, the domestic spending levels reached during the New Deal were maintained as a percentage of GNP, while increasing dramatically in absolute dollar terms. For the years 1933 to 1939, average domestic expenditures were $6.32 billion, or 8.18 percent of GNP; for 1955 to 1960, the same category averaged $37.06 billion, 8.25 percent of GNP. The Eisenhower commitment to domestic spending took two forms. The first, as shown in his 1954 budget, was a genuine commitment to education, health, and highways. This led Holmans to remark:

> In recommending the expenditure of Federal funds for school building and the extension of health insurance . . . President Eisenhower was pursuing a policy which bore considerable resemblance to that of President Truman in 1949 and after. . . . This was an ambitious programme of social welfare and public investment; in this respect 1956 marked the zenith of the influence of "modern Republicanism" in the Eisenhower administration.[37]

This level of spending was attacked in Congress in early 1957 by a coalition of Republicans and conservative Democrats, and many pro-

grams requested by the administration were not passed. This conservative bloc made it even more imperative for Eisenhower to advance the notion of a balanced budget, which he did in his 1956 State of the Union message and all subsequent major economic addresses: "Under conditions of peacetime prosperity that now exist we can never justify going further into debt to give ourselves a tax cut at the expense of our children. . . . a tax cut can be deemed justifiable only when it will not unbalance the budget."[38]

With the recession of 1957–1958, domestic spending increased rapidly because of an automatic increase in transfer payments (primarily unemployment benefits and agricultural subsidies), and also because of increases in housing subsidies and an extension of unemployment benefits advanced by the administration to combat the recession. The combined effect of these spending increases and the anticipation of lower tax collections allowed the administration to head off a proposal by Senator Douglas that taxes should be reduced as a countercyclical policy initiative. Although there was significant support for such action in the country, the new Secretary of the Treasury, Clinton Anderson, reached an agreement with the House and Senate leadership that, because of the threat of deficits, no tax legislation should be passed. Following the Finance Committee's rejection of Douglas' request for hearings, an amendment reducing taxes $50 per taxpayer and cutting excise taxes, which he tried to attach to a floor bill, was easily defeated by a vote of 65 to 23. The issue of further tax reduction was subsequently dropped completely when the deficits of 1958 and 1959 became a reality. Throughout the period, as under Truman, tax reduction was warded off by a firm administration. Although the Truman administration placed greater emphasis on the equity derived from a progressive tax structure, in each administration the fear of deficit-induced inflation played a prominent role. That philosophy changed abruptly in the next two decades, which were marked by simultaneous efforts to reform and reduce income taxes.

Summary and Conclusion

An essential feature of postwar revenue policy is the overriding role of economic factors in policy debates. The most important common factor in the tax policies of the Truman and Eisenhower administrations was the desire to keep deficits down and thus, at least in theory, control inflation. Since expenditures in both domestic and nondomestic areas were at historic peacetime highs, the period was characterized by restraint in tax cutting. At various times the administrations stood

against one of the congressional parties or both in their efforts to halt tax reductions. What is curious and somewhat ironic in this period is the extent to which the initial issues and fears concerning the income tax had shifted. Although Truman took exception to the immediate postwar tax reduction on equity grounds, it is impossible to tell how this consideration weighed against his resolution to balance the budget while also promoting added spending for Fair Deal programs. In the Eisenhower administration there is little evidence of concern for vertical equity; if vertical equity had been an issue, there probably would have been disproportionate and hence regressive tax cuts based on the premise that the structure was too progressive as it stood. The point is that there was little debate of the sort that arose under the Mellon regime or in the early Roosevelt years, when the distribution of wealth and income and its effect on investment and incentives were the heart of the matter.

Two conditions affected this transition. First, by the end of World War II the responsibility for economic stability and growth had been irreversibly placed on the shoulders of the federal government. Second, the magnitude of taxes had grown enormously, as had the perception that shifts in the magnitude and distribution of the tax burden would have an important impact on economic activity. The increased responsibility of government and the perception of the tax system as an important economic policy tool shifted the focus of the discussion from who could and should bear the burden to the questions of timing and the effects of tax cuts and increases.

The irony in this transition is that just as the income tax was becoming a critical policy issue, the classic academic theories of the income tax were becoming irrelevant. Questions of sacrifice, benefit, or ability to pay were now being fought out in the much narrower context of a revenue policy that was primarily directed to reaching the right level of total taxation. Even today's optimal tax theories, which envision elaborate trade offs between equity and efficiency, fail to consider the central issues that drove tax politics during this period. None of these theories are embedded in a macro model, and thus levels of spending and inflation and the fear or acceptance of deficits are never taken into consideration. It is not coincidental that it was also during this period that debates over the classical prescriptive theories were replaced by analysis of the proper structure of the tax code, which meant consideration of the work of Henry Simons. By the 1960s interest in Simons' work had reached a point where actions began to be taken in his name and "tax reform" efforts were guided by his tax base standard.

Chapter 8.
The 1960s
From Tax Stimulus
to Tax Reform

The Eisenhower years stabilized the income tax system for the first time since its creation. The 1954 Internal Revenue Code went essentially unchanged for eight years. Legislation in the sixties was also relatively moderate, although a number of important innovations were introduced, and the tax reform acts of 1964 and 1969 were major pieces of tax legislation, consisting of dozens of major revisions and hundreds, if not thousands, of minor and technical changes. In the seventies, with the simultaneous problems of general economic decline and double-digit inflation, pressure for change was immense and a series of major tax bills were passed with a regularity and speed approaching that of wartime legislation. The tax bills of the sixties and seventies share several characteristics: (1) with one minor exception, all called for tax cuts, usually for both individuals and corporations; (2) they were often touted as "tax reforms"; and (3) with each succeeding bill the tax code became more complex, more cumbersome, but also more adaptable to diverse policy goals.

The Kennedy Tax Bills

Shortly after John Kennedy's inauguration, discussions about tax legislation began under the leadership of Douglas Dillon, Secretary of the Treasury, and Stanley Surrey, a Harvard law professor appointed as Assistant Secretary of the Treasury for tax policy. Surrey had a clear view of the general direction of tax revision. Based on Simons' theory of a comprehensive tax base, the basic goal was to eliminate or reduce the tax loss caused by "structural" tax reduction provisions and use the revenue gained to lower the rates for both individuals and corporations. The basic outlines of this reform effort were worked out by April 1961. Some of the "loophole"-closing reforms provided by the Treasury

bureaucracy were based on studies and recommendations made during the Eisenhower years. However, the faltering state of the economy and Kennedy's desire to take some dramatic action to fulfill his campaign promise to get the nation moving economically led to a two-stage strategy: a quick, simple bill with an emphasis on economic stimulus, and then major tax reform. The problem of long-term decline was traced by Kennedy's economic advisors to slackening growth in productivity, which in turn was linked most importantly to declines in investment in industrial capacity. In later reports and testimony, the administration spokesmen presented data showing a drop in fixed investments for the years 1955 to 1960 (relative to 1947–1954) and a rate of investment just over half that of the European Economic Community (5.5 compared with 9.8 percent). In a chillingly accurate prediction, Dillon argued that without a reversal of this trend, the United Sates would lose its competitive edge in numerous markets.[1]

The action the administration proposed, in an April 20, 1961, speech by Kennedy, was to give a direct tax credit to corporations for investing in capital equipment. The plan was to enact this investment tax credit, along with a limited number of other changes, as soon as possible, with a major tax reform bill to follow in 1962 or 1963. As initially proposed, the administration bill requested an investment tax credit at either 6 or 15 percent for investment over, respectively, 50 and 100 percent of allowable depreciation. In this way the credit rewarded increases over past levels of investment at a higher rate than investment at normal levels. The major provisions to offset this revenue loss (estimated at $430–580 million in the first year) were: (1) repealing the dividend credit and exclusion that had been so controversial in the 1954 act; (2) withholding of dividends and interest at the source; (3) restricting certain forms of business deductions, particularly entertainment expenses; and (4) increasing taxation of American-owned foreign companies, whose profits at the time were taxed only when they were returned to the United States in the form of dividends.[2]

The proposals immediately ran into stiff opposition. The business community, having an underlying suspicion of the Kennedy administration, attacked all of these proposals in the press and in Ways and Means hearings held in May and June 1961. Business was split over the investment credit because it was viewed as a substitute for cuts and depreciation (which Kennedy had mentioned in the campaign) and because it favored large capital-intensive companies. Even some of these companies, such as AT&T, ended up opposing the credit. Organized labor, which had been so instrumental in Kennedy's victory, vehemently attacked both the investment credit and the unified de-

mand by business for liberal revisions in depreciation schedules, while applauding the other provisions. The hotel, restaurant, and entertainment industry and the unions representing workers in these industries teamed up to contest the changes proposed in deductible business expenses.[3]

The political battle over the bill was intense and partisan, but it also demonstrated the parallel abilities of the committee and congressional leadership at that time first to generate bills supported by a majority and then to hold that majority in line against attractive substitute bills and amendments. In this case, which is typical of most subsequent revenue legislation, majority support was ensured by (1) broadening the investment credit to cover excluded industries and all investment (by making it a flat 7 percent of new investment); (2) by pressing the administration to revise depreciation schedules as business requested; and (3) by eliminating the most offensive provisions, those increasing taxation of dividends and interest. In short, the bill was "bought" with greater tax reduction. Ways and Means, under the leadership of Wilbur Mills, broadened the investment credit, dropped repeal of the dividend deduction and credit, and then adjourned in August 1961, sending a clear message to the administration that depreciation revision was necessary before passage would be possible. The administration responded by publishing depreciation revisions for textiles in October and promising to complete other revisions by the summer of 1962. Floor action in March 1962 was short and highly partisan, with Republicans in the perverse position of opposing the investment tax credit. In the end, the House leadership held most Democrats in line. Thanks to their substantial numerical advantage, the bill was passed.[4]

The Senate Finance Committee further sweetened the pot by dropping dividend and interest withholding (which were in the House bill) and liberalizing the provisions affecting foreign corporate taxes and business deductions. These changes, in conjunction with the liberalized depreciation schedules promulgated in July, ensured passage of the bill. As presented to the full Senate after a 9–2 vote in Finance, the bill had broad, moderate support, being opposed only by several fiscal conservatives fearful of deficits and a handful of liberals opposed to dilution of the provisions mentioned above, and the distributive effects of the bill. The result was that the Senate floor debate, which included roll call votes on nearly all the major provisions of the bill, produced no substantive changes other than Finance Committee–sponsored amendments. Of thirteen noncommittee amendments, only one very minor amendment on a business deduction was accepted. Most were defeated by 25 to 30 votes.[5] The conference committee essentially

accepted the Senate version with minor changes. In contrast to the administration's initial proposals, which would have slightly increased revenues, the final bill was predicted by the Joint Committee on Internal Revenue to lose $1.25 billion in fiscal year 1963.[6] Nevertheless, Kennedy signed the bill in October 1962, praising it as "a good start" and emphasizing both its stimulative effect and its contributions to fairness, such as tightening up on expense accounts. Even in this relatively modest bill, provisions pleasing to almost anyone could be found.

Even though it was the first major revenue bill in eight years, passage of the Revenue Act of 1962 did not stir up the excitement that might have been expected, because Congress was looking ahead to the major reform bill that was pending. The administration used the upcoming bill as a prod to move the 1962 act through Congress. As the year wore on, administration pronouncements on the total revenue effects of the forthcoming tax reform changed from vague and noncommittal statements to a firm commitment that revenue-raising tax reform measures would be more than offset by tax reductions. For example, in his January 1962 Economic Message, President Kennedy remarked: "Later this year, I shall present to Congress a major program of tax reform. This broad program will reexamine tax rates and the definition of the income tax base. It will be aimed at simplification of our tax structure, the equal treatment of equally situated persons, and the strengthening of incentives for individual effort and productive investment."[7]

By June the administration had made up its mind on the total revenue effects to be built into the act, deciding that a tax cut was appropriate. In a June 7 press conference, Kennedy remarked that the bill would entail "a reduction in personal and corporate income tax rates which will not be wholly offset by other reforms."[8] In a major economic address in August, which was intended in part to pressure Congress to enact the 1962 Revenue Act, Kennedy stated flatly that such "a bill will be presented to Congress for action next year. It will include an across the board, top to bottom cut in both corporate and personal income taxes." The decision to present it was based on the twin premises that inflation was "no longer a serious threat" and that "the facts of the matter are that our present tax system is a drag on economic recovery and economic growth."[9]

Kennedy's economic planners agreed on the need for the tax cut. By this time they were predicting a sliding economy in 1962, and perhaps beyond, and were still very much committed to a plan for long-term economic growth. The importance of stimulating growth and using and

weighting the tax system toward this end was apparently accepted among this mostly liberal group as early as 1960. In a revealing passage discovered by Ron King in an October 1960 letter from Richard Musgrave (a leading tax expert) to Walter Heller (later head of Kennedy's Council of Economic Advisers), Musgrave wrote:

> To the extent that changes in tax structure are needed to encourage investment, they should not necessarily be ruled out because they interfere with tax equity. In some cases, growth may be the overriding consideration. However, we should be extremely careful to make sure that growth considerations will not be used to increase new loopholes without doing much to help growth. Therefore, any departure from equity must have clear justification in terms of probable effectiveness with regard to growth.[10]

By the second half of 1962, with inflation under control, Kennedy agreed to a deficit as long as it was under Eisenhower's largest deficit ($12.4 billion). The necessity of altering the tax system to create economic incentives was unmistakably reinforced in the 1963 *Economic Report of the President*, which could almost have been written by Andrew Mellon. Kennedy opened his remarks on taxation by stressing that "the citizen serves his country's interests by supporting income tax reductions." Although one would imagine that for most people justifications were unnecessary, Kennedy nevertheless went on to explain: "Tax reductions set off a process that can bring gains for everyone, gains won by marshalling resources that would otherwise stand idle. . . . [T]he tax deterrents to private initiatives have too long held economic activity in check." Tax reduction would address three major problems: inadequate markets, investment incentives, and jobs. In what must have been an intentional omission, there is not a single reference to equity, fairness, tax incidence, or even "loopholes."[11] In this respect, even Andrew Mellon was less single-minded than John Kennedy.

The administration's public emphasis on economic growth and incentives was at odds with some of the actual proposals it introduced in January 1963. It is not clear, however, that these proposals were completely serious, and when they were later dropped, there was little protest from the administration. The proposals called for net tax cuts of $11.3 billion over fiscal years 1964 and 1965: rate cuts to individuals would account for $11 billion and cuts in the corporate tax rates for $2.6 billion, while offsetting reforms would net up to $2.3 billion. The top

individual rate was to be cut from 91 to 65 percent, and at the bottom the rate was to be lowered from 20 to 14 percent. Corporate rates were to drop from 52 to 47 percent for large companies.

Among the most important revenue-gaining reform measures were major changes in capital gains. On the one hand, the administration proposed lower effective rates on business capital gains and a reduced percentage of long-term gains that would be included as income (from 50 to 40 percent). However, these losses were to be more than offset by requiring that long-term gains be held one year rather than six months and by shifting the base value for capital gains acquired by inheritance to the price for assets when purchased rather than the (still) current method of basing them on their value at the time of death. Other major revenue-gaining provisions were reduction of the exclusion for income earned abroad; repeal of the dividend credit and exclusion; reduced benefits from mineral depletion (particularly oil and gas); increased taxes on foreign corporate income; major changes in the treatment of itemized deductions, essentially allowing only deductions that exceed 5 percent of adjusted gross income (i.e., setting a "floor" level); repeal of the exclusion of up to $100 per week in sick pay; and the elimination of certain complex real estate shelters.

At the same time, the administration proposed increasing or creating new tax reduction provisions in the areas of child care, tax treatment of the elderly, moving expenses, income averaging, charitable contributions, and research and development. A minimum standard deduction option would aid primarily low-income taxpayers, who tend not to itemize deductions. As one might have reasonably predicted, given the steady drum beat for tax reduction, nearly all of the provisions that would have gained revenue were either dropped or severely gutted, first by Ways and Means and then by Finance, while nearly all the provisions conferring additional benefits were enacted and in several cases increased above administration recommendations. In the end, structural "reform" would lead not to $3.3 billion in revenue gains, as the administration requested, but to a slight revenue loss. Of the nineteen administration proposals that would have increased taxes, only four were passed; of twenty-seven revenue-lossing proposals, sixteen and a half were enacted.[12]

The basic form of the bill was set in the Ways and Means Committee under the powerful direction of Chairman Wilbur Mills, acting with the cooperation of John Byrnes (R-Wis.), the senior Republican on the committee. Secretary Dillon staunchly defended the administrative program in hearings held by the committee in the summer of 1963. He particularly emphasized the coordinated nature of the capital gains

changes and the general revision in the treatment of deductible items so that only expenses above "floor" percentages of adjusted gross income would count as deductions. This reform was in line with a basic tenet of the comprehensive tax base, which held that such deductions should apply only in cases of extreme expense and hardship. Although complicating the code somewhat, the effect would have been to reduce greatly the number of people itemizing deductions and to eliminate the need to make other revisions aimed at stopping abuses of these deductions. It would have been felt mostly by those at the middle- and upper-middle-income levels. The new minimum standard deduction was designed partially to offset the higher taxes that would result.[13]

The committee was not persuaded by these and most of the other administration arguments. It unbundled the capital gains package and passed a lower rate of 40 percent (for assets held over two years), lowered the alternative rate from 25 to 21 percent, and added a provision allowing unlimited carry-over of capital losses. It dropped the administration's controversial proposal for taxing capital gains at death. Thus, it chose those provisions that taxed capital gains less and ignored those that would have increased the tax rate. The floor on deductions was also dropped, and instead each type of deduction was considered separately by the committee. Medical deductions were liberalized for the elderly, while casualty losses were limited to an amount over $100. A major revenue-gaining change specified that taxes other than state income, sales, and property taxes were no longer deductible. The committee balked at dropping the dividend credit and exclusion, giving the administration less than half a loaf by repealing the 5 percent credit but doubling the exclusion amount from $50 to $100. The only other revenue-gaining provision in the committee bill was a tighter provision for sick pay. On the other hand, the committee went along with almost all the administration's revenue-reducing requests in the areas of child care, moving expenses, minimum standard deductions, income averaging, and so on. It also lowered bracket rates from the 1948 range of 20 to 91 percent to a new range of 14 to 70 percent. In other words, the 1964 Ways and Means bill was extremely generous in tax reductions and scattered those reductions across the entire income spectrum, leaving no one untouched by the bounty of tax reform.

Wilbur Mills was renowned for constructing bills that succeeded on the House floor. After an embarrassing floor defeat early in his chairmanship, he rarely lost a vote, procedural or otherwise. John Manley, who has written the definitive work on the Ways and Means Committee and on Mills himself, attributes this success to Mills's efforts to enlist support from committee members from both parties, to his careful

nurturing of the conservative southern Democrats who could provide the margin for victory or defeat on any bill, and to his ability to tailor his bills to the conservative majorities that ruled the House during most of his tenure.[14] However, another explanation for his success, which is completely compatible with the factors mentioned by Manley, is that bills were constructed in such a way that they provided a broad range of immediate benefits important enough to powerful constituencies that they outweighed any negative factors. For this reason only those with a strong ideological commitment to some general philosophy (be it equity on the left or fiscal responsibility on the right) would vote against the bill. The rest, including the large block of pragmatists in the middle, would be unable to resist.

Mills's opening statement in the two-day floor debate allowed under a closed rule echoed administration philosophy and proved irresistible: "The purpose of this tax reduction and revision bill is to loosen the constraints which the present federal taxation imposes on the American economy." His statement made no mention of equity.[15] The Republicans opposed the bill almost exclusively on the grounds that it was fiscally irresponsible, risking large deficits and inflation in a period of economic expansion. There was little mention throughout the debate of the dozens of structural changes included in the bill. The recommittal motion, designed to elicit the maximum of popular support and provide a campaign vehicle for the next election, required repealing the tax reduction if spending went above specified levels in 1964 and 1965. Mills had counted votes well, however, and the Democratic majority held, with only 26 defections (24 southerners) against an almost perfectly united Republican opposition. That opposition was tied to a spending condition; by supporting recommittal, one could vote for both the principle of tax reduction and balanced budgets. When it came to final passage, 48 Republicans joined in voting for the bill and thus for economic growth tied to tax reduction.[16]

The Senate Finance Committee hearings on the bill spanned three months in the fall of 1963 and included testimony from 132 witnesses. The most important witness was Secretary Dillon, whose only significant objection to the House bill, which he somehow managed to characterize as "generally in accord with the President's proposals," was elimination of the capital gains provisions because of the imbalance created by not changing capital gains at death.[17] Finance obliged on a 12–5 vote but also took the hint and added significantly to the revenue loss. Among other provisions, it passed changes allowing deduction of gasoline taxes, increasing the investment tax credit, authorizing deductibility of interest on installment purchases (which then meant little

revenue loss), excluding $20,000 of capital gains on the sale of homes owned by the elderly, and providing that income earned on royalties on iron ore holdings be taxed as capital gains. When they were finished, revenue-losing "reforms" were over a billion dollars and were offset by revenue gains of over $500 million—a far cry from the net revenue gain of $3.3 billion requested by the administration.

Senate floor action was heated, but the Finance bill emerged with only minor changes. Opposition was led by liberals, who for the only time in the two-year debate over the bill attacked the provision on equity grounds. Crucial votes were registered and liberal positions defeated on capital gains, depletion changes (which were in neither the House nor the Senate bill), dividend credits, and exemption levels. For the first of many times, amendments establishing credits for education were proposed by Senator Ribicoff (D-Conn.) but rejected in several forms. In the interest of speeding debate, Chairman Long conceded a number of amendments that he would later give up in Conference Committee. Final passage was bipartisan, with a vote of 77 to 21.[18]

The Conference Committee favored the House version in most instances and cut back the revenue losses so that structural gains slightly outweigh losses. The revenue effects of the bill and other major postwar tax bills are presented in table 8.1 as they were estimated after passage by the Joint Committee on Taxation (earlier called the Joint Committee on Internal Revenue). Estimates of revenue effects sometimes vary between Treasury and the Joint Committee; because of Treasury's more partisan nature, the latter are usually considered more objective and have proven more reliable over the years. Note that extensions of existing temporary provisions (often involving rate reductions or surcharges) are included. Changes in the standard deduction are listed separately when possible because in theory they have an effect on structural issues (i.e., deductions), but are often considered a part of the basic rate system because in practice they provide a tax exempt floor, as does the personal exemption. It is apparent from the table that for all the technical analysis and detailed discussion in Treasury and the tax committees on structural provisions, the revenue effects of changes in the basic rate components overwhelm changes in structural provisions, even for the major reform or revision acts depicted. As will be shown in subsequent chapters, however, the cumulative effects of structural changes are not inconsequential: structural provisions currently provide tax reductions totaling approximately 60 percent of the revenues collected.

The rate reductions were accomplished by applying across-the-board reductions of existing rates ranging from 20 to 30 percent. Because of

Table 8.1 Estimated Revenue Changes, Major Postwar Revenue Acts (in billions of dollars)

Revenue Act	1954	1964		1969[a]		1975[a]		1976		1978		1981	
Fiscal Year	1955	1964	1965	1970	1971	1974	1975	1977	1978	1979	1980	1982	1983
Structural gains	0	+.9	+1.1	+4.2	+5.0	—	+2.0	+3.0	+3.5	+1.2	+5.4	+2.4	+4.3
Structural losses	-1.4	-.6	-.7	-.5	-.6	—	-4.0	-2.7	-4.7	-1.7	-8.0	-14.0	-29.0
Standard deduction	0	-.3	-.3	0	-1.2	—	-2.6	-4.1	-4.5	[b]	[b]	0	0
Individual rates	0	-6.0	-9.2	+2.0	-3.7	-8.1	-6.7	-10.1	-4.8	-15.6	-27.5	-25.8	-65.7
Corporate rates	+1.2	-1.3	-2.2	0	0	—	-1.5	-1.7	-1.2	-3.2	-7.4	-.1	-.4
Total revenue change	-.2	-7.3	-11.3	+5.7	-.5	-8.1	-12.8	-15.6	-11.7	-19.3	-37.5	-37.5	-90.8

Source: Estimates of Joint Committee on Taxation following final passage of the bills. Estimates include extensions and making permanent prior temporary provisions.

Note: "Rates" include rate schedule and bracket changes, general credits and surcharges, exemptions, low income allowances, and earned income credits. "Structural" includes everything else except changes in the standard deduction, which is listed separately.

[a]Calendar year estimates.
[b]Not available as a separate estimate. Included in rate changes.

the minimum standard deduction and the fact that the lowest rates were cut approximately 30 percent, total tax reduction for the bottom income groups (below $5,000) was significantly greater than for those in the middle and upper income ranges. Thus, the overall impact of the personal cuts was somewhat progressive, although essentially proportional for middle-income groups.[19] Whether this would still be true if it were possible to factor in the incidence of corporate reductions is not clear. It is also unclear in what sense this bill can be labeled a tax reform. If Simons' comprehensive tax base notion is used as the standard—and in numerous conferences, panel discussions, and writings by Treasury tax experts, that standard was invoked—in terms of final provisions, the 1964 act moved the U.S. tax system still further from the baseline Simons established. The only tax reduction devices of any consequence that were eliminated were the dividend credit (but not exclusion) and the deductibility of state excise and license taxes. On the other hand, several new provisions were added (moving expense deduction, income averaging, minimum standard deduction, and capital gains exclusion on the sale of homes by the elderly), and many more were liberalized. Although the administration bill as originally proposed would have had a greater effect on simplifying the code and widening the base, the unmistakable emphasis it placed on economic growth through tax reduction set Congress on the path to broad-based reductions, not tax reform.

The Tax Reform Act of 1969

A major tax bill is an exhausting exercise for all concerned, and after the 1964 act interest in tax legislation subsided for several years. By all accounts President Johnson had little interest in tax policy per se and even less interest in raising taxes to pay for an unpopular war. By 1968, however, with defense expenditures increasing rapidly and with large deficits in the last several years, Johnson was forced to ask Congress for a tax increase in the form of an extension of excise taxes that were due to expire and a temporary 10 percent surcharge on corporate and individual income taxes. Congress was unenthusiastic. Conservatives were angry about the deficits, which they attributed to wasteful Great Society programs, and liberals were against a "war tax" to pay for a war they bitterly opposed. Wilbur Mills, reflecting the conservative point of view, bottled up the bill in Ways and Means, holding out for an increase tied to a spending cut. The most intense lobbying for the bill came from the business community, troubled by fears of inflation, a negative

balance of payments, and, finally, a crisis in gold induced by inflation and trade deficits. It was the last which finally led to action in the Senate, where the tax increase was attached as an amendment to another bill. This forced Mills's hand, and the bill was introduced in the House, but with the provision that the reduction would go into effect only if spending was cut $6 billion below projected spending levels. It finally passed both houses in late 1968, ten months after Johnson's "emergency" request. It was to apply only to 1969 and was expected to raise taxes $10.9 billion. For the fourth time in the brief history of the income tax, a tax increase was induced by war.

Beginning in 1967, Treasury had been working on a major reform package that had been promised by the Johnson administration and was sought particularly by Congressional liberals, whose numbers grew after the 1968 election. However, the proposals that were to become the core of the massive Tax Reform Act of 1969 were held by the Johnson administration until the last minute. Following the election of Richard Nixon, an agreement was reached with Congress that the new Treasury officials would release the proposals without comment and later submit their own plan. Prior to release of the documents in January 1969, the outgoing Secretary of the Treasury, Joseph Barr, made a highly publicized speech warning of a "tax revolt" based on the inequities in the tax code, particularly the "loopholes" that permitted the very rich to avoid taxation. Employing a strategy used successfully by the Progressives forty years earlier, he listed some of the very wealthy individuals who paid no taxes at all.[20] The speech, combined with the Democratic proposals before Congress and the generally liberal congressional environment, set the stage for the first clearly liberal tax bill since 1936— and the last.

As in 1963, Ways and Means hearings were extensive, beginning in February and ending with four days of testimony on Nixon administration proposals submitted in April. Like most congressional hearings, though comprehensive, they conveyed little new information and few surprises. Although the Nixon proposals had an impact in some areas, the bill as finally enacted was very much a congressional bill built around the proposals worked out under the Johnson administration, some of which were also in the Nixon package. The bill as finally enacted is too extensive and touches on too many aspects of the tax code to consider here in great detail. The basic outline of the bill, however, and its differences from the 1964 act, can be shown by concentrating on changes in major provisions measured in terms of revenue.

Most of the changes originated in the Ways and Means bill, although

several were also included in Nixon's proposal. The Ways and Means bill called for general reduction in the rate schedules, partially offset initially by a six-month extension of the surcharge that was due to expire on December 31, 1969, but at 5 rather than the prevailing 10 percent. The committee also recommended increasing both the low-income allowance and the percentage standard deduction but recommended no changes in the personal exemption. The administration's proposals had not included rate schedule reductions, which it felt would produce too high a revenue loss, but they generally agreed with the other proposals, although they preferred a lower level for the standard deduction. In a 180-degree turn from the 1964 bill, both the administration and the House agreed to increase taxation on capital gains and to repeal the 7 percent investment credit. Moreover, in an effort to eliminate the prospect of wealthy individuals avoiding all taxation, which was well publicized after Barr's speech, the administration proposed a complex prevention scheme that would in effect override specific tax reduction provisions if they were used to exclude too much income from taxation. What was proposed, and later modified in the Senate, was to limit the total amount of income that could be excluded from four controversial sources that had been labeled "tax shelters" and to allow only 50 percent exclusion of that income.[21] In addition, total deductions would be reduced by the percentage of income that was ultimately exempted, thus in theory allocating deductions between that income on which tax is paid and that income which escapes taxation.[22]

The Ways and Means bill also included significant changes in complex provisions governing banks and savings institutions and, in what was to be the most controversial change finally enacted, increased taxes on mineral properties, particularly oil and gas. The latter issues were dealt with in the closed sessions of the committee in June and were passed with relative ease (18 to 7) after Mills and Byrnes agreed to vote for lower percentage depletion allowances (from 27.5 to 20.0 percent for oil and gas). The bill also made a host of other changes affecting charitable contributions, real estate depreciation, and "hobby farms." All of these areas had blossomed into fertile tax shelters under the careful cultivation of tax attorneys. Hobby farms remain among my personal favorites. The idea is for wealthy investors to buy farm properties and raise miscellaneous products and animals that qualify for capital gains. During the period of maturation (three years for steers, for example), the property operates at an excludable loss, which offsets other outside income. When the products are finally sold, the income is taxed at capital gains rates. Products with longer maturation periods

and some romantic appeal, such as trees, orange groves, avocados, cattle, and exotic breeds of buffalo, were most appealing. Hog farming was less popular.

The House committee, against the administration's advice, also took another shot at eliminating the tax-exempt status of interest on state and municipal bonds. To compensate for the expected losses to cities and states, tax-exempt status would be replaced by a guaranteed federal subsidy of the interest differential between taxable and tax-exempt bonds. Sensing the uncertainty of this subsidy, which would have required future appropriations, state and local politicians lobbied to defeat the provision and succeeded in having it dropped in the Finance and Conference committees. Thus, the longest-standing and most persistently opposed tax reduction provision survived once again. Other provisions would have fully taxed dividends and repealed the deduction for gasoline taxes. Typically, all the provisions that would have completely eliminated reduction mechanisms were later dropped in the Senate and in Conference.

The difference between 1969 and 1964 was that only a few revenue-losing provisions were enacted, and most of those accounted for small losses. In the process, however, several new benefit provisions were added to the code as a response to political issues of the day. The largest revenue losses came from a liberalization of the recently enacted income-averaging provisions ($300 million) and moving expense deductions ($110 million). New tax reduction provisions allowed accelerated (five-year) amortization of pollution control equipment, expenditures by railroads on rolling stock and grading and tunnel improvement, and renovations of rental property. The Senate added expenditures on coal mine safety equipment to this list. All these provisions originated in policy concerns of the time: tax benefits for pollution control were designed to mitigate the effects of new pollution regulations; railroad improvement and rental aid were central features of the liberal commitment to mass transit and housing; and coal mine safety was an important issue because of recent mining disasters. Finally, a Johnson Treasury proposal that returned to an old liberal idea first introduced by Andrew Mellon suggested a distinction between "earned" and "unearned" income, setting the maximum rate for the former at 50 percent. This "maximum tax" remained even after general rate reductions were dropped in the Senate; thus, the top marginal rates were 50 percent for earned income versus 70 percent for unearned.

Ways and Means finished work on the bill on July 30 with the goal of passing it before the August recess. As an indication of the haste of the process, in the middle of Rules Committee hearings on a closed rule for

the bill, it was discovered by the liberal Democratic Study Group that people with incomes between $7,000 and $13,000 who itemized deductions received very little in the way of tax breaks. In response, Mills hastily called together his committee during the luncheon break of the Rules Committee meeting and added rate cuts that totaled $2.5 billion for this group—an expensive lunch. With this change the rule was granted, and two days of floor debate were scheduled.

Although the bill did not make all of the sweeping changes desired by reform groups, its liberal nature and tone should not be underestimated. In five years the mood of the country and its leadership had changed considerably. Whereas in 1964 Mills had opened debate with an exhortation that taxes were stifling economic growth, he began the debate in 1969 with the comment that if congressmen were concerned over constituent reaction to provisions of the bill, they could "go back to their constituents" and tell them that "if they have been getting preferential tax treatment this legislation will help put them on a level with the less fortunate citizens in the community. Also they could tell the less fortunate taxpayers they are going to get tax relief."[23] The House seemed to agree with Mills because after pro forma votes on committee amendments and predictable rhetorical posturing on the oil depletion provisions, they refused to recommit by a vote of 78 to 345 and voted final passage by 395 to 30.[24]

The Senate made major changes in the bill both in Finance and, in an unusual turn of events, on the floor. Most of the Finance Committee changes relaxed the strict provisions passed by the House; thus, the Senate bill would have lost significantly more revenue than the House bill. The most critical issue in the Senate bill, rejected in Finance but passed over committee objections on the floor, changed the major tax cuts from rate reductions to an increase in the personal exemptions. This change, pushed by liberal Albert Gore, who was used to losing such votes, and the effect of significantly increasing the progressivity of the tax reduction and at the same time adding $2.25 billion to the revenue loss for 1970 and $3.75 billion to the loss for 1971. Gore successfully argued that the bill as written was weighted in favor of middle- and upper-income groups and slighted those who needed tax relief most. He also pointed out that the exemption no longer covered a subsistence income.[25]

Other changes in the Senate Finance bill also overrode reform provisions in the House bill. The most important ones that ultimately survived the Conference Committee were restoration of the gasoline tax deduction and dividend credit and elimination of the provision deleting tax-exempt securities. In response to heavy lobbying by business ex-

ecutives, aided by Secretary of the Treasury David M. Kennedy, who emphasized the bill's probusiness bias, Finance lightened the restrictions on capital gains and depletion. It also dropped the "maximum tax" provision that established a lower tax on earned income, but this was later restored on the Senate floor. Finally, in a major revision of the administration proposal to create a minimum tax, Finance altered the plan to tax excluded income which totaled more than 50 percent of real income. Instead it created a list of *preference items* (excluded dividends, capital gains, tax-exempt interest, the difference between percentage and cost mineral depletion, certain forms of depreciation, etc.) that when totaled were to be taxed at 10 percent after a $30,000 exemption. This provision remained in the bill and became the final answer to the problem of total tax avoidance by some wealthy individuals.

Floor action on the bill was hectic, with climactic votes and debate on the Gore exemption increase (which also adjusted increases in the standard and minimum deductions) and mineral depletion. The vote to raise the exemption from $600 to $800 was a surprisingly lopsided 58 to 37, with 10 moderate Republicans joining 48 Democrats in favor of the proposal. Finance Committee depletion provisions (reducing the current 27.5 percent allowance for gas and oil to 23.0 rather than the House's 20.0 percent) remained, as both votes to cut it further and votes to restore it to 27.5 percent were defeated. Several other amendments were adopted on floor votes. Ribicoff passed another tax credit for education (53 to 32), and the repeal of the investment credit was modified to exempt both the first $20,000 invested (helping small businesses) and investments in depressed areas. All of these provisions were later dropped in Conference. An amendment that survived both the floor and Conference was a provision extending dependent status (and thus an exemption) to foster children. In all 73 amendments were accepted (27 on roll call) and 38 defeated (33 on roll call).

The final Senate bill was estimated to contain about $3 billion more in tax reductions than the House bill. The president immediately declared the revenue loss extravagant and threatened a veto. To avoid that eventuality, the Conference Committee worked closely with Assistant Secretary Charles Walker, who supported less tax reduction. In a rush to complete the bill before the Christmas break, the conferees worked through the night of December 19, 1969, pushed for time even after three years of work on the bill. The final product was easily accepted by both houses and signed by the president on December 30. It was an artful compromise that accepted the basic Senate formula for tax reduction at a reduced level but restored or partially restored many of the structural House provisions, while dropping many of the Senate floor amendments that had conferred additional tax breaks. Those structural

provisions having the greatest effect on revenue are listed in table 8.2. The overall effect as published by the Joint Committee on Taxation is depicted in table 8.1. As can be seen, in contrast with all other bills, the reform provisions account for significantly more revenue change than adjustments in the rates.

Part of the explanation for this outcome was war expenses, although Vietnam had much less impact on government expenditures than previous wars (see figure 7.1). Probably more significant was the liberal atmosphere in the country. The Great Society programs in education,

Table 8.2 Major Structural Changes in the Tax Reform Act of 1969

	1970 Estimated Gain/Loss ($ millions)	
	Individuals	Corporations
Revenue-Gaining Provisions		
Repeal of investment credit	600	1,900
Maximum tax on preference income	290	300
Capital gains	225	105
Lowered mineral depletion	40	195
Reserve requirements for financial institutions	0	225
Treatment of mineral production payments	0	100
All others	25	200
Total gain	+ 1,180	+ 3,015
Revenue-Losing Provisions		
Income averaging	− 300	0
Moving expenses	− 110	0
5-year amortization of railroad property	0	− 105
All others	− 5	− 25
Total loss	− 415	− 130
Net structural change	+ 765	+ 2,885

Source: Joint Committee on Internal Revenue Taxation, *General Explanations of the Tax Reform Act of 1969.* (Washington, D.C.: Government Printing Office, 1969).

income support, health care, civil rights, and job programs preceded this legislation, and the large regulatory reforms in environmental protection and occupational health and safety lay ahead. This spate of liberal legislation lasted less than a decade, but the Tax Reform Act of 1969 fell right in the middle of that remarkable period. At any rate, the outcome of the bill was certainly in the liberal direction. The Joint Committee on Taxation estimated the incidence of the tax changes as highly progressive: tax liabilities were reduced an average of 69.8 percent for those with incomes under $3,000, 33.2 percent for those with incomes between $3,000 and $5,000, but only 1.9 percent for those with incomes between $50,000 and $100,000, and there was an average increase of 7.2 percent for those with incomes over $100,000. Reductions for lower- and middle-income taxpayers were due primarily to higher exemptions and minimum standard deductions, while increases at the upper income levels were mainly due to increased capital gains and the minimum tax on preference income.[26]

Lessons of the 1969 Tax Reform Act

The Tax Reform Act of 1969 was unquestionably the most important piece of peacetime tax legislation up to that time. It also exemplifies several important aspects of contemporary tax politics. First, the form and incidence of the 1969 bill demonstrate the extent to which tax policy is susceptible to ideological trends—trends that complicate partisan influences in tax policy. In five years the basic emphasis in tax reform had completely shifted. The 1962 and 1964 bills, passed under the direction of a supposedly liberal, Democratic president, significantly reduced taxes, and both the rhetoric and the results were extremely favorable to capital formation and business. The 1969 Tax Reform Act reversed this bias. Of the $4.2 billion in structural revenue gains in the 1969 bills, $3 billion came from the corporate side, and of this only $130 million was offset by corporate tax reductions (see table 8.2). This turnaround was not the result of partisan shifts, Congress being only slightly more Democratic in 1969 than in 1963–1964. And, ironically, the latter bill was passed and signed during the administration of Richard Nixon, perceived at the time as the quintessential conservative Republican. One important factor was that many of the changes enacted originated in the proposals of a Democratic Treasury, which had become increasingly liberal under Lyndon Johnson, whose chief tax expert, Stanley Surrey, was firmly committed to a comprehensive tax base approach to the income tax. However, the overriding factors

were not related to party but rather to the need for revenue to pay for the war and reduce inflation and to the perceived mood of the nation as antiwar, antibusiness, and liberal in domestic policy. Taxes were not immune to this mood, and Congress responded with the most liberal peacetime tax bill ever enacted.

The bill also exemplifies the quandary of tax reform, if "reform" means moving toward a relatively simple income tax based on a comprehensive definition of income. Rather than decisive, definitive action to eliminate or curtail basic provisions that erode the tax base, tax reform, true to the incremental approach, often becomes a matter of adjustment and counteradjustment in a cat and mouse game played between clever government experts and tax lawyers. The 1969 farm provisions, for example, tighten taxation of "hobby farmers." A quandary arises because outright repeal of the provisions that are the basis for the tax shelter would hurt the normal farmer, whose income and costs supposedly warrant the special treatment. Even if the provisions are not warranted, the political influence of farm groups would make reform difficult. The result is a complex patchwork set of provisions tailored to farmers with outside income in excess of $50,000—difficult and costly to administer and, of course, awaiting a new set of countermoves by high-priced tax lawyers.

Another example of the difficulty of reform efforts was the unsuccessful proposal to buy off opposition to eliminating tax-exempt securities with a promise of subsidized interest. The exemption of interest on state and local bonds began as a constitutional issue in 1895 but had become a political issue. Simple repeal became impossible as states and cities grew acclimated to tax-subsidized borrowing. From the perspective of state and local officials concerned about their own finances and not tax reform, the carefully conceived subsidy plan was no improvement over existing arrangements, and it involved considerable uncertainty. Although versions of the plan have been proposed several times since, the deterioration of state finances makes the chance of enactment in the near future very unlikely.

Perhaps the best example of both the incremental nature of tax reform and the desperate form it sometimes takes was the creation of the minimum tax applicable to "preference" income. From one perspective this was a charming and ingenious reform in the best tradition of incremental decision making. It was passed as a remedial measure in response to a political outcry against tax shelters. It built on existing provisions rather than traumatically changing the code by deleting provisions to which taxpayers and tax planners had become accustomed. Finally, by creating a list of items, then assessing a percentage

tax after an allowable exemption, the provision became a vehicle for future incremental change. As circumstances and politics changed, the contents of the list, the percentage minimum tax, and the exemption could all be varied, thus fine-tuning the taxes on the very wealthy.

This strategy also exemplifies some of the weaknesses and limitations of incrementalism, however. For one thing, it is a classic example of the problem of complexity. The complexity of the code allows so wide a variation in the treatment of income that wealthy individuals, planning their income for tax purposes, can channel investments and income flows in such a way to avoid most if not all, taxes. And the only response to this is to create a further, even more complex policy that in effect suspends other provisions under special circumstances. This ad hoc jumble of policies not only suffers from an inexplicable internal logic, but must also strike those who suffer under its dictates as illegitimate and somewhat deceptive, thus motivating even more conscientious tax avoidance efforts.

Any reasonable person must wonder if there is not an easier and more straightforward way to tax the rich. The terrible problem is that it is not clear that there is an easier way under a pluralist/incremental system. The inclusion of each of the separate items in the preference list has an internal logic; each item has its protectors in the political system; and, as will be shown in more detail in the next section, each has survived a succession of political challenges. Given these conditions, it is unclear, what the alternative would be, short of radical depoliticization of the revenue process. The form that tax policy is forced to take represents a desperate approach and admits an ultimate inability to reform the tax code in accordance with a more comprehensive tax base. It also symbolizes the futility of using the tax code for redistributive purposes. Although the minimum tax was increased in 1976, the increase was short-lived and was quickly undone in 1978 and 1981 as important items were removed from the preference list and the rate level was lowered. Over the same period a large number of new tax reduction provisions were made available to those with high incomes. So much for taxing the clever rich.

Finally, even though the Tax Reform Act of 1969 was the only major postwar tax bill that increased revenue (at least in its first year), it still provides evidence for the bias of tax politics in favor of tax reduction. The country was in the middle of a war, deficits had been persistent for years, inflation was becoming a continuous concern, and the political mood favored closing loopholes and tax shelters and taxing corporations and the wealthy. And it still took three years of planning and pressure and finally a well-publicized attack on a few people able to avoid taxa-

tion completely to stimulate the enactment of reforms. Even then, the provisions were mostly patchwork rules that did nothing to alter the underlying laws that served as a foundation for abuse. At the same time, five new tax expenditure provisions were created to further politically acceptable goals of the time. In the end, only a strong threat of veto and Treasury's careful monitoring of Conference Committee actions prevented a bill that would have meant substantial tax reduction. It is as if there were a continuous force operating like gravity to push tax legislation in the direction of tax reduction, a force that can be offset only by a diligent and strenuous political effort and that can really be overcome only by the abnormal revenue demands of severe national crisis. After 1969 all resistance was abandoned as the forces favoring tax reduction were supplemented by the effects of inflation.

Chapter 9.
1970–1976
Tax Reduction and
Mixed Reform

The Tax Reduction Act
of 1971

The Nixon administration was am-
bivalent about the first tax legislation passed under its auspices. Although the administration won approval for a number of the proposals
it offered in 1969, many that it had not offered, and to which it was
philosophically opposed, were written into what was basically a congressional tax bill. That was not to be the case in 1971, when the
administration next proposed tax legislation as part of its August economic initiatives. These initiatives followed an intensive planning session at Camp David that established then Secretary of the Treasury
John Connally as a pivotal economic policy maker in the administration.
The economic program announced on August 15, 1971, included a
range of proposals to deal with the economic malaise and inflation that
afflicted the country and about which the administration had attempted
little to that point. To deal with inflation, the president requested an
immediate wage and dividend freeze and expenditure cuts and established a labor-management cost-of-living council. To meet the serious
balance-of-payments problem that had developed, he proposed a 10
percent surcharge on imports, "floating" the dollar from the $35 per
ounce price for gold, and cutting foreign aid 10 percent. To stimulate
the economy, the president suggested a tax cut couched as a Jobs
Development Act. The specific components of this act were to be a
mixture of tax reductions for individuals and businesses, with most of
the cuts going to the latter in the form of a reinstated investment tax
credit; added beneficial options on depreciation, called an Asset Depreciation Range (ADR); and the creation of a new form of tax-exempt
overseas sales organization called a Domestic International Sales Corporation or DISC.[1] The major tax proposals affecting individuals were

for accelerated increases in the exemption and the standard deduction levels that were part of the 1969 legislation.

Hearings began almost immediately, and most participants agreed with Walter Heller, who expressed relief that the administration was going "from a do-nothing policy to a do-something policy."[2] Congress was impatient to take some action to stem the tide of a failing economy and inflated prices, and the tax bill that resulted was therefore put together very quickly. Connally led off House hearings with a classical restatement of the supply side argument that jobs depended on business incentives and capital formation:

> It now takes many thousands of dollars to sustain one job in American industry. . . . In our economic system, profits are prerequisite to attracting and retaining this needed capital. . . . At a time when there is an acute shortage of risk capital—not only in the United States but throughout the world—it is imperative that American businesses . . . generate profits sufficient to attract such capital.[3]

Wilbur Mills countered this supply-side argument with classical demand theory, stating that it was important that the tax increase be spent rather than saved so that demand would be maintained and increased. His recommendation, opposed by Connally, was to increase the low-income allowance (the new name for the minimum standard deduction).[4] Labor also endorsed this proposal, as George Meany flatly labeled the Nixon policy nineteenth-century "trickle down economic theory ."[5] In an atmosphere where taxes were secondary to the debate over wage and price controls, the final Ways and Means bill, put together in only three days of executive sessions, was a compromise of supply- and demand-side approaches. It included both types of tax reductions, although the initial administration proposals for business reductions were scaled down. The investment credit was reenacted at a flat 7 percent rate, rather than a first-year rate of 10 percent followed by 5 percent in subsequent years as the administration had requested. Although the ADR was approved, it was not made retroactive as proposed. The DISC proposal too was cut sharply by making it applicable only to sales of exports above existing levels. Although the bill went along with the president on the standard deduction and exemption increases, as Mills had hinted in the first day of testimony, the low-income allowance was increased by $300 to $1,300. The outcome substantially altered the balance of the tax reductions as proposed by the administration, more than doubling reductions for individuals while

cutting the benefits for corporations approximately 60 percent over the first two years.[6] There was essentially no House floor action. Much to the chagrin of consumer advocates, who noted that the bill provided one of the largest business tax cuts in peacetime, the bill was discussed on the floor for less than two hours and passed by voice vote.

After several weeks of Senate hearings weighted in favor of business witnesses, the Finance Committee met in executive session. It reported a bill very similar to the House bill but with two added provisions, both new to the tax code. The first was a deduction of up to $400 per month for child care expenses; the second, a deduction of up to 20 percent of the wages for employers who hired welfare recipients (known as a WIN deduction). The rationale for the provisions was a desire both to aid those seeking jobs in a period of high unemployment and to make it easier for welfare recipients to get off the dole. One or the other of these goals appealed to almost everyone, and two new tax reduction provisions were born. The only other important change was a compromise with the administration that liberalized the DISC provision by allowing it to apply to 50 percent of all exports, rather than just new exports as in the House bill.

The pattern of Senate floor activity was consistent with that for past bills. A number of amendments were added to the committee bill, most conferring additional tax benefits and most later dropped in Conference. A pitched partisan battle was fought over a political contribution amendment that had little revenue consequence but was critical politically. The Democrats, in debt from the last election but with a large edge in party membership and identification, proposed a one-dollar party "check-off" to support presidential election campaigns. Republicans, with an already large war chest but still awaiting the "emerging Republican majority," bitterly opposed the bill.[7] Of the seventy-six floor votes on the bill, twenty-five were devoted to this issue, with the crucial vote on Senator Pastore's (D-R.I.) amendment passing 52 to 47 on an almost straight-line party vote.

Floor amendments of more revenue importance were also passed: to increase further the personal exemption and low-income allowance; to raise the investment credit (to 10 rather than 7 percent) for investments in rural or central cities where unemployment exceeded 6 percent and for investments in agricultural equipment; and to enact another tax credit for education expenses, this time up to $325 for college or other higher-education costs. A credit for property taxes paid by the elderly with incomes under $6,000 was also easily passed. All of these amendments were later dropped in Conference. One amendment that survived, by Senator Tunney (D-Cal.), changed the child-care deduction

from an itemized deduction to a business deduction, thus making it available to those who use the standard deduction. Numerous roll call votes attempting either to eliminate or to weaken the administration proposals for DISCs and the ADR were all defeated. These new provisions were *not* quietly or deceptively slipped into the tax code.

The final Senate bill would have had the effect of reducing taxes $12.6 billion dollars more than the House bill over the period from 1971 to 1973. Predictably, President Nixon threatened to veto the bill if these levels were kept, and Senate Minority Leader Scott (R-Pa.) predicted that such a veto would not be overridden. In keeping with what was becoming a well-established pattern, Senator Long and other Senate conferees traded away most of the amendments that had been added on the floor. The Conference bill, signed without protest by President Nixon, was almost identical in terms of revenue to the House bill, with a predicted revenue reduction of $25.9 billion over three years. These large effects were achieved with a modest revenue act that was passed in approximately three months. Although the provision changes were few in number, the bill created three new tax reduction provisions and resurrected the investment tax credit. Ten years later, in 1981, it was estimated that the combined annual revenue loss of the ADR system, DISC, and the investment tax credit was $24.8 billion.

1972–1974: Three Years of False Starts

In the next three years, although several major tax bills were begun, there was no significant tax legislation. However, a pension reform act was passed that had implications for the taxation of pensions and savings designated for retirement. During this period, hearings were held on a variety of subjects, including the ill-fated education credit, the possibility of a value-added tax, and, in 1973, general tax reform. The hearings on tax reform were extensive and laid the groundwork for the tax revisions of 1975 and the massive Tax Reform Act of 1976. In those hearings, the comprehensive tax base ideal was lauded as the general standard for income tax changes by the first two witnesses, Joseph Pechman of the Brookings Institution and Stanley Surrey. A number of leading tax experts concentrated on the issue of capital gains. Daniel Throop Smith proposed a sliding scale that would allow more exclusion as assets were held longer. Richard Musgrave and Harvey Brazer argued for either tightening the provisions or completely repealing special treatment of capital gains, with Musgrave opting for a shift to the investment credit (which he helped create) as a preferable stimulus

for the economy. The remainder of the hearings were devoted to oil and gas provisions: the oil lobby argued for a return to the 27.5 percent depletion allowance as a production incentive and, prophetically, a way to reduce U.S. dependence on foreign oil.[8]

Following the hearings, the administration submitted a carefully balanced list of proposals, including several major reform innovations aimed at simplifying the tax code and discouraging high-income tax shelter devices. These included a new form of minimum tax; a limitation on artificial losses (LAL) provision, which limited deduction of investment expenses (depreciation, interest and taxes, etc.) to income earned from an investment in that year; and a miscellaneous deduction provision of $500 to replace deductions for gasoline taxes and certain medical, casualty loss, and employee investment expenses. Of these, the most important and radical was the LAL concept, which would have applied to a range of investments (real estate, oil wells, farms, sports franchises, orchards, etc.). These "shelters" depended on the ability to deduct expenses in full early in a project, while later realizing profits as capital gains or avoiding full taxation by reinvesting in other property. For these investments, deductions for costs and depreciation were usually greater than the income flowing from the property, and thus the investment produced tax losses that were often more than the initial investments. The LAL rule would have limited total deductions from investment projects to the ultimate income derived from the project. Acceptance of the LAL formula would have meant a major restructuring of real estate financing and oil and gas exploration, as well as changes in the other, less important investment areas.

A number of other provisions were also in accord with the goals of simplifying the tax system and broadening the income tax base: repeal of the dividend exclusion, simplification of the child care and retirement credits, a tax subsidy option for tax exempt bond interest, and taxation of foreign corporate income when earned, rather than when repatriated. Changes in the opposite direction suggested the extension of the investment credit to oil and gas exploration (exempted in 1971) and the enactment of previous proposals to allow tax credits for property taxes paid by the elderly and for education expenses. What is curious about this list is that although the innovations were highlighted, the majority of the provisions were old ones, some slightly modified and some exact duplicates of former proposals. Thus, tax reform legislation was beginning to fall into an established and almost institutionalized pattern, with repeated efforts to shift policies along familiar lines. The proposed innovations were not given serious consideration, although some

reemerged later. The entire package was already slated to go nowhere when the highly publicized difficulties of Wilbur Mills became known late in 1973, and hearings were called off as the committee turned to pressing trade legislation.[9]

Legislative activity in 1974 was dominated by energy problems, the OPEC oil boycott, and price and profit increases in oil. Tax politics was tempered by the frequent absence and reduced power of Wilbur Mills and the weakened status of the White House as a result of Watergate. Several Senate committee hearings on oil price increases generated widespread and scathing criticism of the oil companies. The tax advantages of oil and natural gas companies were repeatedly attacked by liberals and moderates alike. Realizing that some tax changes for oil and gas were forthcoming, the administration proposed a moderate change that would have repealed percentage depletion allowances for foreign oil and reduced the extent to which energy royalties and taxes paid to foreign governments could be used as credits against U.S. taxes. Senator Church (D-Idaho) countered this proposal on the Senate floor by arguing that unless credits were disallowed, dropping foreign depletion would have little impact on oil company taxes.[10]

In May 1974 Ways and Means reported out a bill increasing taxes on oil companies by phasing out depletion; restricting foreign tax credits as offsets to U.S. taxes; enacting an energy windfall profits excise tax, but with a "plowback" provision that allowed exemption of profits reinvested in exploration or development; and restricting the use of DISCs for energy resource companies. Liberal Democrats were not satisfied. At the urging of organized labor and public interest lobbies, in an unprecedented move that confirmed Wilbur Mills's declining influence, the Democratic Caucus mandated that the bill should come to the floor under a modified closed rule that would allow votes on amendments by William Green (D-Pa.) and Charles Vanik (D-Oreg.) phasing out depletion and adding other tax-increasing provisions for the oil industry. However, in the final triumph of his career, Mills outmaneuvered the caucus by threatening to take the bill directly to the floor without any rule (which is permitted for revenue legislation), rather than simply restricting amendments to those approved by the caucus. The chairman of the Rules Committee, Ray Madden (D-Ind.), who was a strong supporter of organized labor, was furious but unable to take effective action in his committee, where there was great reluctance to place a volatile revenue bill before an open House. Mills never carried out the threat, as attention in the summer of 1974 turned to other legislative issues and the climax of the Watergate scandal. Most of the

provisions were added to a larger tax reform and reduction bill that was reported out of Ways and Means in November but was never scheduled for floor action.

One important bill of 1974 did have a major impact on tax policy—an impact that was typically destined to grow over the years. As part of a set of pension reforms enacted that year, Congress expanded a 1962 act that had created tax deductible retirement plans for self-employed people and their employees, who could not benefit from the tax-free contributions made by larger employers with formal, regulated pension plans. The argument in 1962 for these "Keogh Plans" (after the sponsor of the bill, Eugene Keogh, D-N.Y.) was one of horizontal equity, though opponents claimed that most of those who would benefit would be upper-income earners, such as doctors and lawyers. Participants could contribute annually to a tax-free retirement account up to 10 percent of earnings or $2,500, whichever was less. In 1974, as a response to inflation and over the objections of liberals, who again questioned the distribution of benefits, the limits were raised to 15 percent of earnings or $7,500.

As part of the same legislation, a new form of tax-free pension plan, called an Individual Retirement Account, or IRA, was established to cover all individuals employed by organizations that did not have formal, qualified pension plans (rather than just people working for those legally termed "self-employed"). The argument was again based on horizontal equity: the desire to cover another segment of the population unable to take advantage of tax-free pension contributions. The limits were set at a modest 15 percent or $1,500, with accounts to be established in a number of authorized financial institutions. The savings would be long-term because taxes would have to be paid and other penalties would be levied on savings withdrawn before age fifty-nine and a half. As will be described below, these accounts were to expand rapidly to new segments of the population in subsequent years. In the process the rationale also changed as the IRA was adopted as a mechanism for increasing the general savings rate and aiding a struggling financial industry.

The Tax Reduction Act of 1975

By 1975 tax issues could no longer be avoided, and a major tax reduction bill was passed in the first eleven weeks of the session, to be followed later in the session by another bill extending these cuts and by

House action on a tax reform bill that would finally emerge in 1976. An odd combination of forces affected the hectic activity during this period. Ignoring the cries of "deficit" by fiscal conservatives in his own party, President Ford, declaring a transition from an emphasis on inflation to an emphasis on jobs, began the year by requesting a $16 billion tax cut. This stimulative policy, which ran counter to the deflationary tax surcharge he had proposed in October, reflected the steep recession that gripped the country. At the same time, however, oil taxes had not yet been changed, and Congress, eager to reassert itself after Watergate, was not about to let an appointed president dictate revenue policy. In addition, liberal changes in congressional organization on the Democratic side of Congress had reduced the power of committee chairmen and party leaders, who now had to be approved by caucus vote. Moreover, the power over House committee assignments had been removed from Ways and Means and turned over to the Policy Steering Committee, and the tax committee was expanded in size. These changes and the liberal outcome of the 1974 "Watergate elections" led to an increased number of liberals on both the Ways and Means and the Senate Finance committees.[11] However, even with this changed environment, there was no question about the direction of the tax bill. The recession and simultaneous inflation (which at 11 percent was pushing people into higher brackets) created an overwhelming consensus for tax reduction. The issues were how much, and who should get what?

The administration proposals were brief and simple: a straight tax rebate of 12 percent for all taxpayers on 1974 taxes; an increase in the investment credit from 7 to 12 percent; a range of increases in taxes on oil, designed to cut consumption but not repeal depletion; and permanent tax cuts for individuals and corporations to offset higher energy costs. The House created its own bill, adding numerous provisions that raised the estimated cut to $17.6 billion, while significantly shifting the reductions to the poor and middle class. A Ways and Means Committee made up of 25 Democrats and 12 Republicans proposed rate structure changes that centered on a 10 percent rebate in 1974, going up to $200 for a $20,000 income, but sliding back to $100 for incomes of $30,000 and over. This dramatically shifted the incidence of the cut from that proposed by President Ford. Also included were a flat credit of $35 per person in 1975 and an increase in the standard deduction and low-income allowance.

A minor provision in the Ways and Means bill was to open the door for a major innovation in the tax system. It established an earned income credit for the working poor. It was initially proposed as a 5 percent credit reaching a maximum of $200 for a $4,000 income and phasing out to

zero at $6,000. There was precedent for such a credit in the 1924 Mellon earned income credit, but that 25 percent credit had not been related to income level (see p. 92). The rationale for the credit was that low-income taxpayers would benefit little from the other relief provisions but would still be affected by the increased Social Security taxes that were to take effect in 1975. An added rationale for some was that the credit would provide an incentive for the poor to remain off welfare. That hook became more important in the Senate Finance Committee, which increased the credit to 10 percent, made it refundable (and thus the first negative income tax), but added the requirement that, like recipients of Aid to Families with Dependent Children (AFDC, or welfare), families had to be supporting a dependent child to be eligible.

Other provisions in the Ways and Means bill were a general increase in the investment credit (to 10 percent rather than the 12 percent proposed by the administration) and other, minor changes in it, and a widening of the lowest corporate bracket, thus aiding small businesses. Under an agreement between the new chairman of Ways and Means, Al Ullman (D-Oreg.), and House Majority Leader Thomas P. O'Neill (D-Mass.), energy taxes were to be split off for later consideration.

The House, however, was not to be put off any longer on the oil issue. The liberal House consensus, combined with the increasing negative publicity surrounding the oil industry, ensured that after almost fifty years of controversy, the oil depletion provisions were about to go. The mechanism for achieving this end was the Democratic Caucus, which voted to mandate a rule allowing a floor vote on Representative Green's proposal to eliminate the depletion allowance for oil and for most natural gas retroactive to January 1, 1975. According to the 153–98 caucus vote, which defied the Democratic leadership, there would also be a vote on a proposal by Charles Wilson of Texas that would maintain the allowance on the first 3,000 barrels of production a day, thus protecting small independent producers. This time, with Mills gone and Ullman claiming that "as chairman of the committee, I don't want to be unresponsive to the majority," the Rules Committee accepted the mandate and also allowed several other votes on the treatment of natural gas producers.[12]

On the floor, the Green amendment won relatively easily, while the Wilson amendment was narrowly defeated. The vote was partisan but somewhat mixed at 248 to 163; Republicans opposed the amendment 44 to 94, but 69 Democrats broke ranks, 52 of them from the South. Although Wilson lost, the Senate later restored a modified exemption for small producers (2,000 barrels a day) but offset this concession by floor votes reducing tax benefits from foreign credits, royalties, and

losses, which were not part of the House bill. In the end, depletion allowances for the large oil companies were for the most part eliminated. All it took was the oil embargo and the quadrupling of oil prices in eighteen months, a liberal Democratic landslide following the worst political scandal in American history, the downfall of a longtime committee chairman at the height of his power, the expansion and "stacking" of the Ways and Means and Rules committees, and a unique revolt in Congress that permitted the membership to overrule party leadership on a critical issue. Tax expenditures as carefully fortified as the depletion allowance do not die easily.

The House bill was passed by an overwhelming majority (317 to 97) once the oil issue was resolved. A Republican substitute that would have enacted only a graduated rebate of up to $430, concentrated in the middle-income ranges, was easily defeated. However, arguments in a minority report supporting this substitute, ignored at the time, were to prove prophetic a few years ahead. They complained that the existing bill was "a bill to redistribute income on a permanent basis" and that the cuts were "not equitably related to the tax burden borne by all Americans. The middle-income American who pays the lion's share of federal taxes receives far too little consideration."[13] The Senate Finance Committee made several major changes in the bill, and further changes resulted from Senate floor actions. Most important, Finance dropped all the oil provisions on two votes of 7 to 10 and 8 to 9. Senator Long still had control of his committee, although he was not to be as fortunate on the floor. Other than this repeal, the committee basically added revenue-losing provisions. It lowered rates in the first four brackets, provided a tax credit option of up to $200 to replace changes in the standard deduction and low-income allowances, altered the earned income credit as discussed above, and liberalized loss carryback provisions for individuals. These changes alone would have added $3.4 billion to the revenue loss in the House bill. The committee also increased the investment credit to 12 percent through 1976 (then set it permanently at 10 percent) but, at the personal request of Senator Long, tied the added credit for investments over $10 million to the creation of company plans to purchase stock for employees (known as ESOPs, or Employee Stock Ownership Plans). This was later retained as a 1 percent added credit when the Conference Committee cut the investment credit back to 10 percent.

There were two provisions tailored to the financial troubles of specific industries. One of these was an extraordinary tax credit, to last through 1976, of 5 percent (up to $2,000) for the purchase of a new or used home. The other, stimulated by the heavy losses in such companies as

Lockheed, Pan American, and Chrysler, extended loss carry-backs for business from three years to eight, thus providing a direct tax subsidy to firms profitable in the past but with recent large losses. Although the tax system had been used over the years to directly aid certain industries (coal, iron ore, timber, agriculture, mineral companies), these provisions had always been rationalized as necessary to offset special circumstances affecting the industry. The rationale for the home credit and carry-back provisions was simply that they would aid depressed industries.

Eleven of these provisions survived floor debate, which was mainly focused on the oil provisions. The debate was compressed into several days in late March because of the impending Easter break. One marathon forty-hour session led to the final compromise and votes restoring the House provisions on depletion and adding the further restrictions on foreign credits and loss deductions. Following complex parliamentary maneuvering, a final compromise was arranged by allowing a per-day exemption of 2,000 barrels, thus sparing the independents. The oil state Senators were resigned to the removal of depletion, and the only uncertain issue was the treatment of the independents. Because of the amount of imported oil, the most important votes were over the treatment of foreign tax credits and losses. Vance Hartke (D-Ind.) led the attack for the liberals and achieved an early vote that was surprisingly one-sided and ultimately sealed the fate of the large oil companies. During the debate, several other provisions were also passed. Two provisions dropped in Conference but enacted in later years changed child care expenses from a deduction to a credit and created a tax credit for the purchase of insulation. A minor provision that survived extended the period for buying a new home without having to pay capital gains from one year to eighteen months.

In the end, despite the oil provisions, the Senate had done it again, almost doubling the estimated House cut to a historic level of $27 billion in the first year. As in the past, the Conference Committee's bill came in much closer to the House level. It accepted the 10 percent graduated rebate for 1974 and a $35 (not $200) tax credit for 1975. The standard deduction increase was cut somewhat from the House proposal (to allow for the $35 credit), but the low-income allowance was the same. The oil provisions generally followed the Senate floor provisions, and the investment credit was raised to 10 percent. New tax reduction provisions were added for home purchases, profitless industries, and ESOPs. The final revenue effects of the Tax Reduction Act of 1975 are given in table 8.1. All of the structural gains came from the taxes on oil and gas, which were to be increased even more later in the year. As

enacted, the bill was a stopgap measure, limited to the year 1975 in anticipation of the major tax reform that was slowly moving through Congress.

"Reform" Proposals and an Emergency Tax Cut Bill

Tax legislation in the latter half of 1975 was extremely complicated. In July Treasury Secretary William Simon appeared before the Ways and Means Committee to present the administration's reform proposals. The proposals were based on an expansion of the Nixon proposals offered in 1973 and included the previously proposed minimum tax formula, the LAL formula, and the $500 miscellaneous deduction. Simon went much further, however, and made some remarkable additional proposals. One set, exemplifying the increasing use of the tax system as a policy tool, was aimed at the administration's goal of supporting the development and construction of coal and nuclear power facilities. The administration proposed special tax incentives for utilities, including an increased investment credit, accelerated depreciation, and deferred taxes on dividends.

More radical were the proposals to encourage "reinvestment in America," as a response to what Simon perceived as a crisis in capital formation. To this end he proposed changes in the taxation of dividends, allowing both individuals and corporations 50 percent tax credits for dividends paid or received. This was also seen as the first step in the administration's plan to integrate the corporate and individual tax codes, a plan which was later presented in the 1977 *Blueprints for Basic Tax Reform*.[14] The other major proposals to promote savings, and theoretically investment, were an expansion of the coverage of IRAs and an increase in the amount of the tax credits they allowed. And, pushing the concept a step further, they also proposed deduction of contributions to special tax-free savings accounts.

Amazing as it would have seemed at the time, over the next six years all the savings provisions, and more, were eventually passed. However, they were not to become part of the Tax Reform Act of 1976 and neither were most of the other administration recommendations. As with most postwar revenue legislation, this was to be very much a congressional bill. Although the residue of Watergate partially explained the impatience to move on these issues, more important was the fact that Congress had been ruminating on tax reform for four years. Major hearings had been held as early as 1973. Many of the changes ultimately included in the second tax bill of 1975 were not new but rather

had been lying dormant for years in the Treasury or the staff files of one of the tax committees or had been incorporated in earlier revision bills that did not complete the legislative cycle.

The administration proposals were not all immediately cast aside, however. After a grueling fall of meetings, political maneuvering, and close votes, Ways and Means finally reported the long-awaited tax reform package on November 12, 1975. The bill combined extension of many of the temporary tax reductions that had been incorporated in the bill passed earlier in the year with dozens of tax revision and "reform" provisions. The extension included the 1975 changes in standard deductions, a slightly altered personal tax credit, and the business cuts and changes in the investment credit. Many of the revisions fit either the reform goal of restricting tax reduction provisions and thus broadening the tax base or the goal of simplifying the tax code. As always, few did both. Although the specific provisions were too numerous to analyze in detail, one major change was the incorporation of the LAL regulation that had been proposed earlier by the administration. The provision was to apply to a number of tax shelter devices involving farms, sports franchises, motion pictures, and oil and gas drilling. Although most of these shelters accounted for relatively little in terms of revenue, the application of the LAL provision to real estate would have made an important difference. However, at the insistence of Joe Waggoner (D-La.), the effect on real estate was minimized by allowing those already involved in real estate to use losses incurred on one property to offset existing income from others.[15] His arguments, which carried a close vote of 20 to 16 in the committee, were that the change would be destructive to a severely depressed industry and that it was unfair to change the rules in the middle of the game.

Other than this major reform, the bill substantially increased and tightened the minimum tax provisions (rather than adopting the new administration's formula), increased taxes on capital gains through a series of modifications, and extended the IRA accounts to employees already covered by existing pension plans (as the administration had requested). An assortment of other revisions, many touted as tax simplifications, were made in the areas of child care, retirement income, moving expenses, sick pay, alimony, and business deductions. Rules governing the taxation of income earned abroad and DISCs, both common reform targets, were tightened, although the resulting provisions were more complicated. The bill also contained numerous administrative and technical provisions.

Under Wilbur Mills's rule, committee reports *were* House bills. Now, however, the legislative process was far from tranquil. Congress in 1975

was a different organization than it had been during the last tax reform drive in 1969. The independence within party ranks and the institutional changes that had taken place weakened not only the committees but also the power of the new chairmen. The trouble came both from Republicans who wanted to tie tax reductions to a spending ceiling, as was proposed in October by President Ford, and from liberal Democrats who felt that many of the provisions did not go far enough in tightening "loopholes." After three very complicated and confusing days before the Rules Committee, a partial closed rule supported by Ullman and the majority of Ways and Means Democrats was passed. It allowed six floor votes on controversial provisions.

When the bill reached the floor, an initial Republican effort to place a ceiling on spending was defeated, and the approved amendments were then taken up. Three minor provisions were passed. One repealed a provision that had been publicly linked to the benefit of a single person (H. Ross Perot, a Dallas millionaire). The two major liberal amendments, lifting the LAL exemption for real estate and further tightening the DISC provisions, were rejected in the wake of intense business lobbying. Joseph Karth (D-Minn.), who offered the DISC amendment, bitterly summarized these votes: "In every instance where there was an organized group to lobby against it, the amendment lost. Where there was no organized group as such, the amendment succeeded."[16] After a brief vote expanding the list of crops exempt from the LAL rules, the bill was passed 257 to 168. The vote was generally along party lines, which Republicans had agreed to maintain following the defeat of the spending ceiling at the beginning of the debate.[17] On its passage, President Ford reiterated an earlier threat to veto any legislation not including a spending ceiling.

The 674-page House bill was passed December 4, 1975. If the Senate was to have any time at all to consider this bill, it could not be passed in the current session. However, if take-home pay was not to be reduced as of January 1 (because of Social Security increases), the tax cuts passed earlier in 1975 had to be extended. Thus, when the Finance Committee met on December 10, a proposal extending the basic tax-cut provisions for six months was quickly approved. These cuts, which would amount to a revenue reduction of about $8 billion, were actually much less than the massive cuts recommended by the administration in October in lieu of major reforms. They were intended to buy political time and were quickly agreed to by the Ways and Means Committee and the full House and Senate.

President Ford, however, refused to sign the bill without the spending ceiling he had requested as part of his tax-cut program. He vetoed

the proposal on December 17, and the veto was sustained in the House when defections of 32 conservative Democrats made it impossible to gain the two-thirds majority needed to override. Ullman and House Democrats who had labored so long on tax issues were furious and threatened obstruction of further action, with no compromise. However, led by Senator Long, the Democratic Caucus agreed to attach a "resolution" to control spending without specifying exact limits—in other words, a meaningless political gesture that would allow members to take a symbolic stance on spending reduction and to vote for tax reduction. Faced with the possibility of no tax cut, which was panicking Republicans and Democrats alike, everyone agreed to this formula. Following quick negotiations, slight alterations in language, and nearly unanimous votes, Ford signed the bill on December 23, just in time for Christmas and just in time to ensure that take-home pay would not go down with the new year. Major tax reforms and revisions were delayed for another year.

The 1976 Tax Reform Bill

The Senate Finance Committee, working from the House reform bill passed in December, reported out a bill at the end of May 1976 following a month of closed markup sessions. Its bill made numerous changes, and, as in the past, most were in the direction of tax reduction, either easing the impact of or eliminating "reform" sections in the House bill. However, it made only one important rate change in the House law. It extended the $35 credit through June 30, 1977, instead of making it permanent, as it was in the House bill. This repeal of the $35 credit, which offered the most progressive means of tax reduction, was immediately attacked by Senate liberals led by Senator Kennedy (D-Mass.).

Among the most important structural changes was the elimination of the LAL provision in favor of another, less restrictive formula. The new formula limited deductions for investment expenses to the amount a partner had at risk and created a "recapture rule" that required payment of depreciation claimed in excess of taxable income received once an asset is sold. For real estate transactions, the bill also limited the amount of construction-period taxes and interest that could be deducted; the plan was eventually to stretch out the amortization of most deductions over ten years. Liberals were angered by these changes and, defending the Republican administration proposal, attacked them unsuccessfully on the floor. They ultimately survived the Conference Committee,

however, and thus the only major administration proposal remaining was dropped.

Another important change by Finance was the elimination of all the provisions relating to capital gains, including a critical House proposal extending the holding period for long-term gains from six months to one year. Although the Conference Committee later restored the House provisions, the Finance Committee change fueled the charge that the legislation was no longer a "tax reform" bill. The committee did, however, increase the minimum tax by raising the rate to 15 percent (the House had passed 14 percent), but offset this and further complicated the provision by an exemption of either $5,000 of preference income *or* the amount of regular taxes paid before the minimum tax was to be calculated.[18] In one of the few floor victories for liberals, the deduction of taxes paid was deleted in exchange for a flat exemption of $10,000. The committee also liberalized the maximum tax by including both income from pensions and investments as "earned income," which then qualified for the lower maximum rate of 50 percent. A limit of $100,000 was placed on investment income. However, a floor amendment by Walter Mondale (D-Minn.) easily eliminated this special inclusion (66 to 17), although pension income remained as earned income.

Other changes that angered reform-minded liberals, but were not dropped even after repeated floor efforts, were retention of the existing exclusion on personal income earned abroad (the House had voted a phased repeal of the exclusion) and an easing of the restrictions passed by the House on DISCs and foreign corporate income. One important revenue-increasing provision dropped the extension of IRAs that had been recommended by the administration and passed by the House. Rather, the committee added a minor increase to $1,750 for already eligible individuals with nonworking spouses. These changes also survived floor challenge and the Conference Committee. Finally, the committee made a series of changes that, in sum, liberalized estate and gift taxes by effectively more than tripling exemptions. The House had made no changes in the estate tax, and although the provisions were cut back in Conference, it was still estimated that the revenue loss as a result of these provisions would amount to $1.5 billion annually by the year 1981. Counting only structural changes in the income tax, the Finance Committee bill would have allowed approximately $2 billion more revenue reduction than the House bill.

The Senate floor debate, which was the longest in history, was a classic tax battle that pitted a group of persistent liberals against more or less the rest of the Senate. It was reminiscent of the floor battles of the twenties and late thirties led by Progressives and liberal Democrats, and

it ended in much the same way—with few victories for the rebellious senators. Over the twenty-five days of debate (June 16–August 6), a reform group of fifteen senators led by Gaylord Nelson (D-Wis.) made a concerted effort to restore some of the original House provisions and to pass a series of provisions more stringent than those in either bill.[19] The major targets singled out by the reform group were the deletion of the LAL provisions in favor of the risk and recapture rules; the changes in the minimum tax, particularly the one allowing the deduction of regular taxes; the addition of investment income as "earned income"; and the taxation of foreign corporate and DISC income.

Chairman Long began the debate by expressing his confusion over the meaning of the term "tax reform." He said: "I have always felt that tax reform is a change in the tax law that I favor, or if it is the other man defining tax reform it is a change in the tax law that he favors."[20] He then defended his committee's actions as getting "at those not paying enough taxes, and not doing the blunder buss sort of thing of hitting innocent victims—not nearly as bad as the House bill or some of these other provisions that people are seeking."[21] Repeatedly using horizontal equity arguments to the effect that reform provisions would harm those in need or in special circumstances as well as those abusing the tax laws, he proceeded to outmaneuver and simply outvote most of the liberal challenges. The effort to reinstate the LAL provisions was defeated on a series of early votes, none of which came closer than a ten-vote margin. The same margin defeated a Kennedy amendment to limit to $20,000 the amount of nonbusiness interest that could be deducted by individuals. The reform liberals were slightly more successful in increasing the minimum tax. In a very complicated series of votes, the Senate finally adopted an equally complex compromise proposed by Senator Allen (D-Ala.) that retained deduction of regular taxes paid and increased the exemption to $10,000 (from $5,000 in the Finance bill) but expanded the preference list and applied the increase to corporations as well as individuals (exempting the timber industry). The Conference Committee later compromised, and *half* of the regular taxes were allowed as an exemption. These negotiations and compromises demonstrate an advantage of a complex provision like the minimum tax when it comes to political bargaining: by carefully tailoring changes and adjusting various aspects of the provision, a little can be given to each side. Of course, the result is an increasing spiral of complexity.

One of the few victories for liberals came on Senator Mondale's amendment to drop investment income from the calculation of "earned" income that would qualify for the reduced maximum rate of

50 percent. To ensure passage, pension income was categorized as "earned," but most of the $30,000 exemption of preference income (which had been completely eliminated by Finance) was restored. Again, the numerous parameters of a hopelessly complex provision facilitated compromise, which in this case was a modest victory for the forces opposed to the broadest application of the 50 percent rate. Senator Kennedy proposed that the entire provision be eliminated and the top tax rate for all income be returned to 70 percent; he was beaten 54 to 24. Five years later the provision was finally eliminated, but not in the direction Kennedy had in mind. Rather, the death of this "loophole," and the distinction between earned and unearned income, would come in 1981 through a bipartisan motion to make the *lower rate* applicable to all income.

On the controversial issues of DISCs and the taxation of foreign corporate income, the liberals came up empty, on the latter winning only a mandate to study the issue further. They were also easily beaten on a host of other amendments, including a proposal by Senator Hathaway (D-Maine), newly appointed to the Finance Committee, that would have done away with the $750 personal exemption and replaced it with a $175 tax credit, which would have significantly shifted the tax burden upward. At the same time, however, an administration-backed proposal to raise the personal exemption to $1,000 was also defeated. Liberals also lost votes by wide margins on higher taxation of oil and life insurance companies; elimination of a long proposal to increase ESOP investment credits; elimination of the deduction of conventions as business expenses (and other efforts to restrict business deductions); and restoration of a House ceiling of $50 on the deduction of gasoline taxes. A belated effort by Senator Kennedy to increase the investment credit to 15 percent and use it as a replacement for the ADR system, which had been added five years earlier, received only 11 votes.

The reform group won an important victory by defeating a Finance proposal for a sliding scale for long-term capital gains that would have increased the exclusion of 50 percent by 1 percent for every five years the asset was held, up to twenty-five years. This proposal, which originated in a suggestion made by Daniel Throop Smith in the 1973 hearings, was defeated by a partisan vote of 39 to 44. Another amendment that had little support but rang like a first-warning bell was a proposal by Senator Taft (R-Ohio) to index the rate schedules for inflation. Senator Long argued against the motion, citing the tax reduction involved and the threat of future deficits. Of the meager 22 votes against tabling the amendment, 19 were cast by Republicans.

Not surprisingly, the reform liberals were much more successful

when they put aside reform measures that closed "loopholes" (which raised someone's taxes) and instead, usually stressing taxpayers' needs, proposed expanding amendments for child care, the retirement income credit, the exclusion of sick pay, and (in a new proposal) the exclusion of employer contributions to prepaid legal plans. The votes on these increased benefits were somewhat partisan, but not close. Unlike the other issues, on which southern Democrats voted overwhelmingly against the proposals offered by the reform group, on these the Democratic majority held, often augmented by liberal Republicans. The obvious heresy of these amendments from a pure reform ideal elicited Senator Long's wry remark that when it came to defining a "loophole," "it all depends on whose ox is being gored."[22]

There was a symbolic and procedural victory for reformers in the midst of floor consideration of the bill. Senator Long called three days of public hearings on the Finance bill, which ended with the Finance Committee's withdrawing twenty minor amendments that reform groups charged aided either specific individuals or very small groups. The hearings were called in response to complaints that the Finance Committee markup sessions had been closed and no records kept, both practices that Long promised to correct in the future. Although Senator Kennedy and tax reform groups hailed this change, it was to do them little substantive good in the years ahead.

The final Senate bill, passed on August 6, 1976, by a vote of 49 to 22 (with 14 of the 22 negative votes cast by northern Democrats), was unsatisfactory to both the reform liberals and such conservatives as James Buckley (I-N.Y.), who lamented the revenue loss and structure of the bill as "the worst possible collection of tax preferences for the lobbied interests."[23] The liberals, in a last-ditch act of defiance, proposed that the word "reform" be removed from the title of the act. Dick Clark (D-Iowa) explained his proposal: "At a time when the American people are questioning the sincerity of Washington and politicians, we cannot afford to pass a tax 'reform' bill which creates new loopholes, which complicates rather than simplifies, and which retains some of the most notorious features of an unpopular tax code."[24] Just before the Clark amendment was defeated (42 to 20), Senator Muskie (D-Maine) recalled a prescient remark made by Senator Long earlier in the year:

> He [Long] said that once you get into tax legislation there is always a majority for "reform" but very seldom a majority—after the special interests have done their work—for any particular reform. It is easy to cut taxes, he told us—and we have—and

very hard to close loopholes. The chairman was absolutely right.[25]

The Conference Committee met for nine days to work out a compromise between the two bills. In a fitting ending for a bill that was four years in the making, a final controversy emerged in Conference and was later fought out on the House floor. The House bill had not included any changes in the estate and gift taxes; it had considered them in a separate bill, which had been blocked on the floor. That bill included a very important provision changing the taxation of capital gains on assets acquired by inheritance by requiring that the gains be based on original cost rather than on market value on the day of death. This provision, which changed the "carry-over basis" for capital gains, had first been proposed by the Kennedy administration (See chapter 8). It would have applied only to assets received after December 31, 1977, and there would have been a $10,000 exemption for personal property and a minimum basis (i.e., an exemption) of $60,000 for each estate. However, even with these exclusions for small inheritances, the provision would have had a profound impact on estate planning, trust administration, and, potentially, the type and rate of investment turnover. It would have significantly increased the taxation of capital assets and the general tax burden of the wealthy.

The Conference Committee agreed to include this provision along with the estate tax changes of the Senate bill. House conferees additionally agreed that a separate floor vote would be taken on this provision. The Republican conferees, Barber Conable (R-N.Y.) and Herman Schneebeli (R-Pa.), led an unsuccessful fight to eliminate the amendment. The key vote was so confusing that Conable and Ullman (who was defending the provision) had to tell members which way to vote as they entered the chamber. The vote carried 229 to 181, primarily because of the overwhelming Democratic majority. There were 52 Democratic defections (42 southern Democrats) against only 9 Republicans. The Senate never voted separately on it, a fact that would haunt the future of the provision, which, as the tide turned against tax reform, was to be first delayed and eventually repealed.

The final provisions of the Tax Reform Act of 1976 are difficult to summarize because of the massive changes involved. One thing is, of course, certain: the bill accounted for a greater cut in taxes than any bill to that time. As shown in table 8.1, the reduction was estimated at $15.7 billion for fiscal year 1977 and $11.6 billion for 1978. Of that amount, most came from the extension of the general tax credit and the lowered

standard deduction. The structural changes added slightly to revenues in the first year, but because of an anticipated growth in the investment credit, they added to tax reductions afterward. Because the provision changes were so complicated, the only estimates of tax changes by income group made by the Joint Committee on Taxation were of those attributable to revisions in what I have defined as "rates" in table 8.1.[26] These were highly progressive at the lower end of the scale because of the effects of the flat credit and the extension of the now-refundable earned income credit (a family of four with less than $6,000 in income could receive $300). Although exact aggregate figures are not available, the distributive effects of individual provisions (to be described in chapter 14), with one major exception, suggest a similar conclusion. As depicted in table 9.1, all the revenue-gaining provisions (with the possible exception of the tightened sick-pay exclusion) affect primarily high-income groups, while the revenue-losing provisions, with the major exception of the investment credit, primarily benefit those in the lower-income category. However, because of the size of the investment credit, for which distribution data are lacking, it is difficult to determine the overall impact of the structural changes in the bill.

Perhaps the best indicator is that while many applauded the sheer passing of such a major bill, no one claimed to be fully satisfied. However, only those on the extreme left and right were openly hostile to the outcome. Analysis of major provision changes corroborates the balance indicated by the estimated revenue effects in table 9.1, with thirty changes increasing and twenty decreasing revenues. Although, as in the past, the bill was only modestly successful in eliminating tax reduction provisions, it did not extend or make permanent the temporary 1975 home-purchase credit and the eight-year loss carry-back rule that was so beneficial to corporations with large losses. It also appeared to eliminate a very large reduction mechanism by calling for the taxation of capital gains at death, though this was not to last. Moreover, although it did increase or expand a number of tax benefits (mostly those favored by liberals), it created only one major tax expenditure item—the exclusion of prepaid legal plans, which still has only a slight effect on revenue.

One undeniable outcome of all of this was that the code became more, not less, complex, as more often than not the effort to reform meant a more careful tailoring of provisions to or away from specific uses. This fine-tuning, which serves to categorize ever more specifically incomes, costs, and circumstances, has the inevitable effect of increasing complexity. The crushing reality of what was happening to the code was discussed on the final day of the Senate debate. Senator Hart (D-Colo.)

stressed not only the complexity of the existing bill, but that of the tax code in general. He noted that in 1926 the code was 136 pages long; fifty years later, the index alone was 125 pages long. He also pointed out that fifty years earlier, the 1040 form had two pages, compared with the thirteen-page form and forty added pages of explanation in 1975. The Senate was apparently moved by these arguments. By voice vote it

Table 9.1 Major Structural Changes in the
Tax Reform Act of 1976: Corporate and Individual Taxes

	Estimate Gain/Loss ($ millions)	
	FY 1977	FY 1978
Revenue-Gaining Provisions		
Increased minimum tax for individuals	1,032	1,135
DISC amendments	468	553
Sick-pay exclusions	380	357
Deductions for business use of the home	207	206
Amortization of construction-period interest and taxes	102	126
Increase in capital gains holding period	33	218
All others (approximate)	778	905
Total gain	3,000	3,500
Revenue-Losing Provisions		
Extension of investment credit	− 1,300	− 3,306
Revised retirement income credit	− 391	− 340
Child care credit	− 384	− 368
ESOP modifications	− 107	− 257
Use of capital gains/losses to offset ordinary income	− 22	− 162
All others	− 496	− 268
Total loss	− 2,700	− 4,700
Net structural change	+ 300	− 1,200

Source: Joint Committee on Taxation, *General Explanations of the Tax Reform Act of 1976* (Washington, D.C.: Government Printing Office, 1977), pp. 15–21, table 2.

resolved to establish a "Commission on Tax Simplification and Modernization."[27]

Finally, despite the bill's essential balance, it failed in two important aspects. Other than the investment credit, the bill did little for capital formation and investment, and many in the corporate community perceived it as an extension of the 1969 attack on business and investment. Second, the bill seemed to do little for the middle class, which was suffering from inflation and the rapid escalation of state and local taxes. The estimated effects of the rate reductions were constant in dollar terms for incomes of $12,500 and higher, and the major structural changes affected those at either end of the income distribution, without much impact on those in the middle. This momentary loss of sensitivity to the middle class and the growing perception of a capital crisis set the tone for the next five years of tax politics.

Chapter 10.
The Carter
Administration

The Building Pressure
for Tax Reduction

The 1977 Tax Reduction
and Simplification Act

It would be inaccurate to describe the tax legislation passed during the Carter administration as a "Carter tax program" as, for example, one can label the 1962 and 1964 bills as "Kennedy tax cuts." Although the Kennedy proposals were significantly modified by Congress, the income tax bills passed in 1977 and 1978 bore almost no resemblance to the legislation proposed by Jimmy Carter. The administration's trouble began with a proposal that emerged from the White House in the first months of 1977 in the midst of a flurry of legislative initiatives. The bill incorporated a $50 rebate on 1976 taxes for each taxpayer and dependent with an extra $50 for retirees. In the wake of unemployment rates of 9.1 percent for 1975 and 8.4 percent for 1976, the rebate had been proposed during Carter's campaign as a mechanism to stimulate demand. The administration also proposed eliminating the percentage standard deduction, increasing the flat deduction to $2,400 ($2,800 for joint returns) and labeling it the "zero bracket amount." To even out the bill and provide a direct supply-side stimulus for the economy, it proposed a choice for corporations of either an increased investment credit (to 12 percent) or a wage credit worth 4 percent of employer Social Security payments. Of these proposals, the only one finally to pass was a version of the zero bracket amount, but with very different numbers.

Both the rebate and the corporate tax reductions were in trouble from the beginning. Although Ways and Means reported a bill that allowed rebates for those with incomes below $30,000, both the vote in the committee and the recommital vote on the floor (which was tied to a

Republican proposal to drop the rebates in favor of permanent tax cuts) were very close.[1] The basic issues were whether the rebate would be large enough to stimulate demand and whether it would have a lasting effect. As usual, opinion varied widely among economists and politicians. Barber Conable, senior Republican on Ways and Means, echoing the new supply-side economics, urged recommittal and permanent tax reduction: "A tax cut of this magnitude is much sounder economic strategy than the bill's rebate-payment scheme which offers neither a sharp stimulative impact nor a permanent reduction upon which consumers can base long term spending."[2]

The corporate reductions were dropped by the committee in favor of a new provision called a New Jobs Tax Credit, which provided employers with credits for a portion of the wages for new employees. Ullman and some of the others on the committee were enthusiastic about the credit as a direct incentive to attack unemployment. One supporter, Abner Mikva (D-Ill.), supported it as a change from "the same old proposals which we know don't work," and added the proposition that: "If it does not work, as indeed, it many not, it is not likely to have a large revenue impact, as will some other ideas if they do not work, because it is an incremental proposal."[3] The Carter administration was not among those initially applauding the innovation, arguing that it was unclear whether it could achieve its objective, that it would subsidize employment that might have occurred anyway, and that if it did work it would serve to lower productivity by distorting the efficient market allocation between labor and capital.[4] On the House floor, in keeping with the philosophy adopted in 1975, the bill was debated under a modified closed rule that permitted votes on the committee proposals on the standard deduction, the jobs credit, the rebate, and a Republican-sponsored recommittal motion with instructions to substitute permanent tax cuts for the rebate. All votes favored the committee recommendations, but the vote on the substitute was close, with 39 of 86 southern Democrats joining all but one Republican in supporting the recommittal motion, which was defeated 194 to 219.

Despite the traditional honeymoon allowed a new president, particularly by members of his own party, the rebate plan was not popular in the Senate either. The Senate Finance Committee managed to keep the provision in the bill on two votes of 8 to 10, but it took a last-minute appearance before the committee by Charles Schultze, chairman of the Council of Economic Advisers, to ensure those votes. In keeping with tradition, the committee added provisions to the bill that further reduced taxes. It accepted the new jobs credit, but gave business the option of choosing instead an increase in the investment credit (from 10

to 12 percent). It also raised the standard deduction to $3,200 for joint returns, but to only $2,200 for single taxpayers. It postponed several provisions of the 1976 tax bill, extending the effective dates for the tougher sick-pay and foreign income provisions and some of the restrictive changes in business deductions.

Four days prior to the scheduled Senate debate on the bill, the administration withdrew its rebate proposal but asked that the business cuts be dropped as well. Although it was widely assumed that the administration feared the defeat of the rebate on the Senate floor, it justified the action as unnecessary now that recovery from the two-year recession was finally under way. The Senate readily dropped the rebate, but not the business cuts. After several votes that pitted Senator Kennedy against Chairman Long, a losing proposition for Kennedy, the investment credit was retained. Reversing his stand in 1976, when he tried to raise the investment credit to 15 percent as a replacement for the ADR, Kennedy tried first to make the credit refundable, thus aiding low-profit or unprofitable businesses, and then, arguing that the credit basically aided large, healthy, capital-intensive industries, proposed that it be repealed entirely. To this latter proposal Senator Long replied: "What's the matter with the *Fortune* 500? They provide good jobs and working conditions. . . . We do not want to limit ourselves to providing the delivery boy job . . . or the job at the corner grocery store."[5] The Senate concurred, and both Kennedy proposals were soundly defeated, the last gaining only 16 supporting votes.

Five votes were taken on the new jobs credit; the first, an administration-backed proposal to delete the provision, was defeated by a vote of 20 to 74. Three amendments were accepted on role call votes: one that increased the credit per employee hired; another that put a cap of $100,000 per firm on the credit, thus making it most useful to small businesses; and a final provision that gave an added credit for new jobs in high unemployment areas. A later amendment by Alan Cranston (D-Cal.) illustrated how tax provisions are tailored to aid specific groups. Passed by voice vote, it provided for higher jobs credits for employers of the handicapped, Vietnam veterans under the age of twenty-seven, and all disabled veterans and low-income persons unemployed fifteen or more weeks or receiving welfare. All of these targeting features, except a bonus for handicapped employees, were later dropped by the Conference Committee, although most would reappear and become part of a modified provision the following year.

Another amendment designed to stimulate jobs through the tax system by offering accelerated depreciation to employers in high unemployment areas, offered by Daniel Moynihan (D-N.Y.), was rejected on

the floor. Also rejected for the second time, by a wide margin (24 to 63), was a Republican-sponsored effort to index brackets, exemptions, and deductions for inflation. Two other amendments were passed. One, which ended up in the final bill and signaled a retreat on oil taxes, repealed the inclusion as a preference item of the deduction of intangible drilling costs; this inclusion had guaranteed at least a minimum tax of 15 percent. A second, later dropped, created a new tax credit of up to $250 for expenses for households that included a dependent over the age of 65. All of these amendments were counter to reform notions, but in each case there was a clearly identifiable rationale for the provision. Given the disenchantment with Great Society programs that had been growing for years and the basic antibureaucracy feeling that Carter had exploited so well in his campaign, the tax system was being used as a micro-policy tool. The policy aspects of the income tax were being extended from general economic incentives and provisions responding to broad conditions of economic hardship to incentives directed at narrow behavior and highly specific cases of need.

In the Conference Committee the administration took a nothing-or-all position: it favored no business reductions of any kind, but, if Congress insisted on the new jobs credits (which was a certainty), it wanted the investment credit increased to 12 percent. In what was to become a typical reaction to Carter tax policy, the committee simply ignored the administration, passing the jobs credit, but dropping the investment credit. It also accepted the extensions in the sick-pay, foreign income, and business deductions and the repeal of the intangible drilling deduction provision, at least until 1978. Combined with extensions of the $35 per person general tax credit, the 1975 corporate tax cuts, the earned income credit, and the increased standard deduction (the Senate version), the estimated reduction in the bill was approximately $11 billion in fiscal year 1978. It was signed reluctantly by the President on May 16 as a stopgap measure, while major reform legislation was being prepared by the Treasury.

The most interesting feature of the bill, which was titled the 1977 Tax Reduction and Simplification Act, was the new jobs credit. It offered a new way to use the tax system for directly stimulating employment and thus was seen as an alternative to direct jobs programs, which had been losing favor in Washington as ineffective and inefficient. In introducing the legislation on the House floor, Al Ullman was very enthusiastic, describing the jobs credit as "a new and simple kind of exciting, dynamic tax concept based upon new jobs." In the same debate, however, Ways and Means member William Steiger (R-Wis.) questioned the provision: "I must say in all honesty that I do not think the commit-

tee . . . at all well understands exactly what implications are in this proposal."[6] A look at an official description of the provision (not the statute itself) certainly leads one to question Ullman's use of the adjective "simple" to describe the credit and suggests that perhaps Steiger was implying that members of the committee did not understand the provision itself, let alone its "implications."

NEW JOBS TAX CREDIT

For taxable years 1977 and 1978, an employer may claim a credit equal to 50 percent of the Federal unemployment tax wage base of employees who represent an expansion of his firm's work force. The credit is subject to four major limitations. First, it is available only for increases in the firm's Federal unemployment tax wage base above 102 percent of its base in the previous year. Second, no employer is entitled to more than $100,000 of credits a year. Third, the employer must reduce his deduction under section 162 for wages as ordinary business deductions by the amount of credit claimed. Fourth, the credit may not exceed 25 percent of the firm's total unemployment tax wage base. In addition, in any given year, the credit may not exceed 50 percent of the difference between total wages paid and 105 percent of total wages paid during the previous year.

If the workers qualifying for the new jobs tax credit are mentally or physically handicapped, the employer is entitled to a bonus tax credit equal to 10 percent of the Federal unemployment tax wage base. This bonus credit may not exceed 20 percent of the general credit earned without regard to the $100,000 overall limitation. However, the bonus credit, unlike the general credit, may exceed $100,000 in a year. In other respects, conditions imposed on the two credits are identical.[7]

What is remarkable about this complicated maze of limits and calculations is that each complication has a specific and carefully drawn rationale designed to prevent unfair advantages either by a particular type of business or clever, tax conscious employers in general. The limitation of the credit to increases above 102 percent of the previous year's unemployment wage base was meant to answer the criticism that it would reward natural growth that would have occurred anyway; the $100,000 limit was meant to cap the benefit for large corporations; the reduction of business deductions by the amount of the credit was

designed to prevent the use of the credit as a tax shelter under which it would pay employers in high marginal brackets to hire workers and not require them to work; the limit of 25 percent of the current year's wages was meant to forestall splitting full-time jobs into part-time ones and thus doubling the credit; and the limit based on the previous year's total wages paid ("50 percent of the difference between total wages paid and 105 percent of total wages paid during the previous year") was meant to limit the advantages accruing to new businesses or businesses that had laid off many workers in the previous year.[8]

Thus, an apparently simple, straightforward concept—providing a wage tax credit to induce new employment—becomes a statutory nightmare that only those backed by the best accountants and attorneys are likely to understand.[9] It has happened repeatedly: legislation based on relatively clear logic and motives (such as the minimum tax, the effort to reward earned, as opposed to unearned, income, and the attempt to prevent abuses of investment incentives), becomes, when put into final form, extremely cumbersome. When it comes to fitting the incentive to a precise type of behavior and population, while at the same time trying to anticipate and thwart the legal maneuvers of those attempting to exploit the provision, what may be simple conceptually becomes unmercifully complex in practice. The irony is that the provision discussed here was the cornerstone of a law entitled the "Tax Reduction and Simplification Act."

The 1978 Revenue Act:
From Tax Reform to Capital Formation

Administration Proposals. Undaunted by its failure in 1977, the Carter administration proposed a comprehensive tax reform package in January 1978. The principles on which the legislation was based were discussed earlier by Emil Sunley, Deputy Assistant Secretary for Tax Policy and longtime Brookings Institution tax scholar. In a presentation in the classic reform tradition, he emphasized the tax changes would be aimed at (1) simplifying the tax system; (2) creating equity, with a particular emphasis on horizontal equity; and (3) aiding growth in investment. In his brief speech before the National Tax Association, he never mentioned the possibility that those goals might conflict. It was even suggested by a follow-up speaker, who was working with Treasury officials in formulating the proposals, that the Carter plan might provide the foundation for integration of the individual and corporate income taxes through its proposal that a portion of corporate tax be considered

as a withholding for dividends paid to individuals. This proposal originated in an administration option paper released in September and was
consistent with the *Blueprints for Basic Tax Reform*, which had been
published the previous year under the auspices of the outgoing Ford
Treasury Department.[10]

When these general principles were reduced to specific reform proposals, they followed very closely the classic formulation for tax reform.
The integration plan was dropped by the administration as too radical,
given that Congress had completely ignored a similar attempt by the
Ford administration in 1975. However, the rest of the administration's
reform package advocated broadening the tax base by eliminating or
tightening tax reduction provisions; this, together with an increased
standard deduction, would also simplify the tax system. The revenue to
be gained from these measures would permit a lower basic rate structure through lowered marginal rates, higher exemptions, general tax
credits, and so on. Incentives for economic expansion would come from
the net tax reduction resulting from the lowering of rates and from the
use of the investment tax credit, which liberal economists at least had
come to agree was the most direct and effective mechanism for stimulating capital investment.

Although in other economic and energy legislation the administration completely abandoned these principles and embraced the program
of Charles Schultze (chairman of the Council of Economic Advisers) to
use the tax system to alter economic behavior,[11] the proposed revenue
bill itself stuck more religiously to reform principles than its predeces-
sors in 1964, 1969, or 1976, and the administration's rhetoric belabored
the reform theme. The basic rate reductions were to take the form of a 2
percent cut in all marginal rates, a shift (and increase) from a personal
exemption to a $240 tax credit for each taxpayer, and a 4 percent cut in
corporate tax rates. Since exemptions are more valuable to those in
higher marginal brackets, switching to a credit would have increased
progressivity. Base broadening was to be accomplished by eliminating
or tightening up on deductions, exclusions, tax shelter devices, and
special corporate provisions. Major changes were suggested in personal
deductions: allowing medical and casualty deductions only when they
totaled more than 10 percent of adjusted gross income, and repealing
the deduction for all taxes except state income taxes (thus encouraging
the most progressive form of state finance).

They also proposed restricting business deductions, particularly entertainment expenses. The infamous "three-martini lunch" and the
case of the businessman who deducted 338 lunches for over $10,000 in
a year were cited repeatedly in presidential messages and news

conferences.[12] The administration further suggested that half of unemployment benefits, which had not been taxable since their inception in 1935, should be taxable for those with incomes over $20,000 a year; that the minimum tax should be increased by eliminating the reduction for taxes paid; that credit unions should be taxed; that tax exemption of industrial development bonds should be reduced; and, backing off somewhat from more extreme proposals, that capital gains income should be more heavily taxed, but only for those with higher incomes. It also brought back the proposal to replace tax-exempt state and local bonds with an interest-rate subsidy. Extension of the at-risk rules and the allowable deduction limit that were passed in the 1976 act as a method of counteracting tax shelters was also proposed. For corporations, in the only major gestures toward stimulating business activity, it proposed fixing the investment credit permanent at 10 percent, extending it to structures, and applying it fully to pollution control investments. However, it also proposed eliminating the deferral of taxes on foreign corporate earnings and phasing out the DISC provisions. The result of these bold proposals for fiscal 1979 would have been a net total of $22.5 billion in income tax reductions (plus $2 billion less in excise and payroll taxes), after $9.5 billion in gains from reform measures.[13]

Several weeks after the announcement of the administration's program, Senator Muskie, in his role as chairman of the Senate Budget Committee, released a report by the Congressional Budget Office that argued that high-income taxpayers (those with incomes over $50,000) got almost a third of the "tax expenditures" in the tax system.* Muskie had been instrumental in 1969 and 1974 in initiating a requirement that the tax expenditure budget be reported along with the regular annual budget on a yearly basis. He had also tried, unsuccessfully, to pass a requirement that any increase in the tax provisions included on the list, and any new items that were proposed, be approved by the appropriate substantive committee in the House and Senate as well as the tax committees. The release of the report, which was expected to generate a lot of headlines, was meant to support the president's reform package and to hasten its consideration in the House.

The result was different, however. Within a month both the *New York Times* and the *Washington Post* published articles that countered

---

* "Tax expenditures" are officially defined as "those revenue losses attributable to provisions of the Federal tax laws which allow a special exclusion, exemption, or deduction from gross income or which provide a special credit, a preferential rate of tax, or a deferral of tax liability." *The Congressional Budget and Impoundment Act* (Washington, D.C.: Government Printing Office, 1974), section 3(a)(3).

Muskie's efforts. The *Times* attacked indirectly in an article headlined "Britain's High Taxes Seen as a Factor in Stagnation," but the *Post* directly rebutted the Muskie article by presenting bold tables demonstrating that although "wealthier persons enjoy the biggest tax breaks and deductions, they also shoulder a disproportionate share of the tax burden."[14] Various interpretations can be and always have been placed on tax numbers, depending on differences in emphasis. In this case, one can look at the percentage of tax reductions or the percentage of taxes paid. The fact that these liberal newspapers were supporting a conservative interpretation should have signaled to the administration that the mood of Congress and the country was shifting rapidly toward lower taxes and away from tax reform. Yet it did not seem to understand the message. Never in the history of the income tax were proposals so out of step with congressional intentions, and never were they so completely defeated.

Congressional Action. Congress began making those intentions explicit in the very first week of Ways and Means markup sessions in mid-April. Those sessions went so badly for the administration that at the end of the week, the leading Democrats on the committee (Ullman, Wagonner, and Rostenkowski, Ill.) went to the White House with the message that tax reform was not in the cards. Ullman then suspended consideration of the bill in hopes that the administration would modify its proposals. There was a solid coalition on the committee that included all the Republicans and at least eight or nine (and often more) conservative Democrats. It defeated the major administration changes in deductions for taxes, medical and casualty expenses, and charities. It even added a provision that extended the charitable deduction by allowing those who take the standard deduction to take a special deduction for charitable giving as well. Although this was eventually dropped by the committee and never restored, the concept would resurface in 1981 with a more favorable outcome. Barber Conable, the senior Republican, summarized the feelings of this coalition and the changes that the administration needed to make with a press conference statement: "The [administration] proposals have a lot of appeal in terms of simplification and structure, provided we don't stick it in the ear of the middle class."[15] While always good political rhetoric, this concern for the middle class had become more pressing because of inflation. It became still more important as the bill progressed, and it carried over as a central issue of the 1980 election and the 1981 tax cut.

While the administration debated whether it should adjust its goals to practical reality, the tax issue exploded with the passage of Proposition

13, which drastically cut and limited property taxes in California. The "tax revolt" had arrived. Normally liberal newspapers and news weeklies ran banner headlines and cover stories about tax protest and dissatisfaction; the polling services discovered, and the news media reported, that the sentiment expressed in California, while varying from state to state, was widespread.[16] At the same time, the business community and a strong bloc in Congress turned again to the problem of capital formation, this time with the added concern that capital gains were artificially increased by inflation. Notable economists had been arguing this case for some time and now began to present it in the popular press as well. Businessmen, like Donald Regan, then chairman of Merrill Lynch, and Frederick Hickman, past Assistant Treasury Secretary for Tax Policy, added pressure through the *Wall Street Journal* and other media sources.[17] But even before Proposition 13 it had become clear not only that the Ways and Means Committee would *not* raise capital gains taxes as the administration had requested, but that a significant reduction would take place.

Despite this crescendo of activity, the administration did nothing, and the Ways and Means Committee, on reconsidering the tax bill in July, shelved the administration proposals. Rather, an agreement was reached between Ullman, Conable, and James Jones (D-Okla.). The last, chairman of the House Budget Committee, had emerged as a swing voter and a compromise Democrat with a more moderate proposal to cut capital gains than the one made earlier by William Steiger. The committee report, supported by all 12 committee Republicans and 13 Democrats, and opposed only by the 12 Democratic liberals, dropped most of the administration's base-broadening reforms and reconstructed the tax cuts by retaining the personal exemption at a higher level and gearing more marginal rate reductions to the middle-income groups. Based on the Jones compromise, the bill increased the capital gains exclusion, dropping the maximum effective rate on capital gains from 49.1 to 35 percent. However, it also indexed capital gains to inflation (on an amendment by Bill Archer, R-Tex.) and added a new provision that allowed a one-time $100,000 exclusion from capital gains derived from the sale of one's home (proposed by Sam Gibbons, D-Fla.). Since the coalition that ended up ruling the committee was more concerned about deficits than either committee liberals or the administration, the bill provided a lower tax cut ($16.1 billion) than the administration requested. This was accomplished primarily by eliminating the general tax credit of $240 proposed by the administration and the existing $35 credit, which was due to expire.

Not until the report was filed in late July did the administration move on to a compromise alternative, which the Rules Committee agreed could be presented on the floor of the House. This proposal, with a modified general tax credit and a complex scheme that would have led to much less revenue loss in capital gains, was openly derided as too little, too late, and was accompanied by charges of legislative ineptness.[18] The administration substitute bill, embodied in an amendment cosponsored by Rep. Corman (D-Cal.) and Rep. Fisher (D-N.Y.) was defeated by a vote of 192 to 225. The floor action included a separate vote on indexing capital gains and a vote on the soon-to-be-famous Kemp-Roth tax cut, which would have cut total income taxes by 33 percent over three years. The latter was defeated after a brief supply-side floor debate in which the Republicans dramatized the unjust and torturous burden on the middle class. The vote was 177 to 240, with only 3 Republicans but 37 Democrats switching sides. However, while temporarily resisting this more radical cut, in an election year that had been labeled the year of the tax revolt, few representatives were willing to risk voting against a tax reduction that would still not quite offset a scheduled increase in Social Security taxes and inflation-induced bracket creep. Thus, the final vote on the committee bill was 362 to 49.

Throughout the postwar period, the Senate has consistently increased the net tax reduction of House revenue bills. Senate action on the Revenue Act of 1978 was no exception and, indeed, extended this pattern to historic proportions. The final Senate bill was estimated to reduce income taxes by $29.1 billion, compared with the House bill of $16.3 billion. The increased tax cuts began in the Senate Finance Committee in a twelve-day markup period in September. Although the committee accepted the basic rate-reduction formula, it enlarged the reduction percentages and, at the same time, consolidated and therefore widened the brackets. Abandoning any pretense of tax reform, it also voted extensions or increases in a host of existing provisions to which the House bill made no reference. Although several provision changes led to more revenue, only one was of any real consequence (dropping the indexing of capital gains). Of the increased benefits that ultimately became law, the most important were (1) delaying until 1980 the new basis for calculating capital gains at death (passed in 1976, but without a separate vote in the Senate Finance Committee or on the Senate floor—see chapter 9); (2) reducing the capital gains rate for corporations from 30 to 28 percent; (3) increasing several pension provisions, including a change extending IRAs by allowing employees to make tax-free contributions to individual IRAs when no formal

retirement plan exists; (4) doubling the credit for political contributions (from $50 to $100); and (5) increasing the amount and income range for the earned income credit. Other changes that also survived the Conference Committee allowed deduction of employer contributions for employee educational expenses; made the additional tax credit for the ESOP plan a permanent feature of the tax code; extended industrial development bonds to water and electrical generation facilities; and made permanent the 1977 provisions eliminating intangible drilling expenses from calculation of the minimum tax.

A number of other provisions would have added to the revenue loss but were dropped in Conference. The most important by far in terms of revenue was an increase in the ADR variation from 20 to 30 percent of the scheduled useful life. Others expanded tax credits for the elderly, added a $500 exemption for the handicapped, increased the WIN credit for hiring welfare recipients, and provided the choice of an exclusion or a tax credit for state and municipal bond interest. A host of other provisions would have benefited specific economic groups (railroads, horse breeders, public utilities, etc.). One curious provision, never to be seen again but exemplifying the potential of the tax system to create change, would have authorized a new form of tax-exempt corporation that would have been publicly owned by all the residents of an individual state. The Conference Committee, adept at terminating "radical" proposals, eliminated this one without debate.

The Finance Committee did, however, approve several House provisions that cut tax expenditures and defeated several major proposals to cut rates even further. In a reversal of earlier stances, it supported the House-passed repeal of the gasoline tax deduction: the energy crisis separated this from the other taxes the administration had wanted to eliminate as deductible items. The committee also supported an administration request and a House provision to scale down the 1977 general jobs credit in favor of a more targeted approach directed primarily at youth unemployment, which had gained a great deal of media attention over the summer. In addition, while increasing the overall reductions allocated for capital gains income, it eliminated the Archer amendment, which had indexed capital gains to inflation. Senator Long personally argued against a tuition tax credit advanced by Senator Roth, convincing the committee that an administration threat to veto any bill including such a proviso was for real. Long advocated a separate bill; however, supporters of the credit were later successful in adding it to this bill on the Senate floor, and it came very close to being accepted in Conference. Finally, on a series of almost straight-line party votes (9 to 8, 9 to 9), Kemp-Roth proposals for a multiyear tax cut of approximately 30

percent were rejected. With the exceptions of the targeted jobs credit and removal of the education credit, all of these actions were later ratified by additional votes on the Senate floor.

In its final form, with an election just over a month away, the Finance bill was irresistible. It was only opposed by two Senators: Senator Nelson, who objected that the bill conferred too many benefits on upper-income groups, and Senator Roth, who objected that the bill helped the rich and the poor, but "in effect created a new class—the middle-class poor."[19]

The Senate as a whole took over where the committee left off, in the end adding $6.2 billion more in tax reductions. The floor session began on October 5, lasting only five days in the rush to adjourn for election campaigning. Of the $6.2 billion in additional Senate cuts, $4.5 billion were due to further reductions in the rate structure, particularly for the middle class (80 percent going to those with incomes between $10,000 and $30,000). Under the final provisions, the average taxpayer would receive a rate reduction of 10.8 percent, compared with 9.0 percent in the Finance bill and 5.6 percent in the House version.[20] The amendment lowering the rates was sponsored by two liberals, Edward Kennedy and Dale Bumpers (D-Ark.). The vote accepting this rate formula followed a vote on a Kemp-Roth three-year, 30 percent tax cut, which was defeated 36 to 60 on a party vote in which 7 Democrats and 7 Republicans switched sides. Later in the session, a bipartisan coalition led by Sam Nunn (D-Ga.), which enlisted Senator Roth, was able to pass a scheduled future tax reduction of 5 percent per year if a stringent set of government spending conditions were met. The amendment was passed on a bipartisan vote of 65 to 20, in part because the prospect of attaining the target goals was so remote. Other than the meaningless resolution that accompaned the 1975 tax bill, this effort to link tax actions to future economic and budget results was historically unique. Later the House supported the notion in a separate vote, but the conferees under a threat of veto watered down the provision to another resolution and a promise to consider tax reduction if the targets should be met. In retrospect it mattered little because spending and deficits far outdistanced the targets. In a final action yet another vote rejected indexing. It was closer this time, with a margin of 53 to 37, but still with only 10 Democrats supporting the amendment.

A number of structural provisions were also affected by floor decisions, and again most served to increase the tax cut. Attempts by the administration to revive tax reforms, particularly those affecting business, were all defeated. Included in the category were votes on DISCs, foreign corporate income, business deductions, and changes in the

ADR. The increases in capital gains included in the Finance bill easily survived a liberal challenge led by Senator Kennedy.[21] Clearly, the notion of tax reform was far from the collective mind of the Senate. Rather, the momentum favored a parceling out of additional tax benefit provisions. To begin, the Senate approved a tuition credit by a wide enough margin (67 to 26) that Carter's threatened veto over the issue was in jeopardy of being overridden. It also passed amendments extending the coverage and hence benefits of industrial development bonds, the investment credit, pension fund exclusion, and the elderly tax credit. It accepted an amendment by Senator Haskell (D-Colo.) restoring the original general jobs credit and eliminating the targeted version that had passed the House and the Finance Committee. This was accomplished by tying the provision to a reduction in the maximum corporate tax rate from 48 to 46 percent. The Conference Committee accepted the latter reduction but went back to the targeted jobs credit approach, which was considerably cheaper but also much more complex and, when implemented, required an elaborate administrative effort to certify eligible workers.

In addition to extending and/or increasing many of the existing tax benefits affecting broad categories of individuals, numerous minor provisions were passed that aided narrower groups: farmers, teachers, Alaskan natives, railroads, magazine, paperback, and record manufacturers, the Gallo winery, two Arkansas chicken farmers, the states of North Carolina and Maryland, and New York City. One reform measure that was upheld was the elimination of the deduction for gasoline taxes, but the reason was clearly extraneous to any reform motive. Other than this single vote, there were no successful actions to add revenue to the existing bill. As in the House, final passage was close to unanimous at 86 to 4.

There was one interesting sidelight to the debate. It began with an effort by Senator Muskie, chairman of the Senate Budget Committee, to pass a general "sunset" provision for direct government expenditures. His proposed new amendment would have automatically terminated spending programs after ten years unless Congress reallocated the funds. Senator Glenn (D-Ohio) attempted to extend the provision to tax expenditures listed in the annual tax expenditure budget. He was supported in the debate by Senator Kennedy but vehemently opposed by members of the Finance Committee. Russell Long warned that such an action would mean much higher taxes, a proposition supported by Lloyd Bentsen (D-Tex.), who concluded that the Glenn proposal assumed "that all income belongs to the government."[22] Although Glenn's proposal survived a motion to table, it was later ruled out of

order, and after it had taken up the better part of two days, a vote of closure was successful and the matter was dropped. Long ended the discussion with a quip: "Sunset sounds good, but home sounds better."[23]

The final Conference bill was a complete renunciation of the Carter tax proposals and any notion of tax reform. Although the bill was much closer to the revenue figures passed by the House and lowered revenues less in the first year than Carter had originally requested, the formula for achieving reductions, the general distribution, and structural changes were very different from the administration program. By my count of administration proposals, it had a success rate of ten out of twenty-three. However, six of the successful proposals were requests to *lower* taxes by increasing the benefits of provisions, while only four of the administration's fourteen requests to tighten provisions were enacted. Several of these, including the one on capital gains, were turned completely around, reducing rather than increasing revenue gains.

Because the proposal to expand the general tax credit was abandoned, the tax cuts were skewed much more to the middle- and upper-income groups than Carter had planned. The shifting of public interest toward the middle class and a reawakened concern for the problem of capital formation and investment (similar to that in the Kennedy years) ensured this outcome. Compared with existing law, the largest cuts in terms of percentages went to those with incomes under $10,000 (since they initially paid very low taxes). However, unlike earlier tax cuts, this one gave all income groups above that level a cut close to the same percentage (around 6.8 percent), with those above $20,000 actually receiving higher percentage reductions than those between $10,000 and $20,000. In absolute dollar terms those in the higher-income groups received much more. Of the total cut, 67 percent went to the 21 percent of the taxpayers who had incomes over $20,000. These results turned the original Carter proposals on their head. Carter initially requested cuts that were uniformly progressive across brackets. His changes were to range from -278.0, -22.6, and -15 percent for incomes under $5,000, $5,000–10,000, and $10,000–15,000 respectively, to -0.9, $+2.2$, and $+5.6$ percent for $50,000–100,000, $100,000–200,000, and over $200,000.

Although the administration had proposed $9.1 billion in net reform gains, in the end structural losses slightly outweighed gains for 1979 and were considerably more than gains in 1980. The reason can be seen in table 10.1, which shows the bill's major revenue-changing provisions. Essentially the only true revenue increases came from the repeal

of the gasoline deduction and the shift to a targeted rather than a general jobs credit. The other revenue-gaining changes, of which there were several, were generally tied to revenue reductions in other aspects of the same provision. The revenue-losing changes were spread across a number of provisions. The table gives a single total for several changes in capital gains and the investment credit. The latter had by this time become extremely complex, with exceptions and varying rates for different types of industry and different forms of investment and an additional credit available through ESOPs. Six changes were made in this set of provisions alone. These were in keeping with the emphasis on capital formation that built up through the legislative session.

Several additional tax reduction provisions passed in 1978 are not listed in table 10.1. I somewhat arbitrarily treat the earned income credit as a "rate" rather than "structural" change on the rationale that it was designed as an integral feature of the rate system (see table 8.1). This credit was expanded significantly and made a permanent feature of the tax code in 1978, changes that were expected to cost $2.3 billion in 1980. The list in table 10.1 does not include a whole series of new provisions, recommended by the administration and enacted as part of the Energy Tax Bill, which were passed on the same day as the revenue bill. These included a 15 percent residential energy credit for insulation and energy conservation expenses (up to $300 per year); a credit for the installation of solar equipment of 30 percent on the first $2,000 and 20 percent on the next $8,000; and a business credit of 10 percent for investment in energy property and certain energy conversion or conservation equipment. It was later estimated that these new provisions reduced revenues by $935 million in fiscal year 1979.[24] They also reflected a distinctly different ordering of priorities from that advanced by the administration in support of tax reform. The tax system was being treated as a vehicle for accomplishing substantive policy goals, and these provisions represented a clear policy choice. As must have been expected, in the next few years energy provisions in the tax code expanded to cover investments in a wide range of alternative energy sources and fuels and to include a much broader range of users.

Other provisions that would have added further revenue losses were not passed. These included the administration's proposal for a tax-based incomes policy (TIP), which offered a complicated tax credit for employees who endured wage increases below an inflationary target. It never received consideration in Congress. If it had passed, combined with the targeted jobs credit, a whole new vista of tax incentives would have opened up. The latest attempt at a tuition tax credit came much closer to passage. It was dropped in the face of a veto threat primarily because conferees disagreed about whether the credit should apply to

primary and secondary education as well as college. Had it passed, not only would it have been expensive, but it would also have opened up the whole field of education as a potential target for tax expenditures. Although this provision has come close to passage several times since the early 1960s and continues to be placed on the agenda, it appears that this is a unique area where the combination of cost, opposition interest groups (public education lobbies), and constitutional questions (parochial schools would be large beneficiaries) seems to forestall final congressional action.

Table 10.1 Major Structural Changes in the Revenue Act of 1978

	Estimated Gain/Loss ($ millions)	
	1979	1980
Revenue-Gaining Provisions		
Repeal of the general tax credit	689	2,458
Repeal of gasoline tax deduction	471	1,237
Alternative minimum tax	—	739
All others	173	—
Total gain	103	748
	+1,263	+5,182
Revenue-Losing Provisions		
Targeted jobs credit plus extension of commitments	−830	−2,941
Combined capital gains reductions	−184	−1,888
Minimum tax changes	—	−1,275
Combined investment credit changes	−275	−706
Exclusion of gain on sale of residence	−165	−415
All others	−342	−760
Total loss	−1,696	−7,984
Net structural change	−433	−2,802

Source: Joint Committee on Taxation, *General Explanations of the Revenue Act of 1978* (Washington, D.C.: Government Printing Office, 1979), from tables I–1, pp. 19–26; I–2, pp. 27–31.

Conclusion. The Revenue Act of 1978 marked the beginning of another major transition point in income tax history. If there ever was a reform era, which one might reasonably question, it ended with a bang in 1978. Although the Carter administration attempted to keep the reform spirit alive, it was, like past administrations, equally willing to use the tax system to solve policy problems in the areas of energy, unemployment, and inflation. Use of the tax system as a basic policy tool had become legitimate. Tax reform meant only that the tax base should be expanded in those specific areas designated by the administration as offering unfair advantages. The reform pretense was not accepted, however, and the definition of "fairness" was beginning to change.

Although the "tax revolt" undoubtedly had an important effect on the final form of the bill, signs of a shift in favor of economic stimulation through tax reductions for business and upper-income groups were plentiful as early as 1976. The first warnings came with defeat of liberal proposals during the long debate over the 1976 Tax Reform Act. The comparatively low rates of U.S. saving and investment and the nation's apparent long-term economic decline were the subjects of discussion and academic analysis throughout the 1970s and had become a major focus of attention under the Treasury leadership of William Simon (see pp. 187–88). It was this building pressure on the government to stimulate the economy, rather than the anticipation of a tax revolt, that led in the spring of 1978 to the Steiger amendments lowering capital gains. On the other hand, the continuing inflation since 1975, which studies revealed had the worst income tax impact on the middle class,[25] created a broad consensus for individual income tax reduction. It was fitting that on the day of final passage of the 1978 act, the *Washington Post* ran an analysis with the headline "The Tax Machine: Despite Major 'Cuts' Rate Stays Remarkably Stable."[26]

Finally, the 1978 Revenue Act is interesting in that it marks the beginning of credibility for the debate over supply-side economics. Because of the tax revolt and the 1978 bill, the Kemp-Roth proposals were given more attention in the press and in Congress. Major stories highlighted Congressman Kemp, not as an oddball football player, but as a possible future presidential candidate. The supply-side theory resurrected an old argument, stated almost precisely fifty years earlier by Andrew Mellon. Kemp explained it on the floor of the House:

> By recreating the incentive to work, save, invest and take economic risks by reducing the percentage of reward for that economic activity taken by the federal government in the form of

taxes, we will have more investment and more economic risk taking. That will expand the total economic activity, expanding the tax base from which federal tax revenues are drawn, providing additional revenues with which to offset federal budget deficits.[27]

In other words, a tax cut would lead in short order to greater, not less, revenue. Although this conclusion was strongly challenged by most economists and by Democrats in both Houses, Republicans sensed a popular issue, and respected tax experts like Barber Conable used the argument to support middle-class tax reductions as noninflationary. Although the specter of deficits and inflation hung over this tax bill and was invoked by the administration in bargaining against the huge Senate bill, those concerns were overshadowed the next time the issue came before Congress, and supply-side theory was the primary economic doctrine.

A Brief Lull

By the end of 1978, the administration's defeat on the tax bill and legislative trouble on a score of other domestic programs made it clear that an era of liberalism was at an end. President Carter's election, based on a campaign against big Washington-based government and the failures of the Great Society, was itself an indication of this swing. However, although his general economic policy had conservative elements (e.g., deregulation and reliance on tight monetary policy), his tax policy was unmistakably liberal, and just as unmistakably rejected. This time the administration learned the lesson and proposed no further tax legislation beyond the windfall profits tax on oil, finally passed in 1980 after three years of struggle. The tax committees were not eager to engage in major tax legislation before the next election, and the few changes they did enact, along with comments from committee leaders and business groups, confirmed the conservative trend that had rushed to the surface in 1978.

In May 1979, in speeches before the U.S. Chamber of Commerce, Senator Long and Representative Ullman agreed that major tax legislation was unlikely before the next election. Long also said that one action his committee would complete was the permanent repeal of the market value carry-over basis for capital gains acquired though inheritance, which he had personally opposed from the beginning. However, he went much further, also supporting additional cuts in capital gains

taxes (from the 28 percent recently enacted to an effective rate of 21 percent); dropping the maximum tax rate of 70 percent on unearned income to the 50 percent rate applicable to earned income; and repealing the double taxation on corporate dividends. To indicate how far the pendulum had swung, both chairmen advocated liberalizing depreciation and the creation of a European-style value-added tax (VAT), which would tax goods and services at progressive stages in the production process.[28] The VAT had long been opposed by liberal tax experts as similar to a national sales tax—that is, regressive—but even worse in that it is completely hidden.

In September the Senate Finance Committee voted unanimously to repeal the carry-over basis for capital gains. Voting for repeal of the measure, which was a cornerstone of the Tax Reform Act of 1976, were such liberals as Gaylord Nelson and Daniel Moynihan. Later in the session, in an incremental move toward Long's stated goal of eliminating double taxation of corporate dividends, a proposal by Senators Bentsen and Dole (R-Kans.) to double the dividend exclusion to $200 ($400 joint) *and* extend it to interest income was passed by a vote of 15 to 2. Both of these provisions were added to the Windfall Profits Tax bill to ensure immediate passage, escape separate consideration by Ways and Means, and avoid a threatened veto. They were enacted along with a half a dozen provisions increasing or creating tax incentives for investment in various energy sources.

As another indication of the new direction in tax politics, a proposal gaining favor in the Senate Finance Committee but judged too important to amend to another bill would have changed the depreciation rules to a "10-5-3" formula, under which buildings could be written off in ten years, light trucks and autos in three, and all other equipment in five. The push for liberalized depreciation and the design of the new rules were the work of a powerful business lobbying group that began meeting informally for breakfast at the Carlton Hotel in Washington. The "Carlton group," as it became known, included Charles Walker and Ernest Christian, tax lawyers who had been high-ranking officials in the Nixon and Ford administrations, Richard Rahn, chief economist for the U.S. Chamber of Commerce, and Mark Bloomfield, who had succeeded Rahn at the Council for Capital Formation. Given the tax expertise of the members, their Washington connections, and the range of business interests covered in the group, they had immediate influence on tax discussions, although their power would not come to full fruition until 1981.[29]

It is symbolic of the change in tax philosophy that Gaylord Nelson, one of the most consistent liberals on the Senate Finance Committee,

was one of the sponsors of the "10-5-3" proposal. He had in the past requested liberalized depreciation, but only for small businesses and then in lieu of increases in the investment tax credit. He was to get his wish in 1981, when the proposal was adopted by both parties as one of the pillars of the Reagan tax cut. Senator Nelson was not around to see it, however, because he was one of the six liberal senators who were casualties of the 1980 elections.

Chapter 11.
Opening the
Floodgates
The 1981 Tax Cut

A Confirming Election

The election results of 1980 took many people by surprise and generated immediate speculation among reporters and political scientists that a major party realignment was beginning. The shock was not simply the election of Ronald Reagan, but the breadth of his victory over a sitting president only six years after Watergate. He carried 44 states and captured 51 percent of the popular vote (to Carter's 41 percent) and all but 49 electoral votes. It is perhaps more important that he brought with him the first Republican Senate majority since 1954, with six prominent liberal senators going down in defeat. Although the Democrats retained majority control in the House, their margin was cut from 277–158 to 243–192, and there was no question that the ideological margin was much closer than that. One of the casualties in the House was Al Ullman, defeated by a well-financed conservative opponent. Dan Rostenkowski, a protege of Mayor Richard Daley of Chicago, became chairman of Ways and Means.

Although a number of factors contributed to the Republican and conservative victories, including the continued holding of the hostages in Iran, the state of the economy, and the general impression that the Carter administration lacked decisive leadership and direction, the tax issue was probably more important than in any previous election. The tax revolt had cooled somewhat, but it was still a salient political issue and undoubtedly *the* issue in many state and local elections. Reagan had made supply-side economics, a proportionate individual tax cut following the Kemp-Roth plan, and a major reduction in corporate taxes the centerpiece of his economic plank. In a dramatic media event on June 25, 1980, he appeared with congressional Republicans on the steps of the Capitol and pledged to enact such a program as his first order of business once elected. Tax cuts were a central element in every

campaign speech, and he pounded away at the issue in the televised debates with Jimmy Carter. Once in office, the administration assumed it had a mandate on taxes. It successfully brought a willing Congress to the same conclusion.

The passage of the 1981 tax cut, to be named the Economic Recovery Tax Act of 1981, was one of the most exciting yet bizarre spectacles in the history of tax politics. The final result—the largest tax cut in history for both individuals and corporations—had more long-term consequences than any previous bill. It was also the least balanced, both in terms of overall incidence and in terms of the mix of provisions passed. A look ahead at table 11.1 shows that only two major legislative changes raised revenue. And one of those was coincidental in that the interest exclusion passed in 1980 was repealed in favor of a more lucrative provision for taxpayers that in 1985 would exclude 15 percent of interest income up to $3,000.

In one sense these results were not surprising. The stage had been set prior to the election for a major tax cut, and one that was clearly going to emphasize savings, investment, and a reduction in the top marginal rates. It was accepted in the previous Congress that work incentives, investment, and risk taking were being stifled by high taxes and that this in turn was the root cause of long-term declines in productivity and real economic growth. The 1978 tax cut sent a clear signal to this effect, and it was reinforced by actions and events in 1979 and 1980. What *was* surprising and in fact somewhat bizarre was the frenzy with which both parties rushed to increase the bounty and their disregard for the fiscal consequences, which have since become so troublesome to the American economy. In short, the bill got out of hand as the dam broke. David Stockman, Reagan's director of the Office of Management and the Budget, in a famous candid interview published in the *Atlantic Monthly* some months after the tax bill was passed, cynically described this degenerative process: "The hogs were really feeding. The greed level, the level of opportunism, was just out of control."[1]

Round One

In retrospect, the initial Reagan Treasury proposal seems extremely modest. Following the tax plank in the Republican platform and the advice of an administration task force headed by Charles Walker, its basic elements were: (1) a 30 percent proportionate cut in personal rates, with a 5 percent cut beginning in July 1981, 10 percent each in

1982 and 1983, and the remaining 5 percent in 1984; (2) liberalized depreciation, although not quite as liberal as the "10-5-3" proposal that had received overwhelming support in the previous year in the Senate Finance Committee; and (3) a three-year phase-out of the distinction between earned and unearned income.[2] By administration estimates, the package would have reduced revenues by $9 billion in fiscal year 1981 and $50 billion in 1982. However, because of a predicted increase in economic activity, the fiscal 1983 deficit was expected to be only $22.9 billion. In presenting these proposals, the president commented that: "The taxing power of government must be used to provide revenues for legitimate government purposes. It must not be used to regulate the economy to bring about social change."[3] In keeping with the practice of the Kennedy, Nixon, and Carter administrations, Secretary of the Treasury Regan promised a second, more comprehensive tax bill when the "economic emergency" had passed and the Treasury had time to work out the details. On this bill, however, the president pressed for immediate action, concurrent with the budget reconciliation that was also being proposed.

Since there was bipartisan agreement on the depreciation increases, the controversial aspects of the proposal were the extension of the rate reduction over several years and the proportionality of the rate reductions. In introducing the proposals on February 18, 1981, Reagan defended these cuts as equitable and as conducive to greater prosperity for all: "Unlike some past tax 'reforms' this is not merely a shift of wealth between different taxpayers. . . . This proposal for equal reduction in everyone's tax rates will expand our national prosperity, enlarge national income and increase opportunities for *all* Americans."[4] Several months later, David Stockman characterized the theory behind the bill and supply-side economics in general in somewhat different terms. He explained that the tax cut was from the outset based on a trickle-down assumption, but that "it's kind of hard to sell 'trickle down,' so the supply-side formula was the only way to get a tax policy that was really 'trickle down.'" More specifically, he linked the across-the-board cut with the effort to bring down the top marginal rate: "The hard part of the supply-side tax cut is dropping the top rate from 70 to 50 percent—the rest is a secondary matter. . . . In order to make this palatable as a political matter, you had to bring down all the brackets. But, I mean, Kemp-Roth was always a Trojan Horse to bring down the top rate."[5]

Trojan horse or not, the Democrats, in some internal confusion and disarray, did not need the hard sell. The Ways and Means Committee began meeting on the bill in late February, and in March Chairman Rostenkowski boldly declared the Reagan plan all but dead. He prom-

ised a Democratic substitute that would increase write-offs even more generously but would target tax relief more to the middle- and lower-income groups and specifically would include a provision to offset the "marriage penalty" that had developed for families with two wage earners. In April Rostenkowski announced the details of the Ways and Means plan, which increased the ante even beyond his initial statement. In presenting the proposal, he declared: "This is not my package, this is not a Democratic package. This is a consensus package. Components came from all the Ways and Means Committee."[6]

To replace the Reagan four-year program, the committee suggested a single-year tax cut, targeted more on the middle class (which was defined as people earning $20,000 to $50,000 a year), and a more liberal standard deduction. Although this would have cost less than the Reagan plan, the committee compensated by proposing an even more liberal depreciation plan and eliminating the distinction between earned and unearned income in one year rather than three. To this was added a 10 percent deduction for the earnings of a working spouse to relieve the "marriage penalty," an increase in the investment credit for building renovation (which would have aided the Northeast, where building stock was older), and an increase in IRA limits from $1,500 per year to $2,000. In what turned out to be one of the most expensive provisions in the final bill, the committee also proposed that IRAs should be made available to everyone. This provision was supported by references to continuing concern over the national savings rate and by the argument that IRAs had become so widespread that it would be unfair if anyone were excluded from the program. This is a marvelous example of a common tax phenomenon: a device created to cover a tax-disadvantaged minority expands until those eligible become so numerous that the remainder are unfairly disadvantaged.

Over the next month positions hardened as disagreement became focused on the multiyear span of the tax reduction and on the question whether the cut should be targeted or proportional. On May 7 the administration's budget resolution, which had been adamantly opposed by the Democratic House leadership, was passed when 63 Democrats, 38 of whom were members of an informal House group called the Conservative Democratic Forum, voted with the administration.[7] The vote changed the game by eliminating the belief that the House had an ultimate veto over administration tax proposals. Behind-the-scenes negotiations led to a series of compromises that slightly reduced the rate cut but expanded reductions in other provisions. The process began with a unique bipartisan meeting between the leaders of the Senate Finance and the Ways and Means committees. The meeting was

arranged by Senator Dole, who had become chairman of the Finance
Committee and was already working independently on a Senate tax bill.
It led the administration to announce a preliminary "compromise"—a
25 percent reduction to begin October 1, 1981 instead of July 1—but the
committee leaders added Rostenkowski's proposals for depreciation
(the 10-5-3 plan), an *immediate* end to the unearned income distinction, and the increase in IRA eligibiity. Also added was a proposal to
lower gift and estate taxes that was supported by Democrats as well as
Republicans.

Dole and Rostenkowski met over the next week, and on May 28 Dole
announced that a core set of agreements had been reached and that full
committee meetings would now be held to work out independent proposals. He reported agreement on a two-year tax cut, although there
were still differences over how the cut would be distributed. The provisions already placed on the table by Rostenkowski and the administration were for the most part included, and *in addition* tax credits for
research and development expenses were raised, the exclusion for
income earned abroad was increased, and Dole's 1980 provision for a
$200 exclusion of dividends and interest was continued. Although it
was historically abnormal for the Senate Finance Committee to take a
forthright public role while Ways and Means was still deliberating, a
pattern that was developing was clear: with each successive round of
bargaining, the bill widened in scope; chips were only added, never
withdrawn.

At this point the legislative confusion escalated. On June 4 President
Reagan renounced the two-year tax cut and stated that he would
support a substitute bill in the House that was to be introduced by
Representatives Conable and Hance (D-Tex.). The latter was a newly
appointed member of Ways and Means and a leader of the Conservative
Democratic Forum. Expressing concern for the effect of the cut on
future deficits, which was a sticking point with conservative Democrats, they presented a package that scaled back business cuts by
revising the very expensive depreciation changes. This reduction
allowed for added provisions to broaden the base of support. In complete
disregard of the president's earlier statement that the tax system should
not be used to further policy ends, the plan kept some version of all the
reductions previously mentioned by either Democrats or Republicans
and, as clear enticement to southern Democrats, extended and increased an exemption for independent oil producers included in the
1980 windfall profits tax.

The business community and the Democrats reacted immediately to
the proposal. A group of business leaders, including most of the mem-

bers of the Carlton Group, met with Treasury and White House officials on June 7 and 8 in what the *Washington Post* later dubbed the "Lear Jet Weekend."[8] With Charles Walker leading the way, the lobbying effort was successful, and on June 9 the administration revised its proposal and restored most of the original business provisions. As a further outcome from that meeting, it was reported for the first time that Treasury tax experts were exploring ways to aid businesses that would not benefit from tax reductions because they were losing money or had past losses that would offset future tax liability (because of carry-forward provisions). The initial discussions focused on extending the carry-forward period for investment credits ten years instead of seven; however, the possibility was also raised of selling unused investment credits and depreciation deductions. Through leasing arrangements, a company with little or no tax liability could sell plants and equipment to a profitable company and then lease them back for approximately the sales price. The profitable company could then take the credits and deductions, paying a portion back to the leasing company for the rights to their tax credits. This strategy was at that time disallowed by the IRS. Supported by the Carlton Group, this practice, known as the "safe harbor leasing rule," survived committee challenges and became part of the 1981 legislation. Over the following year it became the most controversial section of the act as a range of diverse uses and abuses of the provision were quickly devised by tax entrepreneurs.[9]

The Democrats, led by Speaker O'Neill, vowed to fight the bill on the floor and accused the president of stealing most of their tax ideas, of "auctioning" tax provisions, and, in O'Neill's words, of not "understanding the working class" because he surrounded himself with "people only of the upper echelon of wealth in the nation."[10] This latter comment led to a bitter rebuttal by Reagan that increased the existing tension between the president and the Speaker of the House. The administration's strategy of going around Ways and Means to offer a substitute floor bill and O'Neill's angry response to this strategy made a floor showdown inevitable and a bipartisan compromise impossible. The result was to further increase the bidding on tax provisions.

Round Two

The presentation of the revised administration proposal and the promise to offer a substitute bill on the House floor began a new round of bargaining, although this time the bargaining was carried out through separate but parallel actions of the tax committees and the administra-

tion, all of which were working on final legislation. The pace of activity was hectic because the administration was pushing to enact tax legislation before the August break and because the initial Democratic strategy was to vote on the bills as soon as possible to forestall administration lobbying efforts, which had been so successful during the budget reconciliation debates.[11] Although the Ways and Means Committee began markup sessions on June 10, formal committee voting on controversial provisions did not begin until the middle of July. Finance began meeting in late May, submitted a completed report on July 6, and began floor consideration and voting the next week. Thus, the Ways and Means Committee was put in a position where it had to respond to changing proposals by the administration and the Senate Finance Committee and to Senate floor votes and modifications. The result was an all-out bidding war with Ways and Means in an inferior position, particularly after June 25, when a second challenge to the president's budget reconciliation bill failed on a vote similar to that in May.[12] After that loss, which filled the newspapers with stories of inept Democratic leadership, beating the administration on the House substitute bill took on added importance.

In addition to the basic administration formula for a three-year, 25 percent rate cut and accelerated depreciation, the Finance Committee report also reflected the agreements that had been announced by Dole in May. It included the deduction for spousal income and provisions expanding the child care deduction, IRAs, research and development benefits, investment credits for rehabilitated buildings, changes in the treatment of income earned abroad, and the elimination of the 70 percent unearned income rate in the first year. However, responding to the simultaneous pleas from savings institutions, real estate interests, and the building industry (all of which were in severe economic straits), the bill also provided for a new tax-free savings account in the form of a one-year "All Savers Certificate" that would permit up to $1,000 ($2,000 joint) in tax-excluded interest. Although the notion of tax-exempt savings was not new, having been explicitly proposed earlier by the Ford administration, the "All Savers" option came into favor only in the last weeks of June. Although there was controversy over whether the money invested in these special accounts should be specifically targeted for home mortgages, there was broad bipartisan support for the general concept. In fact, the Ways and Means Committee agreed to the proposal before the Finance Committee formally released its report. Chairman Dole expressed doubts about the provision, although he and the rest of the committee voted 20 to 0 for it, and tied the provision to the repeal of the interest exclusion passed in 1980, reverting instead to the $100

exclusion for dividends only. Later, on a Senate floor vote that passed easily and was subsequently accepted in Conference, this sole tax increase was undercut by another new provision excluding 15 percent of all interest income beginning in 1985.

The Finance Committee added further to the revenue loss by liberalizing investment credits for the purchase of used property; creating immediate write-offs, called "expensing," of the first $10,000 of capital assets purchased in any year (an aid to small businesses); and, most important, agreeing to a floor vote on the indexing for inflation (beginning in 1985) of individual income tax brackets, the personal exemption, and the standard deduction or "zero bracket." Although the administration opposed indexing, there was little question, given recent Senate votes and the changed partisan and ideological makeup of the Senate, how such a vote would turn out. The vote, on July 16, was 57 to 40 with 8 Republicans opposing indexing but 14 Democrats agreeing to it.

Considering the postwar tendency for the Finance Committee and the Senate as a whole to inflate House-passed tax cuts, the actions of the committee were hardly surprising and even showed some weak signs of restraint. Chairman Dole began expressing reservations about the magnitude of the deficits that might result from passage of a tax cut of this size. In surprising contrast was the vigor with which the Democrats responded to the cutting frenzy and their apparent eagerness to placate the business community. The Ways and Means bill resembled a set of blocks, haphazardly arranged, with the principal goal of offering a wide enough range of benefits to make it politically irresistible. As the vote approached, the committee backed off from its original two-year, 15 percent rate cuts to authorize a third "trigger" year if economic goals were met on the deficit, interest rates, and inflation (a proposal modeled after the 1978 proposal by Senator Nunn; see p. 211). The business provisions were completely rewritten, offering at least as much in terms of revenue reductions, but proposing that instead of depreciation, the system should be moved toward full expensing of capital investments, eventually lending to full deduction in the year of purchase. The committee's proposal would have phased in the expensing concept over ten years, cut corporate rates from 46 to 34 percent by 1987, and repealed the investment tax credit. Richard Rahn, chief economist for the U.S. Chamber of Commerce and an original member of the Carlton Group, characterized this as "nothing short of astounding. If you'd told me a few years ago that the Democrats would propose expensing, I would have said you were out of your mind."[13]

Beyond the wide range of benefits agreed to in the first round of

bargaining, the committee added a number of benefits targeted at specific industries. Not only did it pass the "All Savers" provision, but it also suggested that for a particular list of depressed industries—autos, steel, airlines, mining, paper, and railroads—unused investment credits should be made refundable as long as the refunds were reinvested. This negative corporate income tax was not in the administration bill or the final law, which favored the safe harbor leasing approach for all industries, but it clearly indicates how far the Democrats were willing to go. The bill also provided special benefits for utilities by allowing an exemption for reinvested dividends; allowed the use of industrial development bonds for the purchase of buses and the payment of other mass transit expenses; aided home owners by increasing to two years the amount of time they had to roll over home sales and still avoid capital gains; and increased the one-time capital gains exemption for the sale of homes for the elderly to $125,000.

In a blatant move to attract crucial votes from conservative southern Democrats, the day after Dole had engineered the defeat of a Senate floor amendment that would have partially excluded independent oil producers from windfall profits taxes, Ways and Means approved such an exemption for the first 500 barrels per day. The administration later countered this offer, in the House substitute bill and as finally passed, the bill contained major benefits for royalty owners, independents, and those operating stripper wells. It also reduced the windfall profits tax on newly discovered oil from 30 to 15 percent by 1986. The combined revenue loss of the oil provisions was estimated at $1.3 billion in 1982 and $1.7 billion in 1983 (see table 11.1 below).

The Finale

The final showdown over the tax bill was politically dramatic but substantively vacuous. The crucial action was in the House, where the basic differences between the administration-backed substitute and the Ways and Means bill were over the third-year "trigger" in the rate cuts, the approach to business depreciation, and the targeting of cuts (the Democratic bill increased the standard deduction and earned income credits). The business community had little time to respond but was lukewarm to the Democratic expensing proposals, preferring the more certain proposals it had helped design. Thus, the basic differences between the bills were not that great, and the climactic vote was mostly symbolic. Although the Democrats were successful in proclaiming after their defeat that Reagan had set his economic program and would have

to live with the consequences, the outcome from either bill would have been similar. The largest and most business-oriented tax cut in peacetime would have resulted from either piece of legislation.

But results mean little when it comes to media drama. On July 23 the administration submitted its final proposals, which accepted most of the Senate provisions, including indexing and a Senate floor amendment that allowed charitable deductions for taxpayers who do not itemize. Given that religious organizations were likely to benefit most from this provision, in a sense the ultimate bid had been made. For good measure the administration added further oil provisions (reducing the windfall profits tax for new oil), a decrease in the holding period for long-term capital assets from twelve to six months (at the request of Representative Hance), and, to cover New England, an energy credit for wood-burning stoves. With that it signaled the end of the bidding and its unwillingness to negotiate further. The *New York Times* headline reporting this final offer read "G.O.P. Tax Strategy in House: All or Nothing."[14]

Although this dramatic flourish implied much greater choice than existed, the administration got it "all." Radio advertisements supporting the administration proposal began on the weekend of July 25. On Sunday President Reagan invited fifteen House Democratic conservatives, whose votes were felt to be critical, to Camp David for "discussions." Twelve later supported the president. On Monday the president went on television during prime time to explain his bill and appeal for support. In what was undoubtedly one of the most politically effective television speeches of recent years, the president extolled the virtues and benefits of the Republican bill first referring to the beneficiaries in mass ("This is the first real tax cut for everyone in twenty years") and then listing them by category: shopkeepers, farmers, small business owners, working people, the savings industry, small independent oil producers, and so on. He fully embraced indexing, stating that "bracket creep is an insidious tax." He then pointed to the difference between the two bills by means of a graph that portrayed the Democratic bill increasing taxes by 1983 (presumably when the trigger failed) and dramatized the difference by declaring that Congress was poised "at the fork of two roads." He ended by suggesting that people contact their representatives in support of the administration bill.[15]

The appeal was successful. On the morning of the vote, July 29, Speaker O'Neill all but gave up on the Democratic bill, commenting: "We are experiencing a telephone blitz like this nation has never seen. It's had a devastating effect."[16] The vote was also devastating; the expected hairline margin evaporated on the key vote as the Conable-

Hance substitute was adopted 238 to 195, with 48 Democrats defecting, including 31 members of the Conservative Democratic Forum. The final vote on the bill was 323 to 107, allowing many more to claim a vote for tax reduction.[17] On the same day, British Crown Prince Charles married Lady Diana Spencer, leading Speaker O'Neill to the cynical indictment: "This has been quite a day for aristocracy: a royal wedding and a royal tax cut."[18]

Because the House and Senate bills were so similar, the Conference Committee met for only one day. Accommodations were quickly reached on differences in child care credits and then on the oil provisions, which neither party seemed eager to claim as its own, each blaming the other for forcing the bidding war that allowed the oil give-backs to reach such an impressive level. As an indication of how far this Congress was willing to cut taxes, several of the Ways and Means provisions not included in either the Senate bill or the House substitute were still accepted in Conference, including the dividend exclusion for utilities (only with a limit of $750 rather than $1,500) and the relatively minor increases in the taxation of home sales. What is more important is what the Conference Committee did not do. In the past the Conference Committee served as a final filter for eliminating large numbers of provisions that had been added at some point in the legislative process, but for which there was little consensus on the tax committees. This filter limited revenue losses and thus balanced the bill. In this case, however, the disjoint legislative sequence, the early agreement on a wide range of relief provisions, and the subsequent bidding war produced bills very similar in philosophy and substance and aborted the moderating influence of the Conference Committee.

The end result of that process is depicted in table 8.1 and table 11.1. As seen in table 8.1, the total revenue loss dwarfs other postwar tax reductions. Assuming that all provisions are allowed to continue and take effect when scheduled, by 1986 the total revenue reduction due to the bill will be approximately $750 billion. The effect on corporations will be to drop their share of federal revenues from approximately 13 percent in 1981 to less than 7 percent in 1986, with a number of corporations receiving negative income tax subsidies through the safe harbor leasing provisions.[19] Also evident in table 8.1 is the fact that the net revenue loss due to structural changes far outweighed that for previous bills. This net change resulted from a number of costly new provisions that were not, as in the past, offset by revenue gains in other areas. A comparison of table 11.1 and tables 8.2, 9.1, and 10.1 clearly demonstrates this point. Also shown in table 11.1 is that the responsibil-

ity for these provisions and thus for the extravagance of the bill must be borne by both parties. If the Economic Recovery Tax Act was indeed aristocratic in character, as O'Neill proclaimed, it was not because the Democrats had lost a noble battle while representing proletarian interests.

Specifically, as depicted in the table, the only revenue-gaining provisions other than administrative changes, were the repeal of the interest exclusion (which was tied to a new provision that will eventually produce substantial losses) and the elimination of a very complex tax shelter based on "straddling" gains and losses in stock and commodity futures over two calendar years. The bill included eight new tax expenditure items. Several minor provisions, such as an allowable deduction of up to $1,500 for expenses relating to adoption, had been around for many years but this time were carried along by the surge. In fact, few of the provisions were really "new" in the sense that they materialized quickly and were pushed through without analysis or adequate understanding. Both the "All Savers" and the IRA provisions were in essence proposed in 1975 by the Ford administration, as was the dividend reinvestment exclusion for utility companies. Safe harbor leasing arrangements had been scrutinized earlier by the Treasury and ruled invalid; depreciation changes were continually under consideration, and the specific 10-5-3 formulation (which was finally closer to 15-5-3) had been the subject of congressional deliberation over the previous two years.

This is not to minimize the magnitude of the changes involved or the avalanche of tax expenditure provisions, which the administration later proposed to extend even further with subsequent tax incentive proposals to support education, urban redevelopment, jobs programs, and economic development in the Caribbean Basin. The most important structural change, the new depreciation system, created broad but uneven sets of benefits. For example, under the new provisions, railroads were allowed to depreciate track from five to fifty years. When these benefits were combined with the accelerated schedules built into the new system, the cash flow of some railroad companies was expected to increase over $200 million in the first year.[20] Further benefits buried in the labyrinth of depreciation rules were revealed over the following months. One result was to increase greatly the profitability of, and thus the participation in, race horse ownership. Under the new rules horses could be depreciated as equipment over three years. This has led resourceful tax entrepreneurs to form limited partnerships for the purchase of pieces of race horses. Thus, moderately wealthy investors

Table 11.1 Major Structural Changes in the Economic Recovery Tax Act of 1981

	Amount ($ millions) Fiscal Year		Institutional Origin	Originating Party
	1982	1983		
Revenue-Gaining Provisions				
Repeal of $200 interest exclusion[a]	566	1,916	Finance	Rep
Tax straddles and related provisions	623	327	Finance	Rep
Sum administrative changes	1,226	2,077	—	—
Total gain	+2,415	+4,320		
Revenue-Losing Provisions				
Accelerated cost recovery system (depreciation)	−6,920	−13,182	Admin.	Both
Sale of tax credits through leasing	−2,649	−3,615	Admin.	Rep
Oil tax reductions[b]	−1,295	−1,727	Admin./W&M	Both
Research and development increases	−505	−728	W&M	Both

Deductions of spouse's earnings	−419	−4,418	W&M	Dem
"All-Savers" interest exclusion	−398	−1,791	Finance	Both
Income earned abroad provisions	−299	−544	Finance	Both
IRA provisions	−285	−1,496	W&M	Dem
Reinvestment of dividends for utilities	−130	−365	W&M	Dem
Building rehabilitation investment credit	−129	−208	W&M	Dem
Charitable contributions deduction	−26	−189	S. Floor	Dem
Child care credits and exclusion	−19	−191	W&M	Rep
All others	−884	−852	—	—
Total loss	−13,958	−29,305		
Net structural change[c]	−11,543	−24,985		

Sources: Joint Committee on Taxation, Committee on Ways and Means Print, August 1981.

[a] In 1985 this exclusion is replaced by a 15 percent exclusion which will lead to an estimated revenue loss of $1,124 and $3,126 million in 1985 and 1986.

[b] Including royalty credits and exemption from windfall profits; reduced tax on newly discovered oil; and exemption for independent producer stripper wells.

[c] Does not include changes in earned income credit or the repeal of the maximum tax rate of 70 percent on unearned income which are included in estimates as rate changes.

(such as doctors) are no longer limited to dull real estate investments. As one of my colleagues remarked, "That is nothing more than democratization of the sport." Alas, it is a sport of kings no longer.

The exact incidence of the tax cuts is even harder than usual to gauge because published estimates depend on calculations that ignore most of the structural changes and all the effects of changes in the corporate tax. Because of the large number of structural and business changes, this is an acute problem for this bill. Nevertheless, estimates by the Joint Committee on Taxation show that at best, without consideration of these changes, the reductions are approximately proportional, averaging close to 25 percent for all income groups by 1984.[21] By this limited estimating procedure, 63.3 percent of the total reductions through 1984 would go to those making $30,000 and over. Prior to the bill's passage, however, that group was paying 63.8 percent of the taxes. Thus, without considering most of the structural changes or the final incidence of business cuts, which would undoubtedly make the reductions more regressive, the outcome was at best a proportional tax reduction. It should be noted, however, that with the exception of the Tax Reform Act of 1969, other postwar tax bills have not deviated all that much from proportionality given the same methods of estimation.

What is historically unique about the 1981 bill is the size of the tax reduction, its multiyear commitment in terms of rate reductions and indexation, and the overwhelming deference to business and upper-income "savings groups." Although these groups have benefited from most postwar tax reductions, in earlier bills there was a degree of moderation that was simply lost in the summer of 1981.

Even in the 1920s, a period the Reagan administration is fond of invoking, revenue legislation was significantly more balanced, and reductions were spread out over four major revenue acts. Moreover, although business taxes were cut dramatically after World War I, during the war years businesses were paying three times the total taxes of individuals (see figure 6.1). Almost exactly the opposite ratio applied in 1981. And, as noted in chapter 5, these bills were less one-sided than the 1981 bill. Congress reacted similarly during the 1920s, pushing for larger reductions than the administration supported; the difference was that Mellon did not give in as easily. There was also more balance to the earlier bills, partly because then the first priority of Congress was to exempt most of the population from income taxes, and thus increasing the exemption was paramount. However, it should also be remembered that Mellon argued for incentives distinguishing earned from unearned, "coupon clipping" income. He proposed a 25 percent tax credit

to reward the former and consistently tried to repeal tax-exempt bonds which encouraged the latter.

Last, and most important, excepting the immediate postwar tax reduction, the tax cuts of 1924, 1926, and 1928 were a reaction to budget surpluses that had accumulated, whereas the 1981 cuts were premised on the supply-side assumption that reductions would lead to enough future revenue to cover government spending (see figure 7.1). Although Mellon argued that this supply-side expansion might occur, he was prudent enough to cut taxes only after a surplus had been realized. How he would have reacted to the fiscal gamble of 1981 tax act is anyone's guess, but I suspect his innate fiscal conservatism, which led him to propose a tax increase in 1931 once the surplus had disappeared, would have left him appalled at the prospect.

The Economic Recovery Tax Act of 1981 was historically in a category by itself. However, its uniqueness does not mean that it resulted wholly from short-term factors. Because of its importance as a legislative landmark and because it is indicative of several long-term historical patterns in tax legislation, let us examine more closely the forces behind the shift toward the efficiency side of the equity-efficiency trade off.

Explaining the Flood

There is a temptation to explain the 1981 tax cut as an aberration of the political process and a coincidental outcome of a number of short-term forces that happened to converge at one time. Such short-term factors were important. The landslide election of Ronald Reagan and the surprise outcome in the Senate stunned congress and allowed the administration a grace period beyond that normally given new administrations. Similarly, the president's fervent embrace of supply-side economic theory served to insulate him from moderating council within his administration that other presidents might have heeded. Another obvious contributing factor was the off-balance, disjointed pace of legislative activity, which allowed and even encouraged the bidding process that led to such an extreme outcome. Thus, idiosyncratic circumstances clearly influenced the 1981 tax cut.

However, it should be remembered that this bill was unique only because it was extreme, not because it established new trends in tax legislation. The tax reductions of 1977 and 1978 were heavily skewed toward stimulating the economy, and one could reasonably argue that the roots of the 1981 tax bill actually go back to 1975 and 1976, when

many reform plans were blocked. Of the possible long-term explanations for this trend, two seem particularly relevant: the effects of inflation and real income growth on taxes, and congressional reforms instituted in the early 1970s.

Income Growth and Increasing Marginal Rates. World War II marked the beginning of the income tax as a mass tax. As was pointed out in chapter 6, even during the war tax analysts were commenting on the reluctance of Congress to tax the middle classes (see p. 121). After the war, however, when the exemption remained low, the pressure increased to control the effective tax rates paid by the large middle-class voting public. The combination of real income growth and inflation that has pushed the middle class into higher marginal brackets is an obvious factor in postwar tax reduction. With inflation in the range of 1 to 2 percent and real income growth at around 3 to 5 percent, tax reductions could be introduced at a moderate pace, as they were from 1954 to 1969. As inflation accelerated in the seventies, income expanded at a dramatic rate, and real income lagged. The bracket creep that resulted, combined with lower purchasing power, created a double motivation for tax reduction. The middle-class family began to be defined as one with an upper income limit of $40,000 or $50,000.

Not only did this group run up against statutory marginal rates that increased rapidly, but in many instances they actually had to pay them. One reason is suggested by figure 11.1, which portrays the average composition of the income from those reporting between $25,000 and $50,000 a year. Not surprisingly, the figures since World War II demonstrate the increasing share of income due to wages and salaries for those in this income range. Since wage and salary income is not as susceptible as business or investment income to exclusions and is less likely to be offset by deductions or business credits of various kinds, effective rates are close to the statutory ones. Thus, the $50,000-a-year government employee in 1980 is in a much different tax situation than the $50,000 doctor, lawyer, or businessman of 1945, and by 1980 there are an awful lot more people at that income level.

The effect on marginal rates of inflation and the changing composition of higher-bracket income is demonstrated in figure 11.2, which is based on an analysis by Eugene Steuerle and Michael Hartzmark.[22] Calculations go back only to 1961 because prior to that the Treasury compiled data on the distribution of average effective rates only, not marginal rates. The figure is a cumulative frequency distribution of actual marginal rates ordered on the basis of increasing personal income.[23] Thus, for 1961 the lowest 21 percent of the returns (in terms of personal income) paid no tax and therefore had a marginal rate of

zero; those between percentiles 22 and 66 were at a marginal rate of 20 percent; those from 67 to 90 were at 22 percent and so on. The proportionality of the tax system for the vast middle-income groups is apparent in the graphs for 1961 and 1969. In 1961, fully 70 percent of those filing tax returns were in a marginal rate of 20 to 22 percent. The graduation increases by 1969, although the middle 50 percent are still at marginal rates ranging from 20 to 24 percent. By 1979, however, the stable middle-class rates no longer exist and a steady and steep marginal progressivity takes over. The political response was to widen brackets, proportionally reduce rates, and create tax reduction devices that, unlike complex real estate or other tax shelters, were readily accessible to

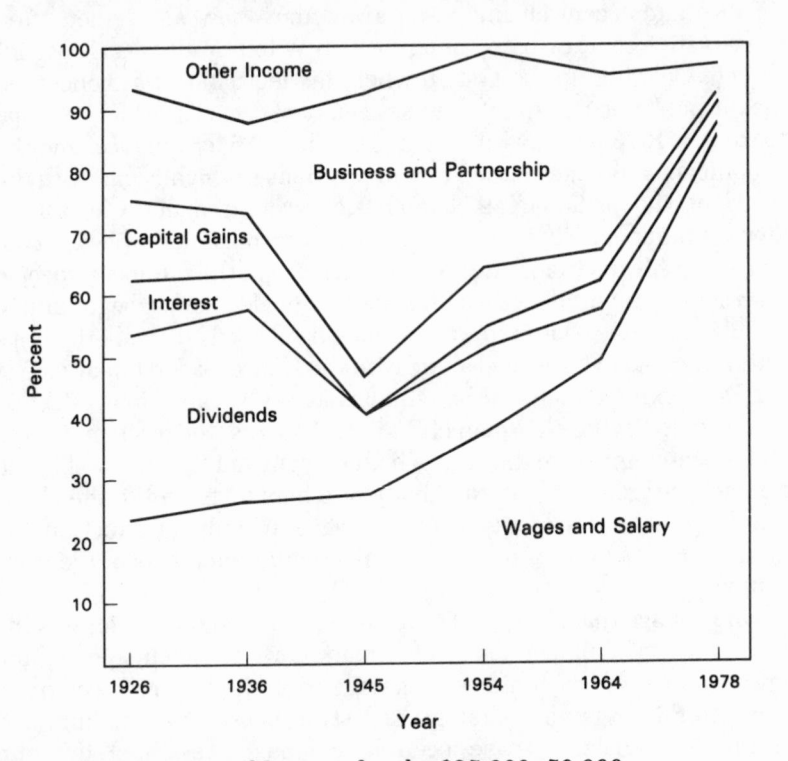

Figure 11.1 Sources of Income for the $25,000–50,000 Income Range, Selected Years 1926–1978

Source: Internal Revenue Service, *Statistics of Income for Individual Returns* (Washington, D.C.: Government Printing Office, appropriate years).
Note: The income ranges for 1926 and 1936 are based on *net* income; all others are based on *adjusted gross* income. The figures for business and partnership income equals net gains minus losses. Capital gains income is based on long- and short-term gains minus losses. For 1945, dividends and interest were reported together.

middle-class wage-earning families. A tax lawyer is not needed to establish an IRA account, purchase an All Savers certificate, or take a spousal deduction.

Congressional Reforms. Although trying to assess the causal relationship between external events and policy outcomes is necessarily a speculative process, the effect of inflation on the pressure to cut taxes is obvious and the effect was constantly discussed in legislative sessions.[24] Less certain is the effect of Democratic congressional reforms, particularly in the House. These liberal reforms, instituted between 1972 and 1974, had the common objectives of opening up the system to public scrutiny and decentralizing power away from a few very senior, often conservative congressmen, among whom Wilbur Mills was always included. Opening up the system where tax legislation was concerned meant public access to markup sessions for tax bills, which became routine in 1973 for Ways and Means and in 1975 for Finance, and the adoption of a modified closed rule in the House, which began with the repeal of oil depletion in 1974 and has characterized all tax legislation since. A number of changes accounted for a decrease in the power of the Ways and Means Committee and an increase in the number of people with significant influence over tax policy. For Democrats, beginning in 1972, committee chairmen were no longer selected on a seniority basis but rather had to be elected along with the House leadership by vote of the Democratic Caucus. Although this has not had any direct effect on the selection of the chairman of Ways and Means (the position went to the senior members in the case of both Ullman and Rostenkowski), the potential for removal and the ability of others to ascend to the chairmanship without seniority may well have an indirect effect on the strategy and actions of the chairman and other members of the committee.

One change that clearly did have an influence on tax politics was the resignation of Wilbur Mills as chairman in 1974, which signaled the end of an era of power almost unparalleled in the history of congress. His careful bargaining strategy and style, consensus building, and pacing of legislation have been meticulously described by John Manley.[25] Although he was criticized by liberal lobbying groups as innately conservative and anti–tax reform, it should not be forgotten that Mills was crucial to the passage of the Tax Reform Act of 1969. It is an ironic twist that the visions of tax reform held by groups delighted with Mills's departure turned sour after he left, with the 1976 act only partially fulfilling reform goals and legislation thereafter completely reversing field.[26]

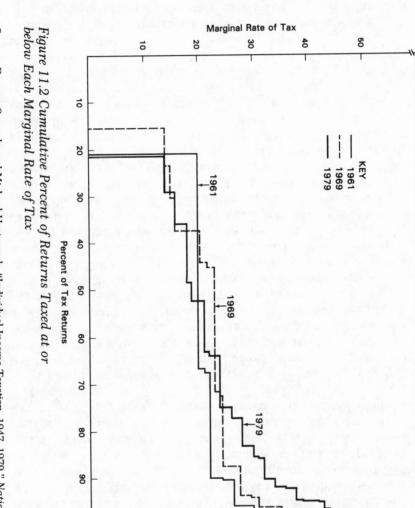

Figure 11.2 Cumulative Percent of Returns Taxed at or below Each Marginal Rate of Tax

Source: Eugene Steuerle and Michael Hartzmark, "Individual Income Taxation, 1947–1979," *National Tax Journal* 32 (June 1981): 156.

Because of simultaneous congressional reforms, it is not immediately apparent what difference Mills would have made, although nothing like the bidding war of 1981 ever took place during his sixteen-year reign as chairman. The most important of these reforms, passed after the "Watergate election" of 1974, removed the power over committee assignments that had been vested in Ways and Means and particularly in the chairman. The Democratic Caucus voted to give this power to the Steering and Policy Committee. At the same time, all House committees were forced to have at least four subcommittees, which, under Mills's rule, did not exist for Ways and Means. Although tax legislation was still decided by the full committee, the six subcommittees that were established further fragmented the power and reduced the general influence of the chairman.

The committee was also enlarged from 25 to 37 members, which at the time, according to one estimate, added 10 new reform-minded liberals.[27] This was thought to be very important for the future of tax reform efforts because it had been a common complaint that members of the tax committees were much more conservative than their respective chambers and were therefore thwarting the true desires of Congress. The Nader congressional study group cited evidence, reproduced in table 11.2, that showed that Finance and Ways and Means members were rated very conservative and atypical of their respective bodies in 1971 by the liberal Americans for Democratic Action (ADA) and the conservative Americans for Constitutional Action (ACA). This is no longer the case. From the 1980 ratings of the same groups for the members of the 1981 tax committees, it is apparent that the committees have become more liberal: their members have higher approval ratings from the ADA and lower ratings from the ACA, and by 1980 they closely matched the averages for the total House and Senate. The flaw in the earlier theory was in assuming that such differences matter. The earlier conservative and unrepresentative committees were essentially responsible for the most liberal tax law in the postwar period, the Tax Reform Act of 1969; whereas the later representative and "liberal" committees produced the most conservative act, the Economic Recovery Tax Act of 1981.

Although it is difficult to assess the effect of congressional reforms on the recent trend in income tax policy, the reforms certainly did nothing to forestall or moderate the tax reductions and the expansion in tax expenditure provisions. Further, it can be argued that they actually facilitated such an outcome. It was assumed that when the political process was opened to the scrutiny of the public, and particularly the

public interest lobbies, the exposure would curtail special interest abuses of the tax code. That theory depended on several heroic assumptions: (1) that the public is really troubled about narrow tax benefits; (2) that people who were troubled could and would be willing to follow the complicated and tedious proceedings (or at least that representatives thought they were following the proceedings); and (3) that they would convey their displeasure to their representatives, who would then restrain their natural inclinations to provide tax benefits.

A more likely alternative scenario is that most people most of the time assume that particularistic benefits are a standard part of politics; that they are very likely not to be aware of, and not to care very much about, what benefits are going to groups other than the ones of which they are members; and that if they were and did, their primary demand would be

Table 11.2 *Average Approval Ratings of Tax Committee Members, 1971 and 1981*

		Americans for Democratic Action[a]	Americans for Constitutional Action[b]
1971			
	House Ways and Means	22%	54%
	Total House	30	43
	Senate Finance	21	67
	Total Senate	41	39
1981			
	House Ways and Means	42	49
	Total House	44	46
	Senate Finance	46	45
	Total Senate	46	45

Sources: 1971—Ralph Nader Congress Project, *The Revenue Committees* (New York: Grossman, 1975), p. 28; 1981—*Congressional Quarterly Weekly Report*, March 21, 1981.
[a]A high percentage is a liberal rating.
[b]A high percentage is a conservative rating.

an equalizing tax break rather than one restricting the largesse due others. If the latter scenario is closer to reality than the former, by opening up the system to public participation and inspection you simply increase the demand for wider benefits. The more tax benefits spread, the easier it is to make claims on the basis of horizontal equity or situations of individual or corporate need. This process is cumulative, and once it becomes clear that the tax system is very adaptable to such claims, it is even more likely to be looked on as a principal source of government subsidy. This process is amplified during periods of declining direct government action, and the openness of the system accelerates the degenerative process.

The same type of case can be made for the fragmentation of power, and 1981 is, I think, a disturbing case in point. The assumption of liberal tax reformers was always that the powerful tax oligarchs (in recent times Mills, Long, and the congressional leadership) were restraining tax reform efforts. It now seems likely that whether or not they were restraining reform efforts, they were also restraining the flood of provisions constantly awaiting any major tax legislation. That the major postwar reform bills were laden with such additions was documented in previous chapters. However, once the position of the chairmen was weakened and the power to add tax provisions was spread out over many centers of influence, trade offs and even judicious restraint became very difficult, as the only power available to chairmen was the power to create policy packages that outbid whatever competing combinations were proposed elsewhere. Just as market competition is thought to lead to consumer benefits through lower prices, so the competition for votes leads to additional consumer tax benefits. Systematic evidence presented in chapter 15 supports this theory by demonstrating that tax actions that originate in the Senate (which has been much less constrained than the House) lead to a significantly higher number of tax reduction changes than actions originating elsewhere in the legislative process.

This general theory, which applies since 1976, if not over the entire postwar period, implies that tax bills are not considered in zero-sum terms, where the advantages accruing to one class are considered disadvantages to another. It suggests that relative comparisons are much less important than ensuring that everyone wins to some extent and that majorities are constructed by bargaining for acceptable additions that secure group support or at least acquiescence. This was the case in 1981, but the rule also applies to some extent to the entire postwar period. During these years the radical prewar shifts in rhetoric

and policy outcomes, which never affected many people, were replaced by a muted conflict fought around the edges of a central concern for maintaining a stable tax rate for the mass middle class. In the process the questions of vertical equity and income redistribution are naturally displaced. Taxation becomes a positive sum game of distributive politics constrained primarily by sensitivity to the middle class.

Chapter 12. Long-Term Patterns and Unsettled Issues

The legislative history of the income tax is characterized by a number of patterns consistent enough to warrant a summary discussion. Some of these patterns were briefly discussed in chapter 5 and have been alluded to at various points in other chapters. One of the most obvious, noted repeatedly, is the highly incremental nature of the change process in tax politics. However, that process has not generated purely neutral or sporadic changes. Some of the most consistent effects of incremental change are portrayed in the preceding history and will be outlined below under the heading "Important Historical Trends in Tax Policy." Others, discussed in the last section of this chapter, are less certain and require further investigation in the following chapters.

Incrementalism in Income Tax Politics

In one of Charles Lindblom's early papers on incrementalism, he focused on spending and taxing decisions as examples of the incremental process.[1] To my knowledge, at that time he had no special expertise or experience in these areas, but either his instincts were acute or he was lucky or, most probably, common knowledge—what Lindblom now calls "casual empiricism"—dictated such a conclusion.[2] For whatever reason, he was correct. The massive literature that has developed on the budget process has done little to alter Lindblom's initial conclusion on the spending side.[3] Similarly, the federal tax system in general, and the income taxes in particular, have also developed in a highly incremental fashion. Although this conclusion is hardly surprising and was essentially an assumption from the beginning of this study, I will invoke the importance of tax policy as an excuse for pulling together the strands of that change process.

Legislative changes in tax policy usually begin as marginal adjust-

244

ments to the existing tax structure. Simple changes in parameters account for most of the modifications and most of the revenue effects. Applicable rates, bracket ranges, exemption levels, standard deductions, depreciation percentages, investment credits, depletion allowances—the list of changes that can be accomplished by simply altering a number is very long. The numbers can also be fine-tuned with changes in increments as small as 0.25 percent. Tax laws can also be easily and marginally altered by expanding or contracting eligible groups, actions, industries, commodities, or financial circumstances. Minerals can be added to or subtracted from the list of those eligible for depletion allowances; various types of income can be included as "preference" income for computation of the minimum tax; the amount and type of income limiting eligibility for retirement credits or the earned income credit can be easily manipulated. Not only can the groups be expanded or contracted, but they can be made to blend into each other by creating rules of diminishing benefits as income or some other circumstance changes. Other provisions can be manipulated by altering time periods—holding periods for capital gains, asset depreciation time ranges, and so on. The tax code offers a variety of easily grasped levers. In this sense, it is an incrementalist paradise, susceptible and seductive to political tinkerers. As a result, most changes in tax bills consist of simple adjustments in existing policy provisions.

However, new structural provisions do arise with some regularity, and every so often one dies as well. But almost without exception, these changes also follow the premises of the incremental model. After the first few years of the income tax, few innovations that had an immediate major impact on revenues were introduced. Most proposals that would have produced major changes either in revenues or in the structure of the tax laws were never even seriously considered. Even during periods of financial crisis, national sales taxes, manufacturing taxes, and consumption taxes were shunned. Large-scale overhauls, such as proposals to integrate the individual and corporate taxes, remained essentially academic execises and never got more than a perfunctory examination by Congress. Even more modest recommendations to begin to move toward such a goal, such as those made in 1975 and hinted at in 1978, were summarily dropped. Similarly, less radical and more constrained proposals, such as Roosevelt's attempt to tax undistributed profits, the Nixon and Carter proposals to create a miscellaneous deduction category, and the multiple efforts, beginning in 1964 to establish a minimum floor under deductions, were easily defeated. Even the short-lived 1976 attempt to alter the carry-over provision for capital gains, which would have meant a substantial change in the tax treatment of property transfers, was too radical an innovation to survive.

The legislative process seems effectively to filter out most proposals for radical changes in structure. In most cases there simply is too much at stake in terms of political futures, money, and established organizational networks (from the Department of the Treasury to rural accountants). Even relatively minor changes set off rounds of seminars, workshops, and written guides that describe and explain the changes to the professional tax community. A major transition in tax concepts would be a financial earthquake that would upset individual and financial dealings in every corner of the nation. Although the accumulation of small changes may radically alter the tax system over a period of time, major transitions, such as current proposals to move to a proportional tax code and in the process eliminate most complicating tax reduction provisions, are simply outside the realm of political possibility.

New provisions—and their numbers have multiplied over the years—are often remedial actions tied to specific problems that arise either from inequities or abuses that have been identified in the tax laws or, increasingly, from external problems that the tax system is being used to address. Deductibility of state and local taxes, the treatment of foreign income, the recently enacted marriage deductions, and the complex regulations governing tax shelters are examples of provisions designed to meet inequitable circumstances or abuses of general provisions. Tax credits for investment, energy, jobs, the elderly, and home purchase are just a few of the long list of tax expenditures intended to address policy problems that arose outside the tax system. IRAs and All Savers Certificates are interesting examples that exemplify both motives.

In addition to being remedial, new provisions are often borrowed from other places or emerge from past proposals. Indeed, the original modern income tax passed in 1913 was a combination of earlier federal laws, state statutes, and the British income tax. Once, in the midst of a heated battle over excess profits during World War II, Robert La Follette, Jr., proposed a major replacement amendment exactly the same as one his father had proposed during World War I. Neither was successful, being judged too radical a departure from existing practice. As I have tried to point out, many other provisions that often appeared to be or were reported as startling new proposals, quickly and carelessly introduced, had actually been recommended in previous congressional sessions. This has been true for nearly all of the new provisions passed since 1976. In taxation, if anything is the mother of invention, it is time.

Finally, new provisions usually (there are exceptions) begin modestly and only later expand to have substantial revenue effects. The growth may occur through incremental legislative actions, as, for example, in the previously discussed cases of IRAs, ESOPs, the earned income

credit, and energy credits; or the provisions may turn out to cost much more than originally envisioned because of inflation or the natural expansion of eligible groups. Inflation has a double effect because it not only drives up the amount deducted or excluded (e.g., Social Security benefits, home mortgage interest, medical costs) but also pushes taxpayers into higher marginal and average rates, making reduction provisions worth more in terms of tax savings. A few provisions, such as the investment credit, were very expensive from the beginning, although in this case there was also considerable expansion in both the rate and the categories of assets allowed (including structures was the big step). Whether or not, as many observers believe, the legislative process is heavily biased in favor of expansion and increase of tax expenditures once enacted requires a more systematic analysis, which is included in chapter 15.

Thus, at any point in time, decisions on tax policy fulfill most of the conditions of the incremental model. They lead to primarily marginal variations in existing structures, with little time spent in consideration of radical proposals; they are remedial in nature, responding to general or particular needs or problems, either within the tax system or without; innovations are often based on or are direct copies of old proposals; and there appears to be an ongoing process of adjustment as new values and objectives are introduced or unforeseen consequences emerge. In all of these respects the structure of the tax code is well suited to the incremental process.

As I have tried to emphasize in the previous chapters, this does not mean that the cumulative effects of these changes are slight. Indeed, in several aspects they are overwhelming. When it began, the individual income tax was an 8-page amendment to a tariff bill of over 800 pages; today the tax code and the rules surrounding it literally occupy shelves. In its first years it was so small a part of our revenue system that it hardly registers in statistics decomposing the sources of revenue (see figure 4.1); today it accounts for over 60 percent of all receipts and almost all revenue for discretionary spending.[4] And although it may appear that this growth is random, uncontrolled expansion in response to idiosyncratic influences, that is not the case.

Important Historical Trends in Tax Policy

Although for several trends summarized below there remain important questions that will be resolved in subsequent chapters, for each the historical evidence seems consistent enough that it can be included as a long-term characteristic of tax politics.

The Complexity and Versatility of the Tax Code. The statement that there is a general trend toward a constantly more complex tax code, and that the code has evolved into a multifaceted policy tool, needs little elaboration and will come as no suprise to those versed in tax policy. The previous chapters are rife with comments, examples, and proclamations of concern. Senator Hart's brief analysis during the 1976 tax reform debate provides as good a set of crude summary measures as is needed to establish the general pattern (see p. 196). The added tax expenditures and revisions in 1977, 1978, and 1981 have only exacerbated the trend.

The chronological history to this point has not established the *rates* of expansion, in terms of both new tax reduction provisions and changes in existing provisions, and this point will require further comment later. A more accurate mapping of the range and uses of the tax system for nonrevenue purposes is also necessary. Finally, a concise analysis of the origin of the code's complexity and an evaluation of its effects remain to be done; these issues are, of course, somewhat dependent on the first two issues. The first two will be a primary concern in the analysis of tax expenditures in chapters 13–15, and the latter two will be discussed in chapter 17.

Tax Policy and Short-Term Revenue Demands. That there is a close relationship between changes in income tax laws and revenue demands is hardly a novel argument, and the evidence for it is overwhelming, at least up to the last decade. World War I transformed the income tax from a Progressive toy into a major source of revenue. Mellon then began a long period of cutting taxes; however, each cut after the initial postwar reduction was in response to a budget surplus. When the surplus turned to deficit, the pressure began to build immediately, and the tax increase of 1931–1932 was the result. Slight increases followed during the thirties as government spending increased and deficits continued. The responses to World War II and Korea, which set the structure and scope of the modern income tax, were described in previous chapters, which also argued that government spending stabilized at a high enough level after the Korean War that it was believed that further tax reductions would jeopardize the economy through deficit spending, a conclusion only very cautiously and grudgingly overruled by President Kennedy.

The seventies and early eighties altered this trend somewhat. First, inflation became an independent force, breaking the link that forced taxes to respond to spending. Although inflation increases revenues and thus allows a tax reduction dividend, it also adds pressure to reduce

taxes by destabilizing the marginal rates paid by the middle class. A second and perhaps temporary deviation is President Reagan's apparent willingness to entertain large deficits, at least in the short term, which has set him apart from the historical tradition of his party and the mainstream of the Democratic Party as well. Whether or not these are temporary aberrations remains to be seen and depends to some extent on possible shifts in the other factors described below.

The reactive nature of tax policy is at best a limited predictor of changes. Primarily, the reaction determines only changes in total revenue and not the way that revenues are to be increased or cut. This does not mean that once the general direction of revenue changes is agreed on, the specifics are merely a matter of political choice. Depending on the amount of revenue involved, certain decisions are more or less predetermined. For example, given the enormous revenues necessary during wars, changes in the exemption levels are to be expected, since the easiest, if not the only, way to get those revenues is to extract increases from a large number of taxpayers. Moreover, the incremental character of policy choices ties current decisions to past ones and limits the scope of any single choice at a given point in time. The sequential aspect of tax policy can, however, produce a major structural change over a short period, particularly in periods of dramatic fluctuations in revenue demand. Thus, although external demands on government explains only a portion of the outcome of revenue changes, they are one key to understanding tax politics, particularly during peak periods of policy transition.

The Tax Reduction Bias. At any given time the equilibrium position, represented by the current status of tax laws is under constant pressure toward less rather than more taxes. This is hardly a startling conclusion: the United States has always been a "tight" tax country, and if the present conservative trend is any indication, the idea that large-scale government is a permanent feature in modern society has not yet been accepted. The brute force evidence demonstrating the bias toward lower taxes is impressive. The only legislated peacetime tax increases in U.S. history have been the Revenue Act of 1932, a slight one-year increase later in the 1930s, and a relatively modest and mostly administrative increase in 1982. As demonstrated by Congress's persistent attempts to force tax reduction during the Truman and Eisenhower administrations, the political pressure for tax reduction is ever present and can overshadow the desire to match revenue to spending during all but the most dire periods. Further, when liberal forces briefly converged to produce tax reform legislation, that reform was purchased at the

expense of overall tax reduction. In the "reform" bills of 1964, 1969, and 1976, initial administration proposals to balance losses with gains or actually to increase taxes were overturned in the legislative process—in 1964 and 1976 the added losses were significant. An even more extreme case occurred in 1978, when the Carter reform proposals were summarily dismissed and net revenue changes were reversed by over $12 billion. Even during periods of war, the succession of tax bills followed a consistent pattern that demonstrated that even before the crisis was over, the forces for tax reduction were in control. Late war tax increases were viciously contested, and postwar reductions were pre-planned.

This bias favoring tax reduction is often explained in terms of reelection incentives that push politicians to increase government benefits; these benefits may at times be restricted on the spending side, but they are always available on the tax side. Given the complexity of tax legislation, it is possible to register support for general tax reduction and particularistic tax benefits while also, at least symbolically, signaling approval for a desired distribution of burdens. Since peacetime tax legislation *is* tax reduction legislation, final votes, which are frequently bipartisan and often approach unanimity, register approval of general tax reduction. Selective tax expenditures offer a means of supporting more refined target populations. As tax expenditure provisions increase, so do the potential changes and adjustments. The fact that floor votes on specific provisions are often not taken can be a further advantage, because representatives who support a final package can pick and choose positions to support as campaign audiences change. The breadth of a major tax bill thus permits a range of actions beneficial to reelection.

Legislative procedures also allow representatives, at their choice, to register either approval or disapproval of the general distributive pattern embodied in tax reductions. Very often "key votes," such as recommittal votes and votes on substitutes that restructure the basic blocks of the tax cut (rate changes, exemption levels, general tax credits, or standard deductions), provide an opportunity for overt expressions of distributive choices. Classic tax battles, such as those of 1946 or 1954, illustrate this form of political maneuvering. Further, since tax reductions can be interpreted differently depending on whether one emphasizes total dollar amounts or reductions as a percentage of taxes paid, almost any legislative outcome can be turned to some advantage. Liberals can simultaneously point to their support for generally lower taxes, particularly provisions aiding working parents, the elderly, home owners, and so on, and rail against the fact that the cut provides x dollars for those at

$10,000 income but 5 x dollars for those at $100,000. Conservatives can support lower taxes, particularly capital formation, savings, and small business provisions, and at the same time state that more should have been done, in that the taxes paid by those at $10,000 were reduced by 5 y percent, but the tax paid by those at $100,000 was reduced by only y percent.

The extent to which such motives actually guide political behavior is impossible to say and, I would think, impossible to research in any rigorous manner. What we do know, however, is that outcomes are consistent with this theory of motivation. Not only have tax bills in the postwar period been tax reduction bills, but for all major legislation, the more actors involved in tax legislation, the greater the tax reduction that results. Congress has religiously passed bills allowing for less revenue than administration proposals, regardless of the party in control of either branch of government or the external circumstances dictating revenue increases or reductions. The pattern has been consistent from Wilson through Reagan. Moreover, the more extensive and open the congressional proceedings, the greater the revenue loss. In every case since 1945 (excepting the 1967 Vietnam surcharge, which was really not debated), the Senate has reduced the revenues of House bills, and actions on the Senate floor have increased the tax reductions approved by the Finance Committee. Thus, the more politics in tax legislation, the more tax reduction.

The bias toward tax reductions has been centered at times by a desire to control deficits. As long as the legislative process was relatively insulated from open-field politics, tax reductions were judiciously paced and moderate in scope. According to James Buchanan and Richard Wagner, this restraint began to erode in the early 1960s with the acceptance of the post-Keynesian notion that it is not actual budget deficits or surpluses that matter but budget balances relative to a hypothetical full employment economy.[5] Since the economy never reaches this level, the effect is to justify deficit spending even in periods of increasing economic activity. On the tax side, the evidence supporting this contention is not particularly strong. The best case is provided by the late 1960s, when most agree that a significant tax increase was needed to pay for the expense of the Vietnam War and the Great Society programs. However, the simultaneous appearance of inflation, congressional reform, and supply-side economic theory has had the effect on tax policy that Buchanan and Wagner attributed to the acceptance of Keynes. The political restraint produced by deficits has at least temporarily subsided as, ever since 1978, tax cutting independent of spending has been the primary concern.

The Influence of the Middle Class. Another persistent, long-term factor in tax politics—the sensitivity of the system to the interests of the middle class—is less obvious than the trends discussed above. In the last chapter it was argued that in recent years tax policy has revolved around the increasing marginal rates for the middle class (see pp. 236–37). That argument was consistent with the changing pattern of effective rates, political rhetoric during the period, and the simple observation that politicians are bound to be particularly sensitive to changes in taxes that affect a middle class that controls the voting majority. What is less apparent is the importance of the middle class in earlier years. We know that before World War II the ultimate in sensitivity prevailed in that the middle class was not subjected to *any* income tax at all. During this period income tax politics revolved around the questions of how much and in what ways to tax the wealthy.

Income taxes began to be collected from the middle class in World War II. Although the middle class continued to be taxed after the Korean War, there is substantial evidence that the effective rates its members paid, at least through the mid-seventies, varied little either between income ranges or over time. Table 12.1 which portrays average effective rates based on reported Internal Revenue Service Statistics of Income for selected years, demonstrates the stability of middle-class tax rates. Because those who do not file returns are not represented in

Table 12.1 Taxes as a Percentage of Adjusted Gross Income Quintiles, Selected Years

Income Quintile	1945	1950	1953	1955	1960	1965	1970	1975
I	1.7	1.9	3.1	2.7	3.1	2.1	1.6	.6
II	6.2	4.4	5.8	5.9	6.5	5.7	7.1	4.7
III	8.9	5.7	8.7	7.9	8.8	7.9	9.3	8.8
IV	10.0	6.8	10.3	9.2	10.2	9.3	11.3	11.2
V	20.7	15.5	18.0	16.8	16.8	15.7	17.6	17.8
All quintiles	14.2	10.2	12.9	11.9	12.5	11.5	13.3	13.1

Source: Internal Revenue Service, *Statistics of Individual Income Tax Returns* (Washington, D.C.: Government Printing Office, selected years).

reported statistics and because the income measured does not include unreported income, exclusions, or tax deductions, these statistics are rough, although the best available. There is no reason to suspect that the errors for any quintile are biased on a year-to-year basis. Because the over-time stability of the middle three quintiles is consistent with the marginal rate stability reported for part of this period by Steuerle and Hartzmark (see figure 11.2), there is no evidence for significant variation in effective rates for middle-class groups until very recently.

The more important consistent errors in estimation occur between income quintiles because exclusions, deductions, and so on occur with varying frequency and have different values at different income levels. As would be expected, when compared with statistics derived from a tax simulation model, which is based on a broader definition of income that takes into account excluded sources of income, the effective rates are generally higher. However, data based on tax models for the years 1966 and 1970 provide even stronger evidence for the narrow variation *between* deciles for middle-income groups. Data for 1966, based on the Brookings Institution model, are depicted in table 12.2. The "variations" in the table refer to different sets of incidence assumptions that must be made to apportion, for example, the burden of corporate taxes.[6] Regardless of whether the most or the least progressive assumptions are made, the average effective rates between the third and the eighth deciles vary less than 4 percent, with less than 2 percent variation for the middle 40 percent of the population.

What is equally striking in these data is that variation *within* deciles, measured by the standard deviation of effective rates around the decile mean, is much lower for the middle-income groups than for groups at either end of the distribution. This means that the effective rates for taxpayers in the same decile are also very similar. One reason is the homogeneous nature of middle-class income, which is derived overwhelmingly from wages and salaries, with a high percentage of taxpayers taking the standard deduction or relatively uniform and consistent itemized deductions and income exclusions (mortgage interest, taxes, excluded employer contributions to benefit plans, etc.). The extreme fluctuations at the lower end of the scale are partly a statistical artifact arising because less taxes are paid and thus more extreme *rate* fluctuations are generated by small variations between taxpayers. However, they are also due to the large variety of income sources at this level and the range of income exclusions, credits, and special exemptions that apply to transfer payments, the elderly, and the working poor. At the upper end there is also considerable variation, as wealthy individuals differentially avail themselves of deductions (particularly for

charitable giving), capital gains, and various sheltering devices.[7] Thus, for those troubled by distortions in horizontal equity (the unequal taxation of equal incomes), the most serious violations occur at both ends of the income distribution, while the middle incomes pay relatively equal rates.

The conclusion drawn from this avalanche of numbers is that there is convincing evidence that for all but the last few years, the income taxes paid by the middle class have always been approximately proportional to their income, and, since Korea, the percentage of income paid as taxes has been quite stable. The remaining issue is political intent. Although part of the explanation is the homogeneous financial situation of this broad middle group, conscious political decisions have also been a

Table 12.2 Average Effective Individual Plus Corporate Income Tax Rates and Within-Decile Variation, 1966

Population Decile	Variant 1C[a] (Most Progressive)		Variant 3B[a] (Least Progressive)	
	Mean Effective Rate	Standard Deviation	Mean Effective Rate	Standard Deviation
First	2.8	26.2	7.3	15.5
Second	4.4	10.3	7.4	12.6
Third	6.2	18.0	8.9	8.2
Fourth	7.3	7.3	9.5	7.6
Fifth	8.0	6.0	10.1	5.7
Sixth	8.5	5.2	10.6	4.9
Seventh	9.1	6.3	10.7	4.8
Eighth	10.1	5.7	11.7	4.7
Ninth	11.0	5.5	12.3	4.7
Tenth	19.5	10.8	17.1	9.1
All deciles[b]	12.4	—	12.8	—

Source: Constructed from Joseph A. Pechman and Benjamin A. Okner, *Who Bears the Tax Burden?* (Washington, D.C.: Brookings Institution, 1974), table 4-9, p. 61; and table 5–2, p. 69.
[a]The assumptions used to apportion taxes under each of these variants are described in Pechman and Okner, chap. 3 and particularly table 3-1.
[b]Includes negative incomes not shown separately.

factor. These decisions included consistent proportional rate reduction, regular increases in personal exemptions and standard deductions, and a reluctance to tamper with important middle-class tax expenditures, even when the revenue loss as a result of these provisions became enormous.

The proportional nature of tax reductions is shown in table 12.3, which depicts changes in marginal rates that apply to taxable income over periods that bracket major postwar tax bills. These changes were computed by calculating percentage differences between the years that define the endpoints of the periods. The general political rule is obvious and requires little comment: with slight exceptions, marginal rates are adjusted proportionately.[8]

The combined effects of these rate reductions and changes in exemptions and tax credits can be estimated by calculating effective rates given certain assumptions. Figure 12.1 depicts calculated effective rates for a family of four, assuming that all income is from wages and salaries and that deductions have already been subtracted. Thus, the only parts of the tax code taken into effect are rates, tax credits, and personal exemptions. The effective rate is merely total tax paid divided by income. Although this formula produces significantly different answers from the effective rates estimated using a tax model, the assumptions are the same over time and thus provide a controlled study of the effects of changes in rates, credits, and exemptions. What clearly emerges and is consistent with the changes in marginal rates alone is the fact that in the postwar period the relative distance between computed effective rates has declined as the rates have been reduced. This narrowing progressivity is precisely what we would expect if the proportionality of rate changes is not offset by distortions in exemptions and tax credits. The negative and combined rate for those at $5,000 and below after 1975 is due to the earned income credit. The figure also demonstrates once again the political tendency to reduce taxes for all categories of taxpayers as incomes increase.

Finally, both changes and nondecisions on tax expenditures have contributed to the stability of effective middle-class rates. The major provisions affecting the middle class (deductions for interest, taxes, medical expenses, and exclusion of employer benefits) are only rarely, if ever, changed. Proposals to cut them back, such as the Carter proposal to eliminate the deductibility of taxes and several proposals to place a percentage-of-income floor under itemized deductions, have been soundly defeated. On the other hand, new provisions that would disproportionately benefit these groups, such as home-purchasing incentives or education credits, have also been limited or in the past resisted, in

Table 12.3 Percentage Changes in Marginal Statutory Rates for Joint Returns

Income	1944–1948	1948–1953	1953–1954	1954–1965	1965–1969	1969–1975	1975–1977
$3,000	−22%	+27%	−11%	−14%	+10%	−9%	−3%
5,000	−21	+27	−10	−15	+10	−9	−4
10,000	−19	+27	−11	−18	+10	−9	−3
25,000	−16	+27	−11	−15	+10	−9	−4
50,000	−15	+18	−4	−17	+10	−9	0

Note: Computed from rate schedules for selected years. Based on marginal rates applied to "taxable income" (after exclusions, deductions, and exemptions, but before tax credits) for endpoint years. That is, the marginal rate for a $3,000 joint income in 1948 was 22 percent lower than in 1944.

part because the potential cost would be staggering. However, as described in detail in chapter 15, to offset increasing marginal rates and thus maintain stability, Congress has recently created such provisions as those permitting IRAs, charitable exclusions for nonitemizers, All Savers Certificates, and the spousal deduction, while also expanding many older middle-income tax expenditures.

This penchant for stability contradicts a number of rational theoretical models relating how tax rates should vary to maximize voter approval. Although they differ in exact formulations, these models often revolve around the median voter and hypothesize shifts of tax burdens to ensure electoral majorities.[9] It would appear that in practice politicians ignore such strategies. Rather, lacking the insight, the information, or the analytical skill of the theorists, they have simply tried to stabilize the taxes of the broad middle class both within and between groups and over time. Until inflation ruined the formula in the 1970s, the political maxim applied to the majority was simple: don't rock the boat.

These long-term trends often push policy choices in different directions. At times the demand for revenue will conflict with the preference for tax reduction and stability for the middle class. During peak crisis periods revenue needs dominate and tend to reshape the revenue system in the process. Since the war, however, the tensions between these forces have been mild, as inflation and real growth provided enough revenue to permit moderate tax cuts, some with offsetting reform, some without, but all aimed at maintaining stable rates for most of the taxpaying public. The changes that began in 1977 may well upset that balance, particularly if indexing is implemented. The implication of this argument, to which I will return in the final chapters, is that one or more of these forces will have to subside. The income tax will either fall short of revenue needs, as it currently appears to be doing; or Congress will have to give up tax reductions, both general and selective; or the stable rates affecting the middle class will have to be replaced by a more progressive structure. That none of these options is politically attractive leads to the supposition that a new tax source will emerge in the near future.

The Redistributive Failure of the Income Tax The relationship between income taxes and income distribution generates misguided complaints from both ends of the political spectrum. Conservatives lament what they perceive to be the actual redistributive effects of income taxation, while liberals argue that the political erosion of the tax base corrupts the real intent of lawmakers. However, there is no evidence either that the

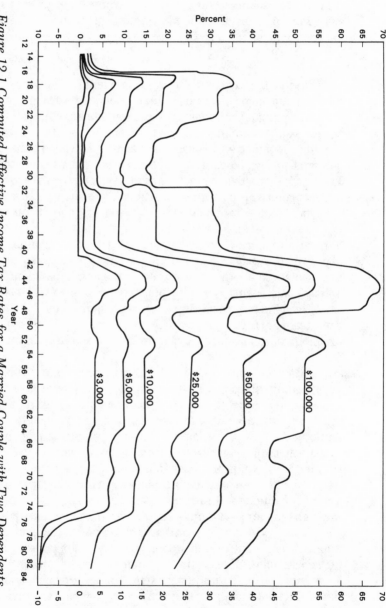

Figure 12.1 Computed Effective Income Tax Rates for a Married Couple with Two Dependents, 1913–1983

Source: Bureau of the Census, *Historical Statistics of the United States: Colonial Times to the Present* (Washington, D.C.: Government Printing Office, 1976), series Y412–39, plus author's calculations.

Note: Income is *net income*, that is, income after deductions (which are therefore not included in the calculations), but before personal exemptions. Income is assumed to derive from wages and salary only.

income tax significantly redistributes income or that there was ever any sustained intention that income taxes should redistribute income. The first of these propositions is well understood, although inflationary effects in the last few years have added some uncertainty; the latter has rarely been discussed but has been a central issue in previous chapters.

The best data supporting the conclusion that income taxes have relatively little effect on the distribution of income are based on the 1966 Brookings tax model, which was later updated to 1970. The average effective tax rates calculated using that model are listed in table 12.2. Although they indicate that for most of the income range actual rates are approximately constant, the table contains no direct information on the effects of redistribution. Table 12.4, which is derived by applying the effective rates in table 12.2 to the distribution of 1966 before-tax income does provide such information. To be conservative and err on the side of redistribution, the most progressive incidence assumptions in the tax model were used (variant lc, table 12.2). Column 2 shows the distribution of income after both individual and corporate taxes have been subtracted. For comparison, column 3 shows the distribution of after-tax income once all taxes have been deducted (income, sales and excise, property, payroll, and motor vehicle).

Some indication of the effects of taxes on income distribution can be gleaned from a simple comparison of decile distributions before and after taxes. There is considerable pretax income inequality: the top 20 percent receive 47.7 percent of the income and the bottom quintile 3.8 percent. Subtracting income taxes borne by these groups, the top 20 percent still have 45.2 percent of the post-tax income, while the bottom 20 have only 4.2 percent. Since the incidence of the total of all taxes other than income taxes is regressive, when all taxes are included, the top 20 percent get 45.8 percent of the after-tax income.

A more precise estimate of inequality can be made by using the GINI coefficient, a commonly used measure of distribution, which is based on deviation from a norm of absolute equality. That norm is defined as the distribution in which cumulative population percentiles receive the equivalent percentage of total income (i.e., equality is achieved when for all xs, x percent of the population also receives x percent of the total income). The GINI coefficient measures the deviation from the norm and has a theoretical range from 0 to $+1$, with $+1$ representing the most unequal circumstance.[10] If one uses calculations based on the decile distribution in table 12.4, the GINI index is only slightly improved by income taxes. The decline from .423 to .398 after income taxes represents an improvement of 5.9 percent in the distribution of income. Including all taxes improves the distribution even less—by

Table 12.4 The Effects of Taxes on the Distribution of Family Income

Population Decile	(1) Pre-Tax Income^a			(2) Minus Individual Income Tax		(3) Minus Corporate Income Tax		(4) Minus Other Taxes^b
	$ Billions	% of Income	Effective Rates (%)	% of Income	Effective Rates	% of Income	Effective Rates	% of Income
1	8.7	1.21	1.1	1.31	1.8	1.34	14.0	1.34
2	19.2	2.67	2.3	2.85	2.1	2.91	14.5	2.89
3	30.6	4.25	4.0	4.46	2.1	4.55	15.5	4.44
4	41.7	5.79	5.4	5.98	2.5	6.12	15.3	5.98
5	52.1	7.24	6.3	7.41	1.7	7.60	14.8	7.45
6	65.2	9.06	7.0	9.20	1.5	9.45	14.2	9.34
7	70.7	9.80	7.5	9.91	1.6	10.17	13.6	10.12
8	88.4	12.27	8.3	12.29	1.8	12.58	13.0	12.59
9	109.2	15.16	8.8	15.10	2.2	15.39	12.3	15.51
10	234.4	32.55	11.4	31.50	8.1	29.88	10.6	30.35
Remaining income	$720.20			$659.36		$631.37		$539.88
Average effective rate of tax category	—			8.45%		3.89%		12.8%
GINI	.423			.410		.398		.404

Source: Pechman and Okner, Who Bears the Tax Burden?, tables 3–2, 4–6, and 4–9.

^aAdjusted family income, incident variant 1c (most progressive), as defined by Pechman and Okner, ibid., chaps. 2 and 3.

only 4.5 percent.[11] Thus, at least in 1966, income taxes had little effect on the distribution of income in the United States.

Whether this conclusion still holds after all the tax legislation and the effects of inflation in the 1970s is difficult to say. As of this writing, the very expensive data base for the Brookings model had been updated only to 1970. In 1970 the effects of income taxes on distribution were even less significant than those in 1966. Although the pretax GINI shows some improvement—to .413 (based on decile calculations)—the post–income tax GINI is only .390, or a 5.6 percent improvement; including all taxes raises the GINI to .395, for a 4.4 percent improvement. Although we know that inflation increased marginal rates somewhat by 1978 (see figure 11.2), and the earned income tax credit provided a slight negative income tax effect, the last two tax bills undoubtedly have countered these effects.

Regardless of the small changes that may have occurred, the early promise of the income tax has not been realized. Part of this failure is due to the fundamental problem that given the degree of inequality in the pretax distribution of income, income taxes are simply too small a percentage of income to have a significant effect. To demonstrate this, consider a hypothetical tax system applied to the 1966 income distribution that allows all taxes other than the income taxes to fall as before, but that levies income taxes only on the top income decile. This would raise the effective rates for this group to 48.5 percent for all taxes paid, while the other 90 percent would pay between 12 and 15 percent. Assessing taxes in this way also has the mathematical property of minimizing the GINI index, thus generating maximum redistribution, given GINI assumptions.[12] The result of this imaginary outside limit would be to reduce the GINI to only .355, compared to a pretax GINI of .423, which would improve the distribution of income by only 16 percent. Although this tax structure would reduce the after-tax income share of the top decile from 30.3 to 21.1 percent, it would only slightly improve the income share of the bottom quintile (from 4.23 to 4.42 percent) and it would reduce the top quintile only from 45.8 to 38.8 percent. Thus, even in the extreme case of applying income taxes only to the wealthiest 10 percent, the impact on income distribution would not be substantial.

What this exercise indicates is that redistribution depends not only on progressivity, but also on the relative pretax distribution and the total amount of taxes paid. Therefore the tendency and bias of tax politics toward lower taxes has an important effect on redistribution as well. Recent legislation, the current confusion in economic theory, and destabilizing tax rates for the middle class magnify this bias. Thus, the

prospect of using the income tax to redistribute income in the near future seems extremely doubtful.

The remaining question is whether this outcome was consciously intended. I have frequently observed in the preceding chapters that the failure to redistribute income has resulted from conscious policy decisions over many years. Whatever progressivity was built into the system, primarily in the form of steeply increasing nominal rates, resulted not from a direct intention to redistribute income but from a dire need for revenue. The basic rate trend was illustrated in figure 12.1, in which the influence of wars and the Depression was obvious.

The same general conclusion emerges in figure 12.2, which is based on actual tax returns rather than the calculated rates used in figure 12.1.[13] The average effective rates depicted are calculated by dividing the total reported income within an income range by the taxes paid by that group. Unfortunately, in 1944 the income base reported by the IRS changed from *net income* (income after deductions but before exemptions) to *adjusted gross income* (income after exclusions but before deductions).[14] There were also some changes in income ranges used. However, even with these differences the general pattern is very similar to that of figure 12.1. The influence of wars is obvious, with by far the most extreme increases in World War II. During that period, for the first time, those reporting under $10,000 paid significant taxes. As described in chapter 5, the only significant peacetime increases in total taxes or progressivity occurred during the Depression, and then the effects were felt almost exclusively by those making over $25,000, who accounted for only about 1 percent of the returns filed. The key to the modern nominal rate structure, which provides the illusion of progressivity, is the Eisenhower administration's reluctance to lower taxes following Korea, an action inspired by a fear of deficits and a fear that a tax reduction intended to stimulate consumption would have been inflationary. In short, the long-term results suggest that whatever progressivity exists in the income tax structure entered through the back door, not as a result of a commitment to equality, but as a response to revenue emergencies.

This inference, based on outcomes, is also supported by the political and legislative history of the income tax. From the 1890s on, there has been a liberal fringe group in Congress that has repeatedly forced the redistributive issue onto the agenda. It has just as regularly been overwhelmingly defeated, primarily on Senate floor votes. The group has varied over time and includes some of the great names in Progressive and liberal lore: the La Follettes, Norris, Couzens, Douglas, Gore, and Kennedy, to name a few. On tax matters they share not only a belief

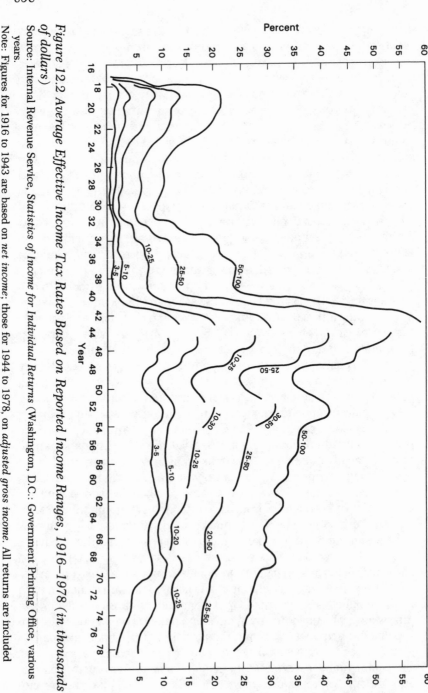

Figure 12.2 Average Effective Income Tax Rates Based on Reported Income Ranges, 1916–1978 (in thousands of dollars)

Source: Internal Revenue Service, Statistics of Income for Individual Returns (Washington, D.C.: Government Printing Office, various years.

Note: Figures for 1916 to 1943 are based on net income; those for 1944 to 1978, on adjusted gross income. All returns are included regardless of filing unit or taxability.

that rates should be progressive and escape provisions for the wealthy limited, but also a resilience to defeat. Although this faction, by presenting liberal extremes and combating conservative ones, has at times shifted tax policy in the redistributive direction, it has remained a minority, and indeed a small minority. It was probably most successful in 1969 and most disappointed in 1976. With slight exceptions, it has been unable to prevent gradual and proportionate rate reductions or the expansion of tax expenditures, some of which it helped create. And thus wartime levels of progressivity have been sharply eroded.

Party competition also fails to produce redistribution through the tax system. Bipartisanship is the rule and Democrats, contrary to expectations, frequently fail to support redistributive policies. Floor voting on tax bills is one indicator of party differences on tax questions. Also important are the party origins of tax expenditures and modifications in tax expenditures, which will be analyzed in chapter 15. The extent of partisanship in voting is some indication of party competition, at least on selective features of tax bills. Table 12.5 provides statistics on both "key" and final floor votes for all major income tax bills through 1981.[15] Because of the importance of war years in establishing the modern income tax system, bills passed in these years have been treated separately. A "partisan" vote as recorded in this table is any vote on which a majority of one party votes in the opposite direction from a majority of the other party. The "Rice Index," a more sensitive measure of party similarity, ranges from 0 to 1. It can be interpreted as the percentage of similarity in the voting patterns of the two parties (i.e., 1 represents an equal proportion favoring a bill in each party).[16]

The data in table 12.5 confirm several expected patterns. First, there is greater bipartisanship during wars than in peacetime. The one exception to this rule is the partisan voting percentage for key votes in the House. Although key House votes are generally partisan, the extreme party differences are evidence that bitter struggles over tax bills can occur even during wars. However, no key votes were recorded for six of twelve war bills, primarily those occurring near the beginning of the war periods. And those bills produced the greatest changes in the tax code. In any event, final passage during war years was nearly always by a substantial bipartisan majority.

Tax legislation during peacetime is more partisan, particularly on key votes, and the House, where less voting occurs and party leadership and discipline are stronger, tends to be more partisan than the Senate in all categories. However, two facts must be noted. It is unclear what key votes represent in terms of the range of consensus that exists across large tax bills. Senate key votes are usually battles over specific provi-

sions affecting rates, excess profits taxes, or exemptions. Although these peak confrontations usually follow expected party lines, with Democrats taking the more liberal position relative to the distribution of burdens, many other votes on special provisions do not follow this

Table 12.5 Partisan Voting on Major Tax Legislation, 1913–1981

	Key Votes		
	War Years	Nonwar Years	All Bills
Percentage partisan			
House	100%	88%	91%
Senate	33%	69%	68%
Mean Rice index			
House	.15	.25	.23
Senate	.76	.47	.56
Number of bills (House/Senate)	(6/6)	(17/13)	(23/19)

	Final Passage		
	War Years	Nonwar Years	All Bills
Percentage partisan			
House	9%	52%	38%
Senate	8%	43%	29%
Mean Rice index			
House	.79	.51	.60
Senate	.64	.59	.62
Number of bills (House/Senate)	(11/12)	(23/23)	(34/35)

Note: Voice votes were counted as bipartisan. Equal percentages yea and nay in a party were included as bipartisan (2 key Senate war votes). Totals between key votes and final votes vary because on a number of bills either no vote was taken or no important and pivotal vote that would qualify as a key vote was recorded.

division, as will be shown in chapter 15. Key votes in the House are in most cases recommittal votes, sometimes tied to substitute provisions, sometimes not. For most bills in both houses, these peak votes afford an opportunity for the parties to stake out political differences while agreeing on the bulk of a tax bill that usually contains general reductions and assorted targeted benefits. That final votes, even during peacetime, show slightly greater party similarity than dissimilarity is an indication of ultimate consensus.

The substantative character of tax bills, particularly in the postwar period, further clouds the simple assumption that Democrats and Republicans consistently battle over redistributive tax issues. Democrats engineered the "efficiency" tax cuts of 1962, 1964, and 1978; supported (against liberal complaints) the mixed Tax Reform Act of 1976 (which was signed by a Republican president); and were equal partners in the "flood" of 1981. On the other hand, the Eisenhower administration maintained the highly progressive tax structure of 1948, and Nixon signed the most liberal peacetime tax bill ever in 1969. Although Democrats tend to stress progressivity more than Republicans, and, as will be shown in chapter 15, they are slightly more inclined to support tax benefit provisions that aid the poor or middle class, there is no consistent political faction of any size, from either political party, supporting redistribution through the income taxes.

This does not mean that parties are inconsequential in tax politics. Indeed, shifts in party control, such as those in 1920, 1932, 1946, 1960, and 1980, often coincide with major shifts of direction and emphasis in tax policy. Even though these shifts are not fully predictable on the basis of party labels, electoral competition does send a signal, or reinforce existing signals, that a policy shift is necessary. That in itself is no trivial accomplishment, however, beyond and even during these shift points, the parties share a great deal—including an uneasiness about a redistributive tax system.

Unsettled Issues

The foregoing discussion skirts several important issues raised in the opening chapter. These issues depend on evidence not accessible in a chronological history. They fall into two general areas: a more detailed analysis of the tax expenditure system and its development, and an evaluation of tax politics in terms of the interests represented, decision-making procedures, and long-term outcomes. A brief comment on these issues will serve as a guide to the chapters that follow.

The Tax Expenditure System. Although the incremental nature of tax politics was easily demonstrated in the previous chapters, it is not as readily apparent where that incremental process has led. That the income tax system has become increasingly complex as tax reduction provisions have been added and modified is not at issue. Extreme cases, such as the New Jobs Credit and the development of IRAs, were highlighted above. However, a closer analysis is needed for a more accurate understanding of the rate of growth in provisions; the effect of this growth on the underlying tax base; and the types of provisions that have contributed most to this expansion. The critical issue is the ultimate impact of this growth in tax expenditures on the capacity to raise revenue. Further, although the overall incidence of income taxes is well known, less is known about how that distribution is generated and particularly about who benefits from the current tax expenditure system. Finally, a more systematic analysis of how tax provisions originate and are modified is necessary. Has there been a recent surge in tax expenditures, and if so, what explains it? Once created, are tax expenditures only expanded, or does oversight also involve restrictions and decreases in benefits? How often are tax expenditures modified or reviewed? Where in the legislative process do changes in the tax code originate? Are changes in general subject to open discussion, adequate analysis, and public votes? Is it possible to determine which party is responsible for which types of modifications?

The Representation of Interests in Tax Politics. There are numerous theories of representation in policy making. The simplest and perhaps most demanding seeks conformity of outcomes with the desires or demands of those governed. Although the difficulty and complexity of this theory will be explored in more detail below, it leads directly to the issue of public attitudes on tax questions. Chapter 16 analyzes attitudes relating to taxes, with specific reference to the historical trends outlined above and the propositions arising in the chapters on tax expenditures. The attitudes explored are related not only to specific trends, but also to the fairness and legitimacy of the income tax system in general.

Decision-Making Procedures. An alternative method of analyzing the issue of representation is to evaluate the procedures by which decisions are reached. If attitudes are mixed, confused, or unknown, procedural assessments become even more important. Although some sense of these procedures can be gleaned from the preceding chapters, more accurate measures will be developed in the analysis of tax expenditures

below. It is also relevant to consider public perceptions of party representation on tax matters.

Evaluating the Outcomes of Tax Policy. A final appraisal of tax politics depends not only on the question of representation, whether in terms of conformity to beliefs or in terms of procedure, but also on the policy results that emerge. Even if policy outcomes seem to conform to majority will and democratic procedures are followed satisfactorily, they may produce a generally pernicious and possibly self-defeating result. The prospect of adequately democratic decision making, yet failed policy, is not a trivial matter. And, for the income tax, it is the conclusion of this book.

Section IV.
The Tax
Expenditure
System

This section analyzes what has in recent years come to be known as the tax expenditure system, or budget. The term "tax expenditure," which is meant to express the idea of government subsidy through the tax system (i.e., parallel to direct government spending) is itself controversial. Those who object argue that the distinction between those tax-reduction provisions that are labeled tax expenditures and those that are not is arbitrary and that the very notion of labeling these provisions "expenditures" implies an assumption that all income inherently belongs to the government. The first of these arguments involves debates about the status of personal exemptions and income exclusions (such as those for moving expenses and alimony) that have never been included in official tax expenditure lists. It also includes the observation that official lists published as a supplement to the budget have varied as administrations change. The second argument involves the debate about the comprehensive tax base. Those who oppose the concept argue that such a base has never existed and observe that a number of tax expenditure provisions have been permanent features of the tax code since the beginning. In many respects this is a semantic debate, in which terminology often masks underlying ideological positions. Those who use the term "tax expenditure" are allegedly "reformers," unafraid of high and progressive taxes; those who do not are believed to savor lower and more proportional tax systems.

I am using the term because it is convenient and because it has become a recognized label covering a broad range of tax laws with the common effect of reducing tax payments. Labeling these laws "expenditures" seems reasonable simply because they were created by explicit

government actions with the intention of increasing income, thus providing benefits for selected individuals and groups. Thus, in both action and result, they are very similar to direct subsidy programs. This similarity is not lost on affected groups, which do not seem to discriminate between forms of expenditures in their lobbying efforts. In addition, and perhaps more to the point for this study, the provisions that are included in the following analysis are important policy statements that cannot be ignored in a study of tax politics. Those who object may substitute any other phrase they prefer, as I have intentionally done throughout this book. The important questions relate to the policies, not the label.

The chapters in this section address three sets of relatively straightforward questions. Chapter 13 provides a description and classification of tax expenditures and analyzes the growth in both numbers of provisions and revenue loss. Chapter 14 considers the distribution of tax expenditures and is devoted to the question of who gets how much from the tax expenditure system. And chapter 15 analyzes the legislative changes that these provisions have undergone. Thus, the enterprise recalls Harold Lasswell's famous description of politics as *Who Gets What, When, and How.*[1]

Chapter 13.
Classification
and Growth
of Tax
Expenditures

Methodology

One of the major problems encountered in studying tax politics is that there is simply so much of it. The federal income tax code comprises over two thousand sections. Selective examples allow one to prove or disapprove almost anything, ranging from a theory that income tax politics is dominated by "long-haired men and short-haired women" bent on socialist redistribution to conspiracy theories that depict a dominion ruled by wealthy and corporate interests. The scope of the tax system is also a problem when one tries to analyze more precise statements about who gets what from the tax code or judgments of the political process where tax changes are concerned. For all of these issues, casual observation is insufficient because the sample is so immense. Unfortunately, the same breadth can also create obstacles to more rigorous study of the income tax system because the number of provisions and changes makes it difficult to summarize general patterns.

The following three chapters are a compromise solution that will, inevitably, lead to some disagreements. The methodology used was, first, to construct an initial set of tax expenditure provisions drawn from official lists of tax expenditures between 1974 and 1982. This set was meant to be close to a comprehensive list of major tax-reduction devices affecting individual and corporate income taxes over those years. Data were collected on each of these provisions, and their origin and subsequent major modifications were systematically mapped.[1] The political source of the provisions and subsequent changes (administration, Ways and Means, IRS ruling, etc.) were noted. The party responsible was determined, either through an identifiable overt action or vote, or

by inference based on committee control.[2] Changes were broken down into separate sets of actions on a single provision when necessary. These changes were then nominally coded as *increasing* or *decreasing* the amount of tax benefit, or *expanding* or *restricting* the eligible group, or as a *neutral* change.[3] Actions were also studied to determine whether votes were taken and, if possible, whether the votes were bipartisan or partisan. Estimates of the revenue loss attributed to the provision and the distribution of that revenue reduction between income groups were then calculated for the years for which they were available. Such estimates are available for most of the provisions on an annual basis beginning in 1975. The most up-to-date estimates of distribution have been obtained from the Treasury Department for 1977, but only for provisions affecting individual income taxes. Details of each of these measurements and problems of interpretation will be noted as the provisions are discussed.

This data set allows for a systematic analysis of a number of important questions concerning the scope and development of income tax policy as well as the political process by which it is generated. The data are such that there are necessarily going to be errors created by measurement problems, missing data, and interpretation (e.g., what constitutes a change, and what constitutes an appropriate tax expenditure item?). My response to these difficulties will be, first, admission and explanation of such problems, particularly when they could lead to serious distortions in the findings; second, concentration on what appear to be "strong" conclusions—that is, conclusions that overshadow even the most pessimistic estimates of errors; and third, when possible, presentation of the data in a complete and basic way in order to allow readers independent conclusions that may differ from my own.

The set of provisions used for most of the analysis to follow includes ninety-one tax expenditure items. I have made some modifications in official lists (which vary over time), including several provisions in combined form that might be listed separately and excluding several provisions that seem to be part of the basic rate structure. Most of the provisions, however, coincide closely with the official tax expenditure budget.[4] The difficulty arises when one tries to summarize changes in what in reality is a very broad area of public policy. To simplify matters, it is necessary to analyze meaningful subsets as well as the tax expenditure system as a whole. The subsets used here are based on size, distribution, and function. Since the functional classification system is used throughout the analysis, the rules defining it will be described in some detail.

Classification of Tax Expenditures

Several methods of classifying tax expenditures have been devised, the most well publicized being the government list based on functional policy areas (energy, natural resources, income security, etc.). Although this system is relevant for policy makers interested in the parallel between direct spending and tax expenditure programs, it is of little use in considering the theoretical issues central to tax debates such as those outlined in chapters 2 and 3. Distinctions between need, equity, and economic efficiency are required. The specific categories used below are need, tax equity, special group benefits, general economic incentives, specific economic incentives, and a sixth, miscellaneous category, which contains those few provisions that cannot easily be classified in any of the other categories.

The classification of a provision is based on its most obvious rationale. Historical arguments are considered in this process, but they are often inconclusive in that a string of rationalizations are often presented for a particular benefit. Some provisions can be reasonably placed in two categories. Nearly all of these cases come down to a determination of whether a provision belongs in the special group category. For this reason a secondary method of classification, which essentially expands the category for special group provisions, was also used in the analysis, and major differences that emerge as a result will be noted in the text or in the footnotes.

The most difficult group of provisions to classify were those affecting the elderly. The question was whether they should be considered "need-based" provisions or benefits going to a special group. Because it is reasonable to assume that the primary rationalization for expenditures targeted on the elderly is economic need and because the analysis of the distribution of benefits (described in the next chapter) indicates that they overwhelmingly aid the poor, I have placed these provisions in the need category in the primary analysis. This category and the others used are defined as follows. The reader may wish to refer ahead to table 13.1, which lists the tax expenditures by category and amount and indicates dual classification when appropriate.

Category I—Need-Based Provisions. This category identifies provisions designed to take into account presumed economic need. Only provisions affecting current conditions of need will be included. Those designed to induce behavior that may ensure against future hardships

(e.g., employer contributions to pensions, health care, life insurance) will be considered incentive provisions (category V). The definition of "need" includes conditions imposing restraints on income-earning potential; extraordinary expenses; situations of economic hardship; and conditions affecting the elderly.

Category II—Tax Equity Provisions. Provisions in this category are designed to either eliminate taxes on taxes or take into consideration expenses accrued in earning income.

Category III—Special Group Benefits. Provisions fall into this category if they meet all of the following criteria:

1. The provision affects a reasonably permanent and identifiable demographic or occupational group;

2. The economic conditions addressed by the provision cannot be assumed to be exclusive to that group;

3. There is no overriding presumption that the benefit is being granted primarily on other grounds.

The first condition applies a restrictive definition to the concept of a group. Without it, every tax provision could be classified as a special group benefit to the extent that it affects an identifiable category of individuals. Moreover, my concern is with the politics of taxation, and thus I am particularly (although not exclusively) interested in groups that might conceivably become organized political interest groups. Three tests apply to this condition: (1) whether the "group" has formal organizations or associations; (2) whether membership in the group is likely to be accompanied by common identifications; and (3) whether membership reflects a relatively permanent condition and not just a temporary economic circumstance. The second condition is designed to give concrete meaning to the term "special." An example is the inclusion in this category of the income exclusion for armed forces benefits or veterans' pensions on the grounds that there are other occupational groups with similar pension and payment plans that do not receive the tax benefit.

The final condition admittedly sometimes requires a judgment call. In some cases the choice between fundamental purposes seems clear (e.g., the exemption for the blind or the exclusion of unemployment benefits); however, it is much more difficult for some other provisions. Since in some cases a provision fulfills the first two conditions but also

has an equally plausible rationale based on need or economic incentives, presuming that these rationales take precedence has the effect of reserving this category (at least for the primary classification) for relatively blatant cases of narrow special interest.

Category IV—General Economic Incentives. The provisions in this category are designed to induce investment and, at least theoretically, to enhance economic growth, and are not exclusive to a particular industry or class of economic producers.

Category V—Specific Economic Incentives. This category includes an assortment of provisions designed to create economic incentives meant to encourage specific forms of desirable behavior other than general economic investment. The distinction between category V and category III involves the nature of organized interests and whether the provision is primarily designed to simply aid a group or to induce a specific activity.

Although the application of this taxonomy requires some judgment calls, most classifications, with the exceptions noted, were obvious, including nearly all of the major revenue-losing provisions listed separately in table 13.2 below.

The Current Scope of the Tax Expenditure System

The Range of Effects. Since many of the provisions listed in table 13.1 have been mentioned in one form or another in previous chapters, the range of the tax expenditure system should come as no surprise. However, even tax experts may benefit from a review of this lengthy list to reaffirm exactly how extensive this policy area has become in terms of the number and variety of organized and unorganized groups or populations affected and the range of behaviors influenced, or at least supposedly influenced, by the tax code. The elderly, students, the blind, the military, the disabled, the militarily disabled, coal miners, timber owners, farmers, veterans, shipping companies, wage earners living abroad, wage earners in two-earner families, parents of students, welfare recipients, the unemployed, and home owners are only some of the categories exclusively affected by one or more provisions. The code provides at least a dozen different mechanisms for encouraging general investment or savings; eight major provisions affecting residential housing; and, by my coding, six or more provisions encouraging various forms of energy production, conservation, and use. The tax laws en-

Table 13.1 The Tax Expenditure System

Tax Expenditure	(1) Year of Origin	(2) 1975 $ Amount ($ millions)[a]	(3) 1982 $ Amount ($ millions)[a]	(4) Distribution Coefficient[b]
Category I—Need-Based Provisions		13,460	30,490	+.308
Exclusion of Social Security—OASI	1941	2,470	9,980	+.535
Deduction of medical expenses	1942	2,315	3,924	−.140
Exclusion of workmen's compensation	1918	505	3,100	+.536
Additional exemption for the elderly*	1948	1,100	2,355	+.196
Exclusion of unemployment benefits	1938	2,300	2,060	+.409
Exclusion of Social Security—survivors' benefit*	1941	450	1,915	+.535
Exclusion of veterans' disability payments*	1917	540	1,360	+.184
Earned income credit	1975	0	1,255	+.955
Exemption of students over 18	1918	670	995	+.162
Exclusion of Social Security—disability payment	1941	275	915	+.540
Deduction of casualty loss	1913	280	800	−.260
Exclusion of public assistance	1913	105	445	+.808
Exclusion of capital gains on home sales of the elderly*	1964	40	415	−.493

Exclusion of railroad retirement*	1935	170	380	+.537
Exclusion of military disability*	1942	70	165	+.559
Exclusion of disability (sick) pay	1954	315	155	+.244
Retirement tax credit*	1954	130	135	+.739
Exclusion of coal miners' disability benefit*	1972	50	95	+.575
Additional exemption for the blind	1943	20	30	+.140
Deduction of adoption expenses	1981	0	10	NA
Excess of percentage over minimum standard deduction	1964	1,385	repeal	+.007
Category II—Tax Equity Provisions		18,185	40,145	−.417
Deduction of state and local taxes	1913	8,490	20,395	−.457
Deduction of real estate taxes	1913	4,510	10,065	−.329
Exclusion state and local bond interest	1913	3,805	6,645	−.818
Child care credit	1954	295	1,120	+.161
Deduction for two-earner couples	1981	0	705	NA
Exclusion of employer-furnished meals and lodging	1918	265	655	+.078
Deferral of taxes on foreign corporate income	1913	NA	520	NA
Deduction of state gasoline tax	1913	865	repeal	−.131

Table 13.1 The Tax Expenditure System (continued)

Tax Expenditure	(1) Year of Origin	(2) 1975 $ Amount ($ millions)[a]	(3) 1982 $ Amount ($ millions)[a]	(4) Distribution Coefficient[b]
Category III—Special Group Benefits		3,345	4,930	+.201
Exclusion of military benefits	1918	650	1,885	+.606
Capital gains for timber income	1943	205	600	−.690
Deduction of noncash agricultural co-op dividends	1913	NA	545	NA
Expensing of farm capital outlays	1916	610	545	−.371
Capital gains for certain farm income	1921	485	460	−.686
Excess bad debt for financial institutions	1947	880	250	NA
Exclusion of GI Bill benefits	1917	255	175	+.710
Exclusion of reinvested utility dividends	1981	0	130	NA
Capital gains on coal royalties	1951	40	105	−.674
Exclusion of veterans' pensions	1917	25	85	+.898

Deferral of tax on shipping companies	1970	70	65	– NA
Exclusion of certain agricultural cost sharing	1954	NA	60	– NA
Capital gains on iron ore royalties	1964	10	20	– .847
Exemption of credit union income	1909	115	5	– NA
Category IV—General Economic Incentives		14,770	57,220	– .622
Investment credit	1962	5,810	20,035	– .266
Capital gains	1921	5,785	18,315	– .683
Asset depreciation range	1971	NA	7,300	– .622
Capital gains at death	1921	NA	5,245	– .683
Research and development benefits	1954	635	2,390	– .798
Dividend exclusion	1916	315	2,185	– .188
Expensing construction-period interest and taxes	1913	1,510	745	– .756
Excess first-year depreciation	1958	275	205	– .753
All Savers Certificates*	1981	0	515	– NA
Depreciation of buildings in excess of straight line depreciation rate	1954	440	285	– .753

Table 13.1 The Tax Expenditure System (continued)

Tax Expenditure	(1) Year of Origin	(2) 1975 $ Amount ($ millions)[a]	(3) 1982 $ Amount ($ millions)[a]	(4) Distribution Coefficient[b]
Category V—Specific Economic Incentives		29,035	101,855	−.240
Exclusion of employer contributions to pensions	1926	5,225	25,765	−.169
Deduction for mortgage interest	1913	5,405	23,030	−.209
Exclusion of employer contributions to health plans	1954	3,275	15,330	−.065
Deduction of charitable contributions	1917	4,770	8,345	−.466
Exclusion of interest on life insurance*	1913	1,545	4,535	−.204
Expensing exploration and development costs*	1917	620	4,145	−.744
Excess of percentage over cost depletion*	1913	2,475	2,750	−.750
Exclusion of self-employed contributions to pensions	1962	390	2,560	−.442
Exclusion of employer contributions to life insurance	1920	740	1,900	−.066
Exclusion of interest on industrial development bonds	1938	175	1,650	−.627
Domestic international sales corp. (DISC)	1971	1,130	1,465	NA
Deduction of charitable contributions to health organizations	1917	NA	1,360	−.634
Tax credit for corporations in U.S. possessions	1921	245	1,200	NA

Deferral of capital gains on homes	1951	255	1,070	−.017
Investment credit for employee stock ownership plans (ESOPs)	1975	0	1,005	NA
Exclusion of interest on housing bonds	1968	0	920	+.574
Deduction of charitable contributions for education	1917	645	895	−.774
Exclusion of interest on pollution control bonds	1969	140	835	−.835
Credit for residential energy expenses	1978	0	670	NA
Credit for new energy technology and alternative fuels	1978	0	595	NA
Exclusion of scholarship and fellowship income	1954	200	465	+.602*
Depreciation of rental housing in excess of straight-line depreciation rate	1954	520	430	−.753
General and targeted jobs credit	1977	0	300	−.264
Investment credit for housing rehabilitation	1978	0	255	NA
Exclusion of employer contributions to accident insurance	1951	50	100	−.064
Exclusion of interest on student loan bonds	1976	0	100	NA
Credit for political contributions	1971	40	80	−.049**
Benefits for preserving historic structures	1976	0	80	−.815
Five-year amortization for housing rehabilitation	1969	105	45	−.815
Credit for employing WIN recipients	1971	10	45	NA
Exclusion of employer educational assistance	1978	0	40	NA
Exclusion of prepaid legal services	1976	0	20	+.161
Deferral of interest on savings bonds	1951	525	−80	−.709
Exclusion of employer child care benefits	1981	0	0	NA

Table 13.1 The Tax Expenditure System (continued)

	(1)	(2)	(3)	(4)
Tax Expenditure	Year of Origin	1975 $ Amount ($ millions)[a]	1982 $ Amount ($ millions)[a]	Distribution Coefficient[b]
Category VI—Miscellaneous Provisions				
Deduction of interest on consumer credit	1913	1,475	13,830	−.379
Safe harbors leasing	1981	1,185	9,285	−.210
Exclusions and deductions for income earned		0	3,450	NA
abroad*	1926	130	985	−.369
Maximum tax on personal services "earned" income	1969	160	repeal	−.935
Total expenditures		80,270	248,470	−.231

Source: U.S. Budgets, Special Analyses for Tax Expenditures.

[a] Estimated amounts include both individual and corporate revenue losses. Those provisions marked with an asterisk were included in the expanded definition of category III as explained in the text.

[b] This coefficient is explained in the text. It ranges from +1 to −1, with +1 representing maximum distribution of the tax expenditure to low-income tax payers. It is based on 1977 distributions of individual income tax returns only. Distributions designated by a double asterisk are based on 1974 distributions.

courage hiring, job seeking, and making a job comfortable and secure, while also offering a helping hand to the unemployed. They encourage health protection, education, life insurance, savings bonds, legal services, and employee ownership. They support giving, caring for children, rehabilitation, retiring, going on public assistance, and, through the earned income credit, going off public assistance. The list is so extensive that at times it is easy to forget that the basic purpose of the income tax is to provide revenue.

Revenue Loss. The revenue lost through the tax expenditure system matches the scope of its effects. Although it is difficult to estimate revenue losses, particularly those associated with exclusion provisions, which are never entered on income tax returns, there is general agreement that the amount is substantial relative to both government outlays and tax revenues.[5] Columns 2 and 3 in table 13.1 give the estimated revenue losses for the fiscal years 1975 and 1982. The former was the first year for which comprehensive estimates were published.[6] The amounts listed for either year suggest a wide variation both between provisions and between categories. However, they also support the general conclusion that everyone benefits to some extent from tax expenditure subsidies. For 1982 provisions range from over $20 billion each for the exclusion of employer contributions to pensions, deductions for mortgage interest and state and local taxes, and the investment credit to currently negligible amounts for credit unions and employer child care and legal services programs. Because of high interest rates, deferral of savings bond interest was actually adding to income tax revenue in 1982.[7]

The revenue totals for each major category in table 13.1 indicate a broad although unbalanced use of the tax code. However, these estimated totals, which are simply the arithmetic sum of the amounts for all the provisions in each category, require a brief explanation. The estimates for individual provisions measure the projected added revenue that would be gained if only that provision were changed while all other aspects of the tax system remained the same. For several reasons, if combinations of provisions were to be repealed, the revenue gained would not necessarily equal the arithmetic sum of losses attributed to each provision separately. Lost revenue for individual items is calculated by taking the estimated income gain for an individual affected by the provision and multiplying it by the taxpayer's marginal rate. These losses are then summed across all taxpayers, or, more accurately, the sample of taxpayers on which most IRS statistics are based. However, if an itemized deduction was repealed, some taxpayers would be better off

using the standard deduction, which means that the revenue to be gained from repealing that provision is not accurately measured by multiplying the amount reported from the deduction by the effective marginal rate. Shifting to the standard deduction offsets part of this gain, and thus the revenue loss is actually less than the simple calculated amount. For individual provisions, the Treasury estimates in table 13.1 take this fact into account. However, more taxpayers would choose the standard deduction option if combinations of deductions were repealed, than if any single provision was. This fact is *not* taken into account in the estimates, and thus the aggregate revenue losses overstate the amount of revenue that would be saved from multiple revisions in deductions.[8]

The marginal rate structure also presents problems of aggregation, but in this case the error is in the reverse direction. The reason is that as provisions are dropped, taxpayers are forced into higher marginal brackets, which means that subsequent changes would be worth more in terms of added revenue. This is particularly true at higher income levels and for provisions such as capital gains and the exclusion of interest on state and local bonds, which primarily benefit upper-income taxpayers. If combinations of provisions are considered, the revenue loss in these cases, would be more than that calculated by simply summing the individual estimates.[9]

Although these problems of estimation could have an important impact on individual policy decisions involving combinations of provisions, this does not mean that the arithmetic totals are useless for comparisons between categories or over time. One reason is that consideration of individual provisions makes sense as an indicator of tax structure and policy changes, particularly in light of the history of tax reform efforts to repeal even single, let alone combinations of, provisions. Moreover, although the exact errors in our aggregate measures are unknown, there is little reason to suspect bias from year to year, and thus trends over time can be accurately detected. For our more theoretical purpose, therefore, these numbers do have significant meaning.

If we concentrate on the 1982 category totals in table 13.1, the most obvious impression again is of the diversity and range of the tax expenditure system. Although the use of the tax system to create specific economic incentives (category V) accounts for the largest amount (41 percent of all tax expenditures), need, tax equity, and general economic incentives all account for substantial sums. This same spread is also evident if we concentrate on the largest of the ninety-one tax expenditures. Each of these provisions, listed separately in table 13.2, repre-

sents a tax loss of 1 percent of income tax revenues or more. These "big ticket" items, which account for almost 79 percent of all tax expenditures, have two general traits in common. They are mass-based provisions that affect large numbers of individual or corporate taxpayers, and they are of long standing: only four of seventeen originated in the postwar period.[10]

Category III is the only group of provisions that accounts for insignificant revenue losses. This is partly because of the narrow definition of special group benefits employed; the provisions fitting this category, while numerous, are all relatively cheap. If the secondary classification system is used (which expands the special group category by including those provisions marked with an asterisk in table 13.1), the percentage of total expenditures for category III is increased only from 2 to 13 percent, despite the fact that several large provisions are added and the number of provisions in the category is increased from fourteen to twenty-eight. Thus, even if the broader definition is used, it is incorrect to perceive the tax expenditure system as primarily a method of distributing hidden benefits to very narrow and highly organized groups. If it were, it might be much easier to deal with, and reform crusades might be more effective. As it is, most of the money is spread very broadly among large segments of the population and corporate world.

This does not mean that tax politics is unaffected by interest group lobbying. Major tax subsidies are often supported by powerful organizations: councils of mayors, governors, and state legislators protect the interest exclusion of state and local bonds (to the advantage of the very wealthy); a range of groups representing the elderly reject even the mildest suggestion that retirement benefits and Social Security be further taxed; and the Chamber of Commerce, the National Association of Manufacturers, and the Business Council variously promote higher depreciation allowances, investment credits, and other business provisions. Similarly, smaller-scale lobbying efforts representing much narrower groups are often successful in altering minor legislative provisions or IRS rulings. Disputes between interest groups are also very important in tax legislation—conflicts over education tax credits, which pit teachers and local government associations against church groups, and debates over the competitive advantages gained by certain businesses through tax provisions come immediately to mind.

Nevertheless, the tax expenditure problem will not be solved by focusing on the influence of narrow interest groups. Excesses in the tax code, such as the infamous provisions written to benefit single individuals or companies, will remain part of the lore and image of tax politics. But in terms of revenue, the tax expenditures that count are

Table 13.2 "Big Ticket" Tax Expenditures

	(1) Amount ($ millions) 1982	(2) % of Tax Expenditures 1982	(3) Average Growth Per Year 1974–1982
I. Need-Based Provisions			
Exclusion of Social Security—OASI	$9,980	4.0%	19.3%
Deduction of medical expenses	3,925	1.6	8.4
II. Tax Equity Provisions			
Deduction of state and local taxes	20,395	8.2	15.4
Deduction of property tax	10,065	4.1	12.7
Exclusion of bond interest	6,685	2.7	7.5
IV. General Economic Incentives			
Investment credit	20,035	8.1	21.5
Capital gains	18,315	7.4	15.1
Asset depreciation range/Asset cost recovery system	7,300	2.9	NA
Capital gains at death	5,245	2.1	NA
V. Specific Economic Incentives			
Exclusion of employer contribution to pensions	25,765	10.4	24.9
Deduction of mortgage interest	23,030	9.3	24.1
Exclusion of employer contributions to health plans	15,330	6.2	23.8
Deduction of charitable contributions	8,345	3.4	10.1
Exclusion of life insurance interest	4,535	1.8	15.8
Expensing of mineral exploration and development costs	4,145	1.7	24.7
VI. Miscellaneous			
Consumer credit	9,285	3.7	27.2
Safe harbor leasing	3,560	1.4	NA
Total	$195,940	78.9%	—

ᵃSee table 13.1, footnote b.

| | | Origin | | Modifications | |
(4) Distribution Coefficient[a]	(5) Date	(6) Source	(7) Party	(8) Increases	(9) Decreases
+.535	1941	IRS	None	0	0
−.140	1942	Finance	Dem.[b]	10	1
−.457	1913	W&M	Dem.[b]	0	3
−.329	1913	W&M	Dem.[b]	0	0
−.818	1913	W&M	Dem.	0	1
−.266[c]	1962	Admin.	Dem.	15	2
−.683	1921	W&M	Rep.	17	14
−.622[c]	1971	Admin.	Rep.	1	0
−.683	1921	IRS	None	0	0
−.169	1926	Sen. Fl.	Dem.	4	6
−.209	1913	W&M	Dem.[b]	0	0
−.065	1954	Admin.	Rep.	0	1
−.466	1917	Sen. Fl.	Dem.	9	5
−.204	1913	Admin.	Dem.	0	0
−.744	1917	IRS	None	5	4
−.210	1913	W&M	Dem.[b]	0	2
NA	1981	Admin.	Rep.	NA	NA
−.308	—	—	—	61	39

[b]Origin based on inference from party control of the committee rather than a specific individual.
[c]Based only on distribution to individuals, who account for relatively small amounts.

those with widely endorsed and solid justifications, long histories, and large potential constituencies. Although many of these provisions began modestly affecting small numbers, in nearly all cases the expansion of these provisions was easily foreseen. Furthermore, such provisions as the exclusion of employer benefits, the exemption of Social Security, and deductions of interest and taxes, while initially modest, were certainly never targeted for narrow special interest groups.

Although the range of the tax expenditure system seems very broad, its magnitude relative to the size of government, the size of the economy, and the total amount of income taxes collected still needs to be explored. That is most efficiently done in the context of analyzing the growth of tax expenditures.

The Growth of Tax Expenditures

Both the number of provisions that allow tax reductions and the magnitude of these reductions are important income tax issues. The former issue involves the problems of complexity, confusion, and control of the tax system; the latter, the question whether the income tax will be able to sustain future revenue needs. The basic evidence on the first of these issues is more conclusive than that on the second.

Growth in Numbers and Complexity. One simple method of understanding the growth of tax expenditures is to study the origins of the current set. This is not a totally accurate measure of change because it does not include provisions that may have been repealed before 1974, which was the starting point for compiling the set of tax expenditures on which this study is based. Although, as was emphasized in preceding chapters, many more new provisions are created than old ones dropped, a number of provisions have been repealed over the years or passed on a temporary basis and allowed to expire. For example, in the early years of the income tax, the incomes of the president, federal judges, and federal, state, and local government employees was excluded, along with certain income in the form of gifts and inheritances. These exclusions were later repealed. Deductions at one time were granted for interest on federal bonds and federal income taxes paid in the previous year. Further, if the many exceptions, exclusions, and special provisions that affected wartime excess profits taxes were included as tax expenditures, this list would grow significantly.

Since World War II, several provisions that would be classified as tax expenditures but do not appear in table 13.1 have also been repealed.

for example, the exemption from taxation of building and loan organizations and cooperative banks in 1951 (leaving only the exemption of credit unions); deductions for customs, excise and miscellaneous state and local taxes and fees in 1964; and the five-year amortization for child care facilities. The one-year tax credit for the purchase of a new home, enacted in 1977, was kept temporary. In the current list, the deduction of state gasoline taxes was repealed during the energy crisis in 1977, and the differentials between the minimum standard and percentage deductions and the earned and unearned rates were technically repealed, although in each case the repeal had the effect of adding to revenue losses.[11]

Yet the number of provisions repealed is not substantial compared with the number of new provisions enacted. Further, some repeals are only technical in that the benefit is broadened to the point that it becomes invisible or is traded for a parallel provision that means less revenue loss.[12] In any event, new provisions are for the most part cumulative, and thus an analysis of the dates of origin of the current list gives us an adequate, if not perfect, measure of the expansion of the number of major tax-reduction provisions available in the income tax codes.

Table 13.3 depicts the dates of origin of tax expenditures broken down by the categories I have previously defined. The totals confirm what is already well known: that a significant expansion in provisions has taken place over the seventy-odd years of income taxation. It is, perhaps, less well understood (and very rarely acknowledged in official statements) that the growth seems to be relatively steady, with almost exactly half of the current list originating prior to or during World War II.[13] Eleven of these provisions emerged from the initial income tax

Table 13.3 Date of Origin of Tax Expenditures

Category	1909–1919	1920–1945	1946–1969	1970–1982	Total
I. Need-based	5	8	5	3	21
II. Tax equity	5	0	1	1	8
III. Special group	6	3	3	2	14
IV. General economic stimulus	2	2	4	2	10
V. Specific economic incentive	7	4	10	13	34
VI. Miscellaneous	1	1	1	1	4
Total	27	18	24	22	91

deliberations of 1909 and 1913. Although the rate of growth may have increased slightly in the last two decades, the increase is modest. The general impression that tax expenditures are a recent phenomenon is further eroded if the origins of the major revenue-losing provisions (table 13.2) are noted. As previously pointed out, only four of seventeen began after World War II.

If there has been a significant change in the pace of tax legislation, it has occurred very recently. Since 1976 thirteen new provisions have been created. This trend also supports the assumption that there has been a recent change in philosophy concerning the use of the tax code to facilitate nonrevenue policy ends. That shift was emphasized in chapters 10 and 11, in which it was argued that although the Carter and Reagan administrations made contradictory statements concerning their tax philosophy, their actions indicated enthusiasm for the use of the tax code to accomplish policy objectives in such areas as energy, housing, urban development, and education. The categorical breakdown in table 13.3 supports the contention that the tax system is being used more frequently for creating both general investment and specific behavioral incentives; however, again the trend goes back further than is often realized. Categories IV and V account for most of the tax expenditures since the Second World War. But although two-thirds of the provisions that offer such incentives have been enacted since the war, only half of those have been created in the last decade. This does not mean, however, that the pressure for such changes is not significantly greater than earlier. The number of pending provisions and proposals of this kind remains large, and the use of tax code for these purposes seems to be equally attractive to both political parties.

Thus, the evidence is mixed for the proposition that tax expenditures have rapidly proliferated in recent years. This should not be interpreted as meaning either that the system has not enlarged considerably over time or that the revenue effects are inconsequential. Indeed, the unchallengeable conclusion that the system has expanded steadily over time may suggest an even more deeply rooted force (and problem) than the temporary fad for using the tax code as a substitute for direct government programs.

The number of provisions alone is not a sufficient indicator of policy complexity. As was pointed out in the last section, complexity multiplies at a much greater rate than the enactment of new provisions. This is because many provisions, once enacted, are modified. The investment credit had only a narrow scope at first, but as its versatility began to be understood, it was expanded and different rates and conditions were added to cover varied and complicated sets of circumstances. Fine-

tuning to achieve refined economic or political effects often adds amendment on amendment to provisions such as capital gains, the expensing and depletion of mineral resources, the minimum tax, and a range of real estate and agricultural provisions designed to contain tax shelters. The result is often that within the scope of a single provision, small policy empires are created that may be thoroughly understood by only small groups of government and private-sector experts. Whether this problem is as serious as current proposals for drastic reforms and enforcement measures suggest will be discussed in chapter 17.

Growth of Revenue Loss of the Tax Expenditure System. Calculation of the size of the tax expenditure system is affected both by the definition of a tax expenditure and by the estimation and aggregation problems discussed above. Since estimating the revenue loss of tax expenditures is a relatively new exercise in government record keeping, the time series involved is very short. However, the Congressional Budget Office (CBO) has calculated tax expenditure aggregates (based on simple sums) going back to 1967. These figures and a calculation of tax expenditures as a percentage of income tax receipts are displayed in table 13.4. Since complete lists of tax expenditures became part of regular government publications only in 1976 (going back to fiscal year 1974), it is not clear precisely which provisions CBO included for 1967 to 1973 in table 13.4. Since 1975 the CBO numbers are very close to the sums for my set of tax expenditures (adjusted for missing data, as indicated in the note to table 13.5). The sharp increase from 1973 to 1975, which cannot be a reflection of changes in the law because there were none of substantive importance during those years, is reasonable given the level of inflation for that period. Thus, the series is probably as good as can be generated under present limitations.

The conclusions drawn from table 13.4 are striking enough to overcome debates over measurement or definitions. In the last fifteen years, the tax expenditure system has grown at a very rapid rate relative to GNP, federal outlays, total receipts, and income tax receipts. By the best estimates available for 1982, tax reduction provisions amounted to 40 percent of all government revenue and 73 percent of the income taxes collected. Moreover, since several major provisions in the 1981 tax bill are to be phased in over several years, and because indexation is scheduled to begin in 1985, these figures could become even more extreme in the very near future, to the point that as much income will be excluded in one form or another as is being collected through the income tax system. The figure of 73 percent of income taxes can be compared to an average of 40 percent for 1967 through 1973. The

Table 13.4 Tax Expenditure Growth, 1967–1982

	1967	1969	1971	1973	1975	1977	1979	1981	1982
Tax expenditure totals ($ millions)	36,550	46,635	51,710	65,370	92,855	113,455	149,815	228,620	253,515
Percentage of GNP	4.4	4.8	4.6	4.7	6.3	6.1	6.4	8.0	8.2
Percentage of federal outlays	20.5	23.7	22.3	24.3	28.5	28.2	30.3	34.6	35.0
Percentage of federal revenues	23.8	24.4	24.8	24.7	33.1	31.7	32.2	37.9	40.4
Percentage of income tax receipts	38.0	37.0	42.1	40.7	56.6	53.2	54.7	65.9	73.5

Source: Testimony, Alice Rivlin, Director, Congressional Budget Office, *Tax Expenditure Limitation and Control*, Hearings before Committee on the Budget, U.S. Senate (November 24, 1981), p. 32. Figures for 1967–1975 are for calendar years, and 1977–1982 for fiscal years; 1982 figures based on Budget Committee estimates. Percentages of income taxes are based on author's calculations using tax expenditure totals listed in the top row.

effects of this revenue shortfall are already being felt, and the budget process and deficits have as a result dominated the legislative activity of the 97th Congress.

Table 13.5 breaks down these increases into the categories that by now should be familiar. Unfortunately, for the reasons stated earlier, the calculations only cover the last eight years. A large proportion of the growth in tax expenditures has taken place over those years, however. The basic conclusions are again quite obvious, although a detailed appraisal of changes in individual provisions, particularly "big ticket" provisions, is also useful. The economic incentive categories have led the recent growth in tax expenditures, even when adjustments are made in published data. Average annual change since 1974 is approximately 20 percent a year in each of these classes.[14] That far outstrips the growth rates for need-based, tax equity, or special group provisions, regardless of the classification definitions used.[15] The result of this growth is reflected in the changing composition of the tax expenditure system. In 1982, 10 percent more of the tax expenditure budget went to provide benefits to generate economic incentives of either a general or a targeted nature, and approximately 10 percent less went for need or tax equity. Since fifteen new incentive provisions have been created since 1970, if these patterns could be extended back to 1967, as in table 13.4, these trends would be even more pronounced.

The shift toward stimulating the economy and using the tax system for targeted policy purposes noted in the previous historical chapters is thus clearly reflected in this more systematic analysis. However, only part of the growth of these segments of the tax code is due to legislative changes, although anticipated future increases will be more directly linked to recent political actions. The reason that politics plays only a partial role is that much of the change is due to growth in major provisions, most of which have not been significantly altered in recent years. Rather, they have grown through the inertia generated by inflation and higher interest rates. For example, the exclusion of employer contributions to pensions and health plans plus the deduction for home mortgage interest have together accounted for 30 percent of the $168 billion increase in total tax expenditures from 1975 to 1982. The average annual expansion of these provisions, at 24–25 percent per year, shifted their proportion of the total "budget" from 17.3 percent in 1975 to 25.8 percent in 1982. Yet no major changes have occurred in these provisions in recent years.[16] The same is true of the exclusion of Social Security income and the deduction of consumer interest: both amounts have grown rapidly of their own accord. Although I do not want to overstate the point, because the growth and the shift in the balance of

Table 13.5 Tax Expenditure Growth by Category

Category	% Dollar Change 1975–1982	% of Expenditures		% of Tax Receipts		Average Annual Change (%) 1974–1982[a]
		1975	1982	1975	1982	
I. Need-based provisions	126.5	16.8	12.3	8.2	8.8	13.2
II. Tax equity provisions	120.8	22.7	16.2	11.1	11.6	12.5
III. Special group benefits	47.4	4.2	2.0	2.0	1.4	4.6
IV. General economic incentives[b]	287.4	18.4	23.0	9.0	16.6	21.2
V. Specific economic incentives	250.8	36.2	41.0	17.7	29.5	19.6
VI. Miscellaneous	837.6	1.8	5.6	0.9	4.0	30.1
All expenditures	209.5	100.1	100.1	48.9	72.0	17.0

Source: Author's estimates based on tax expenditure list and classification in table 13.1.

[a]Missing data in either year eliminate a provision from the change calculation for the year.

[b]Unfortunately, published estimates for two of the largest provisions in this category—capital gains at death and ADRs—are not available before 1977. Estimating these amounts for 1974–1976 by assuming an amount based on their average share of tax expenditures for 1977–1982 changes the calculations for category IV: % Dollar Change 1975–1982 = 185%; % of Expenditures 1975 = 23.5%; % Tax Receipts 1975 = 12.2%. Average annual change is unaffected, so the growth rate of category IV is still substantial.

tax expenditures have resulted in part from conscious political actions, external economic factors are also partly responsible. Since many of the provisions that contribute to expansion under these conditions are of long standing and affect large segments of the population, the prospect of containing these tax outlays is unlikely. The situation is very similar to that posed by entitlement programs, interest payments, and basic defense expenditures on the budget side of the ledger. That these two "automatic" features work in opposite directions has important ramifications for fiscal policy, particularly future expectations concerning the deficit.

Tax Expenditure Growth: How Serious a Problem?

The prediction of doom for the income tax is a standard item in the rhetorical repertoire of many tax experts. Used from time to time to spur change, it is often linked to widely varying conceptions of tax reform. Constant immersion in tax policy seems quite frequently to lead to this gloomy prognosis. It is not, however, a reasonable prospect. The income tax will no more go away than it will be radically reformed. It will never follow the path of tariffs and customs—at least not while I will be caring. But that does not mean that it will be able to do the job alone; and that is an important issue because the alternatives—payroll tax increases, a national sales tax, or a value-added tax—are not very attractive to tax experts. The troublesome aspect of the revenue growth in tax expenditures is their rapid escalation as a percentage of taxes collected. Lest this danger be misunderstood, it is necessary to put it in the broader perspective of taxing potential, and this can be done by relating tax reductions of all kinds to the underlying level of personal income in the country.[17]

Eugene Steuerle and Michael Hartzmark have carefully made such estimates for the period from 1947 to 1979. The results are at first somewhat surprising. Figure 13.1 summarizes their findings. It depicts the various ways in which aggregate personal income is excluded from income taxes. The amounts are depicted as percentages of the total personal income for any year. The less income excluded, the broader the tax base. The surprise is that from a postwar high in 1948, when taxable income was only 35 percent of personal income, the tax base expanded through 1969, at which point close to 51 percent of personal income was subject to taxes. Since that point, if tax credits are included as tax exclusions, the base has contracted somewhat.[18] What this means is that all the clamor over the "erosion of the tax base," much of it based

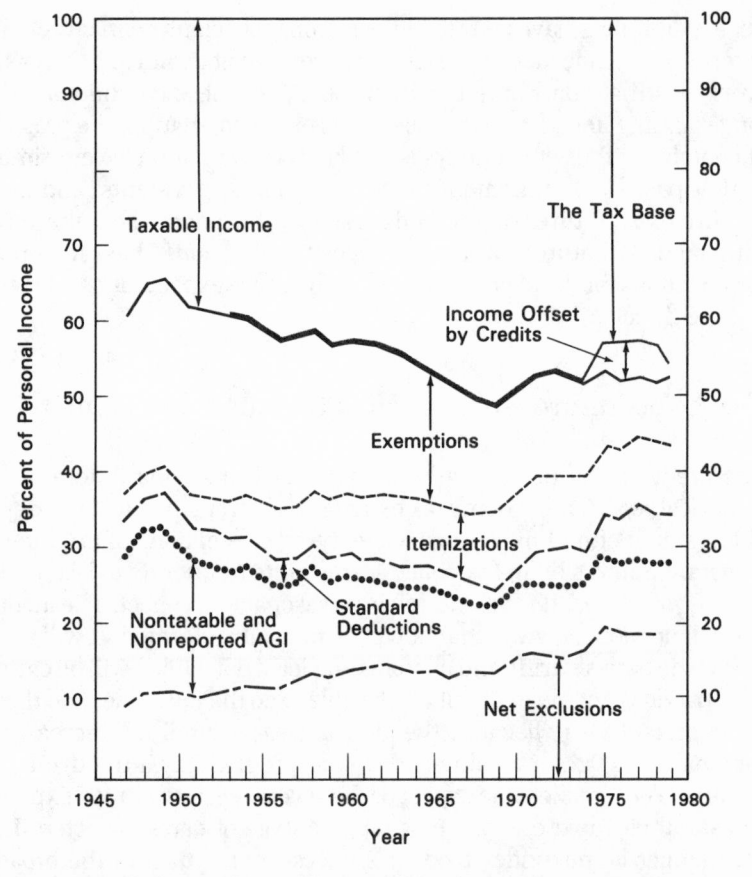

Figure 13.1 Relationship of Personal Income to the Tax Base

Source: Eugene Steuerle and Michael Hartzmark, "Individual Income Taxation, 1947–1979," *National Tax Journal* 34 (1981): 152.

Note: The figure depicts the cumulative percent of income not included in the tax base because of various provisions in the tax code. The percent of personal income remaining at the top of the figure is the tax base.

on analyses similar to that in the preceding pages, is giving an erroneous impression.[19]

The growth of tax expenditures itself is a real phenomenon, as figure 13.1 confirms. The tax base after the war was small because personal exemptions and nontaxable and nonreported income accounted for a substantial amount of the difference between total personal income and the tax base. Through 1959 these two components averaged almost 40 percent of total personal income; since 1970 they have averaged 20

percent. On the other hand, itemized deductions and income exclusions, which account for most tax expenditure losses, have steadily increased, from an average of 16 percent of personal income before 1959 to 27 percent in the 1970s. However, the combined effects of these divergent trends have not led to an erosion of the tax base, but rather to an increase in the total amount of income on which income taxes are levied. Thus, the argument could be made that the increase in tax expenditures is relatively harmless and that the future revenue potential of the income tax is on solid ground.

There is a temptation to counter this general argument by noting that the budgetary politics of the Reagan administration imply that taxing potential as measured in terms of taxable personal income has nothing to do with *political* taxing potential. Chapter 11 was devoted to describing and analyzing the tax-cutting frenzy that swept Congress in 1981. Congressional tax activity since 1981 has been devoted to determining how Congress can live with the results of that tax cut in the face of the unprecedented projected budget deficits. The problem is not only the difficulty of retreating from major tax reductions, but also the realization that federal spending cannot be reduced in large chunks and that a very large core of federal spending (entitlements, defense, and interest) is essentially insulated from serious budgetary action. Although this current crisis may be an ominous signal and may lead to another revamping of congressional budgetary practices, the basic dilemma of maintaining the revenue capacity of the income tax goes deeper. It is rooted both in the historical trends described in the last chapter and in the recent tendency to use the tax code to promote diverse policy objectives.

Until the middle 1970s, first real economic growth and then inflation provided an extended political holiday in tax policy and allowed the luxury of tax reductions and increased government spending with relatively modest deficits. Without substantially altering the personal exemption or the standard deduction, more personal income became subject to taxation. This created an automatic, modest, but broad tax increase for the large numbers of taxpayers at the bottom and middle-income levels, who were still in the lower marginal brackets. This increase in taxable income at the base of the income pyramid provided pressure for cuts in rates and increases in exemptions and standard deductions, as well as an incentive to create and expand specialized structural benefits in the form of tax expenditures. But because of the resistance to tax cuts of the Truman and Eisenhower administrations and leadership control over the tax committees, these cuts lagged behind expanding income, and thus the tax base increased.

As incomes increased, however, first from real growth in the economy

and then from inflation, exemptions and standard deductions began to lose their sheltering effect on middle-class incomes. At the same time those groups began to move up to higher marginal brackets. Together these trends produced overwhelming political pressure for general and specialized reductions, which ultimately led to lower marginal rates, a greatly expanded tax expenditure system, and indexing. Because the base is now shrinking and the only easy way to increase it is to lower personal exemptions and standard deductions (which has never been done in peacetime), we have arrived at a point where lower rates apply to a lower base and, barring real income growth, effective marginal rates are frozen.

Other factors also point toward limited political potential for increasing or even maintaining present income tax levels. Not only has the middle class become extremely sensitive to marginal rate adjustments, but its members have become heavy users of tax expenditures, some of which were once of benefit only to the wealthy. It is no longer only home ownership and its attendant tax advantages that matter to this group. Employer-paid benefits are crucial, and sheltered savings devices will have an equally important impact, as will such provisions as spousal deductions, particularly if they are expanded. A less certain but seemingly sacred trend that also bodes ill for the income tax is the consistent downward tendency of corporate income taxes. Although, as we will see in chapter 16, this trend has less popular support, the alleged link between economic performance and low corporate taxes seems to have been fully absorbed by the public, and thus the percentage of revenue from this source has steadily declined since 1960. Finally, the recent practice of using the tax code for nonrevenue purposes, as indicated by the growth in category V tax expenditures, opens up the system to convenient and potentially unlimited erosion.

The last two of these problems might be overcome by a wave of reform liberalism. However, pressure from the middle class influences both the effects and likelihood of tax reform. Under earlier conditions, when tax reduction provisions and high marginal brackets affected only the wealthy, liberal reforms such as that of 1969 might have both a political chance and, if passed, a significant effect on impending revenue shortfalls. Although it is possible to design reforms that are limited to the wealthy few, to have a meaningful revenue effect, either many of them would have to be enacted or the major economic efficiency provisions in category IV would have to be repealed. Both seem unlikely at this time. Further, one might expect that either opponents of reform or reform zealots would add changes in the middle-class provisions as well. At that point the political ice would become extremely thin.

Chapter 14.
Who Gets What?
The Distribution of
Tax Expenditures

The term "tax expenditure" is used by many synonymously with terms like "loophole" and "tax shelter," which imply narrowly drawn provisions that benefit small groups of wealthy taxpayers.[1] In the last chapter it was shown that the effects of tax expenditures are far from narrow in terms of the groups and functions served. It was also suggested that these provisions have an impact on a broader range of incomes than is usually perceived. That issue is the subject of this chapter. The first part describes various standards by which distributions of tax expenditures can be judged and defines an index, similar to the GINI Index, to measure those distributions. The second part analyzes the aggregate distribution for those tax expenditures for which estimates are available, the varying distributions by expenditure category, and the beneficiaries of individual provisions.

Measuring the Distribution of Tax Expenditures

How one interprets and measures the distribution of tax expenditures depends on the standard of comparison employed. In discussions of equality of income and wealth, the usual standard is an equal division among people. This standard was assumed in the construction of the GINI Index, for example. This standard cannot be used for tax expenditures, however, because relevant data exist only for those filing tax returns. More important, the assumption that tax expenditures should be equally distributed among filers is unrealistic. Tax expenditures offset or reduce taxes due. Since low-income taxpayers pay very little in taxes, the assumption that they should get an equal dollar amount of the tax expenditure pie misrepresents the political intent of these provisions and would mean that many low-income taxpayers would have to receive a lump-sum tax rebate of thousands of dollars. However, be-

cause the standard of equality among persons is so common in equity discussions, distributional effects relative to filers will be included, though not emphasized.

Two more meaningful standards compare tax expenditures benefits to the amount of income earned by different income groups and compare them to the amount of taxes ultimately paid. The first allows one to judge the distribution relative to the notion of a proportional or flat tax rate, and the second allows one to estimate how tax expenditures relate to differing final tax burdens. For both of these standards it is relevant to compare distributions for increasing levels of income. Percentage breakdowns by income group of total tax expenditures and the different classes of expenditures are depicted in table 14.1. Also shown are the breakdowns by income of total returns, adjusted gross income, and income taxes paid.

Several statistical methods can be used to interpret and summarize the basic data presented in table 14.1. One simple method is to create ratios of percentages of tax expenditures to percentages of returns, income, and taxes paid for different income classes. Given a selected standard, one can describe ratios of relative advantage for different income levels, with a ratio of one representing a proportionate share. For example, those with incomes between $5,000 and $10,000 received 7.7 percent of the benefits from tax expenditures, but had 12.3 percent of aggregate income; thus, with a ratio of 0.63, they received less than a proportionate share based on income. However, the ratio based on taxes, of which they pay 5.3 percent, is 1.4.

Although such ratios are useful for conveying the details of distributions, they are not very useful as a summary measure. A summary measure can be based on cumulative frequencies. A distribution coefficient for tax expenditures analogous to the GINI Index can be constructed on the basis of the relationship between the cumulative frequencies of the tax expenditures and the cumulative frequencies of the tax expenditures and the cumulative frequencies of whatever standard (income, taxes, or returns) is selected. Figure 14.1 portrays a Lorenz-type curve for selected tax expenditures. As in a standard Lorenz curve, the data are ordered by increasing levels of income. The axes for this figure are the cumulative frequency of adjusted gross income and the cumulative percentage of tax expenditure benefits. A point of the curve indicates the total amount of a tax expenditure received by those holding a given amount of income. Thus, for point C, taxpayers who account for 80 percent of all the adjusted gross income received only 18 percent of the benefits from capital gains. Since the remaining 20 percent of income is held by the largest earners, and they received 82 percent of

Table 14.1 Percentages of Returns, Income, Taxes, and Tax Expenditures by Income Class, 1977

	Amount ($ billions)	Expanded Income[a] ($ thousands)								Distribution Coefficients[b]		
		0–5	5–10	10–15	15–20	20–30	30–50	50–100	+100	D_r	D_i	D_t
Returns	86.6	26.9	22.3	16.5	13.2	14.0	5.5	1.3	0.6			
Income	1158.5	4.3	12.3	15.3	17.1	25.2	15.1	6.5	4.2			
Taxes paid	158.5	0.4	5.3	10.6	14.5	25.7	19.8	12.0	11.6			
Total tax expenditures	82.3	4.2	7.7	9.1	11.6	19.4	16.7	13.7	17.6	–.59	–.23	.00
Tax Expenditure Classes												
I. Need-based provisions	15.6	17.3	22.0	14.8	13.1	14.7	9.2	5.9	2.9	–.14	+.31	+.52
II. Tax equity provisions	15.1	0.1	1.8	5.9	10.7	22.7	21.2	19.2	18.4	–.75	–.42	–.17
III. Special group benefits	2.2	10.0	26.2	16.7	9.7	7.7	9.5	8.1	11.9	–.26	+.20	+.39
IV. General economic incentives	17.3	0.5	2.2	4.1	5.2	9.7	16.3	20.0	42.0	–.84	–.62	–.44
V. Specific economic incentives	29.3	0.8	4.7	10.1	15.0	26.6	19.0	12.3	11.5	–.63	–.24	+.03
VI. Miscellaneous	2.9	0.4	2.3	5.8	11.7	25.7	21.7	12.2	20.2	–.73	–.38	–.13

Source: Unpublished Treasury Department estimates.

[a] Expanded income is adjusted gross income plus minimum tax "preference income," minus investment interest expense to the extent of investment income. See n. 5 to this chapter.

[b] The coefficients are based on different standards of comparisons as explained in the text. D_r is based on the percentage distribution of *returns*; D_i, the percentage distribution of *income*; D_t, the percentage of *taxes paid*.

the benefits of capital gains, it is clear that this provision is highly skewed in favor of the wealthy. On the other hand, the curve depicting the exclusion of Social Security retirement benefits (OASI) represents a distribution skewed in the opposite direction. For this example, the 45-degree line represents a distribution of tax expenditures that is proportional to the distribution of income.

An exact set of indices (one for each relevant standard on the horizontal axis) can be computed by calculating the ratio of the area between the curve and the 45-degree line (e.g., L_{cg} in figure 14.1) to the total area of triangle *OAB*. The latter measures the maximum possible skewness

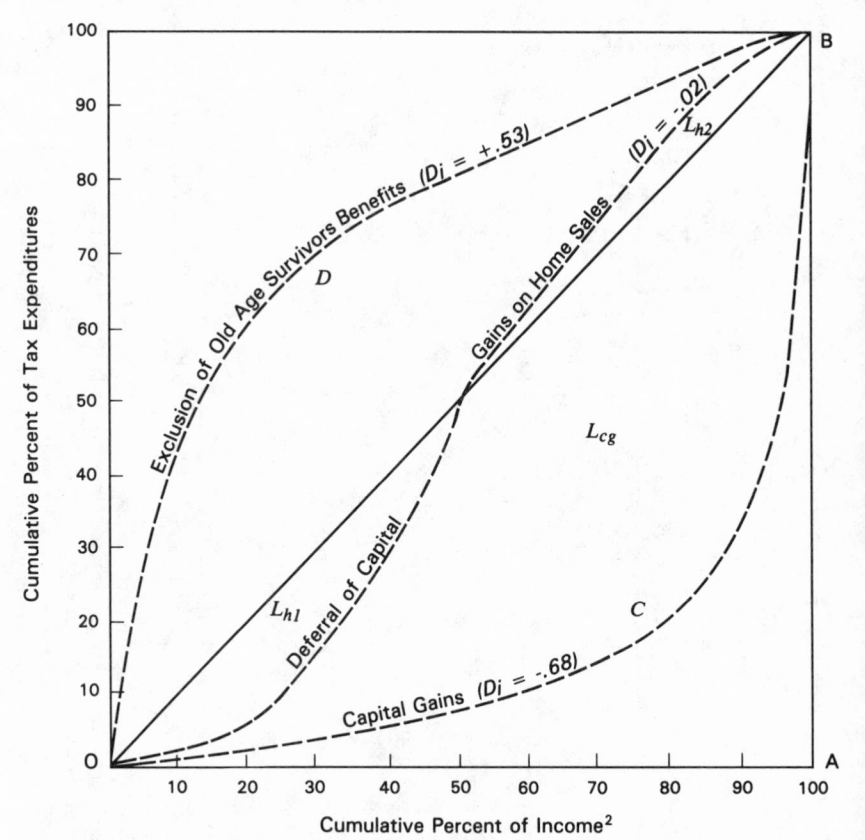

Figure 14.1 Cumulative Frequency Distributions of Selected Tax Expenditures Relative to Income

Source: Unpublished Treasury Department estimates for 1977.
Note: "Income" is adjusted gross income. Units are individual returns ranked from lowest to highest income level.

in the respective direction. In these indices, unlike the GINI, since tax expenditures may disproportionately aid either low- or upper-income groups, the curves may fall on either side of the 45-degree line.[2] Therefore, for this analysis, a negative sign will be used to depict distributions below the 45-degree line and a positive sign for those above it. Thus, the distribution index ranges from − 1, which represents a distribution of benefits accruing entirely to the highest income group, to + 1, which represents a distribution going solely to the poorest. The zero point indicates an aggregate tax expenditure distribution that is proportional to whatever standard is selected.[3]

Who Gets What from the Tax Expenditure System

Although there is considerable speculation concerning who benefits from the aggregate tax expenditure system, there has been little aggregate analysis. The Treasury Department has been tabulating estimates of some tax expenditure distributions since 1971. The first relatively complete set, which includes sixty-seven of the ninety-one tax expenditures used here, was available for the year 1977.[4] The consideration of who benefits from tax expenditures will begin with aggregate distributions. However, these distributions mask considerable variation between types of tax expenditures. As will become clear below, the final result is a system that disproportionately aids those in upper income brackets, but that also provides some benefits for nearly every income class and population or occupational grouping.

Aggregate Effects. The aggregate distribution of tax expenditures is depicted in table 14.1 and in figures 14.2 and 14.3. Table 14.1 provides percentage breakdowns by "expanded income" class. Expanded income, a concept commonly used by the Department of the Treasury, is defined as adjusted gross income, plus minimum tax preference income, less investment interest expense that does not exceed investment income.[5] Figure 14.2 is a cumulative frequency graph of tax expenditures relative to adjusted gross income, and figure 14.3 is the same plot relative to total taxes paid.

The first obvious and overwhelming conclusion derived from table 14.1 is that if the standard of comparison is the total population, the well-off benefit from tax expenditures much more than those in the lower income brackets. The median or fiftieth percentile for tax expenditures occurs at approximately $30,000. However, 95 percent of the tax returns in 1977 were filed by those making $30,000 or less. This

distribution is reflected in the coefficient D_r, which was calculated based on a standard that assumed that each taxpaying unit would receive an equal proportion of tax expenditures. The −0.59 indicates that the area between the curve of total tax expenditures and the diagonal representing proportionality was 59 percent of a distribution that would allocate all tax expenditures to the highest income class (i.e., 59 percent of the area of the lower triangle).

However, if the standard of comparison is either income or taxes ultimately paid, tax expenditures are much closer to a proportional distribution. With income as the standard, higher income groups still

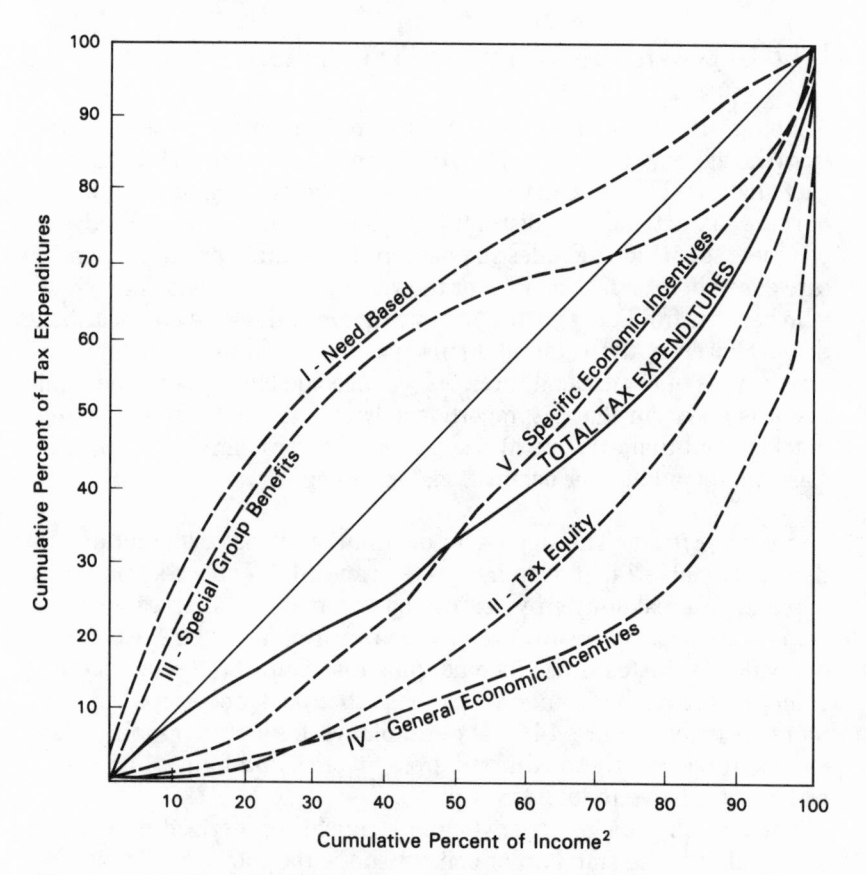

Figure 14.2 Cumulative Frequency Distributions of Tax Expenditure Categories Relative to Income, 1977

Source: Unpublished Treasury Department estimates for 1977.
Note: "Income" is adjusted gross income. Units are individual returns ranked from lowest to highest income level.

benefit in a proportion greater than the income they possess, but the
distribution coefficient (D_i) decreases to -0.23. The distribution and
the area of deviation from a proportional standard are clearly presented
in figure 14.2. If the standard is taxes, the distributional coefficient (D_t)
is exactly zero. This indicates that tax expenditures aggregated across
the population are distributed in direct proportion to the amount of
taxes paid. However, as can be seen in figure 14.3, that aggregate
masks variation across income classes. More precisely, the figure shows
that both lower and upper income groups get a higher percentage of tax
expenditures than the percentage of taxes they pay.

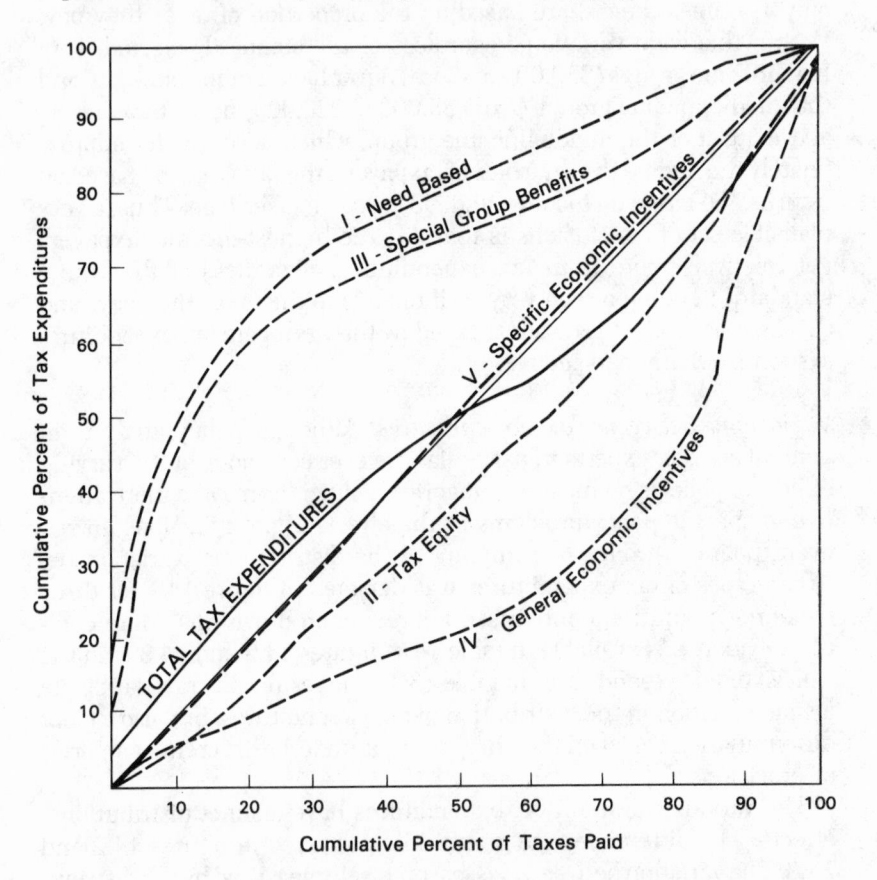

*Figure 14.3 Cumulative Frequency Distributions of Tax Expen-
diture Categories Relative to Taxes Paid, 1977*

Source: Unpublished Treasury Department estimates for 1977.
Note: Units are individual returns ranked from lowest to highest income level.

The distribution of benefits for specific income classes can be analyzed more precisely by calculating "share" ratios based on different standards. Again, the standard selected makes a great deal of difference. For example, those with incomes below $5,000 account for 26.9 percent of the returns but get only 4.2 percent of tax expenditures; thus, on a standard of proportionality between taxpayers, they do very poorly, getting only 15 percent of what would be expected. On the other hand, if the standard is taxes paid, since they pay very little, they receive 10.5 times their share of tax expenditures. At the other extreme, those making over $50,000 get 19.5 times their share based on returns, but only 1.3 times their share based on the proportion of taxes they pay. Within this wide variation, regardless of the standard selected, very high income groups ($50,000 or more) never have a ratio below 1.0, and the middle-income groups (from $5,000 to $20,000) never have a ratio above 1.0. For the middle-income group, which accounts for approximately the middle two quartiles of taxpayers, the ratios are .55 based on returns, .64 based on income, and .93 based on taxes paid. Thus, a very plausible set of conclusions is that: (1) the highest-income taxpayers get relatively more from tax expenditures, regardless of the equity standard; (2) the poor do very well relative to the taxes they pay; and (3) the middle class is disadvantaged by the aggregate tax expenditure system from any perspective.

Variations Between Tax Expenditures. Although policy analysts in general and tax experts in particular are ever conscious of the varying effects of policies on income categories, politicians may be more attentive to specific policy problems or the effects of policy actions on relevant political groups. A sampling of the distributional variation between types of tax expenditures was depicted in figure 14.1 for three well-known and frequently used tax reduction provisions. More complete evidence is available in table 14.2, figures 14.2 and 14.3, and the full list of tax expenditures in table 13.1. The results portrayed indicate a wide variation in the distribution of tax expenditures, but also a clear differentiation based on the purposes that underlie different categories of provisions.

The various classes of tax expenditures have distinct distributional effects. The differences are graphically portrayed in figures 14.2 and 14.3. The variation between classes, precisely measured by the distribution coefficients in table 14.1, is slightly wider when cumulative taxes (figure 14.3) are the standard. The twenty need-based provisions for which distributional data are available, as one would hope, primarily benefit those with low incomes. However, so do those provisions that

are classified as narrow special interest ones, although these latter provisions also benefit some higher income groups as well, whereas almost none of the need-based benefits go to those with higher incomes. Those provisions meant to promote specific economic behavior, which is the largest category in terms of both revenue and the number of provisions (twenty-one), occupy a middle-level position, with large amounts distributed among those with $20,000 to $50,000 incomes. The distribution is almost exactly proportional to the amount of taxes paid at every point in the income distribution. Tax expenditures intended to increase tax equity are more favorable to middle and higher income groups, but by far the most beneficial for the affluent are those designed to promote general economic incentives. This range can be captured by the striking difference between the two extremes that is revealed in table 14.1. Of the total tax expenditures classified as need-based, 67.2 percent goes to taxpayers with $20,000 or less, and only 8.8 percent to those with over $50,000. On the other hand, only 12 percent of the general economic incentives goes to those reporting less than $20,000, while 62 percent goes to those reporting $50,000 or more. This variation is summarized by the spread in distribution coefficients, which for income goes from +0.31 for need-based provisions to −0.62 for those promoting general investment.

The best way to understand how these distributions came about is to relate the aggregates back to the specific provisions listed in table 13.1. The distribution coefficient in column 4 of this table is based on income. The relative position of need-based provisions is evident from the signs of the coefficients of the individual provisions. Only three provisions in category I have negative signs. Of these, the only provision of major revenue consequence is the deduction of medical expenses, which tends to aid the middle-income groups.[6] Exclusions for Social Security, retirement, and survivors' benefits, workers' compensation, unemployment benefits, and public assistance all go to those in the lower-income ranges in a much higher proportion than their share of income would dictate. Because of its built-in income restrictions, the earned-income credit is, as intended, the most beneficial income tax provision for the poor.

A similar but asymmetrical situation explains the oppositely skewed distribution of general economic incentives. None of the nine provisions on which we have data have a positive sign. Further, capital gains, asset depreciation provisions, and research and development incentives, all of which are large, are distributed at the extreme upper end of the income distribution to a degree that is far more than proportionate to the incomes of the wealthy. This category would undoubtedly be even more

heavily weighted toward high-income earners if the incidence of corporate benefits of the investment credit was known or data existed on the
All Savers Certificates, which were designed to have a tax-free interest
of 70 percent of Treasury Bill rates, which makes them attractive only to
investors in higher income brackets. Curiously, the least skewed provision in this category is the exclusion of a portion of dividend income.
This is because the amount of the dividend exclusion is limited and thus
it disproportionately benefits the small investor. However, there is no
escaping the conclusion that stimulating the economy through the tax
system is equivalent to providing substantial tax breaks for the rich.

Generalizations become more complex for the other groups. For
example, the provisions that make up category III, special group benefits, are a widely diverse lot. The most important provision in terms of
revenue, the exclusion of military benefits, is heavily weighted toward
low-income earners, and this has an overpowering effect on the total
distribution in the category. The aggregate distribution would probably
be less weighted toward the lower-income levels if data were available
on the missing provisions, all of which, one would suppose, primarily
benefit upper-income groups. In terms of revenue, however, they do not
account for very much.

The tax equity and specific economic incentive categories also dis-
play this diversity, although in each of these cases some of the large
provisions affect primarily the middle- and upper-middle-income
ranges rather than the rich. This is true for the deduction of taxes (state,
local, and real estate), 48 percent of the benefits going to those with
incomes between $20,000 and $50,000; however, it is not true for the
other sizable provision in the equity category, the exemption of state
and local bond interest, which benefits high-income earners almost
exclusively.[7]

The long and important list of provisions designed to encourage
specific forms of behavior varies as widely in terms of distribution as it
does in terms of the behavior and functions it subsidizes. Once again,
however, the largest of these provisions, currently accounting for over
60 percent of the expenditures in this category, benefits not the very
rich, but the middle- and upper-middle-income, home-owning waged
or salaried employee. The exclusion of employer contributions for pensions and health plans and the deduction for mortgage interest together
account for over 25 percent of all tax expenditures, of which 60 percent
falls within the $15,000 to $30,000 range, and only 14 percent within
the over-$50,000 range.

Disaggregating the overall distribution of tax expenditures creates

a somewhat different impression than the analysis of aggregate coefficients. Although it becomes clear where those with higher incomes gain their relative advantage, one is struck by the diversity of income tax benefits. The poor, elderly, and disadvantaged benefit from a range of income exclusion provisions tailored to their specific condition; the rich benefit from provisions designed to provide general capital incentives for the economy; and middle-class people benefit from deductions for taxes and interest and the exclusion of rapidly expanding employer contributions to benefit plans. Thus, in a very tangible way everyone gets something, a fact that may be more important to politicians than the complicated arguments about relative equity that are the stock-in-trade of the academic.

Summary and Implications

The simple question of who gets what from tax expenditures unfortunately does not have a simple answer. Indeed, there is evidence to support all types of positions, including some that are diametrically opposed, which in itself is a fact important to one's understanding of tax politics. It was shown that if one assumes that the appropriate norm is an equal division of benefits, aggregate tax expenditures are heavily weighted toward high-income taxpayers. However, it was argued that since tax expenditures are not wholly, and perhaps not even significantly, designed to affect income redistribution, other standards of comparison may be more appropriate. The distribution of pretax income and taxes paid are two such standards. It was shown that the overall distribution of tax expenditures is much closer to the distribution of adjusted gross income than to the distribution of returns, and very close to being proportional to the amount of taxes people actually pay.

Shifting the focus from aggregate coefficients that measure the distribution across the total income range to shares for different income levels produces somewhat different conclusions. These tend to vary considerably depending on the standard selected. By any standard the very well-off get more than their share, and, conversely, the middle-income groups always get less. However, there is a significant range in these effects depending on the standard used. For the poor, the range is especially dramatic: if the standard is based on returns, they do very badly, but if the standard is taxes paid, they get, in a sense, more than they deserve. Finally, the purposes behind different tax expenditures are reflected in clearly distinct distributional patterns. The most impor-

tant result of this analysis was to reinforce the widely accepted proposition that creating general economic incentives to save and invest requires conferring substantial tax benefits on the wealthy.

Several implications can be drawn from the distributional patterns of tax expenditures. First, they suggest that the popular impression that the tax system is a welfare program for the rich is based on a great oversimplification. The rich disproportionately benefit because they pay a disproportionate share of taxes and because they control capital, which the government attempts to induce them to invest. Second, and perhaps more important politically, the immense tax expenditure system benefits very large blocs in society, usually in a selective manner. This broad conference of benefits, which is perfectly consistent with electoral incentives for legislators, makes tax reform or even pruning the tax expenditure system an enormously difficult task.[8] Although it is conceivable that congressional majorities could be generated to eliminate some provisions benefiting selective minorities, such actions set precedents and invite political retaliation. Thus, the breadth of the tax expenditure system enhances its self-defense. Indeed, if tax expenditures were the exclusive privilege of the wealthy, containing the system would be much easier. The prospect of large deficits may produce some trimming, but the historical pattern has been one of relentless growth in tax expenditures regardless of deficits. On the basis of the distributional effects described in this chapter, it is difficult to predict that the future holds anything different.

Chapter 15.
Legislating Tax
Expenditures

Discussions of the tax expenditure "problem" often assume that the creation and expansion of tax expenditures result from defects in the legislative process. The common belief is that they are quietly and surreptitiously slipped into tax bills at the urging of well-paid lobbyists representing narrow and wealthy interest groups. Once created they are rarely reviewed and even more rarely terminated; if they are modified, there is a high probability that the change will result in expanded benefits and thus greater revenue loss. Most of these suspected actions take place without adequate legislative overview, broad congressional participation, or recorded votes to allocate responsibility.[1] It is the purpose of this chapter to sort out these claims by analyzing the origin and modifications of the tax expenditures listed in table 13.1.[2] The basic questions are the following ones. How often are tax expenditures created or modified? Is there a consistent pattern to the direction of these changes (i.e., to what extent is there a bias toward expansion of benefits)? Which political parties are responsible for what types of change, and where in the political process do they occur? And how adequate and open is the decision-making and oversight process?

The Creation and Modification
of Tax Expenditures

The growth in tax expenditures was discussed at length in chapter 13. It was pointed out that although the revenue loss from tax expenditures has grown considerably in recent years, enactment of provisions has been a relatively steady process. It was further argued that although a number of tax provisions that today would be labeled tax expenditures have been eliminated from the code over the years, the cumulative effect has been a steady growth in the number and revenue loss because of tax reduction devices. The frequency of changes in tax ex-

penditures was not discussed. As indicated above, however, the popular belief is that tax expenditures are rarely modified, and if they are, it is primarily to increase benefits or expand their coverage.

A systematic analysis of changes in the set of tax expenditures selected for this study indicates that both of these presumptions are overstated. There are a number of tax expenditures that have never been modified, except for administrative or technical changes. These unmodified provisions are listed in table 15.1. Of the 88 provisions in the study, 20 have never been changed once enacted. As the dates indicate, many have existed for some time. Note, however, that most of the provisions that remain unchanged are exclusions of income, which are less likely to be modified incrementally.[3] More interesting perhaps are the types of unmodified provisions. The majority fall into the need-based and special interest categories as I defined them in chapter 13. As shown in the last chapter, and easily verified by scanning the list of beneficiaries in the table, most of these "untouchable" provisions primarily benefit those at the lower end of the income distribution. The few exceptions are minor provisions (in terms of revenue loss) such as capital gains on timber income and coal and iron royalties. The only large provision is the deduction of mortgage interest, which benefits primarily middle-income taxpayers.

In stark contrast to these, some tax expenditures are modified very frequently, with proposals for change raised in almost every session of Congress. Contrary to the standard image, many of the most controversial and the most beneficial for the rich belong to this class. For example, capital gains, which provides more benefit to the very wealthy than any other single provision, has been modified a total of 36 times since its enactment in 1921.[4] Of these changes, 20 represent increases or expanded coverage of the basic provision. Similarly, oil, gas, and mineral tax expenditures, which allow expensing of exploration and development costs and percentage depletion, have been modified 26 times since they were enacted in 1913 and 1917. Again the changes reflect a balance of increases and decreases, with 12 representing increased benefits, 12 decreases, and 2 neutral changes. The provision with the most modifications in proportion to the number of years it has existed is the investment credit tax, which has been repealed twice, has been reenacted or increased 14 times, and has undergone 2 neutral changes since its creation in 1962. Many modification proposals may be introduced, and a provision may be studied in the legislative process many times, before an actual change is made, so that it is difficult in these cases to argue that provisions are somehow lost in the policy-making process. Rather, the pressure to modify at least controversial provisions

Table 15.1 Never-Modified Tax Expenditures, 1909–1978

Category	Provision	Date of Origin
I. Need-based provisions	Exclusion of Social Security disability	1941
	Exclusion of military disability	1942
	Exclusion of veterans' disability	1917
	Exclusion of coal miners' disability	1972
	Exclusion of workmen's compensation	1918
	Exclusion of Social Security survivors' benefits	1941
	Exclusion of public assistance	1913
	Exclusion of railroad retirement benefits	1935
II. Tax equity provisions	Deduction of real estate taxes	1913
III. Special group benefits	Exemption of credit union income	1909
	Exclusion of GI Bill benefits	1917
	Exclusion of veterans' pensions	1917
	Capital gains for timber income	1917
	Capital gains on coal royalties	1951
	Capital gains on iron ore royalties	1964
IV. General economic incentives	Excess first-year depreciation	1958
V. Specific economic incentives	Deduction of mortgage interest	1913
	Exclusion of interest on life insurance	1913
	Exclusion of employer educational assistance	1978

seems to be more or less constant on at least some controversial provisions.

A broader picture of the frequency of change in tax provisions is provided in tables 15.2 and 15.3. Table 15.2 depicts the rate and direction of changes by time period. (The direction of change will be discussed in more detail below.) As is very clear in the table, the number of major modifications in the provisions is far from trivial, and very clearly it has been increasing in recent years. Indeed, over half of the modifications recorded have occurred in the last eleven years, and the figure would rise if the Tax Reform Act of 1969 was included. Part of the explanation for this is the general increase in tax expenditures, due both to cumulative additions to the tax expenditure list and to the higher-than-normal rate of expansion of tax expenditures in recent years. However, table 15.3, which depicts the change process over the life of provisions, indicates that this is only part of the explanation.

Table 15.3 displays the frequency of changes relative to their dates of origin, with the number of changes grouped by period of enactment. The pattern of changes leads to two conclusions: (1) that changes occur throughout the life of a provision; and (2) that the rate of modification has increased dramatically in recent years for both old and new provisions. The first of these conclusions provides strong evidence *against* the proposition that tax breaks, once enacted, are "forgotten" by the system. On the contrary, the evidence suggests an incessant series of changes. Over half of the changes in tax expenditures were made twenty or more years after the provisions were originally enacted, with approximately one-sixth occurring fifty years after the enactment.

The second conclusion is complicated by the fact that provisions enacted between 1970 and 1981 have been modified much more often per year of existence than older ones. This is indicated in table 15.3 by the row labeled "mean number of modifications per year." This could be a "life cycle" phenomenon in which troublesome aspects of provisions are worked out soon after enactment. However, the large number of amendments to older provisions in recent years suggests that a general increase in the pace of tax legislation is the root explanation. The simple fact is that prior to World War II, very few modifications were made in those tax expenditures that persist in today's code. For the 45 tax expenditures created between 1909 and 1945, only 42 changes were recorded prior to 1946. This contrasts with 133 modifications in the same provisions since the war.[5]

Whether this increasing rate of change in tax laws is viewed as beneficial legislative review and oversight or as harmful political indulgence that leads to confusion and complexity in the code and threatens

Table 15.2 Tax Expenditure Modifications by Time Period

Provision	1909–1919	1920–1945	1946–1969	1970–1981	Total
Expanded coverage	1	6	17	43	67
Increased benefit	2	14	34	57	107
Expanded coverage and increased benefit	0	2	5	5	12
Subtotal	3	22	56	105	186
Neutral change	0	2	5	16	23
Restricted coverage	1	2	22	16	41
Decreased benefit	1	8	27	25	61
Restricted coverage and decreased benefit	0	0	2	1	3
Repealed	0	1	2	1	4
Subtotal	2	11	53	43	109
Total modifications	5	35	114	164	318

Table 15.3 Frequency of Changes Based on the Age of the Provision

	Year Provision Originated				
Age of Provision	1909–1919	1920–1945	1946–1969	1970–1981	Total
1–5	8	3	7	21	39
5–10	1	3	26	11	41
11–20	6	18	41	0	65
21–30	5	16	30	0	51
31–40	19	8	3	0	30
41–50	14	24	0	0	38
+50	36	18	0	0	54
Total modifications	89	90	107	32	318
Mean number of modifications per year[a]	.06	.11	.20	.39	.17
Provisions originating in this period	25	18	24	22	89

[a]This variable is the mean of the number of modifications for each provision divided by the number of years the provision has existed. Provisions are categorized by the year of origin. Thus, for example, the average number of modifications per year for provisions originating between 1909 and 1919 is 0.06.

the revenue-raising capacity of the income tax, the finding is important enough to justify speculation as to its cause. The war, as noted in earlier chapters, was a transition point in the history of the income tax, the point at which the tax was transformed from an elite to a mass tax. With the added political pressure of millions of affected voters, the income tax became increasingly politicized. Inflation-induced bracket creep increased the pressure in the 1970s and 1980s to the point that massive legislative changes became an almost yearly event. During this same period, earlier social programs were being seriously questioned and there were repeated attacks (from both parties) on government bureaucracies. A natural course, and the course of least resistance, was to try to use the tax code to accomplish some of the same ends as the social programs as well as new ends in fields such as energy. One important area of new demands was created by a steadily declining national economy. Since direct government subsidy and intervention in industrial decisions has never been easily achieved in the United States, the tax code provided a convenient vehicle for government action. Another plausible factor, suggested earlier as an explanation for the 1981 tax bill, was that the legislative process was now considerably more open, giving many more actors access to the tax laws. Finally, the structure of the tax code that has developed will, through inertia, generate considerably more changes. As the code becomes more complex, in terms of both the number of tax expenditures and the complicated structures of each provision, the potential targets for change increase enormously.

The Direction of Change

A second common belief, as noted at the beginning of this chapter, is that tax expenditures, once enacted, are destined to expand. Systematic analysis of this assumption indicates that there is some truth to the proposition, but that for most of the history of the income tax it is overstated. Table 15.2, in addition to indicating the frequency of changes, details the direction of changes for various time periods. The top three rows of the table represent changes that led to greater revenue loss either through increasing the benefit levels in the provision or by expanding the number of those eligible for an exclusion, deduction, credit, and so on. The last four rows cover changes that raise revenue. Subtotals are given for the respective categories. A comparison of the totals indicates that there is indeed a greater tendency to enact amendments that increase benefits (reducing revenues), but the ratio of

increases to decreases is not as overwhelming as one might expect. The majority of increases and decreases alike represent changes in the value of the provisions rather than alterations of the affected populations. Since adequate estimates of the associated revenue gain or loss are not available for most of the changes, it is impossible to estimate the relative revenue effects of various actions. However, the overall growth in tax expenditures relative to various standards was discussed in detail in chapter 13.

Perhaps more important is the time trend displayed in the table. As discussed above, few changes of any kind occurred before the war. In the period from 1946 to 1969, revenue-losing changes approximately equalled gains. This balance disintegrated in the revenue bills of the seventies and eighties as tax expenditures were increased and broadened much more frequently than earlier. This phenomenon was considered at length in the historical chapters, where it was argued that the combined effects of inflation, tax rebellion, and an opening up of the legislative process were jointly responsible. Thus, in recent years the tax expenditure budget has grown in terms of revenue loss due to new provisions, legislative increases in existing tax expenditures, and inflation-induced increases in the value of provisions.

Both the frequency and the direction of change in tax expenditures vary depending on the type of expenditure. Table 15.4 breaks down the modifications by tax expenditure category. The frequency of change is much higher for tax expenditures designed as economic incentives (categories IV and V). Whether they are general stimulus provisions, such as the investment credit and capital gains, or narrow incentives, such as those designed to stimulate housing or energy conservation, the number of modifications per year is significantly higher than for other types of provisions. Examples discussed above have involved capital gains, oil, gas, and mineral provisions, and the investment credit. Whatever expansion has occurred in economic provisions, and whatever advantages have been gained, they are the result of persistent changes over a number of years.

The ratios of increases to decreases also vary in an interesting fashion depending on the type of tax expenditure. The three smallest groups— tax equity, need-based, and miscellaneous provisions—have actually been decreased more than increased. Changes in category II provisions, which are based on tax fairness arguments and which in the aggregate disproportionately benefit the well-off (see chapter 14), would almost all be decreases if not for the child care credit provision. The eleven increases in benefits are all attributable to this provision, which has had bipartisan support since its introduction by the Eisenhower administra-

Table 15.4 Tax Expenditure Modifications by Category of Provisions

	I Need-Based	II Tax Equity	III Special Group	IV General Economic Stimulus	V Specific Economic Incentives	VI Miscellaneous
Provision increases or expansions	39	11	7	48	69	6
Neutral changes	5	1	1	3	11	1
Provision decreases or restrictions[a]	12	12	10	27	37	9
Total modifications	56	24	18	78	117	16
Mean number of modifications per year[b]	.12	.09	.04	.26	.25	.19

[a]Includes provision repeals.
[b]See table 15.3, n. a, for an explanation of this variable.

tion in 1954. Increases in benefits outnumber decreases in categories IV and V by ratios of 1.76 and 1.86 respectively. On the other hand, while the number of modifications for need-based provisions is less, more than three out of every four changes in these provisions lead to greater revenue loss.

This pattern is further displayed in table 15.5, which breaks down changes based on the coefficient of distribution for the sixty-seven provisions for which such data are available. The results clearly indicate that those provisions which benefit lower-income groups are modified much less frequently. On the other hand, the striking finding is the balance between increases and decreases of benefits in those provisions most beneficial to the rich. Provisions that fall in the middle are altered more frequently and are increased or expanded at the greatest rate.

These results suggest a series of generalizations that run counter to much of the accepted tax lore. First, those provisions which most aid the needy are by far the least likely to be changed once enacted. Provisions that affect the well-off, reflecting the political controversy that surrounds them, are changed much more often, but rise and fall as the political winds shift. Finally, as further evidence of the sensitivity of tax politics to the needs of middle-income taxpayers, those provisions which fall in the middle quartiles are not only frequently changed, but

Table 15.5 Tax Expenditure Modifications by Distribution of Benefits

	Low-Income Quartile	Middle-Income Quartile	High-Income Quartile
Provision increases or expansions	14	121	32
Neutral changes	3	8	9
Provision decreases or restrictions	8	60	29
Total modifications	25	189	70
Mean number of modifications per year[a]	.10	.17	.13
Number of provisions in category	(16)	(34)	(17)

Provisions for which distributional data were available were rank-ordered based on the D_i coefficient described in chapter 14. Column categories represent the first, the second and third, and the fourth quartiles of this set of provisions
[a]See table 15.3, n. *a*, for an explanation of this variable.

the changes are much more likely to be increases in benefits or expansion in the groups eligible for tax reductions. In retrospect, these results are very plausible politically. The provisions that affect the lower-income groups are primarily income exclusion provisions, which are not easy to alter marginally. Provisions skewed in favor of the very rich are the ones that conservatives and moderates tend to define as essential to economic stimulus, but liberal tax reformers attack as "loopholes." As power shifts, so does the treatment of these controversial provisions. Those provisions in the middle are often complicated deductions or credits and thus susceptible to change, yet they affect broad enough income groups that labeling them "loopholes" is politically dangerous. Thus, these provisions are easily altered, and the political incentives are weighted in favor of expansion of benefits.

Responsibility for Tax Expenditures

The responsibility for originating and modifying tax expenditures can be understood in the context of either institutions or political parties. The goals of the analysis that follows are to locate the origin of tax amendments in the political process and then to determine the party affiliation of the initiating agents. The former is easier than the latter. By carefully culling administration or Treasury proposals, committee reports, and floor legislation as it develops, one can readily establish the institutional origin of most proposals.

Determining the party of origin and the party responsible for provision changes is a more difficult empirical problem. Because, at least in the past, many committee meetings were closed and accurate records of both proceedings and votes are not available, inferences sometimes have to be based on majority control of committees. Thus, for example, if the initiative on a proposal cannot be traced to a specific individual or party position, it is assumed that the party controlling the committee is responsible. Floor actions and administration proposals do not require such inferences, although in both cases the actions represent only individual preferences, which may not coincide with the wishes of the party majority. These difficulties suggest caution in interpreting party actions and indicate a fundamental problem in analyzing partisan behavior on tax issues. We will return to the latter problem in the following chapter.

Institutional Roles. The institutional origins and subsequent modifications of tax expenditures are displayed in table 15.6. The most obvious

Table 15.6 The Source of Tax Expenditures and Provision Modifications

	Admin-istra-tion	House Ways and Means	House Floor	Senate Finance	Senate Floor	Confer-ence Com-mittee	Other
Origin of expenditures	18	31	2	11	5	1	19
Modifications							
Increases or expansions	35	73	2	51	21	2	0
Neutral changes	4	10	0	4	4	0	0
Decreases or restrictions (including repeals)	30	55	1	12	5	5	1
Total modifications	69	138	3	67	30	7	1
Total of Origin and Modifications	87	169	5	78	35	8	20

conclusion that emerges is that tax politics are generally congressional politics. Only 18 tax expenditures could be attributed directly to administration initiatives, while 19 came either from nonrevenue legislation or from IRS rulings (13 of the 19 in the "other" category originated with the IRS). Within Congress, 31 originated in the Ways and Means Committee, 2 on the House floor, 11 in the Finance Committee, 5 on the Senate floor, and 1 in conference. These figures may slightly overstate the role of Congress in that the administration may work informally with congressional tax experts to generate proposals, and some administration proposals may have been missed in the coding.[6] However, as Roy Blough and other observers have concluded, just as tax politics in general centers on Congress, so does the tax expenditure "problem."[7]

The congressional role in modifying tax expenditures is even stronger. Of the total modifications recorded in this study, 78 percent began in the legislative branch. Of this percentage, 42 percent began in the Ways and Means Committee, 21 percent in Senate Finance, and 9 percent on the Senate floor. Aggregate figures obscure both time trends and differences in the direction of proposed changes. Dominance by the Ways and Means Committee was greatest in the prewar period. Its declining influence, which accompanied the upsurge of postwar changes in tax laws, was due to the increased tax activity of the executive branch and the Senate. For example, administration proposals accounted for only 5 percent of the changes in the tax code through 1945, but 24 percent since that time. This is consistent with the general transition from a close adherence to the constitutional requirement that tax legislation begin in Congress to a more assertive role by the executive branch. The tax activism of the Senate is a much more recent phenomenon. For 1970 to 1981, fully 37 percent of tax expenditure modifications originated either in Finance or on the Senate floor. This trend was accentuated by the tax legislation of the 1980s, in which the Senate took command of the tax agenda and actually reported legislation before Ways and Means did.[8]

What may be of more importance than the trend toward equal influence in tax policy are the types of changes promoted by the different institutional actors. These differences, also portrayed in table 15.6, indicate that administration modifications are the most balanced in terms of revenue losses and gains. The ratio of revenue losses to gains is only 1.17 for the administration, whereas it is 1.34 for the House and an astronomical 4.24 for the Senate. Of the 97 changes attributed to the Senate, 72 provided tax benefits and only 17 tax increases. Furthermore, floor changes are just about as likely to produce additional revenue losses as those that begin in the Finance Committee.[9] These

systematic data are consistent with the popular notion that the Senate is the locus of influence for well-financed lobbyists promoting a range of "loopholes." More troublesome is the inference that the "openness" of the Senate process, which has operated through the entire postwar period without a closed rule, may create opportunities and irresistible pressure to reduce taxes through tax expenditure provisions. The implication is that congressional policy makers, in their eagerness to respond to constituent desires, lack the restraint needed in tax legislation.

Party Responsibility. Analysis of party responsibility for both initiating and modifying tax expenditures confirms the general conclusion developed in chapter 12 that there are more similarities than differences in party behavior. It is often stated that the tax system provides welfare for the rich. Since the Republican Party is considered the shepherd of the well-off, the assumption follows that Republicans are more likely to be associated with tax expenditures than Democrats. However, a systematic appraisal of changes leads to a different conclusion. If one looks specifically at tax expenditures, the most reasonable conclusion is that both parties share responsibility for the expansion of the tax expenditure system.

Table 15.7 provides aggregate frequencies on policy actions broken down by party responsibility. Democrats bear the most responsibility for the creation of tax expenditures. However, the Republican share (27 percent) is comparable to the percentage of years since 1913 in which they controlled the White House (37 percent) or Congress (23 percent).[10] Thus, the initiation of tax expenditures is approximately proportionate to the opportunity to do so, and it is therefore difficult to argue that either party tends to promote tax expenditures more than the other.

The record of modifications also indicates more similarity than differences between parties. As shown in table 15.7, 78 percent of the changes in tax expenditures can be attributed to Democrats. This again is close to the proportion of time Democrats controlled the policy-making process.[11] The Republicans are more likely to advance tax reduction changes than Democrats, with a ratio of revenue losses to gains of 2.86 (compared with the Democrats' 1.57). However, the number of modifications attributed to Republicans is relatively small, and thus it is not clear how much should be made of these differences.

When party responsibility for different categories of tax expenditures is analyzed, the results are even more surprising. If we consider the origin of tax expenditures, party differences significantly deviated from

Table 15.7 Party Responsibility for Tax Expenditures and Provision Modifications

	(1) Demo- cratic	(2) Repub- lican	(3) Bipar- tisan	(4) None	(5) Un- clear
Origin of expenditures	45	24	1	16	1
Modifications					
Provision increases or expansions	140	40	3	0	1
Neutral changes	14	8	0	0	0
Provision decreases or restrictions (including repeals)	89	14	0	1	1
Total modifications	243	62	3	1	2
Total of Origin and Modifications	288	86	4	17	3

the aggregate percentages only for general economic incentives (category IV). In that case Republicans accounted for five of the eight provisions for which party responsibility could be assigned. Although this difference is consistent with the image of the Republicans as the party of business and wealth, the Democrats did their share for the rich as well. In the other category of expenditures that most benefited the well-off, tax equity provisions, Democrats were responsible for five out of six provisions.

The types of provisions favored by parties are even more mixed when modifications are broken down by category. Again countering the normal image, fully 40 percent of Republican-sponsored increases in benefits fell in the need category, compared with only 16 percent of Democratic actions. Democrats were more likely to be responsible for the increasing use of the tax system to create specific, or targeted, economic incentives (category IV). Forty-two percent of the Democratic proposals that reduced revenues were of this form, compared to only 25 percent of the Republican changes. This result, which is due primarily to the expansion of these provisions in recent years, is consistent with the Carter administration's ambivalent approach to taxes, attacking

"loopholes" while simultaneously supporting a tax incentive approach to public policy (see pp. 214–15 above). It is also consistent with Democratic congressional support for numerous expansions of such provisions in 1978 and 1981.

Overshadowing these refined breakdowns in party differences is the more general conclusion that both parties are prone to expansion of the tax expenditure budget and to increasingly frequent modifications of the tax code. Although both parties attempt to align themselves rhetorically with "tax reform," neither seems to be able to resist the temptation to shovel tax benefits to wide-ranging sets of constituents. It is this penchant for the expansion of the tax expenditure system, exercised over a long policy history, that has produced such uncertainty and complexity and has threatened the revenue capacity of the system.

The Adequacy of Deliberation

The preceding section confirmed that most tax policy decisions originated in the revenue committees, primarily Ways and Means. The historical chapters confirmed that for most of the history of the income tax, this committee-centered process was relatively closed. Both tax committees normally operated in closed executive session, particularly during the final markup of legislation. Detailed records of proceedings and committee votes were not kept. And final legislation was either brought to the floor under a tight closed rule or committee options tended to prevail on floor votes or, later, in Conference Committee negotiations.

These practices bolster the negative image of tax politics as a closed process controlled by a narrow set of tax experts who reach decisions without appropriate political deliberation. Because of the sheer volume of policy decisions over time, and because important information on committee procedures is not available, a rigorous scientific, or even systematic, analysis of this general image is impossible. However, the historical record of floor votes and detailed studies of revenue committee activities suggest that this closed system has been substantially eroded in recent years. There is also evidence that at least on the more controversial tax issues, decisions are rarely made quietly behind closed doors. Finally, there is at least an argument to be made that a more closed system might actually lead to more adequate political deliberation and more acceptable policy outcomes.

Floor Voting on Tax Expenditures. Table 15.8 provides statistics on the frequency over time of floor votes to originate or modify tax expendi-

Table 15.8 Congressional Voting on Tax Expenditures by Historical Period

	1909–1919	1920–1945	1946–1969	1970–1981	Total
Origins					
Total originated	25	16	26	21	88
Some vote taken	5	5	8	13	31
Total voice votes[a]	5	5	7	12	29
Total roll calls[a]	0	0	7	13	20
% bipartisan roll calls	—	—	71%	69%	70%
Modifications					
Total modifications	5	35	114	164	318
Some vote taken	2	15	44	93	154
Total voice votes[a]	2	23	22	24	71
Total roll calls[a]	0	6	32	83	121
% bipartisan roll calls	—	NA	53%	70%	63%

[a]Includes votes in both the House and the Senate; therefore the totals exceed those in the row labeled "Some vote taken."

tures. Although the table combines House and Senate votes, because of the closed rule, the majority occurred in the Senate.[12] "Some vote taken" indicates that at least one vote was taken on an amendment that ultimately passed. The combined totals for voice and roll call votes exceed this figure because of multiple votes on some amendments. Votes on unsuccessful proposals are not included. If they were, the numbers would far exceed those presented. For example, the Senate debate on the 1976 Tax Reform Act included 209 separate votes, of which 129 were roll calls but less than a dozen were tied to changes ultimately enacted. Thus, the table indicates only the tip, although the critical tip, of a much more extensive deliberative process.

The table reveals several interesting patterns. First, to the extent that voting matters, floor deliberation on the origination of tax expenditures is unspectacular. Of the 88 separate provisions included in the sample

used, only 31 were voted on as separate measures. Of the total votes taken, only 20 were roll calls. Although part of the reason for this is that a number of tax expenditures were enacted as part of the original 1913 income tax legislation, which was passed as an amendment to a larger tariff bill, the percentage of separate votes is still relatively small. The percentage is somewhat higher for modifications but is still less than 50 percent.

However, the totals obscure an important and very strong trend over time. Floor voting has significantly increased in the last decade.[13] The increase occurs in both the origin and modification categories. For tax expenditures that originated before 1970, 73 percent were enacted without any floor vote. Since 1969 only 38 percent escaped floor votes. Of the total votes taken, 52 percent occurred in the twelve years between 1970 and 1982. Of the 20 roll calls, 13 were recorded for this period. Sixty-three percent of the modifications enacted between 1909 and 1969 were passed without floor votes, compared with 43 percent since that time. Similarly, of the total votes taken, 63 percent occurred in the most recent period, and of these, 89 percent were roll calls. The irony of this increased "openness" in tax politics, lauded by both Democratic congressional reformers and liberal tax reformers, is that the increase in voting runs parallel to the recent expansion in the tax expenditure system.

One could still argue that even the increased frequency of voting on specific tax provisions is inadequate relative to the scrutiny given other government policies and programs. It is this supposition that seems to be behind many anti–tax expenditure positions.[14] These arguments, almost always stated in general terms, are based on the assumption that policy and program innovations and changes in direct subsidy programs are carefully considered by Congress as a whole. There is reason to question such an assumption, however. For example, what we have learned in the last two decades of research on the budget is that such detailed decisions are almost always the work of committees; that line-item rather than program categories persist; and that to save time and avoid political conflict, the basic incremental "formula" is to begin with last year's outlays and marginally adjust those figures.[15] New programs may be debated in more detail, but often new program legislation only provides general policy outlines, assigning more detailed authority to a specific agency, which then constructs programs that become subject to the normal budgetary review. Although some argue that the recent "decremental" process of budget cuts may be changing this scenario, the lesson as of this writing is that the changes have led to more centralized decisions in OMB or the White House rather than more activity in the Congress.[16]

Thus, when compared to direct budgetary decisions, the rate of voting on tax expenditure issues might be considered extraordinary. To the extent that voting is a suitable indicator of adequate deliberation, tax policy, in recent years at least, may pass the test better than direct subsidy programs.

Breaking down voting patterns according to the direction of changes and the category of tax expenditure reveals other interesting conclusions. As one might anticipate, provision changes that decrease or restrict tax expenditures produce more floor votes and more partisan conflict than those that increase benefits or expand coverage. Of all the modifications that increase benefits (produce revenue losses), only 42 percent were subjected to floor votes. Further, 55 percent of the votes on increases were roll call votes, compared with 83 percent for votes on decreases. Roll calls taken to reduce tax benefits are also more likely to produce partisan splits. As shown in table 15.8, the majority of roll calls on tax expenditures are bipartisan. The pattern has been particularly evident in recent years. Seventy-one percent of votes on modifications increasing tax benefits were bipartisan, whereas 56 percent of votes decreasing them were.

The implication is that "reform" efforts that attempt to tighten tax expenditures are more likely to attract political attention and meet political opposition than efforts to broaden or increase benefits. Thus, if there is a weakness or laxity in the deliberative process, it is on the side of expanding tax benefits. This is consistent with the historical bias toward tax reduction and the accelerating expansion of the tax expenditure system.

The differences in voting rates by type of tax expenditures are also interesting. Consistent with a wide range of other evidence, they indicate that the tax expenditures most carefully scrutinized are those that provide general or specific economic incentives—that is, those usually considered the most controversial by tax reformers. Tax expenditures intended to produce general economic incentives (category IV) were created with floor votes in six cases out of nine. Of the 32 expenditures designed to produce more narrow economic incentives, 14 received floor votes of some kind. Less than 25 percent of provisions in other categories were enacted following floor votes. The voting pattern is more evenly split on modifications, the most significant difference being that need-based provisions (category I) are by far the least likely to lead to a floor vote (only 28 percent do so), whereas changes in general incentives were subject to votes in 62 percent of the cases. This pattern is consistent with data presented above on the frequency and direction of changes.

Thus, need-based tax provisions are the *least* likely to be changed,

the least likely to be decreased or restricted, and the least likely to lead to floor votes. The reverse is true for provisions creating general or specific economic incentives. It is reasonable to assume that a broad consensus exists on need-based provisions, most of which provide a nontaxable income floor for the poor. Congressional scrutiny is more intense for the more divisive provisions, which also tend to disproportionately aid the well-off. This implies that the system is most attentive where it should be and that it is unlikely that the resulting changes in tax expenditures are the quiet work of small groups of congressmen. It is more reasonable to conclude that Congress knows precisely what it is doing when it legislates tax expenditures.

To summarize: although historically floor votes on specific tax provisions are the exception rather than the rule, voting is increasing, and the more controversial provisions of the code are more likely to lead to votes than those related to need and tax equity. The finding that increased voting coincides with the recent increase in the use of tax expenditures and the fact that many roll call votes are bipartisan suggest that forcing public votes may not be a deterrent to the expansion of tax expenditures, as is often implied in the literature. The argument usually refers to the need to open up the system so that blame for tax expenditures can be properly allocated. A more accurate interpretation may be that politicians view tax expenditures as rewards to confer and that they are eager and willing to associate themselves with the conference of such benefits. Thus, opening up the system and encouraging roll call votes serve to expand, not restrict, the tax expenditure system.

Committee Deliberations. Evaluating the thoroughness, balance, and effectiveness of congressional committee deliberations is a difficult task. The public side of committee actions, whether open meetings or public hearings, has been long viewed suspiciously as "Congress on exhibition."[17] Although the possibility of committee orchestration requires a note of caution, an analysis of hearings does provide some indication of the attention span of Congress on particular issues and some evidence as to whose position is being heard most often. Common Cause, in a report questioning the adequacy of congressional oversight of tax expenditures, studied hearings before the Ways and Means and Finance committees for the period from 1971 to 1976. It reported that in that period 193 days of hearings were held before these committees, and 31 additional days before subcommittees.[18] Although this averages over 30 days a year, Common Cause judged this rate of public exposure inadequate. More interestingly, perhaps, it reported the number of witnesses from various organizations who testified on particular tax

expenditure issues. The results of that analysis, reclassified according to my taxonomy of tax expenditures, appear in table 15.9.

Two results of the analysis are consistent with previous arguments in this chapter. First, if there is a category of tax expenditures to which Congress is inattentive, it is the need-based category. Of the twenty-two need-based tax expenditures included in the Common Cause study, there was no public testimony during this six-year period on thirteen. In six years sixty-six witnesses appeared before either committee in reference to these provisions. Not surprisingly, thirty-three of these witnesses were from citizens' groups.

The second conclusion, which also confirms earlier evidence, is that the preponderance of testimony is directed at tax expenditures intended to provide either general or specific economic incentives. Eighty-six percent of all witnesses testified on aspects of these provisions. Part of the explanation for this is that during this period major changes were made in the ADR, the investment credit, and capital gains. These three important provisions alone accounted for 657 witnesses. Similarly, 127 witnesses appeared to comment on the DISC provisions. This attention, which for each provision was followed by vigorous floor debates and extensive voting on particular amendments, is further evidence that changes in important and controversial tax expenditures are not infrequent, private, or accidental.

The other striking aspect of the data presented in table 15.9 is the number of witnesses representing either businesses or trade associations. Fifty-nine percent of all witnesses fall into this category, and most of them appeared on behalf of the economic provisions. Any other result would be surprising because of the direct effects of most of these provisions on various industries. It is reasonable to assume that most of these witnesses supported increasing tax benefits and fought reductions. It should be noted, however, that during the period covered in the Common Cause study, tax expenditures in these categories were expanded considerably and the business community was reasserting itself in Washington. Clearly tax policy was one of its areas of concentration.

Although the Common Cause study did not analyze the content of testimony, a previous study of tax hearings before the Ways and Means Committee did. John Manley's analysis of hearings leading up to the Tax Reform Act of 1964 classified testimony as either pro or con on proposals to raise or lower revenues. What he found was an overwhelming bias in the direction one might expect: for revenue reduction and against revenue increases. In the hearings on proposed changes in capital gains, proposals that would have reduced revenues by liberalizing the provisions were supported by 34 witnesses and opposed by 12;

Table 15.9 Witnesses before the Ways and Means and Finance Committees, 1971–1976

Tax Expenditure Category	(1) Number in Category	(2) No Witnesses	Witnesses Representing					(8) Total Witnesses
			(3) Government[a]	(4) Trade Assoc. or Business	(5) Labor	(6) Experts	(7) Citizens' Groups	
I. Need-based	22	13	9	3	5	16	33	66
II. Tax equity	6	1	25	18	7	17	10	77
III. Special group	12	1	6	41	1	11	3	62
IV. General economic stimulus	9	0	87	471	22	149	40	769
V. Specific economic incentives	25	6	70	440	20	114	39	683
VI. Miscellaneous	3	1	0	12	2	1	0	15
Not classified[b]	3	0	4	5	1	8	0	18
Total	81	22	201	990	58	316	125	1690

Source: Gimme Shelters: A Common Cause Study of the Review of Tax Expenditures by the Congressional Tax Committees (Washington, D.C.: Common Cause, 1978), charts 4a and 4b.

[a] Includes Treasury officials, state and local officials, members of Congress, and other officials.

[b] Three of the tax expenditures included in the Common Cause study are not included in my tax expenditure set. Ten provisions in my study were not in the Common Cause study.

proposals to raise capital gains were opposed by 393 witnesses and supported by only 15. For other revenue-increasing provisions, favorable witnesses were outnumbered by those opposed by a count of 48 to 256.[19] As outlined in chapter 8, Ways and Means responded in this instance by generally reducing the administration's reform proposals. If Manley's conclusions are indicative of a larger trend—and the preponderance of business witnesses in table 15.9 would suggest such a pattern—hearing testimony seems to correspond to the general historical bias toward tax reduction and the expansion of tax expenditures. To the extent that hearings are an adequate test, public deliberation, like public voting, seems to push the system toward greater revenue loss and expansion of the tax expenditure system.

The adequacy of internal committee deliberations defies systematic analysis. There is undoubtedly significant variation between committees and historical periods. The pressure of time, particularly during wars, greatly influences the deliberative process. Similarly, the pace of legislation in general has an influence on staff analysis, committee study, and public input. When the legislative process is rushed, as it was in 1981, provisions are inadequately evaluated.

However, the one major study of the Ways and Means Committee available paints a convincing portrait, at least for the period covered (1933–1966), of a thorough process geared to produce consensus legislation. Manley's classic study argues that the prestige of the committee created an atmosphere of bipartisan professionalism. As others have consistently done, he lauds the expertise and devotion of the staffs of this committee and the Joint Committee on Internal Revenue Taxation. He also emphasizes the importance of committee leadership in the persons of John Byrnes and particularly Wilbur Mills. Manley depicts a free-flowing series of interactions between Treasury, the committee, members of Congress, and lobbyists. The result, according to Manley, was usually a balanced legislative package that invariably produced consensus on the floor of the House.[20]

There are indications that the Finance Committee may be somewhat less deliberate and somewhat more biased toward tax reduction than Ways and Means (see pp. 323–24 above). But Finance has a secondary influence on tax policy, is more often overridden on the floor, and prevails much less often in Conference. Further, in other legislative areas, the Senate has historically served to expand debate and deliberation. The loose and (some would argue) irresponsible nature of Senate deliberation is offset by its contribution in opening up the legislative process. Thus, in some respects the committees have traditionally balanced each other's weaknesses.

In recent years several cracks have appeared in this relatively positive image of committee actions on tax politics. First, with the fall of Wilbur Mills and the weakening of the committee chairmen, a clear source of order and constraint was lost. As a result of the greater influence of the administration and the Senate, the number of relevant actors has increased. This has had the effect of opening up the process and allowing interested groups greater access to the tax agenda. At the same time, tax politics has received more public exposure, and many more provisions have been reaching floor votes.

The standard theoretical response to these trends, by both pluralists and their critics, would be positive. Participation is increasing, the agenda is less rigidly controlled, more actors have more potential access to the policy-making process, and accountability is enhanced by increased voting on specific issues. What is missing in this evaluation of the process is a consideration of results. The assumption is that opening up the system and expanding the democratic process will produce policy results more representative of the desires of the populace, more beneficial to the public interest, or both. The following chapters assess these claims.

Summary

This chapter challenges several aspects of the view that legislative oversight of tax expenditures is inadequate, biased, and relatively closed. It was shown that few tax expenditures go unmodified and that those that do are primarily need-based provisions that exclude income. Similarly, the changes are frequent and have been increasing dramatically in recent years. Although there has always been a tendency for changes that increase tax expenditure benefits to outweigh those that tighten up on revenue losses, it is only in recent years that this bias has become extravagant. Institutionally there has been a parallel shift. Whereas early tax expenditure amendments largely originated in the Ways and Means Committee, in the postwar period and particularly the last decade, more actions originated in the executive branch or the Senate. Party responsibility for tax expenditure amendments appeared to be about evenly split, with similarities outweighing differences. Floor voting patterns sustained this impression, since over 60 percent of the roll call votes passed with bipartisan majorities.

The extent of oversight—reflected in the frequency of change, the balance of changes (the ratio of increases to decreases), the number of votes taken, and the number of witnesses at public hearings—varies

considerably depending on the category of tax expenditures. Need-based tax provisions, which primarily benefit the poor, receive the least attention according to any of these measures. On the other hand, economic provisions, particularly those designed to provide general economic stimulus, are the most frequently modified, the most openly debated, and subject to the most floor votes. Given this conflux of evidence, it seems unlikely that such provisions, which include some of the most important and controversial sections of the code, are enacted or modified without full congressional knowledge of the intent and effects of the legislation.

Section V.
Evaluating
Income Tax
Politics

An evaluation of tax politics, or politics in any other field, can follow two general lines. The differences between them parallel the dichotomy between political theory and policy analysis outlined in the Introduction. An evaluation based on the principles of democratic theory will, in turn, choose between two methods. The first option—and, given modern democratic theory, the most prevalent—is to concentrate not on the outcomes of decisions, but rather on the process by which decisions are reached. The criteria most often considered are: (1) the adequacy of elections; (2) the availability of equal and open access by concerned citizens and groups; (3) the existence of public decisions that allow for electoral accountability; and (4) tolerance of opposition. Empirical research analyzing political processes along these lines has been primarily directed at political institutions and not specific policy decisions. A second method, which is presently receiving greater attention than in the past, is to ask the more fundamental question of whether policy results adequately represent the opinions and attitudes of the public.

The questions addressed in sections III and IV were, to some extent, guided by the first of these methods. Although those sections argued that the commonly held image of tax politics as biased and oligarchic is greatly distorted, it is difficult to generalize beyond that point. Different periods offer somewhat different impressions, and since it is impossible to analyze the relevant behavior directly, the conclusions reached relied heavily on inferences based on outcomes. Given the limitations of time, information, and access to key decision points in most policy areas, this is a general problem that only very narrow case studies can, perhaps, hope to escape. Thus, while procedural theories of democracy prolifer-

ate, empirical studies are limited by the illusive and unmeasurable patterns of influence that envelop complex policy arenas. Perhaps the information provided in the previous chapters will be used by others as the starting point for a more systematic evaluation on procedural grounds.

The second method is the subject of the following chapter. As will become immediately apparent, the difficulties of survey research and the range and complexity of tax issues pose barriers to a definitive answer to the question of how well tax policy represents the wishes of the populace. The available evidence, however, suggests that the basic political patterns and trends in tax policy are in some conformance with at least the views of those who have opinions on income tax policy.

The other general approach—the one based on policy analysis—ignores both the policy-making process and the linkage between popular demands and outcomes and concentrates instead on the characteristics of the policies themselves. This approach depends solely on the specification and defense of a set of independent criteria by which to judge policy results. By its very nature this methodology allows for the possibility that democratically achieved outcomes that conform to popular wishes may be judged to be in error. Although such an appraisal may appear brutally arrogant and will certainly raise the ire of idealistic democrats, in the practical world of policy analysis this is the norm. Rarely do those analyzing public policies search for procedural concurrence with abstract democratic norms or ask whether policy results conform to public opinion. They ask rather what results a policy or program produces, whether the results are "good" or "bad" according to some set of criteria (which may or may not be set by democratic procedures), and whether the results are worth the costs.

This latter approach will be the subject of the concluding chapter. The norms for evaluating the tax system will be those specified at the end of chapter 3. I conclude that the end result of this particular incremental policy-making process, stretched out over a number of years, is unsatisfactory and seriously endangers the primary function of tax policy. That conclusion can be challenged on the grounds that the criteria are invalid or that the results are merely a cost of the democratic process. My final assessment, however, is that the costs are too high and that the only solution is to formulate methods and procedures to insulate tax policy from the demands of the democratic system.

Chapter 16.
Tax Policy
and the
Representation
of Interests

The analysis to this point indicates that the development of tax policy has been characterized by several persistent trends. The first of these is towards tax reduction. Except in periods of war, very few income tax bills have deliberately increased taxes. And this trend has accelerated in recent years, influencing both the frequency and the size of the bills passed. A second trend, also increasing in recent years, is expansion of the tax expenditure system. Although reformers and scholars have long warned of the danger to the tax code of variously conceived tax reduction devices, political decisions have consistently expanded both the number and the revenue impact of these provisions. Finally, as a result of this expansion and the practice of cutting tax rates on a proportional basis, the effective rates of the income tax have remained only slightly progressive, and there is little evidence of a firm, lasting commitment to redistributive taxation. What progression has been built into the tax system has been the result of wartime tax increases, primarily those passed during World War II.

The task of this chapter is to determine whether these three trends are supported by public opinion. A final section will analyze the public's perception of the general fairness of the income tax. The data come from numerous survey sources covering a number of years. However, although some conclusions seem very strong and consistent over time, the reader should be cognizant of several problems in interpreting survey results. First, at times the number of people failing to respond to some questions is small, presumably indicating a lack of knowledge or understanding of the issues. Second, the wording of survey questions is extremely important, and slight changes in language sometimes produce dramatic changes in results. Added uncertainty and ambiguity result from the sheer complexity of the attitudes involved and the

natural contradictions that arise. As the reader will soon appreciate, by selectively choosing data (a fault of scholars and political actors alike), one can find support for nearly any action on tax policy. For that reason an effort has been made to present all the available evidence that focuses specifically on income taxes.

Attitudes Toward the Level of Taxation

Taxes on the Individual. When people are asked simply whether they believe the income taxes they pay are too high, too low, or about right, the responses, as one might predict, tend to favor the "too high" category. As can be seen in table 16.1, which covers responses to this type of question from 1948 to 1978, except in 1949 (when the survey followed the across-the-board tax reduction of 1948), more respondents indicate that their taxes are too high rather than about right. This is true regardless of the wording of the question.[1] Given no other considerations or trade offs to complicate the picture, the majority of Americans consistently perceive the income taxes they pay as excessive.

Tax Levels for Other Groups. The three-year Roper study, commissioned by H. & R. Block, Inc., which is the most detailed study of income tax attitudes available, asked respondents to rate the levels of taxes paid by a series of groups. The results, depicted in table 16.2 for the years in which these questions were asked, cloud the straightforward evaluations of personal tax levels. The most striking findings are the widespread beliefs that middle-income groups pay too much and that high-income groups and large corporations pay too little. In each year over 70 percent of respondents felt that "high-income families" and large corporations paid too little. Further, and more interestingly, the differential evaluations of the amounts paid by middle- and high-income groups were very consistent across income groups. Fully 68 percent of those with family incomes over $25,000 indicated that "middle-classes families" paid too much, and 70 percent of that group claimed that "high-income families" paid too little.[2] In an effort to explain this result, the 1978 survey asked people to define the income range of middle-income families. All groups indicated the middle range as somewhat above the median family income at the time ($15,000), and higher-income respondents selected ever higher and broader ranges. Thus, those making under $7,000 defined (on the average) the middle range as $17,000 to $35,000, while those making more than $25,000 defined that range as $23,000 to $50,000.[3] These definitions

Table 16.1 Attitudes toward the Level of Income Taxes (in percentages of sample)

Question: "Generally how do you feel about the federal income taxes you pay? Would you say they are too high, about right, or too low?"

	1948	1949	1950	1951	1952	1953	1957	1959	1961	1962	1966	1967	1969
Too high	57	43	56	52	71	59	61	51	46	48	52	58	69
About right	38	52	40	43	26	37	31	40	45	43	39	38	25
Too low	1	1	0	1	0	0	0	1	1	0	0	1	0
No opinion	4	4	4	4	3	4	8	8	8	9	9	3	6

Source: *The Gallup Poll* (New York: Random House, 1972).

Question: "Generally, how do you feel about the federal income taxes you yourself pay? Would you say that your income taxes are excessively high, about right, or very reasonable?"

	Total Taxpayers		Total Public	
	1977	1978	1977	1978
Excessively high	55	58	49	51
About right	31	29	28	26
Very reasonable	10	8	10	7
Don't pay taxes (Volunteered)	1	3	12	13
Don't know	2	2	2	2
(N)	(1,656)	(848)	(2,003)	(1,004)

Source: H. & R. Block, Inc., *The American Public and the Income Tax System* (Kansas City, Mo.: H. & R. Block, Inc., 1978), p. 33.

Table 16.2 Attitudes toward the Level of Income Taxes Paid by Various Groups (in percentages of sample)

Question: "Here is a list of some different types of people or groups. (Card shown respondent) Would you go down that list, and for each one tell me whether you think they have to pay too much in income taxes, or too little in income taxes or about the right amount?"

	1977 (N = 2,003)				1978 (N = 2,007)			
	Too Much	About Right	Too Low	Don't Know	Too Much	About Right	Too Low	Don't Know
Middle-income families	69%	25	2	5	74%	20	2	4
People whose incomes all come from salaries	59%	26	3	12	63%	24	2	12
People who own their homes	53%	31	3	12	50%	33	2	15
Low-income families	53%	32	5	10	47%	37	4	13
Small business companies	42%	28	10	20	38%	30	12	20
People who live in rented homes or apartments	38%	33	11	18	37%	31	11	21
Self-employed people	30%	26	17	27	29%	28	15	28
High-income families	8%	10	75	7	7%	9	76	7
Large business corporations	6%	9	72	12	5%	10	72	13

Source: H. & R. Block, Inc., The American Public and the Income Tax System (Kansas City, Mo.: H. & R. Block, Inc., 1978), p. 29.

partly explain the attitudes of upper-income groups, which stretch the definition of middle class to encompass their own income, but not the benevolence of the lower-income groups toward the middle class.

However one interprets these figures, they clearly support the political attention to "middle-class" tax relief that has been so much a part of the rhetoric of tax cutting in recent years. They also rationalize the longer-term practice of maintaining stable, uniform effective rates for the broad middle-income group which has been such an important aspect of postwar tax politics (see pp. 252–57). Less clear, and seemingly much more dangerous politically, is the trend toward corporate tax relief through rate reductions and tax expenditures. Since public hostility toward corporate tax rates is consistent with more general and equally unfavorable attitudes toward "big business," politicians are undoubtedly aware of the danger associated with blatant tax breaks for businesses.

Although corporate tax rates do fluctuate somewhat according to the prevailing political ideologies and economic conditions, in peace time tax policy corporations have been able to prevail much of the time. The reason is probably a combination of vigorous, highly organized lobbying and what can only be called the privileged role of capital in the American economy. If economic conditions are bad, politicians suffer, so they use whatever means are at their disposal to attempt to stimulate investment. This explanation was stated in very clear terms during the recession of 1971 by Secretary of the Treasury Connally when he introduced the administration's stimulative tax program by emphasizing the high capital investment required to sustain jobs (see p. 177). This argument is apparently timeless and will subside only when corporate taxes are eliminated altogether, a condition we may be approaching in the near future.

Attitudes Toward Tax Cut Proposals. In keeping with the general opinion that taxes are too high, when asked specifically about proposed tax cuts or increases, and when no other conditions are raised, the majority consistently favor reductions and oppose increases. For example, in June 1949, 75 percent of those questioned in a national Gallup poll opposed President Truman's proposal to increase taxes by $4 billion.[4] Seventy-six percent opposed a similiar though hypothetical proposal to raise taxes in 1966.[5] When attitudes toward tax reductions are elicited, the majority favor such reductions. In September 1963, of those who had heard about the proposed Kennedy tax cut (52 percent of the sample), 60 percent favored the reduction, 29 percent opposed it, and 11 percent had no opinion.

By 1980 the pressure for a tax cut was even stronger, although the modal response was less radical than candidate Reagan's proposal or the bill that Congress eventually passed. In that year a question on the Survey Research Center's national survey elicited reactions to proposals to decrease taxes over three years by 10, 20, or 30 percent, more than 30 percent, or not at all. The results, along with the perceptions of where the presidential candidates and their parties fell on this issue, are depicted in figure 16.1. They indicate that 78 percent of those who had thought about the issue (59 percent of the sample) favored some level of tax cut, with 39 percent favoring either the 30 percent advocated by Reagan or more. In addition, the perceived differences between Democratic and Republican candidates and parties on this issue were dramatic.[6]

The Problem of Trade Offs. Viewing them in isolation, people tend to choose lower taxes over existing tax levels. However, when faced with a potential trade off involving budget deficits, the national debt, reduced spending levels, or inflation, they become more ambivalent and the preference for tax cuts is not as evident. Indeed, there are strong indicators that the American public is willing to tolerate high taxes when faced with other unpleasant choices. The trade off between lower taxes and higher deficits or debt has been posed in surveys in 1946, 1947, 1953, and 1978. In each case, the majority of respondents favored balancing the budget or reducing the debt rather than cutting taxes.[7] These answers are displayed in table 16.3.

The trade off between higher taxes and reduced spending is not as clear. Attitudes toward spending increases or changes in taxes seem to shift over time, with the type of spending proposed and the political climate toward tax reduction both influencing the results. For example, in both 1958 and 1962 the Gallup Poll asked whether people favored increased public works or lower taxes. In 1958, 46 percent favored public works, 41 percent favored reduced taxes, and 13 percent had no opinion. By 1962, in reaction to the Kennedy tax proposals, these proportions had changed to 28 percent favoring more public works and 59 percent tax reduction, with again 13 percent having no opinion. In 1973 a different question juxtaposed increased spending on social programs with "holding down spending and taxes." In this case 54 percent favored holding down spending, compared with 39 percent favoring more spending on social programs.

A different question, one that does not refer explicitly to income taxes, has been asked since 1975 by the Advisory Commission on Intergovernmental Affairs. The results, depicted in table 16.4, again

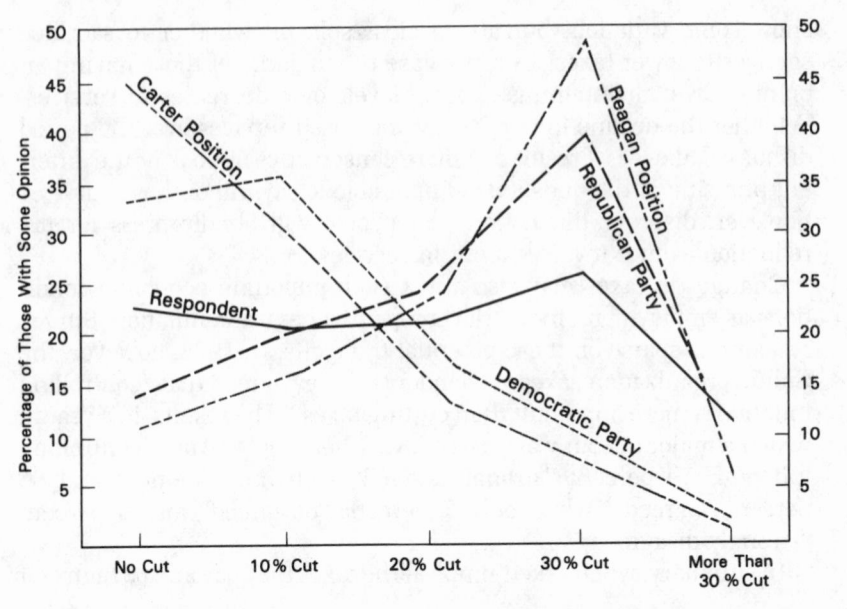

Figure 16.1 Attitudes toward a Proposed 1980 Tax Cut

Question: "Some political leaders think federal income taxes
should be cut 30% over the next three years. Other
political leaders think this would be bad policy for the
government to follow. Do you have an opinion on this
matter, or haven't you thought much about it? (If have
an opinion) Which of these statements best describes
what you would like to see happen over the next three
years? Over the next three years, the federal income
taxes:

1. Should not be cut
2. Should be cut by 10%
3. Should be cut by 20%
4. Should be cut by 30%
5. Should be cut by more than 30%."

Source: *American National Election Study* (Ann Arbor, Mich.: Inter-University Consortium for Political Research, 1980).

show some variation, but also a clear split on whether to sacrifice services to lower taxes. In every case the majority of those having an opinion favor maintaining existing levels over decreases in services. Whether the decline in support for increased services over the period discussed above is a result of a more conservative outlook or the different phrasing of the question is impossible to say. All of these surveys, however, disprove the notion that people will blindly press for tax reduction even it involves a cut in services.

Changes in taxes may also affect such important economic conditions as employment, industrial competitiveness, and inflation. Survey research is sparse on these potential trade offs. In 1978, however, the Gallup organization asked respondents if they agreed that "controlling inflation is more important than cutting taxes." The results, in a year in which a major tax cut was passed, overwhelmingly favored controlling inflation: 19 percent "strongly agreed" with the statement and 66 percent "agreed," while only 7 percent "disagreed" and 6 percent "strongly disagreed."[8]

In summary, when asked simply if the taxes they pay are too high or if

Table 16.3 Attitudes toward the Trade Off between Deficits and Taxes (in percentages of sample)

Questions:

1946,1953 — "What is more important in the coming year, a balanced budget or cutting taxes?"

1947 — "The U.S. has a $1 billion surplus, should we cut taxes or reduce the national debt?"

1978 — "It has been said that tax cuts would lead to a bigger deficit in the federal budget and would make it very difficult for the president to fulfill his promise to balance the budget by 1981. Do you think it is more important to work toward balancing the budget or to cut taxes at this time?"

	1946	1947	1953	1978
Cut taxes	20	38	25	39
Balance budget/reduce debt	71	53	69	53
No opinion	9	9	6	8

Source: *The Gallup Poll* (New York: Random House, various years).

they approve of a potential tax cut, most people respond in the affirmative, expressing particular empathy for the plight of the middle class, which they often broadly define to include themselves. However, when tax reduction is linked to a budget deficit, a reduction in services, or inflation, their attitudes change considerably, and tax reduction may be sacrificed to preserve other values. In these instances the public appears to be taking a more reasonable, moderate, and responsible position than its leaders in Washington. Which set of these beliefs individual politicians chose to emphasize is undoubtedly related to their preconceived notions about tax levels. However, the unquestionable historical bias toward tax reduction suggests that politicians may be underestimating the American public's willingness to sustain high tax levels. In short, the relationship between income tax levels and popular opinion is unclear, but it is certainly not as simple as the dominant wisdom that tax reduction is automatically popular or that holding the line on taxes will result in political damage.

Attitudes Toward the Structure of the Income Tax

The basic thrust of tax reform proposals in the postwar period has been directed at broadening the tax base by paring back or eliminating tax expenditures. The broad-based income concept underlying these

Table 16.4 Attitudes toward the Trade Off between Services and Taxes, 1975–1980 (in percentages of sample)

Question: "Considering all government services on the one hand and taxes on the other, which of the following statements comes closest to your view?"

	1975	1976	1977	1979	1980
Decrease services and taxes	38	30	31	39	38
Keep taxes and services about where they are	45	51	52	46	45
Increase services and raise taxes	5	5	4	6	6
No opinion	12	14	13	9	11

Source: *Changing Public Attitudes on Government and Taxes* (Washington, D.C.: Advisory Commission on Intergovernmental Relations, 1981), p. 16.

efforts was derived from the 1938 work of Henry Simons, which has remained the standard reference for reformers on both ends of the political spectrum. For liberals the proposal is attractive because it curtails provisions that generally favor the well-off; for conservatives the appeal is the promise of a lower and less progressive rate structure; and simplification of the tax code is benefit for both. However, while there appears to be widespread support for this variety of tax reform among technical experts and academics, actual political developments have been in the opposite direction, as the dramatic growth in tax expenditures attests. The present goal is to examine public attitudes on this pivotal issue.

Although evidence from surveys depends partly on how the questions are worded, public opinion generally supports tax expenditures at the expense of technical arguments for tax reform. On the side of tax reformers, Benjamin Page has reported that when people are asked about "tax loopholes" for high-income groups, an overwhelming 88 percent majority favors closing them. In addition, when asked whether they favor closing loopholes or adding a value-added tax, they slightly prefer the former (40 to 38 percent).[9] Moreover, when respondents to the H. & R. Block surveys were asked whether they thought "that we need to broaden the income tax base, which would reduce tax rates by including more types of income," a 48 to 29 percent plurality thought it would be a good idea in 1977, and a 41 to 38 percent plurality thought so in 1978.[10]

However, when questions go beyond these generalities, the results shift dramatically. The H. & R. Block survey of attitudes toward broadening the tax base followed the general query with two specific options. For this purpose the sample of over 2,000 was split. For each half, the deductions and exemptions currently permitted were listed on a card, which also specified that rates ranged from 14 to 70 percent. An alternative plan was then presented that included a $750 exemption for oneself and dependents (with no extra exemptions for the elderly and blind) and deductions only for mortgage interest, real estate taxes, and charitable contributions. The projected rate range was 10 to 35 percent, and it was described as potentially altering the respondent's taxes plus or minus 10 percent. The second, more radical plan allowed no deductions or exemptions, projected rates from 5 to 20 percent, and a plus or minus 15 percent alteration in the amount of taxes the respondent might pay.

In each case, a majority favored the status quo over the alternatives. Fifty-five percent favored the current system, 27 percent favored the less radical alternative, and 8 percent volunteered the information that they would favor the alternative only if it meant for them the same

amount of taxes or less. There was slightly more support for the radical option: 53 percent favored the current system, and 29 percent the alternative; 8 percent favored the alternative only if it meant the same or less taxes. Those who expressed some approval for the plans or said they did not know (46 percent for plan one; 48 percent for plan two) were asked additional questions, prefaced by the statement that the alternative plans would require them to pay either $50 or $75 more in taxes. With this condition support dropped to 15 percent for the less radical plan (from 35 percent) and 16 percent for the more radical version (from 37 percent). Thus, while base broadening and lower nominal rates are attractive in the abstract, when presented with details, the majority of the populace is reluctant to shift from the current system. And if the change is projected to cost the taxpayer even a nominal amount, only a very small minority would be willing to accept tax reform.[11]

The negative opinion of "tax loopholes" is also reversed when specific provisions are the basis of the inquiry. For example, in both 1977 and 1978, the H. & R. Block study asked if respondents considered a list of existing tax expenditure items as "tax loopholes" or "reasonable deductions or nontaxable items." The results are depicted in table 16.5 for each year. The conclusion is striking and highly consistent: *most people support existing provisions as reasonable reductions and not tax loopholes*. The expenditures most likely to be considered loopholes were two of the most controversial on the list: interest income from municipal bonds and half the capital gains profit from the sale of stock or property. The hostility to the latter declined when the question was reworded to indicate that the sale of one's home was included. There was even more support for capital gains in 1977, when a split sample was presented with pairs of options. One set juxtaposed either maintaining the existing 50 percent rate for capital gains (62 percent favored this) or taxing it fully (24 percent). For the first set of options the survey found little variation between taxpayers and nontaxpayers or between those who owned stock and those who did not.[12]

The same type of support for existing tax expenditure policies emerged when respondents were asked about eliminating various tax reduction provisions or adding some that were not currently part of the tax code. For example, when asked which of a list of seventeen tax reduction devices they would favor eliminating "in order to lower the overall tax rate," the only provisions mentioned by over a third of the respondents were the deduction for safety deposit boxes (49 percent) and the deduction for fees paid to someone for filling out tax forms (35 percent).[13]

In both the 1977 and the 1978 surveys, a number of questions were

Table 16.5 Attitudes toward Existing Tax Reduction Provisions as "Reasonable Deductions" or "Tax Loopholes" (in percentages of sample)

Question: "Here are some deductions and exemptions that are now allowed for federal income tax purposes, and some types of income that are not subject to federal income taxes. (Card shown respondent) Some people feel most or at least some, if not all of them, are tax loopholes that work to the unfair benefit of certain groups of people. Would you read down that list and for each one tell me whether it is perfectly reasonable for it to be deductible, or non-taxable, or whether you think it is really a tax loophole?"

	1977 (N = 2,003)		1978 (N = 1,004)	
	Reasonable deduction or nontaxable item	Loop-hole	Reasonable deduction or nontaxable item	Loop-hole
Tax Deductions or Exemptions				
Extra exemptions for blind people	95	3	93	3
Extra exemption for those over age 65	94	3	92	4
Interest paid on home mortgages	90	6	88	7
Property taxes	89	8	88	7
Local and state income taxes	84	11	84	9
Interest paid on loans	84	12	82	13

Local and state sales taxes	84	10	83	10
Gasoline taxes	78	17	76	19
Money paid for child care by working parents	70	23	68	25
Contributions to charity	70	26	65	31
Fees paid for having taxes done by someone else	69	25	61	31
Nontaxable Income				
Social Security income	91	5	88	7
Unemployment benefits	NA	NA	74	19
Welfare benefits	NA	NA	62	29
Interest income from municipal bonds	46	38	43	42
Half the profit (capital gains) from the sale of stock or property	46	39	43	40
Half the profit (capital gains) from the sale of one's home	NA	NA	55	31

Source: H. & R. Block, Inc., *The American Public and the Income Tax System, Summary Report* (Kansas City, Mo.: H. & R. Block, Inc., 1978), pp. 38, 41.

asked to identify attitudes toward adding various provisions to the tax code. Those questions and the responses are summarized in table 16.6. Most of the percentages supporting new tax reduction provisions are very high. A majority opposed only an increased exemption to encourage larger families and deductions for nonitemized charity giving and a working spouse. It is ironic, but perhaps illustrative of the intense political pressure to expand tax expenditures, that the charity and spousal deductions were enacted in the 1981 tax bill.

All of the data reviewed above apply primarily, if not exclusively, to individuals rather than businesses. The margins change considerably when respondents are queried about such practices as business deductions of club memberships, business lunches, gifts, and so on. However, people often felt that even these costs should be partly deductible.[14] These issues had been highlighted in the tax reforms of 1976 and later proposals to limit the "three-martini lunch" and other entertainment and travel expenses. Although they are favorites of congressional tax reformers, the revenue impacts of such provisions are insignificant compared with such major business deductions as the investment credit, depreciation, or interest and tax deductions for corporations. Unfortunately, there is no survey evidence available specifically on these corporate provisions, but the little evidence we have indicates less support for corporate tax reduction devices than for those favoring individuals.

Two conclusions can be drawn from these data, and they spell disaster for comprehensive tax reform efforts unless there is a major change in attitudes. First, just as political rhetoric places politicians of all stripes on the side of tax reform, the majority of people are against "loopholes" in the abstract. Second, people are very reluctant to accept specific reform proposals. They overwhelmingly consider major tax expenditures that affect individual taxpayers as legitimate, and they favor extending tax benefits on a myriad of fronts. Thus, in terms of policy structure, one can only conclude that tax politics is very representative of the wishes of the majority, and perhaps the vast majority. Although one may deride the outcome on other grounds, one must appreciate the dilemma faced by politicians trying to hold the line on tax expenditures and understand the behavior of those not so inclined.

Attitudes Toward a Redistributive Income Tax

Earlier chapters concluded that although political rhetoric varies considerably, policy outcomes over the long term indicate at best weak and ambivalent support for progressive taxation. The specific argument was

made that the progressive structure of the income taxes was essentially the result of wars. Soon after the cessation of hostilities, the dismantling of progressive rates began through proportionate rate reductions and increases in tax expenditure provisions. Although the resulting effective rate structure, which is proportional across most of the income range and slightly progressive at the lower and upper ends, has been lamented by liberals as a perversion of political intentions, the policy choices that created that situation are very consistent over time. With rare exceptions, neither Congress nor presidents have eagerly embraced a redistributive tax policy. Unfortunately, the survey research evidence is not as conclusive on this critical issue as one would hope. The results, which again depend to some extent on the questions asked, seem to indicate uncertainty among many, moderation among most, and polarization for a few.

Over the years a number of survey questions have addressed the general issue of whether government should take responsibility for redistributing income. The results show at best moderate agreement, and some indicate outright hostility. For example, in 1974 the National Opinion Research Corporation (NORC) asked respondents to place themselves on a seven-point scale. One end was agreement with the idea that "government should do something to reduce income differences between rich and poor," and the other was the belief that "government should not concern itself with income differences." Of those expressing an opinion (97 percent), 37 percent placed themselves at the most extreme redistributive position and 59 percent fell in the first three scale positions; 32 percent were in the last three, leaning toward government inaction. Susan Hansen's detailed analysis of this question indicated disproportionate support for redistribution among the lowest-income groups and disproportionate opposition among upper-income groups. The three middle-income categories were very similar to the total population mean. She also found a relatively small correlation (0.21) with party identification, with Democrats more in favor of government involvement than Republicans.[15]

The wording of the question, however, was weak and vague. Neither the extent of redistribution nor the mechanism was spelled out. A similar question posed in a Harris Poll in 1976 elicited simple agreement or disagreement with the proposal that "the federal government try to make a fairer distribution of the wealth of the country." This prospect was opposed by 47 percent and supported by 37 percent, with 16 percent not expressing an opinion.[16]

More specific questions concerning the tax system and redistribution do not adequately clarify this divided and shifting view. In support of a redistributive effect, as we have already seen, a majority of people

Table 16.6 Attitudes toward the Creation of New Tax Expenditure Provisions (in percentages of sample)

	Favor	Not Favor	Don't Know
Income Exemptions[a]			
Income received and placed in special savings account to accumulate enough for a down payment on a loan	64	30	6
Interest on any savings account that is not withdrawn from the bank	58	36	6
Income received and placed in long-term savings accounts until withdrawn	56	36	7
Interest on government bonds	53	40	7
Personal Exemptions[b]			
An extra exemption given a person with a severe physical handicap	84	13	3
Larger exemptions for dependents to encourage people to have children	9	82	8
Give no exemption for dependents to slow population growth	15	74	11
Deductions[c]			
All medical expenses not paid for by insurance as opposed to the present partial deduction	80	15	5
The cost of installing storm windows or home insulation	71	24	5
Money paid for home repairs	60	36	4
The portion of rent paid by apartment or home renters that goes for property taxes and mortgage interest payments[d]	56	34	10
Money paid for household insurance	55	39	. 6

*Table 16.6 Attitudes toward the Creation of New Tax Expenditure
Provisions (in percentages of sample)* (continued)

	Favor	Not Favor	Don't Know
Private school or college tuition fees for children	53	41	6
Money paid for automobile insurance	50	44	5
Contributions to charity even if you don't itemize deductions	40	50	9
Deduction where both husband and wife work because of the extra expenses	36	56	8

Source: H. & R. Block, Inc., *The American Public and the Income Tax System, Summary Reports*, 2 vols. (Kansas City, Mo.: H. & R. Block, Inc., 1977, 1978). The responses in this table come from four different sets of questions. The "favor" column indicates the percentage that favor adding the tax reduction provision to the tax code. Responses may not total 100 percent because of a rounding error.

[a]The exact question from the 1977 survey was: "Now here are some types of income that are now taxable that some people have said should not be taxed. Of course if fewer types of income were taxed, the overall tax rate percentage would have to go up to raise the same amount of tax revenue. Would you go down the list and tell me whether you think it should or should not be taxed."

[b]The responses about the exemption for the handicapped was elicited by this 1978 query: "Some people say that any time a tax deduction or tax break is given to one group the tax rate has to be higher for everyone, and this in effect means that those who don't get the tax benefit are paying for those who do get it. Bearing in mind that more deductions and allowances could mean higher tax rates, would you read down this list and tell me for each one whether it is or is not a tax change you think ought to be made to make the tax system fairer?"

Attitudes toward the increase or repeal of dependent exemptions were tapped by this 1977 question: "Taxes are, of course, used to raise money, but then can also be used to shape or change social behavior. Here are some ways in which taxes can be used for social purposes. Would you please read down that list and for each one tell me whether it is something you think should or should not be done for that purpose?"

[c]The exact question from the 1977 survey was: "Here are some things that are not now deductible for income tax purposes. Of course, if more deductions were allowed, the overall tax rate or percentage would have to go up to raise the same amount of revenues. Would you go down the list and for each one tell me whether you think it should or should not be made deductible for income tax purposes?"

[d]In 1978 this question was repeated using the preamble given note *b* for exemptions for the handicapped. The result was a decline in those favoring the deduction to 48 percent, with 38 percent not favoring the new provision.

feel that taxes for "high-income groups" are too low. However, the definition of high income was much higher than the actual median income and increased as the respondent's income increased. The 1978 H. & R. Block survey asked a number of questions concerning the use of the tax system to further certain social and economic goals. In general people resisted the idea of using taxes to promote such worthwhile actions as working, saving, stimulating depressed industries, or giving up drinking or smoking. This was also true when they were asked if the tax system should be used "to reduce the amount of money those who are better off have, and increase the amount of money poor people have." Only 30 percent felt that the tax system should be used to this end, with another 30 percent favoring doing it through other means and 32 percent stating that it should not be done at all.[17]

Several other questions have been asked concerning the proper rates for the income tax itself. Two such questions were asked in the 1972 and 1976 Survey Research Center presidential surveys. The precise wording of the question, the distribution of respondents' opinions, and their perceptions of the major presidential candidates and parties appear in table 16.7. The question poses a scale ranging between a somewhat vague progressive option, "increasing the tax rate for high income groups," and a flat or proportional tax rate. The results were relatively consistent for both samples and hardly encouraging for those with a predilection for a redistributive tax system. Although the mean was very close to the center of the scale in both years, among those taking extreme end positions, the proportionate tax was favored. In 1972, a more liberal period, a plurality of those having an opinion leaned toward the "tax high income" end (47 to 38 percent); by 1976, 43 percent were on the proportionate side of the middle point. One can only speculate what the result would have been if the question had been asked in 1980, but it is difficult to imagine a more progressive outcome.

The placement of candidates and parties, while difficult for many, indicated a perception of party and candidate separation in the direction we would expect. In all cases the means of the respondents' positions were more moderate than those ascribed to the parties or candidates. In addition, the means in both years were significantly divergent, in the expected directions, for those who voted for the Democratic and Republican presidential candidates.[18] However, except in the case of McGovern, who was perceived by 31 percent as favoring progressive taxation, the percentages of respondents holding extreme positions themselves (1 or 7) are significantly higher than the percentages placing parties or candidates at these scale points. This is partly an artifact of the larger percentages in the middle position, which may have been a further expression of uncertainty about where the parties and candi-

Table 16.7 Respondent, Party, and Candidate Positions on
Progressive Versus Proportional Tax Rates, 1972, 1976 (in
percentages of sample)

> Question: "As you know, in our tax system people who earn a lot of
> money already have to pay higher rates of income tax than those
> who earn less. Some people think that those with high incomes
> should pay even more of their income into taxes than they do now.
> Others think that the rates shouldn't be different at all—that
> everyone should pay the same portion of their income, no matter
> how much they make. Where would you place yourself on this
> issue, or haven't you thought much about this?"
>
> 1. Increase the tax rate for high income groups.
> ⋮
> 7. Have the same rate for everyone.

	1	2	3	4	5	6	7	Mean	St. Dev.	% NA[a]
1972										
Respondent	23	12	12	15	5	5	28	3.94	2.18	14
McGovern	31	19	13	14	8	6	9	3.03	1.56	34
Nixon	10	7	13	25	14	12	19	4.38	1.51	30
Democratic										
Party	15	19	20	22	9	6	8	3.38	1.64	35
Republican										
Party	7	7	12	27	18	14	15	4.44	1.44	33
1976										
Respondent	19	10	11	16	8	7	28	4.18	2.26	16
Carter	15	19	22	22	9	6	7	3.38	1.71	37
Ford	6	6	13	30	20	12	13	4.42	1.61	36
Democratic										
Party	12	15	26	26	9	6	6	3.47	1.59	39
Republican										
Party	4	4	10	32	24	15	10	4.54	1.46	39

Source: *The CPS 1972 American National Election Study* (Ann Arbor, Mich.: Inter-
University Consortium for Political Research, 1973 and 1976).
[a]"Not appropriate." This percentage includes those who have not thought about the
question, those answering "don't know," and those not answering. Percentages for
those answering exclude these individuals and thus add up to 100.

dates really stood. However, it also implies that a substantial number of people held opinions they perceived as beyond the positions of the major parties or candidates.

The results of regression analysis used to estimate and explain the variation in attitudes toward progressivity were not quite as consistent as the distribution of attitudes. The most consistent feature of the models, depicted in table 16.8, is how little of the variation they explain and the uncertainty of the prediction equations. For these two models, which are distilled from a much larger set of independent variables that included age, occupation, education, social class, and others, the R-squared values are very low, indicating that at best 5 percent of the variation in these attitudes can be explained with these variables. A better indication of how much—or, rather, how little—these variables tell us is the standard error of the regression, which indicates the mean error of the predicted values of the dependent variable. One useful comparison, since the units are the same, is between the standard error of the regression and the standard deviation of the dependent variable (see table 16.7). For both 1972 and 1976, the predictions arising from the regression model are, on the average, approximately one standard deviation from the true values—hardly a spectacular result.[19]

The values and significance of the individual coefficients are more interesting, although inconsistent. The signs of the coefficients are almost all as one would predict. Democrats were more likely to favor the progressive alternative than Republicans in both samples. Similarly, those respondents coded as liberals were more likely to be in favor of taxing the rich at higher rates. While the same was true in reverse for conservatives in 1976, the sign is reversed for 1972, and for both years the standard errors are large. Thus, what seems to matter on this issue is identification with a liberal philosophy, conservatives being more split in their judgment.[20] Income entered as a series of dummy variables also has the expected effect, although for 1972 the standard errors are substantial in several cases. Also, the relative sizes of the coefficients indicate a nonlinear relationship, although in both instances belonging to the upper-income quintile has the largest effect on shifting attitudes toward the proportional option.[21]

It is also important to note the size of the coefficients relative to the seven-point scale of the dependent variable. Controlling for the other variables, strong Republicans differed from strong Democrats by only 0.26 points in 1972 and close to one point in 1976. The effects on the predicted dependent variable of the liberal and income dummies are less in each case, never reaching more than 0.7 for a scale with a range of six. To dramatize the point, in 1976, which provides the best esti-

Table 16.8 Regression Analysis of Attitudes toward Progressive Versus Proportional Income Tax, 1972, 1976
Dependent variable: 1. Increase the tax rate for high income groups.

. . . . .

7. Have the same tax rate for everyone.

Independent variables	1972			1976		
	b	s.e. b	t	b	s.e. b	t
Party identification	0.044	0.046	0.96	0.155	0.032	4.89
Liberal dummy	−0.593	0.227	−2.61	−0.287	0.149	−1.92
Conservative dummy	−0.069	0.205	−0.34	0.130	0.135	0.97
Income Quintile 2	0.540	0.325	1.66	0.478	0.218	2.19
Income Quintile 3	0.453	0.314	1.44	0.410	0.208	1.97
Income Quintile 4	0.308	0.287	1.07	0.552	0.211	2.62
Income Quintile 5	0.607	0.300	2.05	0.680	0.215	3.17
R^2		0.03			0.05	
F		2.33			9.43 (df 1407, 7)	
Standard error of the regression		2.28			2.13	

Note: The dependent variables are described in table 16.7. The independent variables are coded as follows:

Party identification is a seven-point scale on which 1 is "strong Democrat" and 7 "strong Republican."

The *liberal dummy* is coded as 1 for those three groups ranging from "extremely liberal" to "slightly liberal." A similar coding is used for the conservative dummy, making the "moderate, middle-of-the-road" category the reference group.

Income is a series of dummies, which break the SRC income groupings as close to quintiles as possible. The lowest-income quintile is the reference category.

mates, a conservative strong Republican in the highest income group would be predicted to have an attitude only two points closer to the flat tax option than a strong Democratic liberal in the lowest income category. Although this difference is not inconsequential, it is clear that attitudes toward progressive taxation do not follow the simple party, ideological, or income lines often assumed in political and academic debates.

Another series of questions, asked for many years by the Gallup Poll, provides a final overview of attitudes toward progressivity. Although the questions are twenty years old, the matching of attitudes with actual policy outcomes is unnerving. Gallup's question elicited the exact dollar amount that respondents felt families in different income groups should pay in personal income taxes. The question and the *median* population responses, converted to a percentage of family income, are shown in table 16.9 for the last three years the question was used. The last column in the table indicates the actual effective income tax rates estimated by Joseph Pechman and Benjamin Okner, using a tax model based on 1966 data. Their calculations describe average effective rates for various income ranges derived from different incidence assumptions (see p. 254). The ranges in that column result from these varying assumptions.

While one might wonder how individuals arrived at these rates, the median figures for the first two surveys are very consistent. The lower amounts in 1962 are a logical shift, given the media attention to the tax cut of that year and the administration's intention to cut taxes further in the next year. For all of the years, there was an extraordinary match between what people said was the optimal level and what the actual effective rates turned out to be. Since income levels were about the same in 1966 and in 1963 (the year projected to in the 1962 survey), it would appear that in terms of medians and averages, there is a very close match between wishes and outcomes and that the match is relatively consistent over time.

These data have complex and ambiguous implications for the question of whether or not the public interest is being represented on the critical issue of progressivity in the tax system. If one adopts the competitive elections model of representation, the results as perceived by the populace are quite satisfactory. The public perceives a clear choice between parties and candidates, and those who vote Democratic see themselves as much closer to the Democratic position (i.e., the position of the Democratic party or candidates) than the Republican position, and vice versa. However, if one accepts the argument presented above, that in actual decision making there has been significant bipartisanship

in tax politics, one could interpret the public's perceptions as cruel delusions generated by superficial symbolic confrontation.

A general criticism of two-party representation from another perspective is that given a preponderance of voters near the middle on an issue, party positions will naturally gravitate toward the middle, and extreme positions will go unrepresented. This problem has long been a concern of pluralists.[22] The data in table 16.7, which resemble a W rather than the classic U-shaped bimodal distribution and which give no indication of intensity of feeling, nevertheless suggest that redistribution politics may be an instance of the problem. In both instances close to 50 percent of those holding a position fall at one extreme or the other, while the parties and candidates are perceived as much closer to the center.

Although this distribution may indicate a failure in representation, it also helps to explain the bipartisan tendencies of tax politics and the political reluctance to take strong stands on redistributive issues. When politicians are faced with the prospect of alienating a significant sector

Table 16.9 Preferred Median Effective Income Tax Rates Compared with Actual Effective Rates, 1957–1966

Question: "Suppose you were a member of the U.S. Congress and it was your job to set the amount of taxes people must pay in the coming year. Let's take a typical family of four—a husband, wife and two children. How much do you think this family, with a total income of $3,000 a year—$60 a week—should pay in personal income taxes next year."

Family Income	Preferred Rates (%)			Estimated Effective Rates, 1966 (%)
	1957	1961	1962	
$3,000	2.0	1.5	0	1–2
$5,000	4.7	4.3	3.0	3–5
$10,000	7.5	7.1	7.2	6–7
$50,000	15.8	14.5	10.0	10–14
$100,000	NA	25.0	20.0	14–18

Sources: *The Gallup Poll*, 3 vols. (New York: Random House, 1972), 2: 1482; 3: 1725, 1800. The estimated effective rates are those in Joseph A. Pechman and Benjamin A. Okner, *Who Bears the Tax Burden?* (Washington, D.C.: Brookings Institution, 1974), p. 59.

of the population through immoderation in either direction, one solution is to diffuse the issue by breaking it down into a large number of apparently unconnected issues. This behavior, characterized in the postwar period by the tendency to reduce rates proportionally and expand the tax expenditure system on a broad front, is politically reasonable, conflict avoiding, and ideally suited to an incremental process. It allows politicians to be responsive to clearly identifiable constituency needs while at the same time avoiding the zero-sum dilemma of income redistribution. Thus, one major criticism of the incremental model—that the system is incapable of generating major policy changes to redistribute income—appears accurate. This behavior, however, appears to be consistent with the division and ambiguity of public opinion on this crucial issue and with the reelection incentives of politicians.

The most telling fact to emerge from these surveys may be the uncanny match between what people say are reasonable income tax rates and the ultimate rates that result once all tax reduction and exemption provisions are included. Although I shrink from an analogy to a hidden hand, it may be that the thousands of decisions and complicated provisions in the tax code produce a centering quality, which arises through a series of adjustments stimulated either by protective, hostile reactions by narrow interests or by overt political initiatives to enact provisions that benefit larger groups. I see no way of adequately resolving such speculations, but it is plausible that the incremental process leads to this unplanned but harmonious result.

The Fairness of the Income Tax System

Although there are some contradictory and ambiguous findings, particularly those related to corporate taxes, there is generally solid evidence of popular support for each of the major features of the development and politics of the income tax. Public attitudes appear to favor lower income taxes, expansion of the tax expenditure system, and a very mild progressivity. However, although these attitudes roughly define the relevant universe of policy changes and options, they are not the whole story. The question is one of the relationship of the parts to the whole: although there appears to be popular support for each major trend in tax policy, there is also considerable dissatisfaction with the system as a whole. When the question turns to the overall fairness of the system and the relative fairness of different types of taxes, the judgment is extremely pessimistic.

The evidence again comes from a variety of sources. The most direct

question concerning fairness was asked in the H. & R. Block surveys that have proven so useful to this point. All three asked respondents if they felt that the present income tax system was "quite fair to most people, or reasonably fair, or somewhat unfair, or quite unfair." The responses (table 16.10) indicate the consistent dissatisfaction of approximately two-thirds of the population. Another question in the 1978 survey asked people to identify, in a list of fifteen policy issues, the one or two they felt were the most important. "Making the tax system fairer" ranked third, named by 23 percent of the people responding. Only lowering crime and fighting inflation ranked higher.[23]

The fairness problem is also central to the public image of tax reform. When asked, "When you hear the words 'tax reform,' which of these things does it mean to you?" 60 percent responded either "to make it fairer for everyone" (47 percent) or "to make it fairer for people like you" (13 percent). Tightening loopholes (29 percent), simplifying tax forms (9 percent), and either increases or decreases in taxes (5 percent each) were considerably less favored alternatives.[24]

Finally, in a well-publicized set of surveys, the Advisory Commission on Intergovernmental Affairs has asked people to identify what they consider to be the "worst tax—that is, the least fair" of a set of taxes:

Table 16.10 Attitudes toward Fairness of the Income Tax (in percentages of sample)

Question: "How do you feel about the present federal income tax system—do you feel it is quite fair to most people, or reasonably fair, or somewhat unfair, or quite unfair to most people?"

	1978	1979	1980
Quite fair	4	3	4
Reasonably fair	25	27	27
Total fair	29	30	31
Somewhat unfair	34	34	36
Quite unfair	33	30	28
Total unfair	67	64	64
Don't know	4	5	4

Source: H. & R. Block, Inc., *The American Public and the Income Tax System*, 2 vols. (Kansas City, Mo.: H. & R. Block, Inc., 1978, 1980), 1: 27; 2: 27.

federal and state income taxes, the sales tax, and the property tax. Since the series began in 1972, the federal income tax and the property tax have vied for the worst tax label. In recent years, with 36 to 37 percent specifying the income tax and 25 to 33 percent specifying the property tax, that label has become firmly attached to the federal income tax. By this measure the sales tax is far and away the least onerous, being selected by only 8 to 13 percent.[25]

Conclusions

As one might anticipate in a complex policy field like taxation, the desires of the governed are difficult to detect, subject to considerable error, and not fully consistent. However, the major conclusion that emerges from the jumble of numbers reviewed above is that the policy decisions that characterize the development of the income tax are representative of at least one level of expressed interest. Unless faced with a dire alternative, people favor lower rather than higher taxes, and politicians have accommodated them. Although favoring base-broadening tax reform in theory, when details are presented they strongly support existing tax reduction provisions and seem eager to expand the tax expenditure system to include new and increased benefits. This contradiction has a parallel in government (or in the behavior of elected officials), where rhetorical calls for tax reform coexist with a persistent stream of policy decisions that make a shambles of any conception of a simplified, broad-based tax. Similarly, the ambivalence toward income redistribution evidenced in the history of the income tax is not inconsistent with the division, uncertainty, and moderation of the populace. Indeed, by one means of estimation, there is an uncanny match between the rates acceptable to the public and actual effective rates.

On another level, however, there is a lingering feeling of malaise about the tax system. The public expresses it in terms of fairness; among policy experts and decision makers, the complaints are both broader and more specific as calls for tax reform come from many quarters. Some emphasize compliance, legitimacy, and simplification; some the inequities of tax expenditures; and some the dangers involved in the increasing use of the tax code as a policy tool. The irony, and the important point for political theory, is that viewed in the long term, the natural reactions of well-meaning politicians, which roughly match the narrow wishes of a majority of the populace, may produce unsatisfactory policy outcomes when viewed as a total system.

Chapter 17.
Democratic
Procedures
and Policy
Outcomes

On several occasions throughout this book I have referred to the various "images" of tax politics. Those images have changed considerably in the six years I have devoted to this book. My early explorations led to an initially favorable image of tax politics as highly consistent with a pluralist/incremental system. I suspected that both the populist image of tax politics as a tightly controlled agenda benefiting the wealthy and economically powerful and the conservative image of the income tax as an American version of redistributive socialism designed to destroy a meritocratic distribution of rewards were radically overdrawn.

The process of enacting taxes, far from being a sweep toward either of the goals implied by these interpretations, was instead a tedious, complicated process of continuous change involving many actors that shifted with circumstances and changes in political power relationships in an effort to balance contradictory sets of values. Most of the key actors were capable experts, willing to compromise, and, when necessary, capable of putting the general interest ahead of more parochial, self-serving interests. Further, the result of this "muddling through," while not fully satisfactory to any specific set of interests, or to any particular tax theory, was a politically acceptable combination of policies that matched the range of demands placed on the system. The tax code could be viewed as a versatile and flexible policy tool, readily conforming to changing needs and changing political will. In other words, in terms of process, responsiveness, and result, the image was positive.

In several important respects that image remains intact as I end this study. I am firmly convinced that the incremental model applies to most tax policy decisions and that the policy-making process is pluralistic in terms of both the number of actors and the range of interests repre-

sented. The actors for the most part are not devious or obsessed with power, but rather seem to be conscientious politicians moved by predictable incentives. I am equally certain that the extreme liberal and conservative images are both distorted. Tax politics has not been dominated solely by the wealthy in a quiet conspiracy to undo a democratically wrought leveling policy. On the other hand, if tax politics is projected as a left-wing march toward a redistributive ethic, the path is totally obscure to me.

However, several generic problems with pluralist/incremental decision making have seriously eroded my initially positive image. The root of the problem is the important value incrementalists place on change and adjustment. Incrementalism is lauded for its ability to shift policy directions, either to meet new demands or to correct ineffective policy efforts. Some proponents also argue that through a series of incremental attacks on a problem, major changes can be introduced without the problems associated with centralized, planned change.

However, the incessant pressure for change can also have a number of negative effects that are seldom discussed. It creates instability, which confuses citizens and makes it difficult for citizens and organizations to anticipate the future shape of laws. More importantly, if tax policy is any indicator, the pressure for change and the inability of the political process to resist it facilitate the creation of a legal structure that is immensely complex, threatens the capacity of government by inducing and indulging claims that extend beyond resource limits, and spreads the actions of government so thin that the central policy goals are often lost as the tangle of programs and provisions grows. This chapter will analyze both the positive aspects of the democratic process in tax politics and the more pathological policy outcomes resulting from the incremental process of change. Although the discussion is generally confined to tax policy, the intent is to stimulate thoughts that might apply to other policy fields.

Process Effectiveness

As I stated in the opening pages of this book, policy analysis is often conducted apart from considerations of democratic theory, and vice versa. Partly because of this, evaluations of ostensibly democratic systems are usually based on procedural norms. One of the general themes of this book is that political decisions that fulfill most of the theoretical criteria of democratic policy making (as described by the pluralist/incremental paradigm) may produce unpleasant policy outcomes when

extended over a long time frame. As a single policy case, income tax policy is particularly relevant because of the widespread belief that the problems that have emerged in tax policy result from a perversion and distortion of democratic procedures. This study has, on the contrary, argued that the decision-making procedures generally fit the theoretical description but that the policy results are still troublesome. The implication is unsettling.

Analysis of procedural democracy occurs at several levels of abstraction. Procedural democracy, in the broadest sense, is related to the role of elections and elite and party competition. In its most rigorous form, informed voters apply either projective judgment of the promises or retrospective judgment of the actions of individual candidates. In the projective form, voters must know their minds on a particular issue, have information concerning the proposed actions of candidates, and fit these two positions together to make their choice. In retrospective voting a similar fit is proposed, but is based this time not on promised actions, but on actions taken by incumbents.[1] The attitudinal evidence presented in the last chapter suggests that voters have great difficulty in meeting the rigorous requirements of either of these models in a field as complex as tax policy. This is certainly the case if one expects judgment to be based on details of tax policy and if the object of that judgment is a congressional candidate. However, at least in recent years, as shown in the last chapter, the population has generally seen the presidential candidates as embodying broad policy differences. Moreover, at least in 1972 and 1980, these perceptions were based on real differences between the candidates; in the latter case the tax issue was critical, and the political system responded to this message.

A more realistic yet still very general model of procedural democracy assumes that political party labels provide information that enable voters to predict policy positions of individual candidates.[2] Whether representation is adequate depends on whether parties adequately represent different positions and that depends on the shape of the underlying distribution of attitudes. If attitudes cluster around one position, parties will project similar stances; if attitudes are dispersed, party positions must be differentiated to accommodate the diversity. If attitudes are complex or unclear, it is difficult to judge the appropriate representative requirement for party positions.

For tax policy it is difficult to assess the adequacy of party representation based on these requirements. Judging from the small handful of surveys that asked people to indicate where they believed political parties stood on tax issues, it appears that most people perceive a substantial difference between parties on the issues of tax cutting (in

1980) and progressivity (1972, 1976). However, on both of these issues, those who place themselves at the extremes on the scales are more numerous than those who perceive either party as holding their own position (see figure 16.1 and table 16.7). More troublesome perhaps is the conclusion reached in earlier chapters that the expected differences in party actions are generally not borne out in practice. Although peak conflicts and the rhetoric of tax politics serve to separate the parties in the anticipated directions, the engine of tax politics is bipartisan agreement on general trends and a reciprocal spreading of tax benefits to broad sets of constituents. Both parties normally support tax reduction and increasing and expanding tax expenditures, and both exhibit ambivalence or distaste toward anything other than mildly progressive effective rates. However, there is also evidence, though not totally conclusive, that the majority of the population supports these trends, and therefore it is difficult to fault the parties for their similarities. In this respect the misperceptions of party differences are harmless illusions in that party actions are more attuned to public wishes than the public is aware. Undoubtedly a multiparty system would better capture the nuances and extremes in public attitudes, but this is true for all policy areas, and the two-party system's countervailing benefits—stability, decisiveness, and moderation—apply as they have applied for over a century in such debates.

Discussions of procedural democracy also occur at a more basic level of discourse that revolves around the actual procedures followed in the decision-making process. The criteria for judging the process at this level include the openness and thoroughness of deliberations, whether individual decisions and stances are publicly recorded, the distribution of power among decision makers, and the adequacy of access for those wishing to petition them. On each of these scores it was argued in previous chapters that the tax-policy-making process is much better than prevailing images suggest and that there is solid evidence, at least for the first three of these criteria, that the situation has improved dramatically in recent years. Most meetings are now open and seemingly endless; the rate of voting, both in committees and on the floor, has increased considerably; and the power of committee chairmen has been greatly diminished in the aftermath of congressional reforms. That these procedural "advances" have been accompanied by a rapid deterioration of the tax base, an increasing tax expenditure system, and a dramatic increase in deficits should by now be well ingrained.

The availability of access and the distribution of influence across affected groups are much harder to judge. As discussed in chapter 1, influence is difficult to define and even more difficult to observe and

measure. The approach adopted in this study has been primarily to work backward, by inference, from results. Those results indicate that the wealthy and corporations have obvious influence on tax policy, but also that special deferrence is shown to the middle class and that all taxpayers, and many nontaxpayers, benefit to a considerable extent from the special provisions that provide exemptions, exclusions, deductions, credits, and preferences. Although access and influence may not be perfectly balanced, they are not confined to a particular set of interests.

Thus, although the procedural aspects of tax policy are far from perfect, some aspects are positive both in terms of criteria of representation of policy positions and requirements of the decision-making process. What remains is to appraise and explain the policy results, and to discuss what corrective actions are appropriate.

Policy Outcomes: A Pathology of Tax Politics

There is one troubling fact that affects judgment of tax systems, particularly if we consider attitudes of taxpayers as one measure of success or failure: no one really likes taxes and almost everyone can justify personal complaints against the taxes he or she pays. If this is so, and I have little reason to doubt the proposition, one's judgment of the tax system should take this into consideration. One conclusion could be that it does a basically unpleasant job as well as we can reasonably expect. Following this line of reasoning, broad dissatisfaction with the "fairness" of the system, which I strategically placed as the final note of the last chapter, is what one would expect and is a poor indicator of the overall inadequacy of the income tax system. This argument has a seductive appeal, particularly for practical-minded realists who charge that academics apply ivory tower expectations to policy problems.

However, I sense that resentment toward the tax system goes beyond intellectual nitpicking and runs deeper than the excessive political rhetoric that surrounds periodic calls for reform. There is something self-destructive in the development of the income tax, something that after many years led Wilbur Mills to describe the tax code as a "house of horrors."[3] Over the years, in trying to respond to the demands of diverse groups, to meet the political needs of decision makers, and—so very important—to correct, adjust, and fine-tune the system, the income tax as a fundamental and ostensibly equitable means of raising revenue has been slowly but continuously eroded. In the process, any possibility of using the tax system to redistribute income—now or, I believe, in the

future—has been lost. What has emerged may be a versatile and flexible policy tool, but it is also a devastatingly complex tangle of diverse legislative provisions and administrative rules. These problems are interrelated. Let us consider them in reverse order.

Complexity. The problem of complexity has entered this study in numerous places. It was recognized as a problem from the first, and prognostications of the destruction of the tax code appeared as early as World War I. Complexity has indeed increased dramatically for both the individual and the corporate tax codes. Ad hoc comments in previous chapters have been directed at the origins and effects of complexity. I now will attempt to draw them together in a more coherent fashion.

The problem is that complexity usually derives from well-intentioned actions and very natural political reactions. This is why everyone complains about the problem, but it gets progressively worse. In budget politics a program often starts out small and gradually increases, a strategy aptly described by Wildavsky as "the wedge of the nose of the camel."[4] There is a direct parallel in tax policy. However, expansion is seldom a matter of simply shifting numbers and readjusting budget allocations (it may not be that simple for direct subsidy programs either). Rather, the expansion, whether in a rate, amount, or time parameter or an eligibility category, often entails rewriting categories or provisions either to safeguard the original recipients or to tailor the new benefits to fit a precise set of circumstances or to avoid abuse. Thus, for example, when IRAs were expanded, they were first extended to specific groups of nonprofit workers (which had to be carefully defined), then they were extended to aid very specialized segments of the work force that were not covered by formal pension plans, and finally, when they were extended in reduced form to everyone, further special provisions were added to cover the work of house spouses. As a teacher, I believe I am presently eligible for three different types of IRAs, although I am not sure.

A similar path was followed as the investment tax credit was expanded. Although several times the flat percentage of the credit was simply increased or decreased, the expansions were often tied to specific, and often complex, actions as the versatility of the investment credit began to be understood. The creation of ESOPs and investment in energy, pollution control equipment, historical structures, and certain classes of rental property all were tied into what began as a very simple concept and policy device. And in each of these areas (and there are more), lengthy rules, lists of acceptable items or practices, and

complicated guidelines to insure compliance had to be established. These provisions were modified in turn as desired incentives changed and as they, following the camel's nose, also expanded.

Complexity also results from efforts to control abuse. Agricultural provisions were previously discussed as an extreme example of an attempt to curtail an undesired tax shelter that arose through a clever and legal use of existing provisions. Other examples are abundant. Business deductions for costs incurred in the production or sale of goods have always been an integral part of the tax system, but so have the yachts, hunting lodges, airplanes, and extravagant entertainment deductions of a small minority. Provisions and rules that draw a legal line are complicated and continually challenged by new situations. Personal exemptions are on their face straightforward, but what of the thirty-year-old child who lives at home with meager income? Or the foster child? Or the elderly parent with assets but inconsequential income? Most would agree that nonprofit charitable foundations like the one that helped to finance this book should be tax-exempt, but what if they cover revenue-generating activities or provide a means to pay exorbitant salaries and fringe benefits that in other businesses would be converted into profit? Real estate provisions, such as accelerated depreciation, inflated interest deductions, and various credits, can all be traced to a desire either to stimulate an industry or to meet a particular housing need. However, when they also serve to shelter the income of the very wealthy and in the process distort the original policy intent, complex lines need be drawn defining a maximum amount of loss that can be claimed and a minimum amount of taxes that must be paid. In all these cases, the original rationale stands, and thus so does the incentive to keep the provision. The solution is to patch the code, to encircle the abuse with restrictions, limits, and extra conditions. The by-product of these rational actions is extraordinary complexity.

A genuine desire for horizontal equity, defined on a case-by-case basis rather than universally, also produces complexity. For example, we want to take into account extraordinary outlays for such things as medical expenses or casualty losses, but we also want to make certain that such expenditures really hurt. The amount of hurt depends on the amount of income; thus, floors are established as a percentage of income, and ceilings may be imposed as well. Similarly, although most would approve of exempting from taxation income transferred to those assumed to be needy (such as unemployment compensation, Social Security benefits, and retirement income), is it fair to others if those receiving such income also have much more? To correct this inequity,

income levels, partial exclusions, and phased-out exemptions are created. Barber Conable (R-N.Y.), leading minority member of Ways and Means, outlined this general problem as follows:

> The desire for equity has compounded our tax system. Nobody started out with the idea to make a complex tax system. In the early 1920's, the system was simple and comprehensive. Maybe a lot of things were not taxed, but at least everybody was taxed about the same way. Then we found that we had a complicated economy, and that the tax code was unfair to some people, so we made exceptions, and then we made exceptions and exceptions.[5]

Finally, complexity has followed in the wake of the tax code's expansion as both a general and a refined policy tool. The resulting provisions are not only abundant but also complex in their own right. Alternative energy devices fall into a number of categories, each of which must be defined—and defined carefully, so that home additions with numerous windows do not receive solar energy credits. The definitions, amounts of credits, and categories will also undoubtedly shift as energy conditions shift. Often they remain past their useful life because, as in direct subsidy systems, attentive and persistent interest groups and industries have become accustomed to their presence. The cumulative effect as more areas are incorporated is ever-increasing complexity.

One of the explanations often given for this problem is that each provision primarily affects a narrow interest that is intensely concerned with the outcome, but there is little incentive for anyone to represent broader interests, which in this instance means working for simplicity in the tax system. This explanation applies in some cases, particularly as tax expenditures expand, but not in all. The quest for horizontal equity, the political mileage to be gained from curtailing abuses, and the real desire to use whatever government means are available to solve pressing problems are all motives that reflect broader interests. Unfortunately, the diagnosis is not as simple as a case of infected interest groups; if it were, yet another crusade to reform their actions might cure the problem.

Rather, the underlying problem is the openness and action-orientation of the pluralist/incremental system. The incentives described above are widespread, and thus well-meaning changes can be introduced at numerous points in the system. Each change can be justified as "marginal" or "remedial," or even as a "reform." The more open the system, the broader the range of interests involved, and the greater

demands on government for change—and change inevitably produces more complexity. Thus, the very responsiveness of the system yields a detrimental result.

Less is known about the effects of complexity than about its growth and origins. Speculation has been rife in recent years that income tax compliance is withering because of the higher marginal rates for middle-income groups, declining perceptions of fairness, and increasing complexity. The electronic media and popular journals have made wild estimates about a massive underground economy, but very little hard evidence existed prior to 1980, when the IRS released preliminary estimates of unreported income for 1976.[6] A more recent report extends that study backward to 1973 and forward to 1979 and 1981. It concludes that although there have been large absolute increases in unreported income, which in 1981 amounted to a revenue loss of $81.5 billion, the percentage of income voluntarily reported has declined only from 91.2 percent in 1973 to 89.8 percent in 1981. This rate of decline (about 0.2 percent per year), however, meant failure to report an additional $40.5 billion in 1981.[7]

Although it is impossible to separate out the causes of noncompliance, some forms are more common than others. Compliance percentages have declined least for simple reporting of wages and salaries. The fastest-growing areas of noncompliance are the underreporting of business income and the overstating of business and personal deductions. Thus, the withholding system is clearly holding up the compliance rate and the most complex areas of the code are reporting the greatest difficulty. There is, then, a tentative support for the popular belief that complexity harms revenue collection.

Redistribution. That the income tax fails to redistribute income in any real sense could be cited as a point in its favor in that, as shown in the last chapter, actual effective rates closely approximate the mean rates people believe different income groups should pay. However, the matter is not that simple. Attitudes are not all that clear; simple conclusions camouflage ambiguity, uncertainty, and inconsistency. Many policy experts from various points on the political spectrum would support a redistributive system, probably based on a negative income tax, in preference to the present array of direct government programs to deal with economic need and poverty. But we have no public opinion data on that option. And one cannot overlook the fact that some notion of vertical equity, progressivity, ability to pay, or simple redistribution has always been at the center of tax discussions, particularly discussions of the merits of the income tax. Finally, if the arguments of this book are

correct, not only has the tax system failed to redistribute income, but even if future attitudes should support such a program, the politics and structure of the income tax make redistribution an unlikely prospect.

There are a number of interrelated factors that render the income tax impotent as a tool of redistribution. First, as outlined in chapter 12, both the historical trends favoring general tax reduction and the deferrence shown the middle classes have a powerful debilitating effect on the redistributive consequences of tax policy. Given the underlying pretax distribution of income, the level of taxation would have to be very large to affect the overall distribution, even if the effective tax rates were extremely skewed against the rich (see p. 261).

Similarly, the apparent goal of maintaining stable, essentially proportional effective rates for the middle-class taxpayer would make it difficult to justify the very high rates for upper-income groups that would be necessary to affect redistribution. It would also make it difficult to "shake down" the distribution in progressive steps that would shift some income from the top to the lower half of the distribution. The first of these possibilities, which maximizes redistribution when measured by the absolute equality norm specified by the GINI Index, is unlikely to be adopted because of the sharp break required between middle- and upper-income classes. Although people seem to favor higher taxes for "upper-income groups," when asked how much higher, they favor only a mild increase over middle-income rates—and tax politics follows the lead. The second possibility, which would have a weaker redistributive effect, is seemingly favored by the populace, which on the average prescribes a mild but smooth progressivity, but is apparently not favored politically. Rather, the political rule has been to reduce rates proportionately for everyone but the people at the very ends of the distribution. Changes at the ends vary according to the political and economic environment. Thus, the historical notion of equality projected in tax policy over the years has been essentially one of proportional burden, with need compelling lower rates for the very poor and with high rates placed on the wealthy only during periods of crisis.

The strong incentives for tax reduction and rate stability for the middle class are not the only dimensions of the problem of using the tax system for redistributive purposes. The nature of the policy-making process is another important component. Redistribution played a relatively important role in the conception of the income tax. Progressives and insurgent Republicans generated broad philosophical discussions of equality, class legislation, and the distribution of income. This rhetoric carried over to the First World War in the form of accusations of war profiteering and calls for sharing the burden of the war in terms of

personal sacrifice and money. Although the same rhetoric flared briefly during the Depression and, in a more muted form, during World War II, as the income tax grew in scope and complexity, the larger issues of redistribution and class confrontation were lost in the details of legislative battles.

This transformation can be explained in part by two developments. The first was that tax bills began to resemble large jigsaw puzzles, the components of which rarely fit a consistent pattern. This meant that individual provisions were treated piecemeal, determined more by their own incremental history than by reference to any standard of redistribution. If progressivity was a factor at all, it was only one among many. Although peak partisan conflicts on particular symbolic issues might invoke the rhetoric of redistribution, the bulk of the tax bill was already decided on wide-ranging technical and particularistic grounds, which probably had more to do with specific horizontal equity questions than matters of overall redistribution. In this way critical tax decisions became insulated from the issue that had played a pivotal role in early tax politics.

The second explanation, not totally unrelated to the first, was that as the tax expenditure system grew, the problem of redistribution, which was often raised in connection with rate changes, was displaced in importance by tax expenditure debates that were essentially distributive in nature. The discussion shifted from consideration of relative advantages to debates over specific needs and desired actions. The elderly on fixed incomes are suffering, the building industry is in the worst slump since the Depression, we need to stimulate energy exploration, and so on. As the use of the tax code for varying purposes expanded, redistribution simply took a back seat to distributive requirements based on need or incentive effects.[8]

Complexity of the tax code also affects its redistributive properties and potential. A policy structure that resembles a very large briar bush is difficult to prune in a purposeful manner. A cornerstone of incrementalism is the ability to effect remedial change to correct policy errors or move in new directions. But think of the time and the range of decisions involved in reforming the tax code. What would be needed is not a battle for tax reform but a sustained war. And as the war progressed, all of the distributive arguments would be raised, compromises would be reached to cut back but ultimately preserve most benefits, and—unless there was a sustained political program unlike any in the postwar period—counterattacks would be likely. Although incremental decision making was able to effect dramatic changes early in the history of the income tax, the structure of the code now would make it much

more difficult to produce significant shifts in collective effects. Steeply progressive nominal rates could be reinstituted, but if our tax models are correct, even this change would be of little consequence so long as the current range of tax reduction devices remained.

A final factor preventing redistribution is more speculative and difficult to state in an analytically rigorous manner. In chapter 3, which discussed and analyzed Henry Simons' comprehensive tax base formula, I described how Simons, when faced with the question of redistribution, merely threw up his hands, renounced efforts to prove its utility, and opted for a simple declaration that the alternative was distinctly unpleasant. Simons' problem and solution have haunted later philosophical discussions of taxation and have been mirrored in the actual politics of taxation. As argued repeatedly in previous chapters, tax policy has reflected an ambivalent and equivocating attitude toward redistribution. One aspect of that ambivalence, which Simons seemed to share, is the almost total lack of a positive ideal of equality. Almost always the arguments for progressivity have been based either on revenue needs or on the privileged position of the very wealthy. The beneficial effects of equality are seldom presented; rather, the arguments are instrumental or simply vindictive. Wars provided the major instrumental rationale, whereas reform legislation was often introduced, as in 1969, by a symbolic attack on abuse, such as pillorying a few wealthy individuals who pay no taxes. Since instrumental conditions change and a belief in meritocracy seem to be well ingrained in the American psyche, both bases for equality have proved to be short-lived. Once the crises that produced such charges were past, immediate efforts to undo the redistributive damage were undertaken.

As with the problem of complexity, the underlying factors preventing redistribution are not alien to the political process; on the contrary, they operate much as the pluralist/incremental model prescribes. Politicians move away from the unpleasant consequences of high tax levels and toward a distribution of benefits to their constituents. Rather than adhering to an abstract ideal of equality, they treat issues on a piecemeal basis, each within its own incremental orbit. Rather than instigating conflict-producing philosophical debates over economic distribution, they resolve differences through particularistic negotiations on narrow, distributive grounds. And rather than promoting some vision of a future state, they act pragmatically in terms of temporary needs and evils.

The large issue that remains is whether these actions are consistent with the true wishes of the governed. Within the confines of this study, I can offer little more to resolve this issue than what was presented in the last chapter. The more important question may be whether the income

tax could be used in the future as a vehicle for redistribution if the majority approved. Given the structure that has developed over time, it appears doubtful. Thus, the most obvious and simple policy mechanism for redistributing income—possibly the only one—has been lost.

Revenue Capacity. I argued at the end of chapter 13 that the income tax system may be seriously strained in the future. In the early postwar period, the tax base expanded because of rising incomes and presidential resistance to tax reduction. During this period most of the erosion of the tax base was the result of tax exemptions and income exclusions (primarily transfer payments). As incomes increased and the middle-class shelters provided by exemptions, exclusions, and the standard deduction were reduced, the tax base expanded, but so did the drive for tax expenditures. By 1969 the tax base was beginning to shrink. Inflationary growth in income in the 1970s cemented these trends and culminated in the 1981 tax cut and indexing provisions. Tax expenditures have taken on a more significant role for the middle class, and barring steep reductions in the personal exemptions, which have traditionally been lowered only in wartime and are presently covered by indexing provisions, the tax base is very likely to continue to decline. If indexing of rates is allowed to take effect as planned—and terrific political pressure will be needed to prevent it—the income tax will eventually lose its capacity to provide necessary revenues. As of this writing, even with the modest increase in tax revenues legislated in 1982 (mostly by tightening administrative provisions), projected deficits for the foreseeable future are on the order of $200 billion per year, or about 5 percent of GNP. As I have argued repeatedly throughout this book, the underlying trends, incentives, and decision processes that led to this result are well entrenched. It appears, therefore, that the politics of income taxation follow a self-destructive path.

Mitigating excuses can be concocted for this apparent long-term policy failure. For instance, it can be argued that government is too large and that, given the power of interest groups, the only way to reduce government size is to cut revenues, which will then force expenditure reductions. But this argument is based on the assumption that government can indeed be reduced in scope. The inability of conservative governments both in the United States and abroad to effect such a change in the last decade is one indicator that most government functions are here to stay. And growth in government may be less a matter of will, belief, or desire than simply a hard reality of modern life.

The difficulty of significantly paring entitlements, defense expendi-

tures, and interest on the public debt has been argued for some time and has been borne out during the most conservative presidency in fifty years. However, there are also more general reasons that budget expenditures cannot be easily reduced, if at all. As family structures change, as occupations become technically and therefore educationally more demanding, as lifespans increase, as the world economy becomes more interrelated, as small organizations are replaced by larger ones, governments simply become more essential. Changing family patterns create demands for more collective services (child care, retraining, financial assistance, etc.). Although the "high-tech" transformation of society has surely been exaggerated, we are rapidly approaching 50 percent college attendance for eighteen and nineteen year olds, up from 7 percent in 1940.[9] An aging population combined with greater family mobility means more, not less, demand for government housing, health care, and general assistance. And demands for subsidy and regulation of the economy come not only from fringe liberal consumer groups, but also from small businesses pitted against large corporations, from industries in declining sectors, and from all businesses faced with foreign competitors perceived as unfairly subsidized by their respective governments. Since these trends are beyond anyone's control, cutting taxes to cut back on government will result only in increasing government debt.

Some offer, as another mitigating argument, that other forms of taxation will grow to make up the revenue gap as the income tax declines. But what kind of taxes? This country has never demonstrated a will to tax estates or inheritances. Shifting taxes to other countries through duties and tariffs would be strongly resisted by both consumers and the corporate world—and even if it is not, the amount of revenue involved is unlikely to be substantial. That leaves taxing consumption, either through a national sales tax or, more likely, a value-added tax, or increasing payroll taxes. Consumption taxes have historically been resisted, and tax experts have compiled a long list of disadvantages associated with either type of tax. Regressivity leads the list, but the new administrative apparatus required would be huge; the effects would be inflationary; such taxes provide no automatic stabilization of the economy; and, at least where value-added taxes are concerned, public opinion appears to be against such a change.[10] Moreover, these taxes would undoubtedly not remain simple, but rather products and services would be differentiated for all the reasons income tax provisions expanded and became more complex. Once this differentiation began, intense interest group pressures similar to those that earlier affected tariff and excise legislation would arise. In short, a complex

maze of tax devices would be born, with a matching amount of political and administrative time devoted to their maintenance and change.

The nonincremental introduction of a new tax is in fact unlikely. It is more likely that the recent trend toward increasing payroll taxes will continue. How far that expansion can go before powerful equity arguments of both a horizontal and a vertical nature are raised is a matter of conjecture. The similarity and overlap between payroll and income taxes is such that once the taxes begin to extract similar amounts from the middle class, the same political pressures that befell the income tax are likely to emerge.

What is certain is that by moving away from income taxes and toward consumption or payroll taxes, we will automatically be excluding more and more wealth and capital income from taxation. Although I argued in chapter 3 that Simons' notion of income as an index of economic power was inadequate in that it failed to consider differential conditions of need, clearly the exclusion of wealth and capital-based income from taxation foresakes any effort to match taxes to economic well-being. Even though the concept of ability to pay is ambiguous (a fact reflected in public attitudes toward it), a crude sense of fairness would seem to dictate that the most well-off should bear a disproportionate share of the tax burden. The failure to preserve a redistributive tax structure and continuing political pressure to reduce taxes have essentially eliminated that possibility.

Remedies, Regressions, and Remissions

The Inadequacy of Tax Reform. At first blush the remedy for these pathologies of the tax system appears to be obvious, if not altogether original. The answer would seem to be a major tax reform effort along standard comprehensive tax base lines, with whatever blend of progressivity in rates the political process might dictate. A stack of such reform schemes are readily available from all corners of the political spectrum. One set of proposals fall under the generic term "flat tax." Most would eliminate most tax expenditures and compress the nominal rate structure. The latest and most prominent is the Hall-Rubushka scheme to reduce the personal income tax form to a postcard allowing (unspecified) business deductions and little else and requiring only twelve lines of information.[11] Income would then be taxed at a single rate close to the current effective rate paid by the broad middle-income groups (12 to 14 percent). The Bradley-Gephardt proposal would have three rate levels

and allow deductions for mortgage interest, taxes, charitable contributions, and payments into IRAs and Keogh plans. Interestingly, few of these proposals discuss excluded forms of income or indirect wages in the form of employee contributions to health insurance, retirement plans, and so on.

Other reform proposals also consider corporate changes. The most grandiose is the Treasury's 1977 *Blueprints for Basic Tax Reform*, which outlines a master plan for eliminating many tax expenditures and at the same time integrating the individual and corporate taxes. This proposal has been less cited in the last several years as attention has shifted to the flat tax and revived expenditure tax, which would be based on a reformed income tax that excludes savings. The latter, which comes in several administrative varieties, has been offered as an addition to the income tax or, more often, as a substitute for it. All these major reforms begin with the premise that the income tax system is in dire straits. I agree with the premise, but am bewildered and somewhat bemused by the remedies.

There is nothing, absolutely nothing in the history or politics of the income tax that indicates that any of these schemes have the slightest hope of being enacted in the forms proposed. In fact, if the past is any guide, reform efforts, whether radical proposals like those above or more modest changes of an incremental variety, are very likely to aggravate the problem over the long run. People and institutions have memories; reforms in one political period are likely to be followed by counterattacks on the tax system in another. Although the reforms might temporarily increase revenues and positively affect redistribution, the few reform bills that have been enacted have had only the slightest impact on these problems when viewed in historical perspective. The main result has been more complexity, which in turn provides more numerous and less visible targets for those seeking specialized tax relief in a later period.

Insulating Policy from Politics. The answer is not to reform the tax system or even to seek immediate policy remedies, but rather to alter the political process to prevent even further regression. The general goal should be, as Allen Schick has compellingly argued, to restore non-decision making—to change the politics of taxation so as to retard and stabilize change.[12] Thus, the goal should be to seek not remedies but merely a remission from the malady. And that requires political, not policy, reform.

Joseph Pechman, who has studied, analyzed, and worried about the tax system for a good many years, has also come to the conclusion that

political reform is the key. However, his solution, which he implies would usher in a tax reform era, is to reform election laws to provide public financing for congressional candidates, thus freeing them from the clutches of special interest groups.[13] If my analysis is correct, this proposal falls far short. Money from any source is only one of the pressures forcing members of Congress to "produce" for their constituents. And for tax politics it is probably a minor consideration when compared with the pressures generated by the large middle class, which dines along with the rich, the poor, and the special interest groups at the tax benefit table. To free representatives from the burdens of electoral finance may prevent some tax abuse, but not the wholesale erosion of the base that comes from income and fringe benefit exclusions, deduction of taxes, interest, the exemption of IRA funds, and broad-based corporate provisions that purportedly aid the economy and indisputably aid large numbers in the business community. And we must assume that the ingenuity of elected politicians in devising new methods to confer such benefits is unlimited. The answer is not to reform the representative process but to insulate policy from it.

Those words do not come easily for one raised in a pluralist tradition, and undoubtedly they will be challenged by many. What is implied is that democracy must be contained—that it must be tempered to prevent elected officials from offering constituents, in good conscience, what those constituents want. The underlying malady is the hyperresponsiveness of the system. It is not that the "electoral connection" is too loose or disjointed; it is that it is too much tied to personal interests, too shortsighted, and too often exercised.[14] Decisions that appear rational and proper in each individual case are in the aggregate and over time a disaster.

An obvious first step is to repeal the reforms enacted in Congress in the early seventies, at least as they apply to the tax committees. These reforms assumed that a more open process with broader participation would lead to more responsible actions, in that efforts to cater to narrow interests would be overruled or would be exposed to political attack. Under the new rules the interests catered to often turned out to be broad ones, but even if they were not, public access, rather than discouraging tax benefits, actually provided politicians with a convenient and appealing platform that they could use to take credit for the measures in a bill that aided their particular constitutents. Some initial reforms would be restoration of the power of the committee chairmen; reduction of the size of committees; and perhaps even the establishment of a subcommittee of Ways and Means and Finance to deal with income tax legisla-

tion. The closed rule should be reinstituted and extended to the Senate. Finally, open committee sessions should be restricted and confined to the early stages of a bill.

Although these changes might restore some order to the legislative process and establish some control over tax spending, the basic incentive structure remains. One way to alter those incentives, at least during conservative periods, is to tie tax expenditure decisions to direct spending, thus attaching the stigma of the latter to the former.[15] In the Canadian format, tax and spending decisions are placed in the same functional "envelope," so that when any program is discussed, whether a tax program or a direct expenditure, the relevant provisions and estimated budget effects are analyzed together.[16] The reader will remember, however, that the modest effort to institute such a procedure in 1976 was soundly defeated on the Senate floor.

The other way to solve the incentive problem is to circumvent Congress altogether. As long as members of Congress perceive their tasks and their rewards as tied to the generation of both broad and specialized legislative benefits, the historical trends in tax politics will persist.[17] And although popular perceptions of Congress as an institution have remained extremely unfavorable in recent years, the very high reelection rates of incumbents must be reinforcing previous behavior. Thus, as long as tax politics remains the prerogative of Congress, the underlying pressures to use the tax code to distribute benefits and offer solutions to specific policy problems will be enormous no matter what institutional changes are made. Therefore, the critical reform must be the insulation of tax decisions from politics, either by creating legal moratoriums that prevent changes in the tax system or by shifting decisions to administrative bodies and executive agencies.

The former strategy has been suggested by Joe Pechman, who nevertheless clings to reform hopes. He recommends a five-year hiatus between "reform efforts," which would be guided by an assemblage of experts.[18] The legal or institutional basis for such a moratorium is not at all clear, however. Proposals to shift decision-making power to the executive branch and to administrative agencies are less common, although there are precedents in related policy fields and the income tax systems of other industrialized countries.

The history of U.S. tariff policy is such a precedent and provides a striking parallel to the problems currently faced by the income tax. Early tariff legislation consumed similar amounts of time and generated the high levels of consternation that have characterized income tax legislation in recent years. E. E. Schattschneider's classic analysis of that policy domain introduced the notion of "reciprocal noninter-

ference" to describe tariff policy. He described the dilemma as follows: "Congress . . . seeks political support for the system, not by giving ample protection to a few industries whose stimulation is required by public welfare, but by giving limited protection to all interests strong enough to furnish formidable resistance to it, and by making a virtue of the means by which the policy is executed."[19] Schattschneider's analysis was confined to a detailed case study of the 1929–1930 Smoot-Hawley Tariff Bill, which set such outlandishly high and broad tariffs that massive retaliation and an eventual halving of world trade followed. Ironically, Schattschneider's critical analysis ended just before Congress admitted its inability to handle tariff affairs reasonably. In the wake of the Smoot-Hawley debacle, stimulated by the Democratic landslide and by the Roosevelt administration in the person of Cordell Hull, then Secretary of State and an unabashed free-trader, Congress enacted the 1934 Reciprocal Trade Agreements Act, which removed tariff decisions from Congress, empowering the executive branch to negotiate tariff changes up to 50 percent of existing rates. The negotiated results were to take the form of executive orders and not treaties, which would have required congressional approval.[20]

Insulation of tax policy from politics is practiced in other countries that remain viable democracies. In both Germany and Canada, to take two well-documented cases, tax decisions are centralized in the executive branch, which serves as both the initiating arm for legislation and a powerful filter for proposals originating elsewhere.[21] On the other hand, British tax legislation is enacted in an open environment very similar to that in the United States. And the results are also similar, as this summary comment by two experts on that system indicates:

> The mess into which the present British tax system has drifted
> has been documented in earlier chapters. Anyone who came
> to it for the first time would regard the present system with
> some incredulity. . . . No one would design such a system on
> purpose, and nobody did. Only a historical explanation of how it
> came about can be offered as a justification. That is not a justi-
> fication but a demonstration of how seemingly individually ra-
> tional decisions can have an absurd effect in the aggregate.[22]

To what degree a shift in tax power from the legislative to the executive branch would stabilize tax policy is an open question. However, peacetime experience indicates that the executive branch has generally maintained greater restraint than Congress. The Mellon Treasury, while reducing taxes steadily in the 1920s, initiated reduc-

tions very prudently, only following government surpluses. And when it was decided that revenue was needed to balance the budget, Mellon and the administration cooperated with Congress in raising taxes in 1932. Most of the Roosevelt administration's initiatives, however symbolic, were geared to increase taxes and close loopholes. After World War II Truman alone resisted tax reduction, finally succumbing to a congressional override in 1948. And the Eisenhower administration followed suit, holding the line on tax changes for eight years despite pressures from both parties to reduce taxes during recessions. Since World War II, as the executive branch has asserted itself more in tax matters, its suggestion for changes in the code have been more balanced than those of Congress (see chapter 15). Even for the monumental Economic Recovery Tax Act of 1981, the initial administration proposals were extremely modest relative to the congressional add-ons of both parties.

In addition to the historical case, a logical argument can be made for greater executive influence. After four years in office, presidents have much more difficulty than congressmen in avoiding responsibility for economic failure. Although presidents try mightily to put the blame for economic problems on an uncooperative Congress or bureaucracy, international events, or simply time lags, evasion of responsibility is difficult, and the audiences to which they must appeal are very broad. Congressmen, on the other hand, can shift attention from the larger issues to the particularistic benefits provided to constitutents, and they can avoid blame by pleading impotence, blaming the administration, or, as Richard Fenno has graphically illustrated, by running against Congress itself.[23]

To the extent that tax changes adversely affect economic conditions—and deficits are the most obvious problem—presidential responsibility for these conditions indicates tax restraints that may not exist for Congress. The next few years, however, may be critical in this respect. If a Republican is reelected easily in 1984 and if the economy is particularly strong, there is no question that the president will claim that tax initiatives were mainly responsible. A Reagan victory might reverse the logic above and set a different course for future aspirants to that office. His reelection could mean that the traditional restraint on tax reduction caused by deficits could be weakened. In that event the tax system would be a slow-moving and wide-open target for all, and even a dramatic shift in power from Congress to the executive branch would be ineffectual in saving the tax system.

The prospects for policy change probably depend more on the course of future political and economic events than on either past actions or

intellectual analysis. If indexing goes into effect and if deficits persist and are linked politically to the economic malaise, then something will be done. The system has adapted in the past, and the capacity to do so remains. Whether the adaptation will be toward a new type of tax, marginal increases in existing taxes, or a change in the political process in the directions I have suggested is anyone's guess. Although the historical policy trends and current political incentives and institutional arrangements all seem to point to the need for political reform, the link between representation and taxes is constitutionally and ideologically ingrained as a sacred right. We may well end up simply paying a higher price for that right than was originally expected.

Epilogue

The central body of this book was drafted in 1982 and 1983. Since that time there has been little major tax legislation. There was a primarily technical bill written in 1982 which did increase taxes some $60 billion, mainly through administrative and compliance changes. This increase was dwarfed by the $750 billion reduction built into the Economic Recovery Tax Act of 1981. Also, all of the major delayed provisions of ERTA, including indexing, have gone into effect. The nation also faces, at least through 1988, annual deficits of over $200 billion.

However, as I write this in early January 1985, it also appears the nation is once again on the verge of revolutionary, nonincremental tax reform. Ronald Reagan was reelected president by one of the widest margins in history. Although the Republican Party did not share this near record victory in congressional or state and local races, few quarrel with the president's popularity and potential power. His Treasury Department, after two years of labor, has produced a base-broadening, modified flat-tax proposal that is more comprehensive than the Gephardt-Bradley or Kemp-Kasten proposals and is nearly as extreme as the Ford administration proposal, *Blueprints For Basic Tax Reform* (discussed earlier). The Treasury plan includes repeal of most deductions, including state and local taxes and all interest; deletion of most income exclusions; and termination of special treatments for capital gains and asset depreciation. The plan, created by the most conservative administration in fifty years, has also been backed by some notable liberals on tax reform, including Joseph Pechman of the Brookings Institution. If enacted in its present form, and then not undone by later legislation, it would truly revolutionize our tax system.

The central argument of this book has been that our political system

has, to this point, been incapable of producing such lasting reform. This time the chips seem about to fall, but that has happened before—in 1969 and 1976—and they did not. Instead, what followed the 1976 effort was a wholesale retreat from tax reform. For the reasons stated in chapter 3, I wish the Treasury well. However, proposals are not laws and I remain highly skeptical that these proposals will become and remain law over the long run. More likely, I would predict some curtailing of tax expenditures (although elimination of very few), a reduction in the number of brackets (which simplifies nothing and will reduce progressivity), and then, in the years ahead a return to the more natural political impulses of conferring both broad and specialized benefits through the tax system. Lasting tax reform will not come without lasting political reform.

Notes
Index

Notes

Introduction

1 Works taking this approach include Joseph A. Pechman, *Federal Tax Policy* (Washington, D.C.: Brookings Institution, 1977); Richard Goode, *The Individual Income Tax* (Washington, D.C.: Brookings Institution, 1975); and George F. Break and Joseph A. Pechman, *Federal Tax Reform: The Impossible Dream?* (Washington, D.C.: Brookings Institution, 1976).
2 Robert A. Dahl, *Who Governs?* (New Haven: Yale University Press, 1961).
3 Theodore Lowi, *The End of Liberalism* (New York: W. W. Norton, 1969).
4 James Q. Wilson, "Problems in the Study of Urban Politics," in Edward H. Buehrig (ed.), *Essays in Political Science* (Bloomington and London: Indiana University Press, 1964), p. 133.
5 This position has been adopted by authors as ideologically estranged as Milton Friedman, *Capitalism and Freedom* (Chicago: University of Chicago Press, 1962); Arthur Okun, *Equality and Efficiency: The Big Trade-Off* (Washington, D.C.: Brookings Institution, 1975); and Charles Schultz, *The Public Use of the Private Interest* (Washington, D.C.: Brookings Institution, 1978).

Chapter 1

1 Major original works in pragmatic philosophy include: William James, *Principles of Psychology* (New York: H. Holt and Co., 1890); John Dewey, *Logic: The Theory of Inquiry* (New York: Holt, Rinehart and Winston, 1938), and *The Public and Its Problems* (Chicago: Gateway Books, 1946); and Charles Hartshorne and Paul Weiss (eds.), *Collected Papers by Charles Sanders Peirce* (Cambridge: Harvard University Press, 1958). A good anthology of Dewey's writings is David Sidorsky (ed.), *John Dewey: The Essential Writings* (New York: Harper and Row, 1977).
2 Robert A. Dahl and Charles E. Lindblom, *Politics, Economics, and Welfare* (Chicago: University of Chicago Press, 1953).
3 See Robert A. Dahl, *A Preface to Democratic Theory* (Chicago: University of Chicago Press, 1956), and *Polyarchy* (New Haven: Yale University Press, 1972).
4 Specifically, the authors refer to Chester Barnard, *The Functions of the Executive* (Cambridge: Harvard University Press, 1938), and Herbert Simon, *Administrative Behavior* (New York: Free Press, 1945).
5 Charles E. Lindblom, "The Science of Muddling Through," *Public Administration Review* 19 (1959): 79–88.

6 David Braybrooke and Charles E. Lindblom, *A Strategy of Decision* (New York: Free Press, 1963), p. 38.

7 Ibid., p. 40.

8 Ibid., pp. 48–54.

9 This list is repeated in almost identical form in Braybrooke and Lindblom, *Strategy of Decision*, chap. 5, and in Charles E. Lindblom, *The Intelligence of Democracy* (New York: Free Press, 1965), pp. 144–52.

10 Lindblom, *The Intelligence of Democracy*, pp. 28–29.

11 Ibid.

12 Charles E. Lindblom, "Decision-Making in Taxation and Expenditures," in National Bureau Committee for Economic Research, *Public Finances: Needs, Sources and Utilization* (Princeton: Princeton University Press, 1961), pp. 314–15.

13 In the second edition of his popular textbook, originally entitled *Pluralist Democracy in the United States*, Robert Dahl, citing the confusion over the term, dropped the word "pluralist" from the title. See *Democracy in the United States* (Chicago: Rand McNally, 1971), p. vii.

14 Lindblom, "Decision-Making in Taxation and Expenditures," pp. 316–18.

15 See, e.g., Lance LeLoup, "The Myth of Incrementalism: Analytical Choices in Budgetary Theory," *Polity* 10 (1978): 488–509.

16 This literature begins with Wildavsky's response to critics of *The Politics of the Budgetary Process*, 1st ed., (Boston: Little, Brown, 1964) who argued that quantitative work was necessary. The highlights for various political units include: Otto A. Davis, M. A. H. Dempster, and Aaron Wildavsky, "Theory of the Budgetary Process," *American Political Science Review* 60 (1966):529–47; Ira Sharkansky, "Agency Requests, Gubernatorial Support, and Budget Success in State Legislatures," *American Political Science Review* 62 (1968):1220–31; John P. Crecine, *Governmental Problem Solving: A Computer Simulation of Municipal Budgeting* (Chicago: Rand McNally, 1969); Peter B. Natchez and Irvin C. Bupp, "Policy and Priority in the Budgetary Process," *American Political Science Review* 67 (1973):951–63; John Wanat, "Bases of Budgetary Incrementalism," *American Political Science Review* 68 (1974):1221–28; Otto A. Davis, M. A. H. Dempster, and Aaron Wildavsky, "Toward a Predictive Theory of the Budgetary Process," *British Journal of Political Science* 4 (1974):1–34; and John F. Padgett, "Bounded Rationality in Budgetary Research," *American Political Science Review* 74 (1980):354–72.

17 Braybrooke and Lindblom, *A Strategy of Decision*, p. 108.

18 Dahl and Lindblom, *Politics, Economics, and Welfare*, 2d ed. (Chicago: University of Chicago Press, 1976), p. xiii.

19 Charles E. Lindblom, "Still Muddling, Not Yet Through," *Public Administration Review* (1979):520.

20 Ibid., p. 521.

21 Ibid. For a more elaborate statement of those positions, see Charles E. Lindblom, *Politics and Markets* (New York: Basic Books, 1977), especially part 4.

22 These arguments have been presented in a number of works. Among the

most often cited are: Peter Bachrach and Morton S. Baratz, "Two Faces of Power," *American Political Science Review* 56 (1962):947–52; Peter Bachrach and Morton S. Baratz, "Decisions and Non-Decisions," *American Political Science Review* 57 (1963):632–42; Jack L. Walker, "A Critique of the Elitist Theory of Democracy," *American Political Science Review* 60 (1966):285–95; E. E. Schattschneider, *The Semi-Sovereign People* (New York: Holt, Rinehart and Winston, 1960); William Connolly (ed.), *The Bias of Pluralism* (New York: Atherton, 1969); Antonio Gramsci, *Prison Notebooks* (London: Lawrence and Wishart, 1971); Lindblom, *Politics and Markets*, and "Another State of Mind," *American Political Science Review* 76 (1980):9–21; Robert A. Dahl, *Dilemmas of Pluralist Democracy* (New Haven: Yale University Press, 1982).

23 Robert A. Dahl, "A Critique of the Ruling-Elite Model," *American Political Science Review* 52 (1961):463–69.

24 The importance placed on checking or controlling leaders is essential to pluralist theory. Domination of decision making by an elite violates the pluralist doctrines of competition and fragmented power. Dahl and Lindblom in *Politics, Economics, and Welfare* argue that the prevention of tyranny by dictatorial leaders is "the number one problem of democracy," (pp. 272–76) and this emphasis has persisted in their later writings, even as other beliefs have changed.

25 Joseph Schumpeter, *Capitalism, Socialism and Democracy* (New York: Harper & Row, 1942), p. 269.

26 Dahl, *A Preface to Democratic Theory*, p. 131.

27 Ibid., pp. 129–30.

28 V. O. Key, Jr., *The Responsible Electorate* (Cambridge: Belknap Press of Harvard University, 1966), pp. 7–8.

29 For excellent reviews and bibliographies of this literature at various stages, see: Richard Brody and Benjamin Page, "The Assessment of Policy Voting," *American Political Science Review* 66 (1972):450–58; Michael Margolis, "From Confusion to Confusion: Issues and the American Voter (1956–1972)," *American Political Science Review* 71 (1977):31–33; and Morris P. Fiorina, *Retrospective Voting in American National Elections* (New Haven: Yale University Press, 1981), chap. 1.

30 The classic article remains Warren Miller and Donald Stokes, "Constituency Influence in Congress," *American Political Science Review* 57 (1963):45–57. For a review of the recent literature, see Barbara Hinckley, "The American Voter in Congressional Elections," *American Political Science Review* 74 (1980):641–50.

31 The classics include Arthur Bentley, *The Process of Government* (Cambridge: Belknap Press of Harvard University Press, 1908); David B. Truman, *The Governmental Process* (New York, Alfred Knopf, 1951); V. O. Key, Jr., *Politics, Parties and Pressure Groups* (New York: Crowell, 1942); Earl Lutham, *The Group Basis of Politics* (Ithaca, N.Y.: Cornell University Press, 1952); and Lester Milbrath, *The Washington Lobbyists* (Chicago: Rand McNally, 1963).

32 This literature begins with Angus Campbell et al., *The American Voter*

(New York: John Wiley & Sons, 1964). The controversy was ignited by Philip E. Converse, "The Nature of Belief Systems in Mass Publics," in David E. Apter (ed.), *Ideology and Discontent* (Glencoe: Free Press, 1964). For recent critiques and a reexamination, see W. Lance Bennett, *The Political Mind and the Political Environment* (Lexington, Mass.: Lexington Books, 1975); and Christopher H. Achen, "Mass Political Attitudes and the Survey Response," *American Political Science Review* 69 (1975): 1218–31.

33 Dahl, *A Preface to Democratic Theory*, chap. 4.

34 This insight is Barbara Hinckley's; see *Congressional Elections* (Washington, D.C.: Congressional Quarterly, 1981), especially pp. 8–14.

35 Richard Spohn and Charles McCollum (The Ralph Nader Congress Project), *The Revenue Committees* (New York: Grossman, 1975).

36 The major exception is the innovative work of Theodore Lowi, particularly *The End of Liberalism* (New York: W. W. Norton, 1969). James Q. Wilson, "Problems in the Study of Urban Politics," challenges the relationship between political structure and policy outcomes. Another work discussing decision theory that emphasizes outcomes is Frank S. Levy, Arnold J. Meltsner, and Aaron Wildavsky, *Urban Outcomes* (Berkeley: University of California Press, 1974).

Chapter 2

1 The best is Harold Groves, *Tax Philosophers* (Madison: University of Wisconsin Press, 1970).

2 Income tax systems that only require filing are voluntary; those in which withholding is used are involuntary. Current discussions of an expenditure tax revolve around a prepayment plan that would tax returns on savings rather than allowing deductions of assets as purchased. See Department of the Treasury, *Blueprints for Basic Tax Reform* (Washington, D.C.: Government Printing Office, 1977), and David F. Bradford, "The Possibilities for an Expenditure Tax," *National Tax Journal* 35 (1982): 243–51.

3 See Richard A. Musgrave, *The Theory of Public Finance* (New York: McGraw–Hill, 1959).

4 The most popular description of this conflict is Arthur Okun, *Equality and Efficiency*. More complicated theories will be discussed later in this chapter.

5 The reverse argument—that the wealthy benefit disproportionately from national defense, government subsidies to industry, and the protection of property in general—can also be made.

6 The principal argument for an expenditure tax is that investment and economic growth are enhanced by lower taxation of returns on assets.

7 The rest of this section is based in part on John F. Witte, "Tax Philosophy and Income Distribution," in Robert P. Solo and Charles W. Anderson (eds.), *Value Judgement and Income Distribution* (New York: Praeger, 1981), pp. 340–79.

8 The pivotal works in this critique are Vilfred Pareto, *Manual of Political Economy*, translated by Ann S. Schweir and edited by Ann S. Schweir and Alfred N. Page (New York: Augustus Kelley, 1971), and Lionel Robbins, "Interpersonal Comparisons of Utility," *Economic Journal* 48 (1938): 634–41.

9 These definitions can also be stated in mathematical terms. Given a general utility function, $U = f(z)$, utility loss or sacrifice at any income level can be expressed as:

$$S = z \cdot t \cdot f'(z),$$

where S is sacrifice, z is income, t is the average tax rate at income z ($0 \le t \le 1$), and $f'(z)$ is the rate of change of utility with respect to income at income level z.

Assuming that C and K are constants, *equal sacrifice* is that tax rate for which $S = C$ for all taxpayers; *proportional sacrifice* is that tax rate for which $s = K \cdot f(z)$ for all taxpayers; and *minimal sacrifice* is that tax rate which minimizes

$$\sum_{i=1}^{n} S_i$$

for n taxpayers.

10 Using the notation and definitions of n. 9:

$$U = f(z) = \log(z)$$

$$f'(z) = \frac{1}{z}$$

Therefore, *equal sacrifice* is:

$$t \cdot z \cdot \frac{1}{z} = c$$

or $t = c$, which is a constant rate.

And *proportional sacrifice* is:

$$t \cdot z \cdot \frac{1}{z} = K \cdot \log(z)$$

$$t = K \cdot \log(z), \text{ which is a progressive rate.}$$

See Arnold Jacob Cohen-Stuart, *A Contribution to the Theory of the Progressive Income Tax*, translated by Johan C. TeVelde (Chicago: University of Chicago Libraries, 1936), pp. 53–60 (originally published in 1889).

11 Using the notation and definitions of n. 9:

$$U = f(z) = \sqrt{z}$$

$$f'(z) = \frac{1}{2} z^{-1/2}$$

Equal sacrifice is:

$$t \cdot z \cdot \left(\frac{1}{2} \cdot z^{-1/2} \right) = C$$

$$t \cdot \frac{z^{1/2}}{2} = C$$

$$t = \frac{2C}{z^{1/2}},$$

which is regressive. *Proportional sacrifice* is:

$$t \cdot z \cdot \left(\frac{1}{2} \cdot z^{-1/2} \right) = K \cdot z^{1/2}$$

$$t \cdot \frac{z^{1/2}}{2} = K \cdot z^{1/2}$$

$$t = 2K,$$

which is a constant rate. See F. Y. Edgeworth, "Minimum Sacrifice Versus Equal Sacrifice," in his *Papers Relating to Political Economy* (London: Macmillan, 1925), pp. 239–40 (originally published in 1910).

12 Walter J. Blum and Harry Kalven, Jr., *The Uneasy Case for Progressive Taxation* (Chicago: University of Chicago Press, 1952), p. 63.

13 Groves, *Tax Philosophers*, pp. 55–58; Henry Simons, *Personal Income Taxation: The Definition of Income as a Problem of Fiscal Policy* (Chicago: University of Chicago Press, 1938), pp. 5–15.

14 T. N. Carver, "The Ethical Basis of Distribution and Its Application to Taxation," in *Annals of the American Academy of Political and Social Sciences* 6 (1895): 95.

15 F. Y. Edgeworth, "The Pure Theory of Taxation," in his *Papers Relating to Political Economy*, p. 110.

16 Ibid., p. 112.

17 For a classic example of such a confrontation, see F. Y. Edgeworth, "Formulae for Graduating Taxation," in *Papers Relating to Political Economy*, pp. 260–70.

18 This was a specific complaint of Carver, who expressed concern that taxes would approach or even exceed 100 percent. See Carver, "The Ethical Basis of Distribution and Its Application to Taxation."

19 Ibid., p. 95.

20 This analysis is based on A. B. Atkinson, "How Progressive Should Income Tax Be?" in Michael Parkin and A. R. Nobay (eds.), *Essays in Modern Economics* (London: Longman, 1973), pp. 90–109. Assuming that ability is a continuous rather than a discrete variable, Atkinson specifies welfare in integral form as:

$$W = \int_0^\infty U_n \left[Z(n) - T(n) \right] f(n) \, d(n).$$

21 J. A. Mirrlees, "An Exploration in the Theory of Optimum Income Taxation," *Review of Economic Studies* 38 (1971): 175–208. For simplicity I
have translated Mirrlees' continuous notation into discrete form.
22 Ibid., p. 186.
23 The reader is reminded that utility is a function of after-tax income, x, and
hours worked for each ability or wage level. The expression $x^a(1-y)$ is thus
composed of income after taxes and leisure $(1-y)$. The full expression,
which is solved for $T(n)$, is:

$$U_n = \log_e [(n \cdot y(n) - T[z(n)])^a (1-y)].$$

By increasing a, income is valued over leisure.
24 R. C. Fair, "The Optimal Distribution of Income," *Quarterly Journal of
Economics* 85 (1971): 551–79.
25 Atkinson, "How Progressive Should Income Tax Be?"
26 For example, Atkinson, following a "suggestion" by Gary Becker, assumes
simply that after-tax income, $z(n, E) = nE^2$, where n is the wage rate index
of ability used before and E is years of education. He admits both the
specialized nature of his model and the simplicity of the assumption. Ibid.
27 Martin Feldstein, "On the Optimal Progressivity of the Income Tax," *Journal of Public Economics* 3 (1973): 56–75.
28 A. B. Atkinson, "On the Measurement of Inequality," *Journal of Economic
Theory* 2 (1970): 244–63. A simple numerical example illustrates these
relationships. Given two classes in society, the marginal utility improvement of the higher class can be expressed as $(U_2 - U_1)/U_1$. The following
table shows how that ratio increases as p is increased and how the marginal
utility drops to almost nothing as p approaches 0.

	Untransformed $(p = 1)$	$p = 2$	$p = 0.5$	$p = 0.01$
U_1	9.00	4.05	6.00	102.200
U_2	16.00	12.80	8.00	102.800
$(U_2 - U_1)/U_1$	0.77	2.16	0.33	0.006

29 Atkinson, "How Progressive Should Income Tax Be?" p. 94.
30 Ibid., p. 107.
31 Ibid.; see also Feldstein, "On the Optimal Progressivity of the Income Tax,"
and Harvey S. Rosen, "A Methodology for Evaluating Tax Reform Proposals," *Journal of Public Economics* 6 (1976): 105–21.
32 See Martin W. Feldstein, "On the Theory of Tax Reform," *Journal of Public
Economics* 6 (1976): 77–104, and Richard A. Musgrave, "ET, OT and SBT,"
Journal of Public Economics 6 (1976): 3–16. The same point is
made by Boris Bittker, "Equity, Efficiency, and Income Tax Theory: Do
Misallocations Drive Out Inequities?" *San Diego Law Review* 16 (1979):
735–48.
33 For example, Atkinson concluded his article with this comment: "The value

of a model such as that discussed in this paper does not lie in the precise solutions obtained. It should indeed be obvious that the specification of the model is inadequate to provide any detailed prescriptions as to what the rate of income tax should be." "How Progressive Should the Income Tax Be?" p. 108.

34 As Feldstein puts it: "The current paper illustrates a common dilemma in economic analysis. Examining an economic question with a more general model often yields new insights but also raises doubts about the conclusion that had been obtained by simpler models. Moreover the greater generality of the model, the more difficult it is to obtain results that are both specific and unambiguous." "On the Optimal Progressivity of the Income Tax," p. 75.

35 Jerry A. Hausman, "Labor Supply," in Henry J. Aaron and Joseph A. Pechman (eds.), *How Taxes Affect Economic Behavior* (Washington, D.C.: Brookings Institution, 1981), pp. 27–84.

36 Gary Burtless, "Comment," in Aaron and Pechman, *How Taxes Affect Economic Behavior*, pp. 81–82.

37 The classic studies are George F. Break, "Income Taxes and Incentive to Work: An Empirical Study," *American Economic Review* 47 (1957): 529–48; Thomas H. Sanders, *Effects of Taxation on Executives* (Cambridge: Harvard University Graduate School of Business, 1951); Robin Barrows, Harvey C. Brazer, and James N. Morgan, *Economic Behavior of the Affluent* (Washington, D.C.: Brookings Institution, 1966); and Sidney E. Rolf and Geoffrey Furniss, "The Impact of Changes in the Tax Rates and Method of Collection on Effort: Some Empirical Observations," *Review of Economics and Statistics* 39 (1957): 394–401.

38 Glen G. Cain and Harold W. Watts (eds.), *Income Maintenance and Labor Supply* (New York: Rand McNally, 1973).

39 Michael Boskin makes this point in his "Comments" on the paper in Aaron and Pechman, *How Taxes Affect Economic Behavior*, pp. 72–75. Note that the "taste" variable is likely to be affected by a number of other variables in the system (job type, career path, education, etc.). Thus, there is an empirical question whether such a completely independent factor really exists and a larger question concerning the range of the distribution. Since Hausman's results are affected by extremes of the distribution on this variable, the latter issue is critical.

40 Ibid., p. 75.

41 See Fair, "Optimal Distribution of Income"; Gary S. Becker, *Human Capital* (New York: Columbia University Press, 1964).

42 Edward F Denison, "The Contribution of Capital to the Postwar Growth of Industrial Countries," in *U.S. Economic Growth from 1978 to 1986: Prospects, Problems and Patterns, Vol. 3: Capital*, Committee Print, Joint Economic Committee, 94th Cong., 2d sess. (Washington, D.C.: Government Printing Office, 1976), provides a review and update of his earlier work.

43 Paul A. David and John L. Scadding, "Private Savings: Ultrarationality,

Aggregation, and 'Denison's Law,'" *Journal of Political Economy*, 82 (1974): 225–49.

44 George M. von Furstenberg, "Saving," in Aaron and Pechman, *How Taxes Affect Economic Behavior*, p. 328.

45 Lester Thurow, *The Impact of Taxes on the American Economy* (New York: Praeger, 1971), p. 26.

46 Arnold Harberger, "Discussion," in Gary Fromm (ed.), *Tax Incentives and Capital Spending* (Washington, D.C.: Brookings Institution, 1971), p. 256.

47 In Aaron and Pechman, *How Taxes Affect Economic Behavior*, p. 129.

48 See Patric H. Hendershott and Sheng-Cheng Hu, "Investment in Producers' Equipment," in Aaron and Pechman, *How Taxes Affect Economic Behavior*, p. 85.

49 Rosen's work (see n. 31 above) is an exception. An interesting analysis of this trend is found in Bittker, "Equity, Efficiency, and Income Tax Theory."

Chapter 3

1 Simons, *Personal Income Taxation*.

2 Numerous "reform" studies have been written with Simons' notion of the comprehensive tax base as the central element. See, e.g., *Tax Revision Compendium of Papers Broadening the Tax Base*, Committee Print, House Ways and Means, 86th Cong., 1st sess. (Washington, D.C.: Government Printing Office, 1959); *Fiscal Policy Issues of the Coming Decade*, Committee Print, Joint Economic Committee, 89th Cong., 1st sess. (Washington, D.C.: Government Printing Office, 1965); *House Ways and Means and Senate Committee on Finance, Tax Reform Studies and Proposals, Part 1* (Washington, D.C.: Department of the Treasury, 1969); and Department of the Treasury, *Blueprints for Basic Tax Reform*.

3 Surrey was instrumental in preparing the 1965 and 1969 reports cited in n. 2. His own views, closely aligned with Simons', appear in his *Pathways to Basic Tax Reform* (Cambridge: Harvard University Press, 1973). Norman Ture deviates from Simons in one critical respect: he would exclude from taxable income either earnings from or income put into savings. However, he writes of his proposed expenditure tax that it "would eliminate the sources of many of the so-called horizontal equity problems in the present law. Apart from [certain] possible exceptions, . . . the tax base would be substantially broader than under present law with far fewer specific or differential provisions reducing the amount of income subject to tax." See Norman B. Ture, "Taxation and the Distribution of Income," in Arlene A. Leibowitz (ed.), *Wealth Redistribution and the Income Tax* (Lexington, Mass.: D. C. Heath, 1977), p. 36.

4 Simons, *Personal Income Taxation*, p. 13.

5 The author of the "modern" faculty tax theory (faculty taxes were originally used in colonial America) was E. R. A. Seligman. Writing in 1894, he argued

for progressive taxes based on the proposition that productive capacity increased at a greater rate than income. In a celebrated passage he argued: "The facility of increasing production often grows in more than arithmetical proportion. A rich man may be said to be subject in some sense to the law of increasing returns. The more he has the easier it is for him to acquire still more." By this reasoning, casually accepted by many others since, more income means greater ability to pay. See E. R. A. Seligman, *Progressive Taxation in Theory and Practice* (Baltimore: Guggenheimer, Weil, 1894), p. 191. Simons dismissed Seligman's theory in one sentence as "totally ambiguous." For added analysis see Groves, *Tax Philosophers*, chap. 4, and Witte, "Tax Philosophy and Income Distribution."

6 Simons, *Personal Income Taxation*, p. 17.

7 Ibid., pp. 18–19.

8 Ibid., p. 50.

9 Imputed rental value is income in kind derived as a benefit from home investment. The theory is that the benefit from such an investment should be counted as income whether received from a tenant or "paid" to oneself.

10 Unrealized capital gains are the changes in the value of capital assets that accrue in a specific time period, whether the assets are sold or not. Taxation of undistributed, or retained, corporate profits was a particularly volatile issue in 1938 because two years earlier, at Roosevelt's urging, a law had been passed to tax such profits. It was never implemented extensively, and it was repealed in the year Simons' book appeared.

11 Simons, *Personal Income Taxation*, p. 205.

12 Musgrave writes, for example: "The defense for the accretion plus consumption concept as an index of equality must rest on its superiority as an equity concept, not as a tool of economics. . . . We conclude that the accretion plus consumption concept of income is the superior measure of tax paying ability, once the income (as distinct from consumption) view has been chosen." "In Defense of an Income Concept," 81 *Harvard Law Review* 44 (1967): 66–67. Goode, also adopting a comprehensive tax base approach, similarly supports the notion of ability to pay as the basis of an equitable tax system and slips easily back and forth between "ability to pay" and "power to consume." See Richard Goode, "The Superiority of the Income Tax," in Joseph A. Pechman (ed.), *What Should Be Taxed: Income or Expenditure?* (Washington, D.C.: Brookings Institution, 1980), pp. 51–53.

13 Simons, *Personal Income Taxation*, p. 205.

14 Ibid., pp. 19–31. This position was in stark contrast to a rival theory promoted by Irving Fisher. Fisher proposed a spending or consumption tax. As with current proposals for "expenditure taxes," Fisher's tax was to be levied on income minus savings. See Irving Fisher, "The Spending Tax," *Bulletin of the National Tax Association* 7 (Oct. 1921): 18–20, and "Income Tax in Theory and Income Tax in Practice," *Econometrica* 5 (January 1937): 1–55.

15 Seligman, *Progressive Taxation in Theory and Practice*.

16 See Jack Nagel, *The Descriptive Analysis of Power* (New Haven: Yale

University Press, 1975), for an excellent summary and constructive definition of power as a causal relationship between preferences and outcomes.

17 Simons, *Personal Income Taxation*, p. 197.

18 Musgrave, "In Defense of an Income Concept," p. 56.

19 Joseph A. Pechman, "Comprehensive Income Taxation: A Comment," 81 *Harvard Law Review* 63 (1967): 66. Pechman is commenting on Boris I. Bittker, "A 'Comprehensive Tax Base' as a Goal of Income Tax Reform," 80 *Harvard Law Review* 925 (1967).

20 Goode, "The Superiority of the Income Tax," p. 51.

21 Simons, *Personal Income Taxation*, pp. 138–39.

22 See, e.g., William M. Goldstein, "The Case for a Tax on Gross Income," *National Tax Journal* 30 (1977): 226; and Harvey E. Brazer, "The Income Tax in the Federal Revenue System," in Richard A. Musgrave (ed.), *Broad Base Taxes: New Options and Sources* (Baltimore: Johns Hopkins University Press, 1973), p. 7.

23 Simons, *Personal Income Taxation*, pp. 19–31.

24 Pechman, "Comprehensive Income Taxation: A Comment," p. 63.

25 Although it might seem easy to compare the costs of raising a dollar of revenue under an income tax, sales tax, property tax, and so on, it is not. A large number of factors—economic, organizational, and political—make such comparisons difficult even within a single state. In addition, there are a range of possible forms for each type of tax, and these forms also affect compliance.

26 The investment tax credit, begun in 1962, allows a credit against taxes for individuals and corporations that invest in new plants and equipment. The asset depreciation range provision allows taxpayers, primarily corporations, to vary depreciation times set for specific asset categories. Tax credit leasing arrangements, permitted under the 1981 tax bill, allow profitless companies that pay no taxes in a given year, and thus cannot benefit from investment credits and depreciation, to sell their credits to profitable corporations. Complex leasing arrangements for capital assets are used to accomplish this. One wonders what language Henry Simons would have used to describe such a provision.

27 In Charles O. Galvin and Boris I. Bittker, *The Income Tax: How Progressive Should It Be?* (Washington, D.C.: American Enterprise Institute, 1969), pp. 61–70.

28 Ibid., pp. 2–3.

29 Philip M. Stern, *The Great Treasury Raid* (New York: Random House, 1964), and *The Rape of the Taxpayer: Why You Pay More While the Rich Pay Less* (New York: Random House, 1974).

30 The list comes from Simons, *Personal Income Taxation*, pp. 210–20.

31 Capital gains that are passed on as inheritance were not in 1938, and still are not today, taxed on total profits from the time originally acquired. Rather, the base for the new owner is the value at the time of death.

Chapter 4

1 This section relies heavily on Sidney Ratner, *Taxation and Democracy in America* (New York: John Wiley & Sons, 1942), chap. 5; Randolph E. Paul, *Taxation in the United States* (Boston: Little, Brown, 1954), pp. 4–29; Roy G. Blakey and Gladys C. Blakey, *The Federal Income Tax* (New York: Longmans, Green, 1940), 2–8; E. R. A. Seligman, *The Income Tax* (New York: Macmillan, 1911), pp. 430–81; David R. Dewey, *Financial History of the United States* (New York: Longmans, Green, 1934), pp. 262–330; and Joseph A. Hill, "The Civil War Income Tax," *Quarterly Journal of Economics* 8 (1894): 416–52.

2 Primitive income taxes existed earlier in the states, beginning with the "faculty" taxes levied on income from professions, trades, handicrafts, and businesses during the colonial period. In the 1840s six states, needing revenue after Jackson and Van Buren had withdrawn federal funds from internal improvement projects, created income taxes. These taxes on salaries and professional income, and in some cases interest and profit, were modest and, because the low rates and the overwhelming proportion of farmers in the population, never accounted for much revenue. They disappeared during the Civil War. See Ratner, *Taxation and Democracy in America*, pp. 51–55; Seligman, *The Income Tax*, pp. 367–98.

3 Ratner, *Taxation and Democracy in America*, p. 72.

4 *Congressional Globe*, 38th Cong. 1st sess., p. 1940. Quoted in part in Ratner *Taxation and Democracy in America*, p. 84.

5 Ratner, *Taxation and Democracy in America*, p. 131.

6 The Populists won only 9 percent of the presidential vote in 1892, but it was believed that Populist sentiment was much more widespread and that votes in critical southern states went to the Democrats only because they made an issue of their staunch support for segregation and the economic structure that had developed during Reconstruction.

7 See Paul, *Taxation in the United States*, pp. 32–39; Ratner, *Taxation and Democracy in America*, pp. 174–84; Blakey and Blakey, *The Federal Income Tax*, pp. 12–17; and Edward Stanwood, *American Tariff Controversies in the Nineteenth Century*, 2 vols. (Boston and New York: Houghton, Mifflin, 1903), 2: 296–359.

8 *Congressional Record*, 53rd Cong., 2d sess., vol. 26 (1894): 3557–68. See also a later speech by Hill on June 21, 1894, recorded on pp. 6611–24 of the same volume.

9 Ibid., p. 6711.

10 Ibid., pp. 6706–16.

11 Cochran's speech was resubmitted for publication in the *Congressional Record*, a common practice today, but unusual in 1894. It appears in vol. 26, Appendix, pp. 462–67.

12 Ibid., p. 1656.

13 Ibid., p. 1658.

14 The key cases were filed in New York federal court in January 1895. One

was *Hyde* v. *Continental Trust Company*, and the other, more important case was *Pollock* v. *Farmer's Loan and Trust Company*, 157 U.S. 429c (1895).

15 *Congressional Record* 61st Cong., 1st sess., vol. 44 (1909): 4400.

16 The vote in the House on July 12, 1909 was 318 to 14, with 55 not voting. *Congressional Record*, 61st Cong, 1st sess., vol. 44 (1909): 4400. In the Senate the vote was 77 to 0. Ibid., p. 421.

17 Ratification by the states is analyzed by Paul, *Taxation in the United States*, pp. 68–70. See specifically p. 69, table 6.

18 Ratner has an excellent brief description of those studies and their effects. See Ratner, *Taxation and Democracy in America*, pp. 303–14.

19 Ray S. Baker and William E. Dodd, *Public Papers of Woodrow Wilson*, 6 vols. (New York: Harper and Brothers, 1925), 3:1–6.

20 *Congressional Record*, 63d Cong., 1st sess., vol. 50 (1913): 1246.

21 Ibid., p. 3840.

22 The law was based on the 1894 statute but also reflected some features of the British income tax passed in 1910 under Lloyd George and the state income tax passed by Wisconsin in 1909.

23 Detailed analysis of the income tax during World War I can be found in Charles Gilbert, *American Financing of World War I* (Westport, Conn.: Greenwood Press, 1970), and Jerry Waltman, *The Evolution of the Income Tax: A Public Law Perspective* (forthcoming), chap. 2.

24 *Congressional Record*, 64th Cong., 1st sess., vol. 53 (1916): 10514.

25 Longworth's reply is in the same volume, pp. 10529–31.

26 See Waltman, *The Evolution of the Income Tax*, pp. 46, 49–50.

27 Quoted in Blakey and Blakey, *The Federal Income Tax*, p. 123.

28 The vote was 211 to 196, with Republicans unanimously opposed (0 to 188) and Democrats favoring the bill 210 to 4. *Congressional Record*, 64th Cong., 2d sess., vol. 54 (1917): 2440–42.

29 The recommittal vote was defeated 28 to 51, and the bill was passed 47 to 33. On both votes there were only 2 Republican defections. Ibid., p. 4524.

30 *Congressional Record*, 65th Cong., 1st sess., vol. 55 (1917): 2045.

31 See Gilbert, *American Financing of World War I*, p. 87.

32 Ibid., pp. 83–99; Waltman, *The Evolution of the Income Tax*, pp. 158–75; Ratner, *Taxation and Democracy in America*, pp. 372–93; and Blakey and Blakey, *The Federal Income Tax*, chap. 6.

33 See Gilbert, *American Financing of World War I*, for details concerning the revenue effects of various changes in the law.

34 Ibid., pp. 98 and 114.

35 Ibid., pp. 114–15.

Chapter 5

1 The most complete treatment of taxation between 1920 and 1932 is in Blakey and Blakey, *The Federal Income Tax*, chaps. 8–12.

2 All quoted in Andrew Mellon, *Taxation: The People's Business* (New York: Macmillan, 1924), pp. 123, 129.

3 Ibid., p. 12.

4 Ibid., p. 16.

5 Ibid., pp. 56–57.

6 Blakey and Blakey, *The Federal Income Tax*, p. 218.

7 Quoted in Mellon, *Taxation*, pp. 85–86. Adams expanded this argument in a famous article entitled "Should the Excess Profits Tax Be Repealed?" *Quarterly Journal of Economics* 35 (1921): 363–93.

8 *Congressional Record*, 67th Cong., 1st sess., vol. 67 (1921): 563.

9 What Mellon meant by "earned" income is not perfectly clear, although he meant to exclude interest, dividends, and capital gains. Rather than define it precisely, Congress simply opted to exclude the first $5,000 of taxable income as long as total taxable income was not over $10,000. Thus, the provision ended up as a low-income credit rather than a preference for a type of income, as Mellon had desired.

10 The *New York Times* reported that the Garner bill would have meant a revenue loss of $559 million, compared with a reduction of $341 million provided in the Ways and Means bill. The Longworth plan was a compromise; its estimated reduction was $446 million. See Blakey and Blakey, *The Federal Income Tax*, p. 237.

11 An estate tax is levied on inheritance. The gift tax made it impossible to avoid the estate tax by transfering property prior to death.

12 Noted in Ratner, *Taxation and Democracy in America*, p. 424.

13 Since state inheritance taxes had been higher than the federal estate tax, raising the credit greatly reduced federal estate tax revenue. This lasted until the Roosevelt administration reversed the policy once again. An excellent analysis of these effects is in Blakey and Blakey, *The Federal Income Tax*, pp. 272–74.

14 The problem of taxing mineral industries is complicated by the argument that investment in mineral property is similar to investment in equipment or plants by other industries. Plant and equipment expenditures cannot be subtracted from net income because they are assets of a company. However, as they wear out or depreciate, a percentage of the original value is deductible from income. Initially, the parallel for minerals was accomplished by establishing the worth of the property on discovery (or, later, worth as of 1913) and then depreciating this amount relative to expected income or the "depletion" of the asset. This procedure proved unworkable because of the difficulty of assessing worth on discovery, and so it was decided instead to allow a deduction based on a percentage of the value of the minerals extracted during the tax year.

15 *The Annual Report of the Secretary of the Treasury of the United States for the Fiscal Year Ending June 30, 1928* (Washington, D.C.: Government Printing Office, 1928), p. 23.

16 *The Annual Report of the Secretary of the Treasury of the United States for*

the Fiscal Year Ending June 30, 1931 (Washington, D.C.: Government Printing Office, 1931), pp. 28–29.

17 A 25 percent *deduction* of earned income would allow $1,250 of the first $5,000 to be excluded from taxable income. A *credit* would allow 25 percent of taxes due to be subtracted from the total taxes due. The deduction would be more beneficial only for those paying a marginal rate greater than 25 percent. Because of the prevailing rates and the ceiling on the use of the earned income provision ($20,000), no one was in this category; thus, switching to the deduction would increase revenues.

18 *Congressional Record*, 72d Cong., 1st sess., vol. 75 (1932): 6816.

19 Ibid., p. 7329.

20 See Blakey and Blakey, *The Federal Income Tax*, for a discussion of this debate.

21 This included Senators Borah, Norris, Couzens, and Robert La Follette, Jr., who had replaced his father as the Senate's most radical member where tax policy was concerned.

22 John Morton Blum, *From the Morgenthau Diaries: Years of Crisis, 1928–1938* (Boston: Houghton Mifflin, 1959), p. 301.

23 *Congressional Record*, 74th Cong., 1st sess., vol. 79 (1935): 9659.

24 In Blum, *From the Morgenthau Diaries: Years of Crisis, 1928–1938*, p. 303.

25 The House bill proposed only token graduation, from 13.5 to 14.5 percent. The administration had requested a graduated tax from 10.75 to 16.75 percent.

26 Paul, *Taxation in the United States*, p. 195.

27 Democrats favored the bill 263 to 11, and Republicans opposed it 4 to 82. *Congressional Record*, 74th Cong., 2d sess., vol. 80 (1936): 6367.

28 Quoted in Blum, *From the Morgenthau Diaries: Years of Crisis, 1928–1938*, p. 317.

29 In the campaign Landon repeatedly attacked the bill as "the most cockeyed piece of tax legislation ever imposed in a modern country." Morgenthau defended the legislation in a major speech just before the election. He argued that the administration bill was based "upon the democratic principle of ability to pay . . . we lowered the effective rates of taxation on small individual incomes and on small corporation incomes, but we raised and made more fully effective the rates of income taxes on those best able to pay." Landon's comment is quoted in Paul, *Taxation in the United States*, p. 192; Morgenthau's in Blum, *From the Morgenthau Diaries: Years of Crisis, 1928–1938*, p. 320.

30 Reported in Paul, *Taxation in the United States*, p. 203. Paul was the highest ranking tax expert in the Department of the Treasury during this period.

31 Blakey and Blakey, *The Federal Income Tax*, p. 444.

32 *Congressional Record*, 75th Cong., 3d sess., vol. 83 (1938): 5183.

Chapter 6

1 *Congressional Record,* 76th Cong., 3d sess., vol. 86: 8021–22.
2 Quoted in Paul, *Taxation in the United States,* p. 263.
3 *Congressional Record,* 76th Cong., 3d sess., vol. 86: 12172.
4 The Treasury objection was primarily that those industries with base period profits as high as 30 to 50 percent above average could still escape paying excess profits tax. The objections are stated in Paul, *Taxation in the United States,* pp. 270–72.
5 "Hearings before the Committee on Ways and Means," 77th Cong., 1st sess., April 24, 1941 (Washington, D.C.: Government Printing Office, 1941), p. 3.
6 This is Paul's assessment. See *Taxation in the United States,* p. 272.
7 That debate, which occurred intermittently in July 1941, is summarized by Paul. Ibid., pp. 274–76.
8 This second reduction reduced the joint exemption from $2,500 in the prewar period, but dropped the single exemption only from $1,000.
9 *Congressional Record,* 77th Cong., 1st sess., vol. 87: 7280–88.
10 Ibid., p. 7377.
11 Details of these proposals are given in Blum, *From the Morgenthau Diaries,* 3: 35–36; Paul, *Taxation in the United States,* pp. 296–99; and *The Annual Report of the Secretary of the Treasury for the Fiscal Year Ending June 30, 1942* (Washington, D.C.: Government Printing Office, 1942).
12 This administration debate is described in Blum, *From the Morgenthau Diaries,* 3: 41–42.
13 Paul, *Taxation in the United States,* p. 299.
14 *Congressional Record,* 78th Cong., 1st sess., vol. 88: 3723.
15 This incident is described in Blum, *From the Morgenthau Diaries,* 3: 45–48; Paul, *Taxation in the United States,* pp. 291–94; and Roy Blough, *The Federal Taxing Process* (New York: Prentice-Hall, 1952), p. 415. Blough worked with Paul in Treasury to produce the proposal.
16 Paul, *Taxation in the United States,* p. 318.
17 Quoted in Blum, *From the Morgenthau Diaries,* 3: 51.
18 Paul, *Taxation in the United States,* pp. 333–34. The quotation is from Paul's testimony at hearings before the Ways and Means Committee on February 2, 1943. See "Hearings before the Committee on Ways and Means on Revenue and Revision of 1943," 78th Cong., 1st sess. (Washington, D.C.: Government Printing Office, 1943).
19 President of the United States, *Budget Message for the Fiscal Year Ending June 30, 1944* (Washington, D.C.: Government Printing Office, 1944).
20 *Congressional Record,* 78th Cong., 1st sess., vol. 89: 4448.
21 This incident and the resulting bill are described in Blum, *From the Morgenthau Diaries,* 3: 71–72.
22 See Paul, *Taxation in the United States,* p. 356.
23 The text of the president's veto message is reprinted in *The Annual Report*

of the Secretary of the Treasury for the Fiscal Year Ending June 30, 1944, also in the *Congressional Record,* 78th Cong., 2d sess., vol. 90: 1958–59.

24 Quoted in the *New York Times,* February 26, 1944.

25 Only 88 Democrats and 5 Republicans in the House supported the president. In the Senate, 1 Republican and 13 Democrats voted against override. See *Congressional Record,* 78th Cong., 2d sess., vol. 90: 2013 and 2050.

26 Edward D. Allen, "Treasury Tax Policies in 1943," *American Economic Review* 34 (1944): 718.

27 Paul, *Taxation in the United States,* p. 381.

28 See Joseph A. Pechman and Benjamin A. Okner, *Who Bears the Tax Burden?* (Washington, D.C.: Brookings Institution, 1974), for a discussion of this problem and a solution.

29 Richard A. Musgrave and Tun Thin, "Income Tax Progression, 1929–48," *Journal of Political Economy* 56 (1948): 498–514.

Chapter 7

1 Quoted in the *New York Times,* August 12, 1946, in a report of a Knutson address given on August 11.

2 *Congressional Record* 93: 2726.

3 Quoted in Paul, *Taxation in the United States,* p. 456.

4 Text of speech quoted in the *New York Times,* August 1, 1947.

5 Calculations in A. E. Holmans, *United States Fiscal Policy 1945–1949: Its Contribution to Economic Stability* (London: Oxford University Press, 1961), p. 72.

6 The vote to recommit was rejected 197 to 237, with only 4 Democrats voting against the motion and 2 Republicans for it. However, more Democrats (40, of whom 32 were southern) switched on final passage, while the Republicans held their ground.

7 A detailed analysis of these votes compared with the later vote to override the president's veto is contained in Holmans, *United States Fiscal Policy,* p. 79.

8 The text of the veto message is contained in *The Annual Report of the Secretary of the Treasury for the Fiscal Year Ending June 30, 1947* (Washington, D.C.: Government Printing Office, 1947), pp. 244–46, and in the *Congressional Record,* 80th Cong., 1st sess., vol. 93: 7277–78.

9 Descriptions of these events are included in Holmans, *United States Fiscal Policy,* pp. 79–82, and Paul, *Taxation in the United States,* pp. 473–78.

10 Ways and Means report on H.R. 4790. *House Report No. 12-74,* 80th Cong., 2d sess., 1948.

11 *Congressional Record,* 82d Cong., 1st sess., vol. 97: 11731.

12 Holmans, *United States Fiscal Policy,* p. 95.

13 Tax reduction was a plank in the Republican platform in 1948 and was prominently featured in many Republican campaigns.

14 The Keynesian influence in Treasury is discussed in Paul, *Taxation in the United States*, pp. 516–21, and in Holmans, *United States Fiscal Policy*, pp. 110–19, 196–97.

15 It turned out that business activities and personal income were being sheltered under the tax-exempt cloak of charitable organizations. One common device was to transfer corporate land, buildings, and other assets to tax-exempt organizations, which would then lease them back to corporations at a favorable rate. A similar situation arose involving foundations that lent money to or purchased assets from family members or donors at favorable rates.

16 Republicans voted 21 to 9 for the George substitute, while Democrats were split 21 to 27 against it. See *Congressional Record*, 81st Cong., 2d sess., vol. 96: 14060.

17 Ibid., p. 16152.

18 E. Gordon Keith, "The Excess Profits Tax Act of 1950," *National Tax Journal* 5 (1951): 206.

19 The president's message on signing the bill is contained in *The Annual Report of the Secretary of the Treasury for the Fiscal Year Ending June 30, 1951* (Washington, D.C.: Government Printing Office, 1951), p. 439.

20 The message was printed in *Congressional Record*, 78th Cong., 2d sess., vol. 90: 10626–30.

21 *Congressional Record*, 82nd Cong., 1st sess., vol. 97: 6893.

22 Ibid.

23 The estimate was made by Senator Douglas in the course of the debate. See *Congressional Record*, 82d Cong., 1st sess., vol. 97: 11710.

24 Ibid., p. 11720. In the debate, the senator also sarcastically attacked the increasing number of items qualifying for mineral depletion, concentrating his attack on "oyster shells—if oyster shells and clam shells can be included in the bill, then anything can be included. Why not include duck feathers? Or canary birdseed, or dried beetles, or anything?" Ibid., p. 12318.

25 Up to this point special provisions had governed farm cooperatives and mutual savings banks, both of which were ostensibly owned by their members. They differed from other cooperatives and corporations in that retained earnings not paid out as dividends were untaxed. The 1951 act taxed these retained earnings. Not surprisingly, some of the arguments for such taxation came from their competitors. Efforts to remove tax-exempt status from credit unions failed, however, and they have retained it to this day.

26 *The Annual Report of the Secretary of the Treasury for the Fiscal Year Ending June 30, 1951* (Washington, D.C.: Government Printing Office, 1951), p. 491.

27 Holmans, *United States Fiscal Policy*, p. 179.

28 The Republicans held a 221 to 211 majority but had a 15 to 10 vote advantage on Ways and Means.

29 "Hearings before the Committee on Ways and Means on the Excess Profits Tax on Corporations," 81st Cong., 2d sess., June 1, 1953 (Washington, D.C.: Government Printing Office, 1953), pp. 1–6.

30 These proposals are included in *The Annual Report of the Secretary of the Treasury for the Fiscal Year Ending 30 June, 1954* (Washington, D.C.: Government Printing Office, 1954), p. 44, and the *Budget of the United States for the Year Ending June 30, 1955* (Washington, D.C.: Government Printing Office, 1955), pp. 16–23.

31 This process is described in great detail in Eugene N. Feingold, "The Revenue Act of 1954: Policy and Politics" (Ph.D. dissertation, Princeton University, 1954).

32 See *Congressional Quarterly Almanac*, 1954 (Washington, D.C.: Congressional Quarterly, 1955), p. 478.

33 Printed in *The Annual Report of the Secretary of the Treasury for the Fiscal Year Ending 30 June, 1954* (Washington, D.C.: Government Printing Office, 1954), pp. 221–24.

34 See Feingold, "The Revenue Act of 1954," chap. 4, for a detailed description and analysis of these maneuvers. An account of Senate floor actions is contained in *Congressional Record*, 83d Cong., 2d sess., vol. 100: 8999–9030.

35 See Holmans, *United States Fiscal Policy*, p. 238.

36 Testimony of Secretary of the Treasury Humphrey before the Senate Finance Committee. His statement is printed in *The Annual Report of the Secretary of the Treasury for the Fiscal Year Ending 30 June, 1955* (Washington, D.C.: Government Printing Office, 1955), pp. 26–27.

37 Holmans, *United States Fiscal Policy*, p. 299.

38 The text, presented by the president's advisors, is printed in *Congressional Record*, 84th Cong., 2d sess., vol. 102: 137–43.

Chapter 8

1 These figures are from Dillon's testimony, reprinted in "Hearings Before the Committee on Ways and Means on the President's 1961 Tax Recommendations," 87th Cong., 1st sess., May 3, 1961, vol. 1, pp. 21-37.

2 Pages 3–17 ibid. give the text of Kennedy's tax message.

3 Ibid., vols. 1 and 2.

4 A key vote defeated a Republican substitute that would have dropped both the investment credit and withholding of dividends and interest. It was defeated 190 to 225, with all 163 Republicans favoring passage, but only 27 Democrats. Final passage was 219 to 196, with 1 Republican and 34 Democrats voting against their parties. See *Congressional Record*, 87th Cong., 2d sess., vol. 108: 5432.

5 The Senate debate took place between August 25 and September 6, 1962. See *Congressional Record*, 87th Cong., 2d sess., vol. 108, parts 13 and 14. An extensive description is also available in David J. Stern, "Congress, Politics and Taxes: A Case Study of the Revenue Act of 1962" (Ph.D. dissertation, Claremont Graduate School, 1965); and in *Congressional*

Quarterly Almanac, 1962 (Washington D.C.: Congressional Quarterly, 1963), pp. 500–508.

6 Reported in *Congressional Quarterly Almanac,* 1962 (Washington, D.C.: Congressional Quarterly, 1963), p. 479.

7 Reproduced in *Public Papers of the Presidents, John F. Kennedy, 1962* (Washington, D.C.: Government Printing Office, 1963), p. 58.

8 Ibid., p. 457.

9 Ibid., pp. 6111–17.

10 This quotation is in Ron King, "The Supply-Side of the New Frontier: A Study in Presidential Economics," mimeographed, June 1982, p. 22.

11 *Public Papers of the Presidents, John F. Kennedy, 1963,* pp. 57–71.

12 These calculations are based on substantive proposals only. Technical amendments with no revenue effects were excluded. Multiple changes in a complex provision were counted as separate proposals. For example, changes in the exclusion percentage and holding period for long-term capital gains would be counted as two proposals. Partial success scores reflect compromise solutions. A full presentation of these procedures, with success scores for postwar administrations, is contained in John F. Witte, "Congress Versus the President on Tax Policy," in James P. Pfiffner (ed.), *The President and Economic Policy* (Philadelphia: Institute for the Study of Human Issues, 1984).

13 The exact proposal was to establish a 4 percent floor for all medical and casualty deductions and a 5 percent floor for remaining personal deductions (taxes, interest, etc.). Mr. Dillon's testimony and that of many others can be found in "Committee on Ways and Means, Hearings on the President's 1963 Tax Message," 88th Cong., 1st sess., 1963.

14 See John F. Manley, *The Politics of Finance: The House Committee on Ways and Means* (Boston: Little, Brown, 1970), and "Wilbur D. Mills: A Study in Congressional Influence," *American Political Science Review* 62 (1969): 442–64.

15 Mills, quoting President Kennedy for support, listed five problems: wartime tax rates, deficits, unemployment, obsolete equipment and unused plant capacity, and balance of payments. See *Congressional Record,* 88th Cong., 1st sess., vol. 109: 17905–9.

16 The final vote, on September 25, 1963, was 271 to 155. Forty-eight Republicans defected from their opposition position, while 126 held firm. Twenty-nine Democrats voted against the bill, 26 of them from the South. See *Congressional Record,* 88th Cong., 1st sess., vol. 109: 18119.

17 "Hearings Before the Finance Committee on the Revenue Act of 1963," part 1, 88th Cong., 1st sess., October 15, 1963, p. 121.

18 Republicans were split (21 in favor, 10 against), as were Democrats (56 in favor and 11 against). See *Congressional Record,* 88th Cong., 2d sess., vol. 110: 2393.

19 See Joint Committee on Internal Revenue Taxation, *General Explanations of the Revenue Act of 1964* (Washington, D.C.: Government Printing Office, 1964), or *Congressional Quarterly Almanac,* 1964 Washington, D.C.: Congressional Quarterly, 1965), p. 520.

20 His testimony was given before the Joint Economic Committee, 91st Cong., 1st sess., January 17, 1969. His statement is reproduced in *Congressional Record* 115: 2772. There was also a summary and editorial analysis in the *Wall Street Journal*, January 20, 1969.

21 The original administration proposal for this "minimum tax" was to limit tax-exempt income to 50 percent of "total income," which was to be defined as currently included gross income, plus appreciation of property given to charities, the excess of mineral depletion allowances over actual costs, certain farm losses, and excess depreciation on real estate (i.e., the difference between accelerated and straight-line depreciation). The Senate Finance Committee instead adopted the "preference list" approach described on p. 170.

22 The administration proposals are outlined in *The Annual Report of the Secretary of the Treasury for the Fiscal Year Ending 30 June, 1969* (Washington D.C.: Government Printing Office, 1969); the House bill is in Tax Reform Act of 1969, Report of the Committee on Ways and Means to Accompany H.R. 13270, August 2, 1969.

23 In sharp contrast to Mills's introduction of the 1964 act, his primary theme now was that "taxpayers are interested in improving the tax system because they have reason to believe that there are those who are not carrying their fair share of tax burden based upon ability to pay." *Congressional Record*, 91st Cong., 1st sess., vol. 115: 22562.

24 The recommittal vote was supported by 44 Republicans, but opposed by 141. Only 34 of 238 Democrats opposed it. On final passage only 10 Republicans and 20 Democrats objected. See ibid., pp. 22808–9.

25 Ibid., p. 362–63.

26 Joint Committee on Internal Revenue Taxation, *General Explanations of the Tax Reform Act of 1969* (Washington, D.C.: Government Printing Office, 1969).

Chapter 9

1 The ADR proposal established ranges for depreciation periods, thus allowing corporations further choice in how fast assets could be depreciated. DISCs were complex legal entities that were meant to stimulate export sales. Income generated through these international sales office subsidiaries was not taxed until it was distributed to the parent company, which for a portion was never.

2 Joint Economic Committee, *Hearings on the President's New Economic Program*, 92d Congress, 1st sess., August 19, 1971, pp. 3–21.

3 Testimony before the House Ways and Means Committee, September 8, 1971. Quoted in *Congressional Quarterly Almanac*, 1971 (Washington, D.C.: Congressional Quarterly, 1971), p. 435.

4 Ibid.

5 Ibid., p. 436.

6 Joint Committee on Internal Revenue Taxation estimates indicated that Ways and Means increased the tax cut for individuals in FY 1971 and 1972 from the $2.2 billion proposed by the administration to $4.6 billion, while reducing the corporate reductions from $12.8 to $7.6 billion. See Joint Committee on Internal Revenue Taxation, *Summary of the Revenue Act of 1971, As Passed by the House of Representatives*, 92d Cong., 1st sess., October 7, 1971 (Washington, D.C.: Government Printing Office, 1971).

7 The reference is to a book by Kevin R. Phillips, *The Emerging Republican Majority* (New Rochelle, N.Y.: Arlington House, 1969), which was widely cited at the time.

8 *Prepared Statements, Panel Discussion on Tax Reform, Panels I–II*, Committee Print, House Ways and Means, 93d Cong., 1st sess. (Washington, D.C.: Government Printing Office, 1973). Smith's comments are in panel 1, pp. 53–67; Brazer's in panel 2, pp. 1–18; and Musgrave's in panel 2, pp. 19–29.

9 Wilbur Mills's escapades with exotic dancer Fanny Fox, which ended unceremoniously in the Washington Tidal Basin, led to the public disclosure of his alcoholism. He remained in Congress until his defeat in the 1976 primary but resigned as chairman of Ways and Means.

10 The arrangements oil companies made with foreign countries varied widely. In all cases the companies paid the governments fees based on the volume of oil removed. Generally the "royalties" were judged to be taxes paid to foreign governments; hence, they could be credited against U.S. taxes. Church's point was that since the fees were generally high enough to offset nearly all overseas profits, repealing depletion would have no effect unless changes were also made in the treatment of royalties.

11 The 1974 elections produced Democratic majorities of 291 to 144 in the House and 60 to 37 in the Senate. The composition of both tax committees and the House Rules Committee also became more liberal. In the House this came about because congressional reforms abolished the control of Ways and Means over committee assignments and increased the size of key committees, adding liberal Democrats to fill the new positions. Similarly, liberal Democrats in the Senate gained control of the Steering Committee, which led to Finance Committee seats for Floyd Haskell (D-Col.) and William Hathaway (D-Maine), both strong supporters of tax reform (both were defeated in 1978). See Thomas Reese, *The Politics of Taxation* (Westport, Conn.: Quorum Books, 1980), pp. 151–57, for a discussion of this change. See pp. 238–42 for a general discussion of the effects of congressional reform on tax politics.

12 *Congressional Quarterly Almanac, 1975*, p. 101.

13 *House Report on H.R. 2166* (H. Rept. 94–19).

14 Department of the Treasury, *Blueprints for Basic Tax Reform.*

15 Under general LAL rules, deductions for new investment projects were limited to the eventual income derived from that project or property. Wagonner's amendment removed that restriction for real estate by allowing deductions from new projects to offset income from existing projects for those already in the industry.

16 Quoted in *Congressional Quarterly Almanac, 1975*, p. 152.

17 The vote was split as follows: Democrats—225 for, 57 against; Republicans—32 for, 111 against. Southern Democrats voted 40 for, 49 against.

18 The minimum tax, created in 1969 (see pp. 167–68), was at that point an "add-on" tax that was not truly a minimum tax because taxpayers with preference income over the exemption level had to pay the 10 percent tax regardless of other taxes they might owe. It was this fact that led to the proposal that regular taxes be added as exemptions. If these taxes had been credited instead of exempted, the tax would have been a real minimum tax.

19 The reform group consisted of Senator Nelson and Senators Hartke (D-Ind.), Mondale (D-Minn.), Hathaway, Haskell of the Finance Committee, along with Hollings (D-S.C.), Mathias (R-Md.), Brooke (R-Mass.), Clark (D-Iowa), Gary Hart (D-Colo.), Phillip Hart (D-Mich.), Huddleston (D-Ky.). Humphrey, Kennedy, and Proxmire (D-Wis.). It is important to note that of this group, only six remained in the Senate after 1980. Of the nine others, two retired and seven were defeated in reelection bids. Curiously, of the six remaining four chose to run for the presidency in 1984.

20 *Congressional Record*, 94th Cong., 2d sess., vol. 122: 18553.

21 Ibid., p. 18542.

22 Ibid., p. 18559.

23 Ibid., p. 26191.

24 Ibid., pp. 26193–94.

25 Ibid., p. 26188.

26 See U.S. Congress Joint Committee on Taxation, *General Explanations of the Tax Reform Act of 1976* (Washington, D.C.: Government Printing Office, 1977), pp. 22–23, tables 3 and 4.

27 *Congressional Record*, 94th Cong., 2d sess., vol. 122: pp. 26, 131–32.

Chapter 10

1 The rebate barely survived a February committee vote of 20 to 17. The recommittal vote was defeated 194 to 219, with Republicans united 140 to 1 in favor of recommittal, and Democrats somewhat split at 54 to 218.

2 *Congressional Record*, 95th Cong., 1st sess., vol. 123: 6635.

3 Ibid., p. 6593.

4 *Congressional Quarterly Almanac*, 1977 (Washington, D.C.: Congressional Quarterly, 1978), p. 104.

5 *Congressional Record*, 95th Cong., 1st sess., vol. 123: 12470.

6 Ibid., pp. 6585–86, 6588–89.

7 *Tax Expenditures*, Committee Print, Senate Committee on the Budget (Washington, D.C.: Government Printing Office, 1979).

8 For a description of these rationales and the legislative history of this provision, see Emil M. Sunley, "A Tax Preference Is Born: A Legislative History of the New Jobs Tax Credit," in Henry J. Aaron and Michael J. Boskin (eds.), *The Economics of Taxation* (Washington, D.C.: Brookings Institution, 1980), pp. 391–408.

9 The results of the provision confirmed this observation. Tax consultants offered to search company files for past hirings that qualified for the credit. These specialized entrepreneurs then took a cut (usually 40 percent) of the tax credits acquired for the company. See Lance de Haven-Smith, "Evidence on the Minimal Management Principle of Program Design: Implementation of the Targeted Jobs Tax Credit," *Journal of Politics* 45 (1983): 711–30.

10 See Emil M. Sunley, "Administration's Tax Program," and John S. Nolan, "Administration Tax Reform Plan: Integration of Corporate and Personal Tax for Dividends," in *Proceedings of the National Tax Association, November 1977* (Columbus, Ohio: National Tax Association—Tax Institute of America, 1978), pp. 4–10.

11 See Charles L. Schultze, *The Public Use of Private Interest* (Washington, D.C.: Brookings Institution, 1976).

12 See, for example, President Carter's tax reduction and reform message to Congress on January 20, 1978. *Public Papers of the Presidents, Jimmy Carter, 1978*, vol. 1 (Washington, D.C.: Government Printing Office, 1979), p. 165.

13 Computed from a document in *Public Papers of the President, 1978*, 1:177, table 2. Also summarized in *Congressional Quarterly Almanac, 1978*, p. 225.

14 *New York Times*, March 13, 1978. The *Post* article was titled, "Richer Half of U.S. Pays 94% of All Income Taxes." *Washington Post*, March 13, 1978.

15 Quoted in *Congressional Quarterly Almanac, 1978*, p. 227.

16 For example, the *New York Times* ran major tax revolt articles on June 11, 12, 13, 15, 17, and 18. The revolt was termed a "tidal wave" in a June 19 *Newsweek* cover story, which reported the finding of a national poll that only 30 percent of the population did *not* favor "a proposal in your state to cut or limit property taxes—even if it means a reduction in certain local services, or an increase in other forms of tax." *Newsweek*, June 19, 1978, p. 22.

17 See, for example, Martin Feldstein, Jerry Green, and Eytran Sheshinski, "Inflation and Taxes in a Growing Economy with Debt and Equity Finance," Harvard Institute of Economic Research Discussion Paper 481, (1976); Michael K. Evans, "Taxes, Inflation and the Rich," *Wall Street Journal*, August 7, 1978; and Frederick W. Hickman, "For Indexing Capital Gains," *Wall Street Journal*, September 25, 1978.

18 House Speaker Tip O'Neill in a rare speech on a policy matter, while supporting the administration amendment, complained that the administration had been "tardy in bringing tax legislation to this body." The conservative Democrat Joe Wagonner labeled it "nothing but a disruptive practice," and Republican John Anderson (Ill.) called it a "thirteenth hour late-blooming Blumenthal bill." See *Congressional Record*, 95th Cong., 2d sess., vol. 124: 25419, 25491, and 25493.

19 Quoted in *Congressional Quarterly Almanac*, 1978, p. 234.

20 Joint Committee on Taxation, "General Explanation of the Revenue Act of 1978" (Washington, D.C.: Government Printing Office, 1979).

21 Kennedy's amendment would have kept the exclusion percentage for capital gains at 50 percent rather than the Finance bill's 70 percent. It was defeated 10 to 82, with only the most liberal Democrats in the Senate voting for the status quo. See *Congressional Record*, 95th Cong., 2d sess., vol. 124: 35262–63.
22 Ibid., p. 34524.
23 Quoted in *Congressional Quarterly Almanac*, 1978, p. 240.
24 Estimates are from "Tax Expenditures," in *Special Analysis G of the U.S. Budget for 1981* (Washington, D.C.: Government Printing Office, 1981).
25 "The Inflation Tax: The Case for Indexing Federal and State Income Taxes" (Washington, D.C.: Advisory Commission on Intergovernmental Relations, 1980).
26 *Washington Post*, October 16, 1978.
27 *Congressional Record*, 95th Cong., 2d sess., vol. 124: 25501.
28 Referenced in *Congressional Quarterly Almanac, 1979*.
29 See "How a Lobbyist Group Won Business Tax," *Washington Post*, January 17, 1982.

Chapter 11

1 Quoted in William Greider, "The Education of David Stockman," *Atlantic Monthly*, December 1981, p. 5.
2 The proposal also increased investment credits for certain forms of property by virtue of the fact that the assets were now included in a more accelerated depreciation class. Bringing down the maximum rate for unearned income from 70 to 50 percent also has a derivative effect on capital gains, which are considered unearned income. At 70 percent, after a 60 percent exclusion for long-term gains, the effective rate is 28 percent; this drops to 20 percent at a marginal rate of 50 percent.
3 "Address Before a Joint Session of Congress on the Program for Economic Recovery," February 18, 1981. In *Public Papers of the Presidents, Ronald Reagan, 1981* (Washington, D.C.: Government Printing Office, 1982), pp. 108–15.
4 Ibid., p. 112.
5 Greider, "The Education of David Stockman," pp. 46–47.
6 Quoted in *Congressional Quarterly Weekly Report*, May 16, 1981, p. 869.
7 The crucial House vote was 253 to 176, with all 190 Republicans and 63 Democrats supporting the president's substitute budget bill.
8 *Washington Post*, January 17, 1982.
9 Although the intention was to aid unprofitable and depressed industries, obviously the profitable organizations that "bought" tax breaks also benefited, or the sales would not have gone through. In some cases, international companies with large overseas profits but little American tax liability were able to become "sellers" of tax credits: Occidental Petroleum was a well-publicized example. Another common arrangement was for governmental units, which have no tax liability, to sell facilities (such as offices or sports

complexes) or equipment (rail cars or buses) to profitable companies and then lease them back. The profitable companies again got the tax breaks in exchange for lower costs to the government agency.

10 Quoted in the *New York Times*, June 8, 1981.

11 House Speaker O'Neill made a comment to this effect on a June 7 television show. Later in the debate, as the August recess approached and an administration victory loomed, the Democrats were accused of the opposite strategy of stalling to delay the vote. See *Washington Post*, June 8, 1981.

12 A series of close votes were taken. On June 25 a vote to accept a substitute rule for floor action that would allow only a vote on the total Gramm-Latta package was passed 214 to 208, with support from 188 Republicans and 26 Democrats. The next day the entire package of amendments was passed en masse by a vote of 217 to 211, with 188 Republicans and 29 Democrats supporting the substitute.

13 Quoted in *Congressional Quarterly Weekly Report*, June 27, 1981, p. 1137.

14 *New York Times*, July 24, 1981, p. 1.

15 The text of the speech appears in the *New York Times*, July 28, 1981, p. 36.

16 Quoted in *Congressional Quarterly Weekly Report*, August 1, 1981, p. 1374.

17 The final vote was bipartisan; Republicans voted for the bill 190 to 1 and Democrats 113 to 106. The southern coalition was in effect, with northern Democrats opposing the bill 64 to 97, but southern Democrats favoring it 69 to 9.

18 *New York Times*, July 30, 1981.

19 Joint Committee on Taxation, *General Explanations of the Economic Recovery Tax Act of 1981* (Washington, D.C.: Government Printing Office, 1982).

20 *Wall Street Journal*, October 28, 1981.

21 The range of reductions through 1984 as percentages of taxes that would have been paid without the 1981 bill vary from 20.9 percent for those with incomes over $200,000 to 27.1 percent for those with incomes between $5,000 and $10,000. For people between these income levels, reductions are tightly bunched around 25 percent. See Joint Committee on Internal Revenue Taxation, *General Explanations of the Economic Recovery Tax Act of 1981*, p. 23, table 4.

22 Eugene Steuerle and Michael Hartzmark, "Individual Income Taxation, 1947–1979," *National Tax Journal* 34 (1981): 145–66.

23 "Personal income" is the current income received by individuals from all sources, minus their personal contributions to social insurance. It includes transfer payments and also certain nonmonetary types of income, chiefly estimated net rental value to owner-occupants of their homes and the value of services furnished without payment by financial intermediaries and food and fuel produced and consumed on farms. For an explanation of various income measures, see *Statistical Abstract of the United States 1981* (Washington, D.C.: Government Printing Office, 1982), pp. 417–19.

24 One of the most interesting examples was a long discussion on the Senate

floor of indexing. Senator Armstrong (R-Colo.), who was one of the main supporters of the bill, argued strenuously that the middle class was adversely affected by inflation and presented a series of tables showing the increasing marginal rates from 1950 on of those with incomes at the twenty-fifth, fiftieth, and seventy-fifth percentiles. He summarized the results, which are very close to those in figure 11.2, as follows: "I stress that these are people whose income is half the median. So the idea or charge, or allegation that, in some way indexing is for the rich or for high-income families is simply not borne out to any degree, not even one iota, by the facts." *Congressional Record*, 97th Cong., 1st sess., vol. 127: S-7664–65.
25 Manley, *The Politics of Finance*, pp. 98–150, and "Wilbur D. Mills: A Study in Congressional Influence," pp. 442–64.
26 See, e.g., Spohn and McCollum, *The Revenue Committees*.
27 Ibid., p. xviii.

Chapter 12

1 Lindblom, "Decision Making in Taxation and Expenditures."
2 The concept of "casual empiricism" is explicitly defined in Lindblom and Cohen, *Usable Knowledge*, p. 12.
3 Aaron Wildavsky, *The Politics of the Budgetary Process* (Boston: Little, Brown, 1964).
4 As was shown in figure 4.1, Social Security taxes are growing rapidly as a percentage of federal receipts. However, these funds, although included in total receipts, are earmarked for Social Security programs. Thus, government outlays other than Social Security programs are primarily supported by income taxes.
5 James M. Buchanan and Richard E. Wagner, *Democracy in Deficit: The Political Legacy of Lord Keynes* (New York: Academic Press, 1977).
6 The major issue where the income taxes are concerned is whether corporate taxes fall on the owners of capital (in the form of lower dividends), consumers (as higher prices), or employees (as lower wages). The most progressive variant assumes a greater burden for those who own capital.
7 For the best study of the causes of variation within income groups, see Joseph J. Minarik, "Who Doesn't Bear the Tax Burden?" in Aaron and Boskin, *The Economics of Taxation*, pp. 55–68. He demonstrates the extent to which deductions, and particularly charitable deductions, create variation in effective rates at upper-income levels. See specifically figs. 5, 6, and 9.
8 A possible problem with this conclusion is that the marginal rate structure is not only affected by rate percentages but also by bracket widths, which have also varied over time. The use of single income points is not sensitive to such changes. However, the generally proportionate pattern of postwar marginal rate reductions is also evident in figure 12.2, which depicts changes in average effective rates for income ranges based on reported statistics.

9 See, for example, Allan H. Meltzer and Scott F. Richard, "Why Government Grows (and Grows) in a Democracy," *Public Interest* 52 (1978): 111–18.

10 The GINI Index equals twice the area depicted in figure below. The curve defining that area is called the Lorenz curve. It depicts the cumulative percent of the population ordered in terms of increasing income on the horizontal axis. The cumulative percent of income they hold is depicted on the vertical axis. The 45-degree line represents absolute equality (i.e., the first 20 percent of the population have 20 percent of the total income, the first 50 percent have 50 percent of the total income, and so on). The larger the area between the curve and the 45-degree line, the greater the inequality.

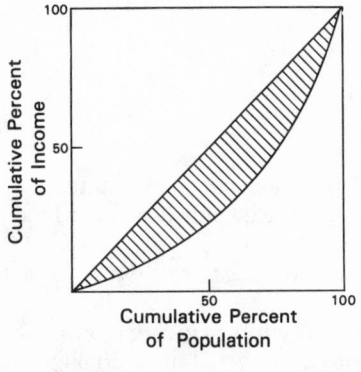

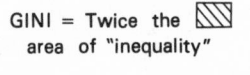

GINI = Twice the area of "inequality"

Cumulative Percent of Income

Cumulative Percent of Population

11 Since the GINI Index is defined in terms of area, using continuous distributions, error is built in when one aggregates income measures: because an average is used for any aggregation, the deviation from the 45-degree line will always be understated when income is aggregated, and thus actual inequality will be greater than measured. The larger the unit of aggregation, the greater the error. Pechman and Okner used a more refined unit (percentiles) and therefore computed the pretax GINI to be 0.437 (compared with my 0.423). Percentage changes in the GINI will be only slightly affected by different units of aggregation, however.

12 Maximizing redistribution in this way would be out of the question politically, but it demonstrates the point. This criterion does maintain aggregate pretax rank orderings of income for the 1966 distribution because even if all income taxes are subtracted from the top decile, this group will still have more income than the ninth decile. In other assimilations that were performed with higher hypothetical tax rates, it became possible for after tax income in the ninth decile to be higher than in the top pretax decile. Thus, the rule was that taxes would be extracted from individuals in the highest decile until they were equal in income to the individuals in the ninth, then both would be taxed equally, and so on. This redistributive formulation conforms to Edgeworth's famous minimum sacrifice theory, described in chapter 1.

13 The same limitations apply to these statistics as to those for table 12.2. See the discussion on p. 253.
14 The drop in effective rates for 1944 is an artifact of the change in the income base. Since adjusted gross income is higher than net income, the effective rates are lower.
15 The process of selecting key votes requires informed judgment. Interest groups rate congressmen on votes selected according to the specific interests of those groups. I suspect that some political scientists who perform broad sweeps of congressional votes may tend to simply pick the most divisive votes. In this case congressional debates in both houses were carefully reviewed, and care was taken to select the most pivotal motion. In most cases this was relatively easy, especially in the House, where recommittal votes are often the only votes before final passage.
16 The Rice Index is calculated by taking the differences in the party proportions of yea votes and subtracting that from 1.0. For example, if Democrats vote 70 yea to 30 nay and Republicans 45 to 55, the index is: $1.0 - (0.70 - 0.45) = 0.65$. This measure was proposed by Stuart A. Rice in *Quantitative Methods in Politics* (New York: Knopf, 1928), pp. 209–11.

Introduction–Section IV

1 Harold Lasswell, *Politics: Who Gets What, When, How* (New York: Meridian Books, 1958).

Chapter 13

1 Although there was no way to precisely define "major" modifications, the modification was generally included if it was important enough to be separately listed in any of the documents, reports, and analyses that accompany tax legislation (*Congressional Quarterly* summaries, "General Explanations" written by the Joint Committee on Internal Revenue, or the Treasury's yearly summary of tax action). Rule changes made by IRS were not counted except when a rule created a major provision, which is not that uncommon. Since many provisions are made up of several sections, conditions, or parameters that can be varied independently, each of these changes would be coded and counted separately. Thus, for a provision like capital gains, four or five changes might be made in a single bill.
2 The party coding based on inference when the exact sponsor or committee voting results were unknown, was either "strong" or "weak," with the cutoff being 60 percent of the seats going to one party. For a number of computations in this section, this distinction was dropped.
3 The rule here is that if a change only increases or decreases the amounts specified in a provision, it *increases* or *decreases* the benefit for an existing set of eligibility rules. If changes affect eligibility rules, the provision is said

to be *expanded* or *restricted*. If neither was apparent, the change was coded as *neutral*; and if both, it was coded as both.

4 The "Tax Expenditure Budget" is published annually as a special appendix to the federal budget. The lists vary somewhat from year to year as judgments in Treasury or the Congressional Budget Office change. The actual count of provisions is somewhat arbitrary. For example, beginning in 1977 separate provisions were established for charitable contributions to health, educational, political, and general organizations. Similarly, the various types of investment credits are listed separately: ESOP, housing rehabilitation, pollution control, and so on. Several exclusions from income, including alimony and moving expenses, are not listed as tax expenditures, because they are considered—arbitrarily, to be sure—expenses in earning income. I have combined provisions in the energy area that are sometimes listed separately (e.g., conservation and production incentives). The need to stabilize a set of expenditures dictated these choices. The set used is very inclusive of provisions existing between 1974 and 1981. Revenue totals given here are very close to official estimates, even when there is minor variation in the numbers of provisions due to my listing and combination decisions.

5 The most accurate estimates, given the limits discussed in the text, are for those items that come directly from tax returns. Since most excluded income (Social Security, employer contributions, etc.) is not reported, it must be estimated with a tax model that merges tax information with other income data by matching characteristics of "simulated" taxpayers. The estimates for new provisions on which no data exist are also very error-prone. The fact that IRS income statistics are always three years out of date affects a number of recent provisions. Since multiple years are reported in the special appendix of the budget, to minimize error, I used the latest available years, which in most cases were still estimates because actual amounts of revenue loss were not yet available.

6 Published estimates for a few provisions go back to 1967. Estimates for a small list of provisions began to appear on a regular basis in the 1976 FY budget, going back to 1974. The first relatively complete estimates were those for 1975.

7 The explanation for this apparent sleight of hand is this: if deferral of taxes means that taxes paid later are actually higher than they would have been if paid on an annual basis, a net gain to the Treasury results.

8 To give some idea of the magnitude of overestimation relative to an assumption of repeal, the 1982 estimate for total itemized deductions when simply aggregated would be $81.3 billion, while the combined effect of total repeal of these provisions would be a revenue gain of only $62.3 billion. This later estimate is taken from "1982 Special Analysis G," *Appendix to the Budget of the United States* (Washington, D.C.: Government Printing Office, 1983).

9 For a thorough discussion of these problems, see "1982 Special Analysis G," pp. 209–13.

10 Furthermore, dating the origin of the exclusion of employer contributions to
    health plans to 1954 is somewhat misleading. IRS rulings had allowed this
    exclusion from the inception of such plans, which, of course, spread slowly
    as employers began to adopt them. The 1954 rewrite of the total code
    embodied and thus formalized this and a number of other provisions.
11 It was initially assumed that the original percentage standard deduction was
    the norm and the minimum standard deduction an added benefit for those
    who selected that option. Similarly, since the original rate structure set a 70
    percent rate for the top bracket, an alternative 50 percent rate for earned
    income was considered a tax benefit when it was enacted. In each case the
    differences were counted as tax expenditures. The expenditures dis-
    appeared when the differential was eliminated by repealing the original
    provisions (the percentage standard deduction and the 70 percent rate). In
    both cases this resulted in less revenue.
12 The cases described in n. 11 are examples of broadening an initial provision
    to the point that the tax expenditure is eliminated. An example of a parallel
    benefit is the repeal of the tax-exempt status of building and loans and
    cooperative banks in 1951. Although their net income became taxable, they
    were given and still enjoy significant preferential deductions, relative to
    other banks, in the percentage of loans they can deduct as ostensible bad
    debts.
13 These data differ significantly from congressional testimony given by Alice
    Rivlin, in which she cites a growth in tax expenditures from 1967 to 1981 of
    50 to 104. Since no tax expenditure lists were presented in her testimony, it
    is impossible to evelute her figures, although they appear to be exaggerated
    for both years. See "Tax Expenditure Limitation and Control Act of 1981,"
    Hearings before the Committee on the Budget, United States Senate, 97th
    Cong., 1st sess., Nov. 24, 1981 (Washington, D.C.: Government Printing
    Office, 1981), p. 25.
14 Missing data for either year eliminated the provision from the calculation of
    growth; thus, 1974 data could be used. The average growth figure is a
    weighted average, which is equivalent to calculating the aggregate change
    from year to year for all provisions in a category for which data appear in both
    years. Initiation and repeal of provisions are counted in the category totals
    and hence the growth rates. The yearly changes are then averaged to
    produce the figures in the table.
15 Using the expanded classification system for category III, the 1974–1982
    average growth for category I is 11.5 percent and for category III, 13.2
    percent. It should be noted that the change in category was effected by
    dropping the provision for the "excess of minimum over the standard
    deduction" when the "zero bracket" was created.
16 Note that IRAs are included as employer contributions to self-employed
    pensions. These have undergone dramatic legislative changes in recent
    years.
17 Personal income is a broad concept defined in national income accounting

as "current income received by persons from all sources minus their personal contributions for social insurance." Thus, wage income, proprietary and rental incomes, dividends and interest, and transfer payments are all included. For an explanation and breakdown of personal income components, see the *Statistical Abstract of the United States 1981* (Washington, D.C.: Government Printing Office, 1982), pp. 417–18, 427.

18 Tax credits pose an analytical problem in that general tax credits, such as those that applied to each taxpayer in the mid-1970s, are really an aspect of the rate system. However, many other credits, including retirement, child care, and investment credits, are structural tax-exclusion provisions and should be subtracted from the taxable base. While Steuerle and Hartzmark do not distinguish between these forms, they do show tax credits as a separate entity. See Steuerle and Hartzmark, "Individual Income Taxation, 1947–1979."

19 For example, see Joseph A. Pechman and Benjamin A. Okner, "Individual Income Tax Erosion by Income Classes," in *The Economics of Federal Subsidy Programs*, a compendium of papers submitted to the Joint Economic Committee, part 1: *General Study Papers*, 92d Cong., 2d sess. (Washington, D.C.: Government Printing Office, 1972), pp. 13–40.

Chapter 14

1 This chapter is based on John F. Witte, "The Distribution of Federal Income Tax Expenditures," *Policy Studies Journal* 12 (1983): 131–53.

2 The standard Lorenz curve depicts the cumulative percent of the population on the vertical axis and the cumulative percent of income on the horizontal axis. Since the population is ordered in terms of increasing income, any given cumulative population percentile must be less than or equal to the same income percentile. See n. 10, chap. 12 for an explanation of the Lorenz curve.

3 In those few cases where the distribution crosses the 45-degree line, such as the deferral of capital gains in home sales (depicted in figure 14.1), the index is computed by subtracting the smaller area (L_{h1}) from the larger (L_{h2}), then computing the ratio and attaching the sign of the larger area. Such a distribution reflects a provision that disproportionately benefits middle-income groups in the range where the switch occurs. Although developed independently by the author, the general concept of this index was first reported by Daniel Suits for measuring the distribution of tax burdens. A detailed description of the calculations appears in Daniel B. Suits, "Measurement of Tax Progressivity," *American Economic Review* 67 (1977): 747–52.

4 I thank Tom Vasquez of the Tax Analysis Division of the Department of the Treasury for making available the estimates by income groupings. For all subsequent analyses I alone am responsible.

5 The "preference" list for computing a minimum tax is an ad hoc list that includes many provisions that benefit high-income groups and are used to avoid or defer paying taxes. The major provisions on the list include one-half the excluded portion of capital gains, the excess of percent over cost depletion for mineral extraction, accelerated depreciation on property, and income realized by exercising stock options. The effect of this income concept is to "spread out" adjusted gross income by adding income that accrues to upper-income groups while not adding excluded income (such as Social Security) that primarily benefits people at the lower-income levels.

6 The breakdown of medical deductions is as follows: 20.0 percent goes to those with incomes under $15,000; 46.1 percent, $15,000–$30,000; 18.3 percent, $30,000–$50,000; and 15.6 percent to those above $50,000.

7 The reason is that the rate of return on tax-free bonds is only appealing to those in high marginal brackets. For others after-tax yields are higher on taxable bonds.

8 See David R. Mayhew, *Congress: The Electoral Connection* (New Haven: Yale University Press, 1974); and Morris P. Fiorina, *Congress: Keystone of the Washington Establishment* (New Haven: Yale University Press, 1977).

Chapter 15

1 See, e.g., Spohn and McCollum, *The Revenue Committees*; Stanley Surrey, *Pathways to Tax Reform*; Common Cause, *Gimme Shelters* (Washington, D.C.: Common Cause, 1978); Thomas Reese, *The Politics of Federal Taxation* (Westport, Conn.: Quorum Books, 1980).

2 There is a slight difference between the tax expenditure set used in this chapter and the set used in chapter 13. All charitable deductions are considered together in this chapter. In the previous analysis, deductions exclusively for education and health were treated as separate tax expenditures. This difference accounts for the differences in total frequencies reported.

3 Exceptions are the exclusion of unemployment insurance and Old Age Survivors Benefits for families with high incomes. Half of these benefits were made taxable in 1978 and 1982 respectively.

4 Only "major changes" were included in this analysis. These include provision changes that served to modify either the coverage or the structure of a provision. For example, for capital gains this category could include changes in the exclusion percentage, the maximum alternate rates, definitions and holding periods for long, short, or intermediate gains, or the definition of eligible assets. Technical changes and IRS administrative changes or rulings were not included.

5 These figures are somewhat distorted by not including provisions that existed during the prewar period but have been repealed since. However, the list of such provisions is not long, and therefore the basic conclusion holds. See pp. 288–90 for the list of repealed provisions.

6 Errors of two types are possible in determining the institutional origin of actions. First, there are errors of omission in which a proposal made at one point in the policy process is overlooked in a document search. This is most likely to occur with Treasury or administration proposals, which are first revealed as part of a Ways and Means report. Such proposals are not documented as systematically as those occurring in committee reports. Second, the formal presentation of proposals may often be preceded by informal initiation and/or agreement between institutional actors. The first problem was given special attention in a secondary search of administrative documents. The latter is not susceptible to remedial solution, and one must assume that such errors exist.

7 Blough, *The Federal Taxing Process*, p. 13.

8 The history of the 1981 act in chapter 11 describes this reversal. However, the tax increase of 1982, which is not included in this analysis, provides even stronger evidence. Ways and Means never even presented a proposal for that act: the Conference Committee worked only with Senate-passed legislation.

9 A study of tax expenditures by Common Cause for 1971–1976 confirmed the Senate's penchant for proposing tax reduction amendments. They analyzed proposals only, whether enacted or not, and found that the Ways and Means Committee proposed 27 amendments that would have increased tax expenditures and 33 that would have decreased benefits. On the other hand, Finance proposed 39 increases and only 14 decreases, and Senate floor amendments added 37 more increases, offset by only 12 decreases. See Common Cause, *Gimme Shelters*, p. 38, chart 6.

10 The reader is reminded of the coding method described on p. 286 above. Of the 69 "party" tax expenditures, 36 were coded by identifying the sponsors of provisions, and 33 by inference based on the party in control of the institution originating the provision.

11 The party origin of modifications could be directly assessed for only 40 percent of the changes. The coding of the remainder was based on the party in control of the initiating institutions. Of the number that originated in the 1913 act, however, most were coded according to committee control but were clearly the work of the Democrat-controlled subcommittee that wrote the original income tax amendment.

12 Of the total votes taken to establish tax expenditures, 90 percent occurred in the Senate. For modifications, the Senate figure is 80 percent.

13 Tracking down votes before the creation of the *Congressional Quarterly* in 1948 is a time-consuming process that requires extensive review of the *Congressional Record*. Missing data are therefore more likely for the prewar period. However, strenuous efforts were made to locate votes that initiated tax expenditures, and the amount of missing data should be minimal. Coding was difficult only in the case of approval of amendments en masse, which was more common in the prewar period, and in the case of routine and often uncontested voice vote approval of amendments sponsored by the

Finance or Ways and Means Committee. En masse amendments were not coded as specific votes, but committee-sponsored votes were.

14 See, e.g., Common Cause, *Gimme Shelters*; Surrey, *Pathways to Tax Reform*; and Stanley Surrey, "Tax Incentives as a Device for Implementation of Government Policy: A Comparison with Direct Government Expenditures," in Joint Economic Committee, *Federal Subsidy Program Papers*, 92d Cong., 2d sess. (Washington, D.C.: Government Printing Office, 1972), pp. 74–105. An earlier version of the last paper was published in 83 *Harvard Law Review* 705 (1970).

15 See Aaron Wildavsky, *The Politics of the Budget Process*, 2d ed. (Boston: Little, Brown, 1974); Dennis S. Ippolito, *Congressional Spending* (Ithaca, N.Y.: Cornell University Press, 1981); and Allen Schick, *Congress and Money: Budgeting, Spending, and Taxing* (Washington, D.C.: Urban Institute, 1980).

16 Schick, *Congress and Money*; Allen Schick, "The Politics of Budgeting: Can Incrementalism Survive a Decremental Age?" paper given at the Annual Meeting of the American Political Science Association, Denver, September 25, 1982.

17 The reference is to the famous epigram of Woodrow Wilson: "Congress in session is Congress on public exhibition, whilst Congress in its committee-room is Congress at work." Woodrow Wilson, *Congressional Government* (Cleveland: World Publishing, Meridian Books, 1956), pp. 68–69.

18 Common Cause, *Gimme Shelters*, p. 16, chart 1.

19 Manley, *The Politics of Finance*, p. 363, table 7.1, and p. 370, table 7.5.

20 Ibid., particularly chaps. 2–5.

Chapter 16

1 That study consisted of three national surveys, performed in 1977, 1978, and 1979. Summary reports and detailed tabulations are available from H. & R. Block, Inc., Kansas City, Mo.

2 Roper Associates, *The American Public and the Income Tax System: Summary Report* (Kansas City, Mo.: H. & R. Block, Inc., 1977), p. 22.

3 Roper Associates, *The American Public and the Income Tax System: Summary Report* (Kansas City, Mo.: H. & R. Block, Inc., 1978), pp. 31–32.

4 *The Gallup Poll*, 3 vols. (New York: Random House, 1972), 2: 824.

5 Ibid., 3: 2005.

6 The Roper study commissioned by H. & R. Block for 1980 contained a similar question. It asked specifically whether people favored the Kemp-Roth one-third cut in taxes with no reduction in government services. Although only 53 percent felt that such a cut was possible, 67 percent of the population favored the proposal. See *Third Annual Tax Study, Vol. 2: Detailed Tabulations* (Kansas City, Mo.: H. & R. Block, Inc., 1980), pp. 61–66. For both the SRC study and the Roper study, income level appeared

to have only a slight effect on attitudes. For the SRC question, difference of means between quintiles proved insignificant at the .05 level. For the Roper question, both the lowest and highest income category registered 65 percent approval, with the $15,000–$25,000 level showing greatest approval at 69 percent.

7 Survey evidence also supports the willingness of the population to pay for wars through higher taxes rather than borrowing. In 1941, 70 percent chose higher taxes while only 18 percent felt that borrowing was the way to pay for higher defense costs. In 1950 and 1951, 51 and 48 percent favored taxes, while 26 and 24 percent favored borrowing. The American public seems to be consistently opposed to deficits and increases in the national debt.

8 *The Gallup Poll*, February 16, 1978. Reported in the *Washington Post*, February 17, 1978.

9 Benjamin I. Page, "Taxes and Inequality: Do the Voters Get What They Want?" Discussion Paper 423–77, Institute for Research on Poverty (Madison, Wis.: The Institute, 1977), p. 5. The surveys he refers to are respectively a 1972 Harris Poll and a 1976 Advisory Commission on Intergovernmental Affairs survey.

10 The questions were not identical from year to year. In 1977 the wording was: "Some people have said that we need to *broaden* the income tax base and *reduce* the tax rate or percentage. That is, some types of income that are not now taxed *should* be taxed, fewer deductions and exemptions should be allowed and at the same time the tax percentage would be lowered. How do you feel about this—would you like to see the tax base broadened, or don't you think this is a good idea?"

In 1978 it was changed to: "Some people have said that we need to broaden the income tax base, which would reduce tax rates by including more types of income. That is, some types of income that are not now taxed would be taxed, and fewer deductions and exemptions would be allowed. Broadening the tax base could simplify the tax return, and reduce taxes for those who don't have many deductions, exclusions, exemptions or allowances, while raising taxes for those who have a number of deductions, exemptions and allowances. *In some cases, taxpayers, regardless of income, would pay more in taxes and in other cases, taxpayers, regardless of income, would pay less in taxes. How do you feel about this?* Would you like to see the tax base broadened in this way, or don't you think this is a good idea?" (Italics added)

The addition of the underlined sentence undoubtedly was part of the reason fewer people supported the broad-based tax in 1978 than in 1977. See Roper Associates, *The American Public and the Income Tax System* (1977), p. 40, and *The American Public and the Income Tax System* (1978), p. 63.

11 Roper Associates, *The American Public and the Income Tax System* (1977), pp. 41–43.

12 Taxpayers in fact by 26 to 24 percent favored taxing capital gains at the full rate and only slightly favored not taxing them at all (57 to 54 percent). Stock

owners also were more willing to tax capital gains at the full rate (26 to 23 percent), but fewer of them were unsure of the issue (6 percent "don't know" to 10 percent). See ibid., pp. 38–39.

13 Roper Associates, *The American Public and the Income Tax System* (1978), p. 64.

14 Ibid., p. 89. The highest percentages opposed deductions for the following costs: Christmas gifts for customers (89 percent), "travel to conventions outside the United States in a place where the company does no business" (76 percent), and "the costs of tickets to the theatre, sports events, the symphony, etc. when entertaining a business customer" (75 percent). On the other hand, less than a majority favored fully taxing child care (22 percent), required uniforms (27 percent), union dues (35 percent), or the cost of getting home from work (49 percent). The last has never been deductible.

15 Susan B. Hansen, "Public Opinion and the Politics of Redistribution," paper delivered at the Annual Meeting of the American Political Science Association, Chicago, Il., September 2–5, 1976. See especially tables 1, 2, and 6.

16 Quoted in Page, "Taxes and Inequality," p. 6.

17 Roper Associates, *The American Public and the Income Tax System,* (1978), p. 75.

18 The means for 1972 are as follows: McGovern voters, 3.60; Nixon voters, 4.23. For 1976 the figures are: Carter voters, 3.83; Ford voters, 4.45. Difference of means tests are significant in each case at the .01 level or better. Partisan choice also affects people's judgments about the positions of candidates and parties on this issue. In general, the distortion (relative to population means) results in partisans viewing their candidate or party as closer to themselves and perceiving the opposition's position as more extreme than does the general population. The latter effect is the more striking and consistent of the two. For example, Nixon voters viewed Nixon as more moderate than did the population as a whole (4.23 to 4.38), but they viewed McGovern as more extreme in his support for progressivity (2.70 to 3.0). Similarly, McGovern voters placed Nixon closer to the proportional tax end (4.91) and McGovern closer to their own position than did the general population (3.10). The end result in both years was that voters perceived greater distance between the candidates and parties than nonvoters did.

19 Slightly higher R-squared values were achieved by including a number of other variables, but even with these variables, for which the estimated coefficients were very uncertain (t-ratios less than 1.0), the R-squared value never broke 0.07, and the standard errors of the regression were almost unaffected. The best estimate was achieved by taking the square root of the dependent variable, which essentially dampened the effect of the proportional tax end of the scale. However, again the gains were modest, and since the problem with the scale seems to be that it limits expression of extreme positions (i.e., one might believe in a head tax concept or an extremely progressive system and not be able to register those thoughts), this transformation cannot be easily justified.

20 In both years there were significant differences in attitudes between those claiming some Democratic affiliation (strong, weak, or independent leaning toward the Democratic side) and those claiming Republican affiliation, and between those identifying themselves as liberals and conservatives. The means, with the population means for reference, are as follows:

	1972	1976
Total population	3.94	4.18
Democrats	3.85	3.92
Republicans	4.22	4.56
Liberals	3.43	3.79
Conservatives	4.07	4.51

The relevant differences are all significant at the .01 level.
21 Income was coded in "raw form" into eighteen categories in 1972 and twenty in 1976. Use of the original categories created lower t-ratios. For 1972 the t value was well below the 0.1 level of significance. Analysis of means also indicated a nonlinear relationship that was better modeled using dummy variables.
22 See, for example, Dahl, *Preface to Democratic Theory.*
23 Roper Associates, *The American Public and the Income Tax System* (1978), p. 53.
24 Ibid., p. 50.
25 "Changing Public Attitudes on Government and Taxes, 1981" (Washington, D.C.: Advisory Commission on Intergovernmental Relations, 1981), p. 4.

Chapter 17

1 For a concise description of those two theories, see Fiorina, *Retrospective Voting in American National Elections*, chap. 1.
2 See Barbara Hinckley, *Congressional Elections* (Washington, D.C.: Congressional Quarterly, 1981), especially chaps. 1 and 2.
3 Quoted in Sven Steinmo, "The Political Economy of Taxation: Taxing in Britain, Sweden, Germany and the United States," paper delivered at the Annual Meeting of the Western Political Science Association, Seattle, March 23–26, 1983.
4 Wildavsky, 3d ed., *The Politics of the Budgetary Process*, p. 11.
5 Quoted in Steinmo, "The Political Economy of Taxation."
6 See Singleton B. Wolfe, "Magnitude and Nature of Individual Income Tax Noncompliance," *Proceedings of the Annual Conference of the National Tax Association* 73 (1980): 271–77.
7 Testimony of Philip E. Coates, Commissioner of Internal Revenue, the Senate Finance Committee *Hearings on the Administration's FY 1984 Budget Proposals*, June 23, 1983, pp. 98–121. See especially items 1–3. The

IRS also commissioned a study to measure noncompliance but dropped the project after a pilot study because of inherent methodological problems.

8 This argument casts some doubt on the characterization of tax policy as redistributive politics. See Theodore Lowi, "American Business, Public Policy, Case Studies, and Practical Theory," *World Politics* 16 (1964), pp. 667–715; Lester C. Thurow, *The Zero-Sum Society* (New York: Basic Books, 1980); and James Q. Wilson, *American Government* (Lexington, Mass.: D. C. Heath, 1980), pp. 419–21.

9 *Statistical Abstracts of the United States, 1982–1983* (Washington, D.C.: Government Printing Office, 1983), p. 140.

10 This proposal was first published in the press on December 10, 1981, on the editorial page of the *Wall Street Journal*.

11 Allen Schick, "The Three-Ring Budget Process: The Appropriations, Tax, and Budget Committees," in Thomas E. Mann and Norman J. Ornstein (eds.), *The New Congress* (Washington, D.C.: American Enterprise Institute, 1981), pp. 288–329.

12 Pechman, *Federal Tax Policy*, p. 48.

13 Mayhew, *Congress: The Electoral Connection*.

14 This suggestion has been made often in both political and academic circles since Senator Muskie first proposed it during debate on the 1974 Budget Reform and Impoundment Act, which called for the estimation and publication of a tax expenditure "budget." Recent academic support has been provided by Robert W. Hartman, "Making Budget Decisions," in Joseph A. Pechman (ed.), *Setting National Priorities: The 1983 Budget* (Washington, D.C.: Brookings Institution, 1982), pp. 221–50.

15 See, for example, Alice Rivlin's testimony during the Senate Finance Committee hearings on tax expenditures. See "Tax Expenditure Limitation and Control," pp. 24–29.

16 The envelope concept is described in detail on pp. 16–41 ibid.

17 Although the provision of particularistic benefits has been discussed by Mayhew in *The Electoral Connection*, the benefits he describes were either direct constituent services or "pork barrel"-type distributions from bureaucratically allocated funds. My argument is that major legislation is also highly susceptible to these types of incentives.

18 Pechman, *Federal Tax Policy*, p. 48.

19 E. E. Schattschneider, *Politics, Pressures, and the Tariff: A Study of Free Enterprise in Pressure Politics, as Shown in the 1929–30 Revision of the Tariff* (New York: Prentice-Hall, 1935), p. 145.

20 For a discussion of the Smoot-Hawley Tariff and the 1934 act, see Robert A. Pastor, *Congress and the Politics of U.S. Foreign Economic Policy: 1929–1976* (Berkeley: University of California Press, 1980), pp. 84–93.

21 The Canadian case is described by David A. Good, *The Politics of Anticipation: Making Canadian Federal Tax Policy* (Ottawa: School of Public Administration, Carleton University, 1980). Curiously, after describing the Canadian system as insulated from direct legislative politics and highly controlled by the Finance Ministry, he recommends opening up the system

and moving toward the U.S. model. The German system is described in Steinmo, "The Political Economy of Taxation: Taxing in Britain, Sweden, Germany and the United States."

22 J. A. Kay and M. A. King, *The British Tax System* (Oxford: Oxford University Press, 1978), p. 246. In another study of British tax policy, Simon James and Christopher Nobes stress the constant changes in policy: "One of the most notable characteristics of the British tax system is that it is under continual change. Writing about it is like trying to hit a moving target." *The Economics of Taxation* (Oxford: Philly Allen, 1978), p. 135.

23 Richard F. Fenno, *Home Style* (Boston: Little, Brown, 1978).

Index

DESIGNED BY RICHARD HENDEL
COMPOSED BY MODERN TYPOGRAPHERS
DUNEDIN, FLORIDA
MANUFACTURED BY EDWARDS BROTHERS, INC.
ANN ARBOR, MICHIGAN

Library of Congress Cataloging in Publication Data
Witte, John F.
The politics and development of the federal income tax.
Includes index.
1. Income tax—United States—History. 2. Income tax—Political aspects—
United States—History.
I. Title.
HJ4652.W69   1985   336.24′0973   84-40506
ISBN 0-299-10200-9